BLACK FIRE
This Time

Volume 1

DR. KIM McMILLON, EDITOR
KOFI ANTWI, ASST. EDITOR

WILLOW BOOKS
a Division of AQUARIUS PRESS
Detroit, Michigan

BLACK FIRE THIS TIME

Volume 1

© 2022 AQUARIUS PRESS

All rights reserved. No part of this publication may be reproduced, stored in a retrieval system, or transmitted in any form, or by any means, electronic, mechanical, recording, photocopying or otherwise without the prior written permission of the publisher.

Editor: Kim McMillon, PhD

Assistant Editor: Kofi Antwi

Disclaimer: This is a collection of original works and reprints. The views and opinions within this collection are solely the creators' and do not necessarily reflect the opinions and beliefs of the editors and publisher, nor its affiliates.

Cover source image: "To Be Free" (1971) by Barbara Jones-Hogu (1938-2017). Silkscreen on paper. *Art of the SSCAC,* 2008.

Cover design by Aquarius Press LLC

ISBN 978-1-7379876-7-3
LCCN 2022933531

 WILLOW BOOKS, a Division of AQUARIUS PRESS
www.WillowLit.net

AQUARIUS PRESS LLC
PO Box 23096
Detroit, MI 48223

Printed in the United States of America

Contents

Editor's Notes	Dr. Kim McMillon	xiii
Foreword	Ishmael Reed	xv
Introduction	Dr. Margo Natalie Crawford Let's Do It Again: The *Black Fire* Remix	23
Nikki Giovanni	No Complaints	29
	Rosa Parks	30
	Vote	32
James Baldwin	Amen	33
	Blues for Mister Charlie (excerpt)	34
Gwendolyn Brooks	to the Diaspora	46
	The Boy Died in My Alley	47
	Infirm	48
Haki Madhubuti	We Are a Hated People	49
Dr. Doris Derby	Signs of Spring	52
	Earth Child	53
Askia Touré	Sun Ra Resurgent	55
	Legacies: A Redemption Song	57
	The Way	57
Umar Bin Hassan	Water	59
Amina Baraka	Hip Songs	59
Ishmael Reed	The Luckiest People in the World	61
Wanda Coleman	Emmett Till	65

Eugene B. Redmond	BAM!: Pre-, Present, & Post-Black Arts Movement	70
	Long Distance Warriors, Dreamers & Rhymers	71
	"Be My Brother Forever": Maya Angelou & The Invention of a FriendShip, 1970s-Style	72
Aishah Rahman	The Mojo and The Sayso, Act One, Scene 1	78
Henry Dumas	Knees of a Natural Man	92
	Love Song	93
	Son of Msippi	94
Michael Simanga	Haiku for Sonia Sanchez	96
	A Tribute to Amiri Baraka	96
	Ntozake Shange Say	98
Charlotte "Mama C" O'Neal	I Almost Lost My SELF!!!	100
Margaret Walker	For My People	104
	For Gwen—1969	105
Tom Dent	Ritual Murder, ACT 1	107
Lucille Clifton	shapeshifter poems	123
	fury	125
Quincy Troupe	Duende	126
Dudley Randall	On Getting a Natural	127
	A Poet is Not a Jukebox	128
	Booker T. and W.E.B.	130
Aneb Kgositsile	For Dr. Ron Milner	133
	Amiri Baraka: A Remembrance	135
	Prayer Cave in Bahia	136

Melba Joyce Boyd	To Darnell and Johnny	137
	"It Could Have Been Me": President Obama said in response to the murder of Trayvon Martin	138
Everett Hoagland	Sister Say	140
	A Big B.A.M. Theory of Creation	142
E. Ethelbert Miller	1865	145
	Lost in the Sun	145
	Love the Ghost in Me, Shonda, Hold Me Dear	146
Jerry W. Ward, Jr.	Poem 77	147
	The Poem Undone	147
	Somewhere Near Charlottesville	148
Opal Palmer Adisa	They Will Not Take You	149
	Knee on Neck/Race on Hate	151
	Queen Mother to Future I	154
Charlie R. Braxton	Another Mississippi Murder	155
	Babylonian Consequences	158
	Songs That are Sacred and Pure	158
Karla Brundage	Black Arts Movement	160
	Take Her Down	162
	The Revolution will be Televised	164
Amber Butts	Ruin	167
Zakiyyah G.E. Capehart	MRI…My Reasonable Imagination	172
	Fires in Oakland	173
Kalamu Chaché	Mothers Speaking About Their Sons	175

Meilani Clay	black woman is god, part 1	177
	black woman is god, part 2	178
Cole Eubanks	The Other N-Word	179
Tanji Gilliam	Act Three, Scene One	181
Lisa D. Gray	No Beats	188
	Dust Men: A Haiku	189
Quincy Scott Jones	All Lines Matter	189
	knives of peace	191
Venus Jones	Plight	193
Margaret Porter Troupe	Mourning the dead	195
Judy Juanita	Bruno was from Brazil: a prose poem	197
	I first see LeRoi Jones in the flesh	198
devorah major	downpressors	204
	city values	205
	writing love	206
Lenard D. Moore	Summer Blues for George Floyd	208
	8 Haiku	209
	Haiku Sequence	210
Denise Nicholas	Freshwater Road, Chapter 3 (excerpt)	211
Aldon L. Nielsen	Note to "In a Class with Baraka"	221
	In a Class with Baraka	222
Halima J. Olufemi	Power	223
	Tired of Running	226
Mozel Zeke Nealy	EXULANSIS	230
	Marching Papers	231

Dr. V.S. Chochezi	Black Girls Bop	232
	Black is beautiful	233
	Fabric of the Universe Pledge	235
Allison E. Francis	We are	236
	Night Hawks	238
	Chocolate cake (8:46)	239
Bryant B. Bolling	What it is to Be A Man	246
Staajabu	The Tude	247
	The Message	248
Tongo Eisen-Martin	A Good Earth	250
	I Imitate You	253
Ewuare Osayande	Our Afros Are Us	256
	Black Phoenix Uprising	257
Darlene Roy	BAMtized	261
	Pen Felt Around the World	261
	Black Arts Movement Warrior	261
Wanda Sabir	Night Rain	262
Kalamu ya Salaam	THE MAN WHO WROTE I AM	265
	NINA SIMONE	269
	my father is dead. again.	275
Landon Smith	Oxymorons in Margins	280
Kathryn Takara	Stolen Jewels	282
	Sweet Honey in the Rock	284
Michael Warr	What Not to Do (an unfinished poem)	287
	Back to the Ark (Axum, Ethiopia) 1978-2020	291

	The Armageddon of Funk: In Memory of James Brown (1965-2006)	291
Katrina Washington	Queen	293
	Myth	293
Lolita Stewart-White	the only black women she can think to compare me to	294
	Dear Miss Jeantel:	295
Camille T. Dungy	This'll Hurt Me More	296
	Metaphor of America as this homegrown painted lady chrysalis	298
	Jamestown 2019	298
QR Hand, Jr.	dopey poetry in the rhetoric of blood	299
	Defense Offense Back Fence	300
	Gruencjipersnoots	302
Tony Bolden	Blues People (For Amiri, Billie & Ella Nem)	304
brian g. gilmore	amiri baraka, d.c. space, 1989	307
	come back charleston blue (for larry neal)	308
	amadou	310
Keisha-Gaye Anderson	Black is Not Enough	311
Curtis L. Crisler	What Mamie Till Gave the World	313
	Before the (Re)showing of Medgar Evers, His Son Sits Alone	313
Amoja Sumler	Peace Be? (for Nikki)	314
Alan King	The Land of Innocence	317
Ron Milner	Black Theater—Go Home!	320
Connie Owens Patton	Kindling	325

Charlois Lumpkin	Neo Kwansaba in Barakan Verse	326
	Atomic Remedy (for Jayne Cortez)	327
	Kwansaba for Maya	327
Darrell Stover	Look Back: Amiri the Blues God Lives	327
	Be We We? for Amiri Baraka and Larry Neal	333
	Another Trane	334
James E Cherry	Mississippi: A History	335
	Eliza Wood	337
	Nocturnal Poetics	339
Raymond Nat Turner	Essential Work	340
	It's capitalism, baby...	341
Thurman Watts	Mbombe's Glass	343
C. Liegh McInnis	What Good Are Poems?	347
	Us From Dirt	348
Dr. Liseli A. Fitzpatrick	Amazing Grace	352
	seen and heard	353
	"reach the reacher" (For Val Gray Ward, Queenola Valeria)	354
Paulette Pennington Jones	Flying African Survival Song for Roi	356
	emmett till saga	366
	hello as much as goodbye	369
Val Gray Ward and Francis Ward	The Black Artist— His Role in the Struggle	372
Megha Sood	asphyxiated	380
Lamont Lilly	All Natural	382

	assata: general shakur	383
	in baltimore	384
Joanne V. Gabbin	Excerpt from "Introduction," Furious Flower: African American Poetry from the Black Arts Movement to the Present	386
Tureeda Mikell	If I Hadn't	394
Pamela D. Reed	James Baldwin's "Everybody's Protest Novel," Distilled to its Essence: Richard Wright and Harriet Beecher Stowe, A Marriage Made in Hell	399
Clenora Hudson Weems	Chapter 1: The Need for a Definitive Africana-Melanated Womanism Paradigm and the Question of Interconnectivity versus Intersectionality	413
Mona Lisa Saloy	7th Ward Daily Fare: of Black Creole Talk	424
	Resurrection Sunday, Tree Top visits	424
	Years ago Before the Storm	426
Elaine Brown	Joshua's Tree	429
Akua Lezli Hope	IGBO LANDING	430
	IGBO LANDING 2	432
	On Design	435
Linda D. Addison	MetaGender Machine	436
	Neo-Americans	436
Jewelle Gomez	Gilda Dreaming Awake	439
	Eleanor Bumpers* Reminds You: This is Not the Titanic…	441
Halifu Osumare	The U.S. Has Always Been About US	443
	Dancing in Blackness, A Memoir (excerpts)	444

Elijah Pringle III & Aileen Cassinetto	How To Launch An Ad Campaign Using Black Bodies	451
Lakiba Pittman	We Come to Heal the World	454
	I am the Instrument	454
Antwoinette Ayers, Kathryn Bentley, Dr. Connie Frey Spurlock and Dr. Sandra E. Weissinger	Beloved by Many; Abandoned by Some: The Undying and Unwavering Spirit of East St. Louis, Illinois, A Cultural Clap Back	457
Avotcja	Sanctuary	467
	Never Alone	468
	On Romanticism	469
Amiri Baraka	Legacy	471
	Ka'Ba	471
Sonia Sanchez	A Poem for Sterling Brown	474
	Just Don't Never Give Up on Love	475
	I'm Black When I'm Singing, I'm Blue When I Ain't (Excerpt from Act I)	478
Afterword	Carole Boyce Davies Already Missing the High Priestess of "Talking Back"—A Tribute to bell hooks	490
Text Permissions and Acknowledgments		492

Editor's Notes

There is enormous joy in the creative process, whether drafting a poem, building a house, creating or listening to music, or appreciating the moment, the realization that we are a part of something larger, the human race. The creative fires dwell within us all, representing our greater connection to spirit. *Black Fire—This Time* is the creative flame encompassing writers committed to telling their stories, and their resistance to conforming to ideological notions of what it means to be Black, and what to do with that realization.

In 2013, as a graduate student at UC Merced, I taught a course on "Theatre and Social Responsibility." I wanted my students to understand and appreciate the writings of Amiri Baraka, Sonia Sanchez, Askia Touré, Lorraine Hansberry, and so many others. A student questioned whether the plays we were reading by African Americans qualified as theatre. He equated theatre with Shakespeare, but not necessarily Lorraine Hansberry. What was beautiful about this teachable moment was helping the entire class understand that theatre and what it means are unique to each person. There are no right or wrong ways to create and say, "This is theatre for me."

For too long, we have lived in a liminal space where the art and culture of Black people is not always seen for its worth, its beauty, its magic. I say "magic" because of the power of words. The words, "Black is Beautiful, Black is Powerful, and Black is Home" fueled the dreams and hopes of an entire race. Words were used to shine a light on a people maligned, hurt, enslaved for the color of their skin without seeing the beauty represented in Black bodies and minds.

With *Black Fire—This Time*, we are asking our readers to see not just the beauty on the pages, but the beauty in yourselves, that you are standing in this moment, in this time when so much of our world is examined for how much of it is threatened. Similar to the 1960s, marginalized voices demand absolute freedom from the limits placed by those claiming absolute power. But we as Black people come from a tradition rooted in the earth with the understanding that real power is given by the creator.

We as the human race have the right to create with words, with stories, with sounds, with each other. And that is what *Black Fire—This*

Time has done. We have used words to create, to bring together voices in celebration of Blackness. *Black Fire—This Time* pays homage to *Black Fire*, edited by Amiri Baraka and Larry Neal, and published in 1968, a time when Black people and minorities, in general, were treated as second-class citizens.

As the editor of *Black Fire—This Time*, I threw the shells and spoke to the ancestors on Blackness, inclusivity, and words that speak truth, whatever that may be. I heard the voices of Nikki Giovanni, Sonia Sanchez, Val Gray Ward, Liseli Fitzpatrick, and the daughters of Aishah Rahman, Lucille Clifton, Gwendolyn Brooks, and so many others saying, "We heard the communal call," and have answered it with our hearts, our dreams of Blackness in all its colors, in all its rainbows, in all its power. We are builders with words waiting for our new home.

Black Fire—This Time represents a new era in Black literature where there is a knowingness that we have the tools and the power to uplift ourselves. Educator and sociologist Anna Julia Cooper says, "Only the BLACK WOMAN can say 'when and where I enter, in the quiet, undisputed dignity of my womanhood, without violence and without suing or special patronage, then and there the whole Negro race enters with me (26).'" It is fitting that the publisher of this collection, Heather Buchanan, is a Black woman. *Black Fire—This Time* uplifts Black women throughout this anthology because we understand that when we walk through that door as Black women seeking freedom, equality, and self-determination, it shall forever remain open for those in need.

We are here to open doors. We require absolute acceptance of the changing face of Blackness and the need for those of African descent throughout the diaspora to know and understand that age, sexuality, gender, and the rules of who may enter no longer apply. Please walk through our doors where the power of words sings in our hearts as James Weldon Johnson's "Lift Ev'ry Voice and Sing" permeates the atmosphere...

We are determined to tell our stories, our history that calls for our ancestors to bless this home, built the first day we touched soil that was not African and had to learn to build a home that encompasses all our brothers and sisters throughout the world. This earth, this world, is our home. We created this home with our words representing who we are as a people. The ancestors greet us as we step into the world of our creation, rooted in access and self-determination. And the ancestors say, *Ashé*.

—*Dr. Kim McMillon*

Foreword

Alain Locke of the 1920s—and Amiri Baraka and Larry Neal of the 1960s—produced anthologies that were reports about the state of Black writing arts at the time of their publication. Dr. Kim McMillon's *Black Fire—This Time, Volume 1* (2022) provides an update. Notable prior works are *The New Negro* (1925), *Black Fire* (1968), *Confirmation: An Anthology of African American Women* (1983), *African American Literature* (2004), *The Norton Anthology of African American Literature* (most recently 2014) . . . and published this year, *The Tribes Anthology*, edited by me and the artist Danny Simmons. McMillon's anthology shows that the 2020s might be the new Golden Age of Black writing.

From The New Negro *to* Black Fire

Amiri Baraka wrote in *Freedomways* magazine that the idea for New York Black Arts began in the Umbra Workshop, founded by Calvin Hernton and Tom Dent. Though Umbra published notable authors like Julian Bond, Oliver Pitcher, Robert J. Williams, Lerone Bennett, Calvin Hernton, Joe Johnson, Tom Dent, David Henderson, LeRoy McLucas, Lloyd Richardson, Askia Touré, David Henderson, Dudley Randall, Ree Dragonette, Conrad Kent Rivers, Lorenzo Thomas, Ann Allen Shockley, Ishmael Reed, LeRoi Jones, Jayne Cortez, Nikki Giovanni, Bob Kaufman, Tom Weatherly and Jay Wright, critics appear to ignore its literature and only seem to be interested in a falling out between Black Nationalists and Integrationists. While literary disagreements and even bitter feuds have occurred in white literary magazines from *The Partisan Review* to *The Paris Review*, both are known primarily for their literary content. When Baraka needed assistance establishing The Black Arts Repertory Theater in Harlem, he called upon Umbra members William and Charles Patterson and Askia Touré, whose poem, "Dawnsong," heralded a return to Black tradition.

One of the differences between *The New Negro* and *Black Fire* is that of style. Locke's prose is so florid that it's difficult to follow, while Neal and Baraka's are to the point. While poets like Claude McKay chose a lofty diction in their writings, the majority of contributors to *Black Fire* chose the language of the streets. Stanley Crouch wrote:

> The fifties were cool
> fewer niggers carried knives
> more bought cadillacs
> and conked their hair
> McNeeley was a messiah
> with a tenor full of fonky niggers
> motel money and stuffed toilets (395).

Before the publication of *Black Fire*, (subtitled *an anthology of Afro-American Writing*) Black writers, if they wanted to sell books, had to cater to a white Liberal audience. The sales line was that "Blacks don't buy books," which continues to be a marketing strategy (yet there seems to be a high demand for what novelist Elizabeth Nunez calls "girlfriend" books). According to Baraka's autobiography, the Black Arts were also undermined by internal divisions. Nevertheless, Black Arts brought the arts to the people of Harlem—theater, poetry, and music—and The Black Arts model was exported throughout the nation.

Before the Black Arts Movement, Black authors received awards, prizes and chairs at universities and colleges based on their ability to mimic the writing styles of white authors, chiefly men like Eliot, Hemmingway, Henry James and Faulkner.

Black Fire proposed new models. In his anthology, Jimmy Stewart recommended Babalawo, Shaikhs, or Weusi Mchoro, which he saw as a rejection of "the white aesthetic." Larry Neal, in his "Afterward," wrote:

> There is a tension throughout our communities. The ghosts of that tension are Nat Turner, Martin Delaney, Booker T. Washington, Fredrick Douglass, Malcolm X, Garvey, Monroe Trotter, DuBois, Fanon, and a whole panoply of mythical heroes from Br'er Rabbit to Shine. These ghosts have left us with some very heavy questions about the realities of Black life in America (639-640).

No women are listed among the heroes, however. *Black Fire* included some of the bad habits we "warriors" grew up with and as a result, more works by women were not included.

Black Fire nevertheless was a historic breakthrough. Though it represented men flexing their literary muscles, it inspired feminist and multicultural writers. When Black male authors found their voices, others found theirs. The Black Arts Movement introduced thousands to a literature neglected in their Colonial classrooms, and it inspired thousands to write themselves. Though the Black Arts Movement was denounced and still distorted by the mainstream critics because it freed Black writers from Establishment restraint, the efforts of Dr. Kim McMillon and others have created a resurgence.

Unlike *The New Negro,* which was seeking patrons, *Black Fire* not only brought literature to thousands but inspired thousands to write. Young writers were instructed to take their inspiration from African models: Muslim, Yoruba and other cultures, but also the Black streets and music. David Henderson based his classic poem "Keep On Pushin'" printed in *Black Fire* on a 1964 song recorded by The Impressions. In the book, some of the writers view Black musicians as the leading purveyors of Black culture.

Black Fire was a book in which "Black men were Gods," and the supreme deities were Malcolm X and Marcus Garvey.

In the 1970s, women expressed their frustrations with their omission. Their dissent came in the form of plays like *For Colored Girls* (excerpts of which were first published by Al Young and me in 1974); books like *Black Macho* and the *Myth of Superwoman* by Michele Wallace and Toni Cade Bambara's *The Salteaters*; works by Paula Giddings, bell hooks, Mary Helen Washington and Marie Brown; and agents like Faith Childs. With *Confirmation,* Amiri and Amina Baraka made up for women being overlooked by male editors.

Scholars like Barbara Christian and Nellie McKay were able to acknowledge the literary power of Black women in *The Norton Anthology of African Literature.* Patricia Liggins Hill, Bernard W. Bell, Trudier Harris, William J. Harris, R. Baxter Miller, Sondra A. O'Neale and Horace A. Porter supplemented the Norton with their own version of the canon. On the west coast, Al Young and I published Black women in our *Yardbird Reader.* My small press published not only Black women but women from other ethnic backgrounds. I published Native American writer Joy Harjo, current United States poet Laureate, and Mei Mei Berssenbrugge, 2021 Pulitzer Prize finalist and recipient of the Bollingen Prize in the same year. In a review of *Yardbird Lives,* an anthology that Grove Press produced which was a summation of our work on five issues of *Yardbird,* Maya Angelou saluted our pioneer work. The review appeared in the issue of *The Saturday Review of Literature* (Nov. 11, 1978).

Black Fire—This Time (2022)

Dr. McMillon's collection is a follow-up and an expansion of all that has preceded *Black Fire—This Time,* which includes the pioneers as well as new voices. She has managed to print the works of writers belonging to multiple generations. Icons like Tom Dent, Amiri Baraka, Margaret Walker, Lucille Clifton, Wanda Coleman, Henry Dumas, James Baldwin, Aishah Rahman, QR Hand, Gwendolyn Brooks, Dudley Randall; brilliant and outstanding veterans Haki Madhubuti, Eugene B. Redmond, Quincy Troupe, Mona Lisa Saloy, Opal Palmer Adisa, Everett Hoagland, devorah major, Kathryn Takara, Kalamu ya Salaam, Jerry Ward, E.Ethelbert Miller, Askia Touré, Sonia Sanchez, Nikki Giovanni, Avotcja, Wanda Sabir, Melba Boyd, Ron Milner, Amina Baraka and Elaine Brown; and members of the younger generation Karla Brundage, Allison E. Francis, Tongo Eisen-Martin and C. Liegh McInnis. Some of the Black Arts pioneers like Amina Baraka as well as those who were contemporaries like Nikki Giovanni are still going strong. Giovanni is represented in this anthology with a powerful poem, "Rosa Parks":

> This is for the Pullman Porters who organized when people said they couldn't. And carried the Pittsburgh Courier and the Chicago Defender to the Black Americans in the South so they would know they were not alone. This is for the Pullman Porters who helped Thurgood Marshall go south and come back north to fight the fight that resulted in Brown v. Board of Education because even though Kansas is west and even though Topeka is the birth place of Gwendolyn Brooks, who wrote the powerful "The Chicago Defender Sends a Man to Little Rock," it was the Pullman Porters who whispered to the traveling men both the Blues Men and the "Race" Men so that they both would know what was going on.

But it was left to the late Aishah Rahman to include a literary slam dunk:

> Every night I lay out your striped blue suit and your Van Heusen shirt with the rolled collar and your diamond stick pin and your patent
> leather wingtips and your ribbed silk socks and your monogrammed hand embroidered linen pocket handkerchief hoping that you will come to church with me.

Dr. Kim McMillon has benefitted from the oversights of *The New Negro* and *Black Fire*. She has built on the pioneering efforts of both. In twenty years or so when future anthologists produce an anthology that will reflect a future state of Black writing, they will find this one hard to surpass.

—*Ishmael Reed*

BLACK FIRE
THIS TIME

"… the master's tools will never dismantle the master's house. They may allow us to temporarily beat him at his own game, but they will never enable us to bring about genuine change."

—Audre Lorde

Introduction

Let's Do It Again: The *Black Fire* Remix

In 1968, Amiri Baraka and Larry Neal edited *Black Fire*. This groundbreaking anthology of poetry, essays, drama and short stories propelled the Black Arts Movement forward. The Black Arts Movement was at its height at this moment, in 1968, as Baraka and Neal gathered a wide range of voices that would capture the most nuanced movements within the movement. Now, in 2022, we have *Black Fire—This Time*, and Kim McMillon is the wondrous curator. The practice of anthologizing literary movements is the practice of historicizing, creating expected and unexpected affinities, and revealing the flow, layering, and rupture that cannot be fully mapped.[1]

Black Fire—This Time shows that the Black Arts Movement never ended. The mix of 1960s and 1970s BAM art and more contemporary art honors the flow of the art of the Black Power Movement into, through, and around the art of the Black Lives Matter movement. For example, Haki Madhubuti's twenty-first century poem "We Are A Hated People" moves into, through, and around his 1960s and 1970s BAM poetry. The end of this twenty-first century *Black Fire—This Time* poem most clearly echoes BAM poetics when Madhubuti evokes an inwardness tied to a black mirror—"look in the mirror. say your last name." In Madhubuti's classic Black Arts poem entitled "Gwendolyn Brooks" (1969), the black mirror stage produces a collage-like layering of the infinite possibilities and limitations moving within the name "Black" that gained the force of electricity during the Black Arts Movement. We feel this electricity when Madhubuti, in this poem "Gwendolyn Brooks," writes, "into the sixties/ a word was born" and then creates a collage of blackness:

> black doubleblack purpleblack blueblack beenblack was/
> black daybeforeyesterday blackerthan ultrablack super/
> black blackblack yellowblack niggerblack blackwhi-te/ man/
> blackthanyoueverbes ¼ black unblack coldblack clear/black my

momma's blackerthanyourmomma pimpleblack/fall/ black so black we can't even see you black on black in/ black by black technically black mantanblack winter/black coolblack 360degreesblack coalblack midnight/ black black when it's convenient rustyblack moonblack/black starblack summerblack electronblack spaceman/. . .black blackisbeautifulblack i justdiscoveredblack negro/black unsubstanceblack.[2]

It is hard to read these words with any pause. The tribute to Gwendolyn Brooks, one of the guiding voices of the BAM, demands that a reader experience this part of the poem as a state of trance, an ecstatic process of purging that ends with the liquid blackness signaled by "unsubstanceblack."

Black Fire—This Time reignites the fire of the Black Arts Movement. When the original *Black Fire* was published in 1968, Amiri Baraka and Larry Neal framed more than an anthology. They paused as the art of the Black Power Movement was unfolding and curated a *non*-exhibit of the range of voices that were shaping this mid-1960s and early 1970s movement. They wanted *Black Fire* to be what James Stewart, in the anthology's opening essay "The Development of the Black Revolutionary Artist," describes as the "non-matrixed form" (a non-enclosed form).[3] *Black Fire—This Time* continues this practice of anthologizing the type of art that is too open to be contained, too explosive to be the type of book that can be held and read if you are not ready to feel what Gwendolyn Brooks describes as "the dissonant and dangerous crescendo." These words appear in Brooks's poem "to the Diaspora." This poem is one of the many layers of this anthology that teach readers how to hear the dissonance within Black Arts poems that, on the surface, may sound like a familiar, always recognizable, type of black representational space. When Brooks describes this black representational space as "dissonant" and "dangerous," she hails the work that this anthology is doing. The "dissonant and dangerous crescendo" in this anthology is the sound of the Black Arts Movement that never ended. As this anthology combines BAM poetics and the art created after this movement, we hear the sound of a movement that never ended. *Black Fire—This Time* teaches us how to hear the echoes that never stopped.

Black Fire—This Time is a remix that continues the groove of the original 1960s and 70s Black Arts jam session. Baraka and Neal began

Black Fire with the opening note:

> It is obvious that work by: Don Lee
> >Ron Milner
> >Alicia Johnson
> >[. . .]
> >Carolyn Rodgers
> >Jayne Cortez
> >Jewel Latimore
>
> Shd be in this collection. [. . .] The frustration of working thru these bullshit white people   shd be obvious.⁴

This anthology continues this unfinished work, this awareness that there is no way to include all of the voices that are a part of *Black Fire—This Time*. Gwendolyn Brooks' poem "to the Diaspora" is one of the many poems, in this anthology, that teach us how to grasp the power of the unfinished. Brooks writes, "Your work, that was done, to be done to be done to be done." *Black Fire—This Time* embodies this spirit of the revolutionary Black art that was done, was redone, and what still needs to be done.

As *Black Fire—This Time* opens up space for Gwendolyn Brooks' triple consciousness of what is "to be done to be done to be done," crucial space is given to a vision of what Linda D. Addison calls "MetaGender." In the poem "MetaGender Machine," Addison delivers the vision that fully disrupts the limitations of the original 1968 *Black Fire* that marginalized the voices of black women. In the midst of the omnipresent performances of reclaimed black patriarchal masculinity, many black women were brave and created space within the Black Arts Movement for radical black feminism. We hear this radical gender work when Toni Cade Bambara begins her pivotal 1970 anthology *The Black Woman* with Nikki Giovanni's image of the castration of black women. By deciding to include "Woman Poem," by Nikki Giovanni, as the first poem, Bambara immediately makes *The Black Woman* a response to the rhetoric of castrated black men. Whereas Moynihan argues that black men have been castrated by black matriarchs, in the opening poem, Giovanni writes, "It's having a job / they won't let you work / or no work at all / castrating me / (yes it happens to women too)."⁵ The radical edge of this poem is Giovanni's insistence on this unacknowledged castration that happens to black women. Addison's "MetaGender Machine" extends Giovanni's refusal of the Black Power anti-black woman response to the white power that castrates black men. Some of the Black Arts patriarchal nationalist discourse imagined black women's bodies as the receptacle of black male freedom dreams (black women's bodies were imagined as the most local alternative nation-state in this black patriarchal nationalism). When Addison, in "MetaGender Machine," writes, "What is my homeland, where can/I live, a place of comfort, perhaps/not this planet or the next, but/ I continue to search, to/morph until I am what I am to be....," we hear the *black feminist fire this time* meeting Giovanni's black feminist fire in the beginning pages of Bambara's *The Black Woman*. The black feminist energies on the edges of the Black Arts Movement become more legible when *Black Fire—This Time* allows us to hear BAM literature alongside art that is not recognized as being a part of the legacy of the BAM. "MetaGender Machine," when read as a part of the full flow of energy created in this anthology, offers a way of understanding the sound technology of Black Arts (the 1960s and 70s movement and its afterlife) as a call to "split, revise, break into pieces" (the line in "MetaGender Machine" that is a description of "living outside the boundaries" of gender and the line that captures Larry Neal's call for the refusal of the trauma of double consciousness in the afterword of the original *Black Fire*). Neal and Baraka arranged *Black Fire* so that the last note heard would be Neal's insistence that the Black Arts Movement was hailing artists who did not view blackness as the Du Boisian idea of "two warring ideals in one dark body," with no "true self-consciousness."[6] The "MetaBlack" machine that Neal hails in the *Black Fire* afterword, like Addison's "MetaGender Machine," defies the investment in binaries and boundaries.

brian g. gilmore's poem "come back charleston blue (for larry neal)" stands out in this collection as one of the most compelling twenty-first century tributes to the Black Arts Movement. This tribute to Larry Neal (like many of this collection's tributes to Black Arts Movement icons) teaches us how to understand the moodscape that connects *Black Fire* during the 1960s and 1970s to *Black Fire—This Time*. The moodscape of "come back charleston blue (for larry neal)" is a sorrow song yearning to be a sweet love song. gilmore conveys the horror of the 2015 Charleston church shooting and the sweetness of a woman keeping her lover's razor for years and waiting for the return of his "delicate" hands. The dedication "for larry neal" (embedded in the poem's title as if it must be read as more than a typical dedication) asks readers to try to hear the overlapping of 1960s and 1970s Black Arts poetics and the emergent poetics that are defining the first decades of the twenty-first century. gilmore imagines a razor that is also a star: "sharpened & still shining, like/a star at night in/a place called harlem." This language begs to be compared to Neal's move away from the aesthetic warfare often championed by the Black Arts Movement. In *Black Boogaloo* (in a final short note in the last pages of the poetry volume, a final note from the author), Neal writes: "Poems are ways into things, the opening of the natural spirit in us. Poems do not shoot guns; they are spiritual cohesives, tightening us up for the future war, if there be one, and giving us the strength to build a nation. These are dimensions of our consciousness: ourselves extended as far as current possibilities allow."[7] For Neal, the *Black Fire* is the feeling of not being contained, of feeling "ourselves extended."

This anthology both honors and extends the Black Arts Movement. The wonder of the experimental impulse that overdetermined the BAM was the constant play with the creation of new forms. The call for "form," in "The Narrative of the Black Magicians," is one of the most lucid examples of the BAM's understanding of *form* as the anti-formulaic. Neal chants, "form child. form in the rush of war./ form child. form in the taking of life./ form child. form in the sun's explosion."[8] As Neal and Baraka co-edited *Black Fire*, they became curators of formlessness. They wanted the anthology to document a movement and to hail more movement within the movement. *Black Fire—This Time* continues this movement work when it puts a spotlight on the emergent art of the contemporary era. Michael Warr's "What Not to Do (an unfinished poem)" begs to be read alongside Claudia Rankine's *Citizen*. Both texts have an expanding memorial list (memorials to those who have been murdered by police brutality and other acts of white supremacy). Rankine expands this memorial in each new edition of *Citizen*. The constantly expanding memorial list will need a new page soon. The book is unfinished. The memorial to the murdered, in the most recent 2020 edition of *Citizen*, ends with the names "Ahmaud Arbery, Breonna Taylor, George Floyd, Rayshard Brooks."[9] The typeface becomes lighter and lighter as the list progresses as if the sound of the names will fade as people become numb to this ongoing murder. Since 2018, Warr's poem has continued to add the names of a fraction of black people unjustly killed by the police.

As *Black Fire—This Time* creates vital correspondences across the courtyard and closed windows that separate the Black Arts Movement and our 21st century moment, we feel the intensity of the *swell* as the poetry, essays, stories, and plays in this volume burst out of any enclosure and make us feel the black aesthetic movements that will never stop moving. During the 1960s and early 1970s Black Arts Movement, artists were committed to representing blackness, but the impulse to represent blackness often became inseparable from the impulse to experiment with new ways of representing blackness. The Black Arts Movement set in motion a new understanding of the inseparability of black representational space and black experimental space. *Black Fire—This Time* continues this powerful work of the simultaneity of black representation and black experimentation.

This book is "skintight"—the word Sonia Sanchez uses in "A Poem for Sterling Brown." Sanchez gained her visionary poetic wings during the Black Arts Movement. Through the decades, her voice has continued to soar. *Black Fire—This Time* ends with her resonant voice. Her description of Sterling Brown captures the spirit of the "skintight" black gathering that this book becomes: "skintight with years/ a world created/ from love."

—Dr. Margo Natalie Crawford

Notes

[1] Arthur Jafa's theory of "flow, layering, and rupture" is cited in: Tricia Rose, *Black Noise: Rap Music and Black Culture in Contemporary America* (Middletown, CT :Wesleyan University Press, 1994), 38.

[2] Don L. Lee (Haki Madhubuti), "Gwendolyn Brooks," in *Directionscore: Selected and New Poems* (Detroit: Broadside Press, 1971), 88–90.

[3] LeRoi Jones and Larry Neal, eds., *Black Fire: an anthology of Afro-American Writing* (New York: William Morrow, 1968), 5.

[4] LeRoi Jones and Larry Neal, eds., *Black Fire: an anthology of Afro-American Writing* (New York: William Morrow, 1968), n.p.

[5] Toni Cade Bambara, ed., *The Black Woman: An Anthology* (New York: Penguin, 1970), 13.

[6] W. E. B. Du Bois, *The Souls of Black Folk* (New York: Penguin, 1995), 45.

[7] Larry Neal, *Black Boogaloo: Notes on Black Liberation* (San Francisco: Journal of Black Poetry Press, 1969).

[8] LeRoi Jones and Larry Neal, eds., *Black Fire: an anthology of Afro-American Writing* (New York: William Morrow, 1968), 314.

[9] Claudia Rankine, *Citizen: An American Lyric* (Minneapolis: Graywolf Press, 2014), 135.

Nikki Giovanni

Nikki Giovanni is an American poet whose writings range from calls for black power to poems for children. Giovanni has written more than two dozen books, including volumes of poetry, illustrated children's books and three collections of essays. Her book *Racism 101* includes bold, controversial essays about the situation of Americans on all sides of various race issues. Other books include *Bicycles* (Poems), *Chasing Utopia (Poems), A Good Cry (Poems)* and *Make Me Rain (Poems)*. Giovanni has received 29 honorary degrees, with another expected in January 2022. She has received 21 honorary doctorates and a host of other awards, including Woman of the Year titles from three different magazines and the Governors' Awards in the Arts from both Tennessee and Virginia. Rosa, her biography of legendary civil rights activist Rosa Parks, won Caldecott Honors and the Coretta Scott King Medal for best-illustrated book. Other books include the collection of adult poetry *Acolytes* and the novel *On My Journey Now: Looking at African American History Through the Spirituals*. Three of her volumes of poetry—*Love Poems, Blues: For All the Changes,* and Quilting the *Black-Eyed Pea*—were winners of the NAACP Image Award in 1998, 2000, and 2003. Since 1987, Giovanni has taught writing and literature at Virginia Tech, where she is a distinguished professor.

No Complaints
(For Gwendolyn Brooks, 1917—2001)

maybe there is something about the seventh of June: Gwen,
Prince and me . . . or maybe people just have to be born at some
time . . . and there are only three hundred sixty-five days or three
sixty-six every four years or so . . . meaning that some things
happen at the same time in the same rising sign . . . and the same
houses in Gemini . . . but some of us might also consider the
possibility of reincarnating revolving restructuring that spirit . . .
reshaping that spirit . . . releasing that spirit . . . tucking the useless inside and when the useless pushes out again we restructure
again and poetry and song and praisesong go on . . . because it is
the right thing to do

we always will cry when a great heart . . . a good soul . . . one of
the premier poets of her age restructures . . . reincarnates . . .
revolves into a resolve that we now carry in our hearts . . . as all

great women and men are alive . . . not by biology but remembrance . . . and that's all right . . . as the old folk say . . . because as long as they stay on the lips . . . they nestle in our hearts and those souls which are planted . . . continue growing . . . until generations not knowing their touch . . . their voice . . . or even the fact that some Chicago poets are terrible cooks . . . but always fun to eat with . . . will tell tales of having met someone who knew someone who once watched a basketball game . . . in which some Chicago poet cheered for Seattle at the request of some Virginia poet who wanted more games . . . while Mr. Blakely was amazed that a Chicago poet was even watching a game . . . and didn't we miss him as he slipped away watching baseball . . . and what a way to go . . . though we then did sort of know . . . that once gone . . . he would call the woman he loved

and so we come to no more phone calls at six a.m. to chat ... and no more Benihana when we are all in New York . . . and no more gossiping and questioning and trying to make sense of a senseless world . . . no more face-to-face . . . only the poetry which is a great monument from this Topeka daughter to the world . . . and yet . . . there can be no complaints in this passing . . . no sorrow songs . . . no if onlys . . . it is all here: the work the love: the woman: who gave and gave and gave . . . no complaints of too long or too hard . . . no injustice of accident or misunderstanding of disease . . . just one great woman moving to the next phase . . . and us on the ground . . . giving Alleluias

Rosa Parks

This is for the Pullman Porters who organized when people said they couldn't. And carried the Pittsburgh Courier and the Chicago Defender to the Black Americans in the South so they would know they were not alone. This is for the Pullman Porters who helped Thurgood Marshall go south and come back north to fight the fight that resulted in Brown v. Board of Education because even though Kansas is west and even though Topeka is the birthplace of Gwendolyn Brooks, who wrote the powerful "The Chicago Defender Sends a Man to Little Rock," it was the Pullman Porters who whispered to the traveling men both the Blues Men and the "Race" Men so that they both would know what was going on. This is for the Pullman Porters who smiled as if they were happy and laughed like they were tickled when some folks were around and who silently rejoiced in 1954 when the Supreme Court announced its 9—0 decision that "separate is inherently unequal." This is for the Pullman Porters who smiled and welcomed a fourteen-year-old boy onto their train in 1955. They noticed his slight limp that he tried to disguise with a doo-wop walk; they noticed his stutter and probably understood why his mother wanted him out of Chicago during the summer when school was out. Fourteen-year-old Black boys with limps and stutters are apt to try to prove themselves in dangerous ways when mothers aren't around to look after them. So this is for the Pullman Porters who looked over that fourteen-year-old while the train rolled the reverse of the Blues Highway from Chicago to St. Louis to Memphis to Mississippi. This is for the men who kept him safe; and if Emmett Till had been able to stay on a train all summer he would have maybe grown a bit of a paunch, certainly lost his hair, probably have worn bifocals and bounced his grandchildren on his knee telling them about his summer riding the rails. But he had to get off the train. And ended up in Money, Mississippi. And was horribly, brutally, inexcusably, and unacceptably murdered. This is for the Pullman Porters who, when the sheriff was trying to get the body secretly buried, got Emmett's body on the northbound train, got his body home to Chicago, where his mother said: I want the world to see what they did to my boy. And this is for all the mothers who cried. And this is for all the people who said Never Again. And this is about Rosa Parks whose feet were not so tired, it had been, after all, an ordinary day, until the bus driver gave her the opportunity to make history. This is about Mrs. Rosa Parks from Tuskegee, Alabama, who was also the field secretary of the NAACP. This is about the moment Rosa Parks shouldered her cross, put her worldly goods aside, was willing to sacrifice her life, so that that young man in Money, Mississippi, who had been so well protected by the Pullman Porters, would not have died in vain. When Mrs. Parks said "NO" a passionate movement was begun. No longer would there be a reliance on the law; there was a higher law. When Mrs. Parks brought that light of hers to expose the evil of the system, the sun came and rested on her shoulders bringing the heat and the light of truth. Others would follow Mrs. Parks. Four young men in Greensboro, North Carolina, would also say No. Great voices would be raised singing the praises of God and exhorting us "to forgive those who trespass against us." But it was the Pullman Porters who safely got Emmett to his granduncle and it was Mrs. Rosa Parks who could not stand that death. And in not being able to stand it. She sat back down.

VOTE

It's not a hug
Nor mistletoe at Christmas
It's not a colored egg
At Easter
Nor a bunny hopping
Across the meadow
It's a Vote
Saying you are
A citizen
Though it sometimes
Is chocolate
Or sometimes vanilla
It can be a female
Or a male
It is right
Or left
I can agree
Or disagree but
And this is an important but
I am a citizen
I should be able
To vote from prison
I should be able
To vote from the battlefield
I should be able
To vote when I get a driver's license
I should be able
To vote when I can purchase a gun

I must be able
To vote
If I'm in the hospital
If I'm in the old folks' home
If I'm needing a ride
To the Polling Place
I am a citizen
I must be able to vote
Folks were lynched
Folks were shot
Folks' communities were gerrymandered
Folks who believed
In the Constitution were lied to
Burned out
Bought and sold
Because they agreed
All Men Were Created Equal
Folks vote to make us free
It's not cookies
Nor cake
But it is the icing
That is so sweet
Good for the Folks
Good for Us

JAMES BALDWIN

James Baldwin was an essayist, playwright, novelist and voice of the American Civil Rights Movement known for works including *Notes of a Native Son*, *The Fire Next Time* and *Go Tell It on the Mountain*. Baldwin published the 1953 novel *Go Tell It on the Mountain*, receiving acclaim for his insights on race, spirituality and humanity. Other novels included *Giovanni's Room*, *Another Country* and *Just Above My Head*.

Amen

No, I don't feel death coming.
I feel death going:
having thrown up his hands,

for the moment.
I feel like I know him
better than I did.
Those arms held me,
for a while,
and, when we meet again,
there will be that secret knowledge
between us.

Blues for Mister Charlie (Excerpt)

NOTES FOR BLUES

THIS PLAY HAS BEEN on my mind—has been bugging me—for several years.

It is unlike anything else I've ever attempted in that I remember vividly the first time it occurred to me; for in fact, it did not occur to me, but to Elia Kazan. Kazan asked me at the end of 1958 if I would be interested in working in the Theatre. It was a generous offer, but I did not react with great enthusiasm because I did not then, and don't now, have much respect for what goes on in the American Theatre. I am not convinced that it is a Theatre; it seems to me a series, merely, of commercial speculations, stale, repetitious, and timid. I certainly didn't see much future for me in that frame-work, and I was profoundly unwilling to risk my morale and my talent—my life—in endeavors which could only increase a level of frustration already dangerously high.

Nevertheless, the germ of the play persisted. It is based, very distantly indeed, on the case of Emmett Till—the Negro youth who was murdered in Mississippi in 1955. The murderer in this case was acquitted. (His brother, who helped him do the deed, is now a deputy sheriff in Rulesville, Mississippi.) After his acquittal, he recounted the facts of the murder—for one cannot refer to his performance as a confession—to William Bradford Huie, who wrote it all down in an article called "Wolf Whistle." I do not know why the case pressed on my mind so hard—but it would not let me go. I absolutely dreaded committing myself to writing a play—there were enough people around already telling me that I couldn't write novels—but I began to see that my fear of the form masked a much deeper fear. That fear was that I would never be able to draw a valid portrait of the murderer. In life, obviously, such people baffle and terrify me and, with one part of my mind at least, I hate them and would be willing to kill them. Yet, with another part of my mind, I am aware that no man is a villain in his own eyes. Something in the man knows—must know—that what he is doing is evil; but in order to accept the knowledge the man would have to change. What is ghastly and really almost hopeless in our racial situation now is that the crimes we have committed are so great and so unspeakable that the acceptance of this knowledge would lead, literally, to madness. The human being, then, in order to protect himself, closes his eyes, compulsively repeats his crimes, and enters a spiritual darkness which no one can describe.

But if it is true, and I believe it is, that all men are brothers, then we have the duty to try to understand this wretched man; and while we probably cannot hope to liberate him, begin working toward the liberation of his children. For we, the American people, have created him, he is our servant; it is we who put the cattle-prodder in his hands, and we are responsible for the crimes that he commits. It is we who have locked him in the prison of his color. It is we who have persuaded him that Negroes are worthless human beings, and that it is his sacred duty, as a white man, to protect the honor and purity of his tribe. It is we who have forbidden him, on pain of exclusion from the tribe, to accept his beginnings, when he and black people loved each other, and rejoice in them, and use them; it is we who have made it mandatory—honorable—that white father should deny black son.

These are grave crimes indeed, and we have committed them and continue to commit them in order to make money.

The play then, for me, takes place in Plaguetown, U.S.A., now. The plague is race, the plague is our concept of Christianity: and this raging plague has the power to destroy every human relationship. I once took a short trip with Medgar Evers to the back-woods of Mississippi. He was investigating the murder of a Negro man by a white storekeeper which had taken place months before. Many people talked to Medgar that night, in dark cabins, with their lights out, in whispers; and we had been followed for many miles out of Jackson, Mississippi, not by a lunatic with a gun, but by state troopers. I will never forget that night, as I will never forget Medgar—who took me to the plane the next day. We promised to see each other soon. When he died, something entered into me which

I cannot describe, but it was then that I resolved that nothing under heaven would prevent me from getting this play done. We are walking in terrible darkness here, and this is one man's attempt to bear witness to the reality and the power of light.

James Baldwin
New York, April, 1964

Cast of Characters
(in order of appearance)

ACT I

MULTIPLE SET, the skeleton of which, in the first two acts, is the Negro church, and, in the third act, the courthouse. The church and the courthouse are on opposite sides of a southern street; the audience should always be aware, during the first two acts, of the dome of the courthouse and the American flag. During the final act, the audience should always be aware of the steeple of the church, and the cross.

The church is divided by an aisle. The street door upstage faces the audience. The pulpit is downstage, at an angle, so that the minister is simultaneously addressing the congregation and the audience. In the third act, the pulpit is replaced by the witness stand.

This aisle also functions as the division between WHITETOWN and BLACKTOWN. The action among the blacks takes place on one side of the stage, the action among the whites on the opposite side of the stage—

which is to be remembered during the third act, which takes place, of course, in a segregated courtroom.

This means that RICHARD's room, LYLE's store, PAPA D.'s joint, JO's kitchen, etc., are to exist principally by suggestion, for these shouldn't be allowed to obliterate the skeleton, or, more accurately, perhaps, the framework, suggested above.

For the murder scene, the aisle functions as a gulf. The stage should be built out, so that the audience reacts to the enormity of this gulf, and so that RICHARD, when he falls, falls out of sight of the audience, like a stone, into the pit.

In the darkness we hear a shot.

Lights up slowly on LYLE, staring down at the ground. He looks around him, bends slowly and picks up RICHARD's body as though it were a sack. He carries him upstage drops him.

LYLE: And may every nigger like this nigger end like this nigger—face down in the weeds!

(Exits. BLACKTOWN: The church. A sound of mourning begins. Meridian, Tom, Ken and Arthur.)

MERIDIAN: No, no, no! You have to say it like you mean it—the way they really say it: nigger, nigger, nigger! Nigger! Tom, the way you saying it, it sounds like you just might want to make friends. And that's not the way they sound out there. Remember all that's happened.

Remember we having a funeral here—tomorrow night. Remember why. Go on, hit it again.

TOM: You dirty nigger, you no-good black bastard, what you doing down here, anyway?

MERIDIAN: That's much better. Much, much better. Go on.

TOM: Hey, boy, where's your mother? I bet she's lying up in bed, just a-pumping away, ain't she, boy?

MERIDIAN: That's the way they sound!

TOM: Hey, boy, how much does your mother charge? How much does your sister charge?

KEN: How much does your wife charge?

MERIDIAN: Now you got it. You really got it now. That's them. Keep walking, Arthur. Keep walking!

TOM: You get your ass off these streets from around here, boy, or we going to do us some cutting—we're going to cut that big, black thing off of you, you hear?

MERIDIAN: Why you all standing around there like that? Go on and get you a nigger. Go on!

(A scuffle.)

MERIDIAN: All right. All right! Come on, now. Come on.

(Ken steps forward and spits in Arthur's face.) ARTHUR: You black s.o.b., what the hell do you think you're doing? You mother—!

MERIDIAN: Hey, hold it! Hold it! Hold it!

(Meridian wipes the boy's face. They are all trembling.) (Mother Henry enters.)

MOTHER HENRY: Here they come. And it looks like they had a time.

(Juanita, Lorenzo, Pete, Jimmy, all Negro, carry placards, enter, exhausted and disheveled, wounded; Pete is weeping. The placards bear such legends as Freedom Now, We Want The Murderer, One Man, One Vote, etc.)

JUANITA: We shall overcome!

LORENZO: We shall not be moved! (Laughs) We were moved tonight, though. Some of us has been moved to tears.

MERIDIAN: Juanita, what happened?

JUANITA: Oh, just another hometown Saturday night.

MERIDIAN: Come on, Pete, come on, old buddy. Stop it. Stop it.

LORENZO: I don't blame him. I do not blame the cat. You feel like a damn fool standing up there, letting them white mothers beat on your ass

—shoot, if I had my way, just once—stop crying, Pete, goddammit!

JUANITA: Lorenzo, you're in church.

LORENZO: Yeah. Well, I wish to God I was in an arsenal. I'm sorry, Meridian, Mother Henry—I don't mean that for you. I don't understand you. I don't understand Meridian here. It was his son, it was your grandson, Mother Henry, that got killed, butchered! Just last week, and yet, here you sit—in this—this—the house of this damn almighty God who don't care what happens to nobody, unless, of course, they're white. Mother Henry, I got a lot of respect for you and all that, and for Meridian, too, but that white man's God is white. It's that damn white God that's been lynching us and burning us and castrating us and raping our women and robbing us of everything that makes a man a man for all these hundreds of years. Now, why we sitting around here, in His house? If I could get my hands on Him, I'd pull Him out of heaven and drag Him through this town at the end of a rope.

MERIDIAN: No, you wouldn't.

LORENZO: I wouldn't? Yes, I would. Oh, yes, I would.

JUANITA: And then you wouldn't be any better than they are.

LORENZO: I don't want to be better than they are, why should I be better than they are? And better at what? Better at being a doormat, better at being a corpse? Sometimes I just don't know. We've been demonstrating— non-violently—for more than a year now and all that's happened is that now they'll let us into that crummy library downtown which was obsolete in 1897 and where nobody goes anyway; who in this town reads books? For that we paid I don't know how many thousands of dollars in fines, Jerome is still in the hospital, and we all know that Ruthie is never again going to be the swinging little chick she used to be. Big deal. Now we're picketing that great movie palace downtown where I wouldn't go on a bet; I can live without Yul Brynner and Doris Day, thank you very much.

And we still can't get licensed to be electricians or plumbers, we still can't walk through the park, our kids still can't use the swimming pool in town. We still can't vote, we can't even get registered. Is it worth it? And these people trying to kill us, too? And we ain't even got no guns. The cops ain't going to protect us. They call up the people and tell them where we are and say, "Go get them! They ain't going to do nothing to you—they just dumb niggers!"

MERIDIAN: Did they arrest anybody tonight?

PETE: No, they got their hands full now, trying to explain what Richard's body was doing in them weeds.

LORENZO: It was wild. You know, all the time we was ducking them bricks and praying to God we'd get home before somebody got killed—(Laughs) I had a jingle going through my mind, like if I was a white man, dig? and I had to wake up every morning singing to myself, "Look at the happy nigger, he doesn't give a damn, thank God I'm not a nigger—"

TOGETHER: "—Good Lord, perhaps I am!"

JUANITA: You've gone crazy, Lorenzo. They've done it. You have been unfitted for the struggle.

MERIDIAN: I cannot rest until they bring my son's murderer to trial. That man who killed my son.

LORENZO: But he killed a nigger before, as I know all of you know.

Nothing never happened. Sheriff just shoveled the body into the ground and forgot about it.

MERIDIAN: Parnell will help me.

PETE: Meridian, you know that Mister Parnell ain't going to let them arrest his ass-hole buddy. I'm sorry, Mother Henry!

MOTHER HENRY: That's all right, son.

MERIDIAN: But I think that Parnell has proven to be a pretty good friend to all of us. He's the only white man in this town who's ever really stuck his neck out in order to do—to do right. He's fought to bring about this trial—I can't tell you how hard he's fought. If it weren't for him, there'd be much less hope.

LORENZO: I guess I'm just not as nice as you are. I don't trust as many people as you trust.

MERIDIAN: We can't afford to become too distrustful, Lorenzo.

LORENZO: We can't afford to be too trusting, either. See, when a white man's a good white man, he's good because he wants you to be good. Well, sometimes I just might want to be bad. I got as much right to be bad as anybody else.

MERIDIAN: No, you don't.

LORENZO: Why not?

MERIDIAN: Because you know better.

(Parnell enters.)

PARNELL: Hello, my friends. I bring glad tidings of great joy. Is that the way the phrase goes, Meridian?

JUANITA: Parnell!

PARNELL: I can't stay. I just came to tell you that a warrant's being issued for Lyle's arrest.

JUANITA: They're going to arrest him? Big Lyle Britten? I'd love to know how you managed that.

PARNELL: Well, Juanita, I am not a good man, but I have my little ways.

JUANITA: And a whole lot of folks in this town, baby, are not going to be talking to you no more, for days and days and days.

PARNELL: I hope that you all will. I may have no other company. I think I should go to Lyle's house to warn him. After all, I brought it about and he is a friend of mine—and then I have to get the announcement into my paper.

JUANITA: So it is true.

PARNELL: Oh, yes. It's true.

MERIDIAN: When is he being arrested?

PARNELL: Monday morning. Will you be up later, Meridian? I'll drop by if you are—if I may.

MERIDIAN: Yes. I'll be up.

PARNELL: All right, then. I'll trundle by. Good night all. I'm sorry I've got to run.

MERIDIAN: Good night.

JUANITA: Thank you, Parnell.

PARNELL: Don't thank me, dear Juanita. I only acted—as I believed I had to act. See you later, Meridian.

(Parnel exits.)

MERIDIAN: I wonder if they'll convict him.

JUANITA: Convict him. Convict him. You're asking for heaven on earth.

After all, they haven't even arrested him yet. And, anyway—why should they convict him? Why him? He's no worse than all the others. He's an honorable tribesman and he's defended, with blood, the honor and purity of his tribe!

(WHITETOWN: Lyle holds his infant son up above his head.) LYLE: Hey old pisser. You hear me, sir? I expect you to control your bladder like a gentleman whenever your Papa's got you on his knee.

(Jo enters.)

He got a mighty big bladder, too, for such a little fellow.

JO: I'll tell the world he didn't steal it.

LYLE: You mighty sassy tonight.

(Hands her the child.)

Ain't that right, old pisser? Don't you reckon your Mama's getting kind of sassy? And what do you reckon I should do about it?

(Jo is changing the child's diapers.)

JO: You tell your Daddy he can start sleeping in his own bed nights instead of coming grunting in here in the wee small hours of the morning.

LYLE: And you tell your Mama if she was getting her sleep like she should be, so she can be alert every instant to your needs, little fellow, she wouldn't know what time I come—grunting in.

JO: I got to be alert to your needs, too. I think.

LYLE: Don't you go starting to imagine things. I just been over to the store. That's all.

JO: Till three and four o'clock in the morning?

LYLE: Well, I got plans for the store, I think I'm going to try to start branching out, you know, and I been—making plans.

JO: You thinking of branching out now? Why, Lyle, you know we ain't hardly doing no business now. Weren't for the country folks come to town every Saturday, I don't know where we'd be. This ain't no time to be branching out. We barely holding on.

LYLE: Shoot, the niggers'll be coming back, don't you worry. They'll get over this foolishness presently. They already weary of having to drive forty-fifty miles across the state line to get their groceries—a lot of them ain't even got cars.

JO: Those that don't have cars have friends with cars.

LYLE: Well, friends get weary, too. Joel come in the store a couple of days ago—

JO: Papa D.? He don't count. You can always wrap him around your little finger.

LYLE: Listen, will you? He come in the store a couple of days ago to buy a sack of flour and he told me, he say, The niggers is tired running all over creation to put some food on the table. Ain't nobody going to keep on driving no forty-fifty miles to buy no sack of flour—what you mean when you say Joel don't count?

JO: I don't mean nothing. But there's something wrong with anybody when his own people don't think much of him.

LYLE: Joel's got good sense, is all. I think more of him than I think of a lot of white men, that's a fact. And he knows what's right for his people, too.

JO (Puts son in crib): Well. Selling a sack of flour once a week ain't going to send this little one through college, neither. (A pause) In what direction were you planning to branch out?

LYLE: I was thinking of trying to make the store more—well, more colorful. Folks like color—

JO: You mean, niggers like color.

LYLE: Dammit, Jo, I ain't in business just to sell to niggers! Listen to me, can't you? I thought I'd dress it up, get a new front, put some neon signs in—and, you know, we got more space in there than we use.

Well, why don't we open up a line of ladies' clothes? Nothing too fancy, but I bet you it would bring in a lot more business.

JO: I don't know. Most of the ladies I know buy their clothes at Benton's, on Decatur Street.

LYLE: The niggers don't—anyway, we could sell them the same thing.

The white ladies, I mean—

JO: No. It wouldn't be the same.

LYLE: Why not? A dress is a dress.

JO: But it sounds better if you say you got it on Decatur Street! At Benton's. Anyway—where would you get the money for this branching out?

LYLE: I can get a loan from the bank. I'll get old Parnell to co-sign with me, or have him get one of his rich friends to co-sign with me.

JO: Parnell called earlier—you weren't at the store today.

LYLE: What do you mean, I wasn't at the store?

JO: Because Parnell called earlier and said he tried to get you at the store and that there wasn't any answer.

LYLE: There wasn't any business. I took a walk.

JO: He said he's got bad news for you.

LYLE: What kind of bad news?

JO: He didn't say. He's coming by here this evening to give it to you himself.

LYLE: What do you think it is?

JO: I guess they're going to arrest you?

LYLE: No, they ain't. They ain't gone crazy.

JO: I think they might. We had so much trouble in this town lately and it's been in all the northern newspapers—and now, this—this dead boy—

LYLE: They ain't got no case.

JO: No. But you was the last person to see that crazy boy—alive. And now everybody's got to thinking again—about that other time.

LYLE: That was self defense. The Sheriff said so himself. Hell, I ain't no murderer. They're just some things I don't believe is right.

JO: Nobody never heard no more about the poor little girl—his wife.

LYLE: No. She just disappeared.

JO: You never heard no more about her at all?

LYLE: How would I hear about her more than anybody else? No, she just took off—I believe she had people in Detroit somewhere. I reckon that's where she went.

JO: I felt sorry for her. She looked so lost those last few times I saw her, wandering around town—and she was so young. She was a pretty little thing.

LYLE: She looked like a pickaninny to me. Like she was too young to be married. I reckon she was too young for him.

JO: It happened in the store.

LYLE: Yes.

JO: How people talked! That's what scares me now.

LYLE: Talk don't matter. I hope you didn't believe what you heard.

JO: A lot of people did. I reckon a lot of people still do.

LYLE: You don't believe it?

JO: No. (A pause) You know—Monday morning—we'll be married one whole year!

LYLE: Well, can't nobody talk about us. That little one there ain't but two months old.

(The door bell rings.)

JO: That's Parnell.

(Exits.)

Gwendolyn Brooks

Gwendolyn Elizabeth Brooks was an American poet, author, and teacher. She won the Pulitzer Prize for Poetry on May 1, 1950, for "Annie Allen," making her the first Black American to receive a Pulitzer Prize. Throughout her prolific writing career, Brooks received many more honors. A lifelong resident of Chicago, she was appointed Poet Laureate of Illinois in 1968, a position she held until her death 32 years later. She was also named the Poetry Consultant to the Library of Congress for the 1985–86 term. In 1976, she became the first Black woman inducted into the American Academy of Arts and Letters.

to the Diaspora

When you set out for Afrika
you did not know you were going.
Because
you did not know you were Afrika.
You did not know the Black continent
that had to be reached
was you.
I could not have told you then that some sun
would come,
somewhere over the road,
would come evoking the diamonds
of you, the Black continent—

somewhere over the road.
You would not have believed my mouth.
When I told you, meeting you somewhere close
to the heat and youth of the road,
liking my loyalty, liking belief,
you smiled and you thanked me but very little believed me.
Here is some sun. Some.
Now off into the places rough to reach.
Though dry, though drowsy, all unwillingly a-wobble,
into the dissonant and dangerous crescendo.
Your work, that was done, to be done to be done to be done.

The Boy Died in My Alley
to Running Boy

The Boy died in my alley
without my Having Known.
Policeman said, next morning,
"Apparently died Alone."

"You heard a shot?" Policeman said.
Shots I hear and Shots I hear.
I never see the Dead.

The Shot that killed him yes I heard
as I heard the Thousand shots before;
careening tinnily down the nights
across my years and arteries.

Policeman pounded on my door.
"Who is it?" "POLICE!" Policeman yelled.
"A Boy was dying in your alley.
A Boy is dead, and in your alley.
And have you known this Boy before?"

I have known this Boy before.
I have known this boy before, who ornaments my alley.
I never saw his face at all.

I never saw his futurefall.
But I have known this Boy.

I have always heard him deal with death.
I have always heard the shout, the volley.
I have closed my heart-ears late and early.
And I have killed him ever.

I joined the Wild and killed him
with knowledgeable unknowing.
I saw where he was going.
I saw him Crossed. And seeing,
I did not take him down.

He cried not only "Father!"
but "Mother!
Sister!
Brother."
The cry climbed up the alley.
It went up to the wind.
It hung upon the heaven
for a long
stretch-strain of Moment.

The red floor of my alley
is a special speech to me.

Infirm

Everybody here
is infirm.
Everybody here is infirm.
Oh. Mend me. Mend me. Lord.

Today I
say to them
say to them
say to them, Lord:
look! I am beautiful, beautiful with

my wing that is wounded
my eye that is bonded
or my ear not funded
or my walk all a-wobble.
I'm enough to be beautiful.
You are beautiful too.

Haki Madhubuti

Haki Madhubuti received an MFA from the University of Iowa and served in the army from 1960 to 1963. A member of the Black Arts Movement, Madhubuti has published more than 20 books of poetry, nonfiction, and critical essays, and his work has been widely anthologized. Influenced by Gwendolyn Brooks, Madhubuti writes experimental, free-verse, politically charged poetry with a staccato rhythm. Over the span of his career, his poetry has shifted its focus from the personal to the political. Early work with the Student Non-Violent Coordinating Committee (SNCC), the Congress of Racial Equality (CORE), and the Southern Christian Leadership Conference (SCLC) inform his activist poetics. In December 1967, Haki R. Madhubuti met with Carolyn Rodgers and Johari Amini in the basement of a South Side Chicago apartment to found Third World Press, an outlet for African-American literature. Over the years, this press would publish works for Pulitzer Prize for Poetry-winning author Gwendolyn Brooks, as well as Amiri Baraka, Sonia Sanchez, and Pearl Cleage.

We Are A Hated People

before george floyd, breonna taylor and millions of Black "others"
was emmett till. i, a yellowBlack boy of 13 was slapped into
our Black reality upon reading and selling out of my jet magazines
of 9/15/55 that horrified a world with the images of the teenager
emmett till who had been crucified by white supremacist christian
cowards in money, mississippi.
his slaughter was not just a killing,
it was ritual, a lesson and an open message to Black people,
this was a repositioning of boundaries,

the putting of butchering hands on a Black boy
by white men who came in numbers;
as sterling a. brown writes, "not by ones,
not by twos, but by tens" high on their
racial righteousness and numbers took a
radiant possibility—emmett—in the dark of
a mississippi night and brutally lynched him,
on a lie told by a white jane crow woman to her jim crow men.
his body returned to chicago unrecognizable.

not just the bullet in the face or
the hatchet splitting his head,
separating eyeball from eyeball, or the forced
ejection of thirty teeth from his mouth,
leaving only his two front teeth partially holding
his tongue hanging loosely from his face like a
child screaming for mercy before the
final death blow and drowning.

this was a "nigger stay in your place" statement
from a psychopathic, racist, disturbed, frightened people,
of a state, in a nation, that has never respected or
acknowledged Black people as human and sacred souls.
this national killing, this execution, this ritual murder of our native son,
a developing young Black spirit touched hearts across the nation.
It is not just an awakening, it was a
national unignorance-ing of a traumatized people.
we, products of a native-Black culture,
less than a century removed from chattel enslavement
now confronted our enemies 20th century end-game:
white supremacy, nationalism, rage, fear,
economic annihilation, violence, hatred, and terminal ignorance
imprisoning us in its murderous confederate directives.
apartheid America was public news,
state news, national and world news.
the Black community nationwide
put on muscle, shoes and resistance.
earth shaking was beginning,
Black volcanoes and hurricanes erupted across the nation.
mamie till took the memory of her son—

refusing to let his death become history's
forgotten page.

there is a 400-year herstory / history of people of African ancestry,
Black people, now also native to this land the only land we know
whose labor, intelligence and ingenuity built this nation and it
has never been acknowledged or compensated.
Our story in its most poetic, scholarly and musical telling
needs to be preached, loudly told, noted, sung, recorded
and proclaimed in all Black churches, taught in all
our early educational institutions, HBCUs, as a topic
of conversation in beauty and barber shops, at breakfast and
dinner tables making connection between Black Lives Matter
to Black her/history and future. proactive self-knowledge.

always remember, if our struggles and battles reveal anything,
it will be the contradictions and treachery of the nation's
leaderships and actions: the non-lethal response and minimal
arrest during white peoples' insurrection on January 6, 2021 against
the nation's capital; the 30,000 lies told; half million coronavirus deaths
and the homicidal incompetence of the 45th president/commander-in-chief.
if george floyd was white and a Black officer was on his neck,
hard to ever imagine, that Black officer, in this culture would be dead.
in the western world yes, Black Lives Matter, however white lives
matter more. If we ever forget that western world fact—
we are in trouble, deep, deep trouble.
look in the mirror. say your last name.
if you do not know who you are
anybody can name you and in america, they will.
it is difficult to love a country, in all of its complexities and possibilities
that doesn't love you.
we must become whirlwinds against their evil.
fighting, demanding and securing fresh water, clean air and
Yeses for tomorrow's children of the world.

Dr. Doris Derby

Dr. Doris Derby is an American activist, documentary photographer, and retired director of Georgia State University's Office of African American Student Services and Programs and Adjunct Associate Professor of Anthropology. She was active in the Mississippi civil rights movement, and her work discusses the themes of race and African American identity. She was a working member of the Student Nonviolent Coordinating Committee (SNCC), as well as co-founder of the Free Southern Theater, and the founding director of the Office of African-American Student Services and Programs. Her photography has been exhibited internationally. Two of her photographs were published in *Hands on the Freedom Plow: Personal Accounts by Women in SNCC*, to which she also contributed an essay about her experiences in the Mississippi civil rights movement. Derby lives in Atlanta, Georgia, with her husband, actor Bob Banks. They are active leaders in their community and members of local and national organizations.

Signs of Spring

Crocus, Forsythia, dogs, police dogs,
Slight breeze, warm air, suddenly but,
Greatly disturbed by raging flames
In the night.
Screams nighttime, daytime,
all the time, growing louder
Crimson buds with new leaves,
and new thorns
While black men, women and children
Still not able to breather, walk right.
Fluffy white clouds unexpectedly turn dark
Loom overhead and thunder with danger.
Repeatedly destroying the life which was before;
Which was to come, and which is still in sight.
Worn, dark brown trees, without warning
Bring forth the new branches,
showing red, blue, whitish berries
As die-hard racists normally bring forth the blood
Of black and brown children,
with all their might.
Nature yields unknown fruits,
often strange but strong

They give inner strength to those who partake of them
And help undo that which is wrong.

Earth Child

Earth Child,
Fear not
Your rags,
Your mirror
Your beautiful
Blackness is
Clothed in
The pearl
Blue skies
Golden sun
Green leaves
Of our
Pregnant mother
We and the beautiful brown, black, red earth are one.

Askia Touré

Askia Muhammad Abu Bakr el Touré is one of the founding members of the Black Arts Movement of the 1960s and 1970s. As a poet, editor, and activist, Touré helped define a new generation of black consciousness that sought to affirm through the arts the community's African heritage as a means to create an uplifting and triumphal identity for the modern black experience. Touré is the author of several books of poetry and has been published in numerous anthologies.

Touré was born as Rolland Snellings on October 13, 1938, in Raleigh, North Carolina. He spent his early childhood, along with his younger brother, in La Grange, Georgia, where he lived with his paternal grandmother until the age of six. At that time he moved with his family to Dayton, Ohio. Although he spent the remainder of his childhood in Ohio, he made frequent trips back to North Carolina and Georgia to visit relatives, and the South had a profound influence on his early poetic images.

Touré wrote his first poem in the seventh grade, but after his teacher insisted that he could not have been the actual author of the work, he was duly dissuaded from further writing at the time. He attended public school and graduated from Dayton's Roosevelt High School in 1956. By that time, Touré had begun singing in nightclubs, imitating the doo-wop style of popular 1950s groups such as the Ravens and the Platters. Although he considered heading straight into the music business, after graduating Touré decided instead to join the Air Force, serving from 1956 to 1959.

Upon his discharge from military service, Touré headed to New York, and from 1960 to 1962 he studied visual arts at the Art Students League of New York. In 1963 Touré, working with illustrator Tom Feeling and artist Elombe Brath, helped produce a brief, privately published illustrated history of Samory Touré, who resisted French colonialism in Guinea in the 1800s and was the grandfather of Sékou Touré, former president of Guinea who successfully led his country's struggle for independence from the French in the 1950s. This publication marked the beginning of his life-long interest in the history of Africa.

In 1962, Touré began providing illustrations to *Umbra* magazine, whose staff included several prominent poets, authors, and activists. Here, in this company he began to focus on his poetry and to develop his own poetic style. Turning first to W.E.B. De Bois for inspiration, Touré's influences eventually came from a broad range of writers, including Irish poet William Butler Yeats, Chilean poet Pablo Neruda, and Harlem Renaissance writer Langston Hughes, among others. Ultimately, Touré found his poetic home in the rhythm, phrasing, and tonality of black music, with particular homage paid to the jazz saxophone of John Coltrane.

During the early 1960s, Touré solidified his growing role as a leader of the emerging Black Arts Movement by working with several new black arts publications. From 1963 to 1965 he served on the editorial board of Black America, the literary arm of the black nationalist Revolutionary Action Movement (RAM). For the following two years he was on the staff of *Liberator Magazine*, and then he served as an associate editor on the staff of *Black Dialogue*, which had begun publication in the spring of 1965. Eventually, the *Journal of Black Poetry* (now *Kitabu Cha Juai*) emerged from *Black Dialogue* and Touré was named editor-in-chief. Through all these forums, Touré sought to redefine black identity and strengthen the movement against racial injustice and oppression.

Touré was deeply affected by the assassination of Malcolm X on February 21, 1965. In response he joined with influential scholar Larry Neal to founded the newspaper *Afro World*, which went to press just one week after Malcolm X's death. That spring Touré, again partnering with Neal and took the Black Arts Movement to the streets of Harlem by organizing the Harlem Uptown Youth Conference. They invited artists from the Black Arts Repertoire Theatre School to perform music, poetry, and plays in the blocked-off streets of Harlem. Among the many Harlem-based artists, Touré performed some of his own poetry in this massive block party. This event spawned the creation of Harlem's Black Arts School.

SUN RA RESURGENT

Horns arouse deathless
Beauty, resurrect
Possibility, Here
in the human universe.
Primordial laughter flows
in fiery voices
mastering
Magi language: lean
saxophones scream into
Wonder-realms,
Sun Ra—hip, robed, magical—invokes
Nommo: giving voice to space
between notes, beyond
rhythmic time. An elegance,
a singular flare: a meteorite's
unearthly glare connecting
Worlds. Sun Ra, lord
of cosmic possibility,
In a "universal" reign
claiming vast destruction:
empires cast in Nordic tones
crumble into dust.
Yet Ra invokes
miracles—*hekas*, power-chants—
resurrects, from slave-hordes,
Ancient Kemet on the Nile.
Nommo: sound as text,
Parables in Ra's Eye,
Rising in the "West".

Sound: a blaring trumpet
as miracle.
Sound: ancient masters
blast sonic truths
against Evil's greatest lie. Set,
noble heroes,
alias the "West".

Sun Ra,
In the after-glow,
again invokes Nommo
to cleanse
the atmosphere, ignite the Da.
Yes, folks, this is a Wonder-song,
a chant of mythic saints, Ancestors
surging
in your blood.
But, after Set's demise, beyond
Armageddon, Dawn
invokes responsibilities
within our lives.
Here,
Sun Ra smiles,
between notes,
asking that we always
remember Self
as Heritage;
Challenge Evil, resurrect
Godhood, through this
Cosmic Music, this
Blazing genius-gift
linking
with Eternity,
through fire, blood and tears.
Sun Ra's
Promise blazing like a comet
In the
       Melanin Universe
of our minds.

LEGACIES: A REDEMPTION SONG

How will they see us, these coming generations?
Will they grasp the subtelties of this marathon,
this Long War? How has this "Slave" race
survived our great Holocaust; and what is the
transformative level, spiritually, from slave-songs
To the renowned complexities of "Jazz"?
from Nat Turner to Duke Ellington, from Ellington
To Miles, and beyond, to 'Trane, Pharaoh, Sun Ra,
and the vast Cosmos. An upsurge of legendary
Masters creating a whole Atmosphere, a living
Tradition: at once hip, holistic, visionary, spiritual:
a divine act of "Seeing" into the very depths
of being fully human: grasping the Zen-like
phenomena of mature improvisation, creating
a rhythmic, dialectical Universe, an Empire
of Sound against Cosmic Silence, entering
the Void…What we're describing is the hidden
soul of a people, Its inner language, Will
expressed sonically, a living Magic, if you will,
which creates a Godly consciousness,
embodies a Nation of Shamans—Guerilla Maroons—
to stand against the rape of Paradise by
legions of assassins and imperialist wolves.

THE WAY

Love
Is
the canvas,
this growing
toward
internal
knowing/being
One with
all things. This
Shamanic
being. Life as

black lines
against
The page's
snow. The
Way so
strange, It
changes:
flowing, as
jungle
rivers, into
warm seas.
This Way
into things,
this Path
of which
Larry sung…
Solo deep
moments
filled with
wonder,
solitutde,
and bliss.

Umar Bin Hassan

Umar Bin Hassan joined the Last Poets in 1969 and continues to troubadour the world with them as well as performing spoken word. In mid-1993, he released his first solo album, *Be Bop or Be Dead*, produced by Bill Laswell. Hassan combined rap, house, and jazz elements on the record. He later went on to record *To the Last* which was also produced by Bill Laswell.

In 1994, Bin Hassan appeared on the Red Hot Organization's compilation CD, *Stolen Moments: Red Hot + Cool*, appearing on a track titled "This is Madness" alongside Abiodun Oyewole and Pharoah Sanders. The album was named "Album of the Year" by *Time*.

In early 1999, Umar performed spoken-work at the legendary Snaps-N-Taps in Columbus, Ohio and met Carl Zero, local area reggae promoter and owner of Roots Records. The two worked together with several musicians and released the *Life is Good* CD on Stay Focused Recordings.

Water

A walk to the water. Each step a journey into trust. The past needs a friend to believe in. The music in our strides have put our games to sleep, we hope. The truth flashes by in the trail of a Comet. The ancestors speak in volumes. We arrive at the dock. Old slaves seeking a new freedom. The intrusive skyline invades our privacy. We turn to the water. The Africa in you speaks to the Africa in me. I hear a harmony in your voice... A harmony I haven't taken time to listen to before. I then realize that the closeness in your touch has just been a few sincere words away. I begin to feel strong and at ease watching you watch the water. I'm growing... I'm getting better. The struggle has not been in vain. For the first time in my life I don't need the unnecessary to make me feel like a man in your prescence slowly takes me out to Sea on gentle waves of confidence... Be blessed and be loved!

AMINA BARAKA

Amina Baraka co-edited *Confirmation: An Anthology of African American Women* with Amiri Baraka.

Hip Songs

did you ask me
who was the hippest singer
in the world well,
i'd go so far
as to say
it was the first slave
that gave a field holler
& a shout in the field
i mean thats
what i would say
i'd say the hippist singer
must have been
the local gospel group over yonder there
down the country road while pickin cotton

& they tell me little willie james father
was the hippist blues singer in town
& they say his mama got her freedom once
the master heard her screaming and crying song
but you know
the hippist singer i heard
wassa dude in new Orleans
playing a piano & singing a kinda different tune
although....
in Chicago there was this fast singing woman
w/a blues bottom & a lotta rhythms behind her
she was hip
now I've heard some hip singers
i know a hip song
when i hear one
you know w/hip lyrics & all
but, let me say this
one of the hippist singers
i ever heard
was a poet
singing
"Don't Say Goodbye to the PorkPie Hat"

Ishmael Reed

Ishmael Reed is the winner of the prestigious MacArthur Fellowship (Genius Award), the renowned *L.A. Times* Robert Kirsch Lifetime Achievement Award and the Lila Wallace-Reader's Digest Award. He has been nominated for a Pulitzer and finalist for two National Book Awards and is Professor Emeritus at the University of California at Berkeley and founder of the Before Columbus Foundation, which promotes multicultural American writing. The American Book Awards, sponsored by the foundation has been called The American League to the National Book Awards' National League. He also founded PEN Oakland which issues the Josephine Miles Literary Awards. PEN Oakland has been called "The Blue Collar PEN" by the *New York Times*. Ishmael Reed is the author of more than thirty titles including the acclaimed novel *Mumbo Jumbo*, as well as nonfiction, plays and poetry. His other novels include: *The Freelance Pallbearers; Yellow Back Radio Broke Down; Flight To Canada; The Last Days Of Louisiana Red; Reckless Eyeballing; The Terrible Twos; The Terrible Threes; Japanese By Spring; Juice!;* and *Conjugating Hindi*.

The Luckiest People in the World

A hard time for you is not
Having enough kegs for
Your fraternity party, or
Hearing that your luxury cruise
Has been cancelled while
Our ancestors had to go
Without beer and didn't
Come over here on yachts
They weren't part of no regatta
They came in slave ships
And coffin ships

A hard time for you is when
Others are crowding
Out your bandwidth but
Suppose that you were
A Mexican American citizen
Sent across the border because
Herbert Hoover blamed
You for his Depression
Or how about a Guatemalan
Child thrown in a cage
And separated from
Its parents, permanently
If this happened to your Child
You'd be in a rage

If you think things are bad now
Because the price on your
Hi tech stocks dipped
Imagine that you're a Chinese
Girl kidnapped and sold
On the streets of
San Francisco
It's 1860 and the 6 Companies
Let strangers mangle
You for 75 cents
Yet you're upset because
Your spouse's Chanel

Wasn't delivered in
Time for the dog show

What of the other Chanel
The one taken by
An immigrant in a leaking boat
That was supposed to take him
From Libya to Italy and the
Boat capsizes and all he
Sees are black fins swimming toward
His children
Chanel that

Hell, if times get tough
You have Grubhub and
DoorDash or Walmart
Can get you groceries
In two hours when you
Reach for Peach Melba
Think of the long
Lines of cars as
People await their food
Allotments and it's 95 degrees
and your children didn't
Eat yesterday and you've
Been unemployed for a
Year and the nurses
Working in the near
By hospital have to
Use trash bags for
Gowns
The government believes
That CoVid is a Chinese
Hoax

If you think you got it bad
Suppose you were an inmate
In San Quentin
and CoVid
Is jumping from cell to cell
After having left a nursing

Home, the end for those
Who fought two wars and
Survived two depressions
Think of this as you put
Your $100 designer mask over
Your nose and chin

Your daughter has to
Attend a state school because
She was turned down by Princeton?
Girls in other countries
Get acid thrown into their
Faces if found reading books
Or they're too busy
To think about a book
Because they are slaves in
India, Africa and cases even
Pop up in the United States
From time to time
Isn't she better off than
Those kidnapped by Boko Haram or
Isis or another group
Of over armed idiots
High on testosterone
Smelling themselves
Roaming the world
Looking for a fight

Americans, even
Though you might
Be led by an over
The hill vaudevillian
Who has a hole in
The sole of his soft
Shoe and streaks of
Makeup on his collar
And lacks grog and
Is trailed by a roll
Of toilet paper
As he boards Air Force 1
Even though your

Lead evangelists romp
From motel to motel In their underwear
Even though some
Boy Scout leaders
And some Catholic
Bishops get off on children

Unlike people in the
Rest of the world
Who hold their children
As they starve in their arms
Who drink from water that
Animals and humans defecate
In
Whose lands have become
Deserts and sink under water
Because of your insatiable
Greed for toxic energy
You live a charmed life
You always win the lottery
The daily double
3 bells in a row in Las Vegas
Yet you whine grouse
Bitch and moan when
Your lives are mirrored In the
Streisand song
You are the
The Luckiest People in
The world.

WANDA COLEMAN

Wanda Coleman—poet, short story writer, novelist, and essayist—was born and raised in South Central Los Angeles. Coleman was awarded the prestigious 1999 Lenore Marshall Poetry Prize for *Bathwater Wine* from the American Academy of Poets, becoming the first Black woman to ever win the prize, and was a bronze-medal finalist for the 2001 National Book Award for Poetry for *Mercurochrome*. *Wicked Enchantment: Selected Poems* appeared in 2020, edited and introduced by Terrance Hayes. *Heart First into This Ruin: The Complete American Sonnets* appeared in 2022, introduced by Mahogany L. Browne.

EMMETT TILL

1

river jordan run red

rainfall panes the bottom acreage—rain
black earth blacker still

blackness seeps in seeps down
the mortal gravity of hate-inspired poverty
Jim Crow nidus

*the alabama the apalachinola the arkansas the aroostook
the altamaha*

killing of 14-year-old
stirs nation. there will be a public wake

works its way underground
scarred landscape veined by rage
sanctified waters flow
go forth

the bighorn the brazos

along roan valley walls blue rapids
wear away rock
flesh current quickly courses thru
the front page news amber fields purple mountains
muddies

*the chattahoochie the cheyenne the chippewa the cimarron
the colorado the columbia the connecticut the cumberland*

waftage

spirit uplifted eyes head heart
imitation of breath chest aheave

that grotesque swim up the styx
level as rainwater culls into its floodplain

the des moines

blood river born

2

ebony robe aflow
swathed hair of the black madonna
bereft of babe

the flint

that hazel eye sees
the woman
she fine mighty fine
she set the sun arising in his thighs

the hudson the humboldt the illinois

and he let go a whistle
a smooth long all-american hallelujah whistle
appreciation. a boy

the james the klamath

but she be a white woman. but he be
a black boy

*the maumee the minnesota the mississippi the missouri
the mohican*

raping her with that hazel eye

the ohio

make some peckerwood pass water mad
make a whole tributary of intolerance

*the pearl the pesos the pee dee the penobscot
the north platte the south platte the potomac*

vital fluid streaming forth in holy torrents

think about it. go mad go blind
go back to africa go civil rights go go

the red the white the green

run wine

3

silt shallows the slow sojourn seaward

they awakened him from sleep
that early fall morning
they made him dress
they hurried Emmett down to the water's edge

the roanoke

after the deed
they weighted him down
tossed him in
for his violation

*the sacramento the salt the san juan the savannah
the smoke*

from the deep dank murk of consciousness a birth
oh say do you see the men off
the bank dredging in that
strange jetsam

the tennessee the trinity

a lesson
he had to be taught—crucified (all a nigger
got on his mind) for rape by eye that
wafer-round hazel offender plucked out
they crown him

the wabash

cuz she was white woman virtue and he
be a black boy lust

the yazoo the yellowstone

oh say Emmett Till can you see Emmett Till
crossed over into campground

spill tears
nimbus threatening downpour
sweetwater culls into its soulplain

come forth to carry the dead child home

4

at my mouth forking

autumn 1955, lord!
kidnapped from his family visit
lord!
money road shanty
lord!
his face smashed in
lord! lord!
his body beaten beyond cognition
river mother carries him
laid in state
sovereign at last

that all may witness true majesty
cast eyes upon

murder

the youth's body too light
was weighted down in barbed wire & steel

dumped into the river agape a ripple a wave
(once it was human)

aweigh. awade in water. bloated
baptized

and on that third say awaft
from the mulky arm of the tallahatchie
stretched cross cotton-rich flats
of delta

*on that third day
he rose*

and was carried forth to that promised land

Wanda Coleman, "Emmett Till" from *Wicked Enchantment: Selected Poems.* Reprinted by permission of Black Sparrow Press. Copyright © 1990, 2020 by Wanda Coleman.

Eugene B. Redmond

Eugene B. Redmond, emeritus professor of English and Black Studies at Southern Illinois University Edwardsville, was named Poet Laureate of East St. Louis in 1976. That same year Doubleday released his "critical history," *Drumvoices: The Mission of Afro-American Poetry*. Earlier—1967-69—he taught with Katherine Dunham and writer Henry Dumas (1934-1968) at SIU's Experiment in Higher Education. He also helped found Black Studies Programs and weekly newspapers, including the *East St. Louis Monitor*, where he wrote weekly columns and editorials. As literary executor of Dumas's estate, and with assistance from Toni Morrison, Maya Angelou, Quincy Troupe and Amiri Baraka, Redmond edited several volumes of his late friend's writings. These included *Ark of Bones* (short fiction), *Knees of a Natural Man* (poetry), *Jonoah and the Green Stone* (novel) and *Echo Tree* (short fiction). While/after serving as Professor of English and Poet-in-Residence in Pan African/Ethnic Studies at CSU-Sacramento (70's-80's), Redmond won an NEA Fellowship, a Pushcart Prize, an Outstanding Faculty Research/Teaching Award, and two American Book Awards. He also co-directed CSUS's Annual Third World Writers and Thinkers Symposium. Third World Press published his *Arkansippi Memwars* in 2012.

BAM!: Pre-, Present-, & Post-Black Arts Movement

Between Askia's
Pyramids & The Projects
Africa stumbled, got lost
In Middle Passages &
Discovered Arkansippi

Between Zora & Maya
Strange Fruit's Morning Heartache met
Gwen Brooks's Bronzeville

Between Richard Wright
& Ta Nehesi Coates LOOMed
The Black Arts Movement

Between Black is Beautiful
& George cum Breonna
Black Lives Matter sang:

Amiri, Sonia,
Ankh Dumas, Haki, Alice, Ra,
Toni(s)—Amanda(la)!

Long Distance Warriors, Dreamers & Rhymers

In memory of my parents,
John Henry Sr. & Emma Jean (Hutchinson) Redmond
(& for Mahmoud El Kati)

O classical mammas & poppas: soular-centered lovers &
Parents of Drum Scripture & Pyramid:
Nile-cool & Benin-blue Songhaifiers:
   hip—& pre-Hip/Hop—diasporan daddies
          & honey-in-the-rock divas:
               ship-huddled & cattle-hurried
       across the Ethiopian Ocean. O epic parents:

Fine brown arks war-poised & prayerful.
Long-distance
Dreamers & W.E.B.'s souljahs smelting ancestral ore
into double-conscious Rhymes
       of epic Passage
          epic Pain
               epic Spillage.

Lo, you "stolen" legacies
Rocking burdens beside the Mississippi
& creeping or racing
              like Ogun's archers & Harriet's scouts
                  through steal-away nights:

Militantly upright,
or shape-shifty,
your winged whisperings
arming us with clouds of joy
that "swing low" & "fetch high":

  Olmec & Soul Trek Nat Turner & Sojourner
  Paul Laurence Dunbar & James Weldon Johnson
  Hughes's Blues Mahalia & Maya B.B. & Cee Cee
  Mary Bethune & Henry Dumas & Duke's Jive
  Zora Neale & Larry Neal Cullen & Hayden
  Elijah & Umoja Gwendolyn & Aretha
  Kenyatta & Mandela Nyere & Amiri Nina & Sonia
  Toni & Terri Malcolm & Jesse
  Katherine & Latifah Juju & Jesus.

O parents of Mem/Wars & Love-Mergers: ritual (!) clickings
storefront-saviors cornbread-fantasies hambone & banjo
        railroad & gumbo Thurgood's legions King's cadres
of Orators...O epic parents of mother-shore & father ore
        smelting generations of fine brown arks
        Ntu battle & prayer: warriors dreamers rhymers.

"Be My Brother Forever": Maya Angelou & the Invention of a FriendShip, 1970s-Style
A Hook Up Haiku

Nineteen Seventy:
"Brother be, I'll sister thee,"
Maya sang to me.

The Loss—her passing—is Huge, Huger than the Leap of Fate she took to co-invent her place on the planet.
        (But that's a whole nother chapter
        for a whole nother tome.

It suffices to say, simply & Hugely:
Maya's gone.)
She was 41. I was 32. It was the fall of 1970. Sacramento (CA) City College. (We'd exchanged glances and nods at "cause"-inflected rallies, arts events and sundry moments in the late Sixties. But whether in New York or Los Angeles, no other "moment" would be like this one.)
Her exact words were:
"Eugene, be my brother forever!"

A tall order from a tall woman, it came during our first full contact. Right after Maya Angelou had slung her songified language at—and *plie'd* to—an SRO throng for more than an hour. Initially I was smacked aback by this uncaged bird, this leggy goddess, this poet, actress, dancer and former cast member of *Porgy and Bess* and—with <u>James Earl Jones</u>, <u>Cicely Tyson</u>, <u>Roscoe Lee Browne</u>, *et al*—the New York production of Genet's *The Blacks*. But I quickly readied for her request-into-perpetuity, thinking, "brother?" "forever?" . . . *Shiddddd* . . . *nuttin but sumpn to do*. After all, hadn't I just done *time*—60s-style—in East St. Louis (aka "East Boogie"), Illinois? Followed by a year's stop-off at Oberlin College (Ohio) as writer-in-residence, where I'd met poets Russell Atkins, Norman Jordan and James Kilgore—in nearby Cleveland? And Calvin Hernton—who would replace me at Oberlin, and later date Angelou in the 1980s? Hadn't I, among other Black Arts Movement (BAM) self-assignments, spent the last years of the 60's frequently delivering elegiac/eulogistic poems & polemics for fallen warriors, many felled under questionable circumstances? (And when there was even a fraction of an iota of a suspicion about causes of the "fall" of one of our comrades—e.g., Henry Dumas (1934-1968)—hadn't we chalked our charges up to "healthy paranoia"?) Hadn't I—as a faculty member at Southern Illinois University's Experiment in Higher Education in East St. Louis—worked with colleagues, artists and students like Dumas, Katherine Dunham, Edward Crosby, Julius Hemphill, Oliver Jackson, Joyce Ladner and Sherman Fowler to help conceptualize and implement the new Black/African American Studies Movement? (And wouldn't this same Sacramento City College—the one where Maya had just delivered her

mixed-genre, high/low art jeremiad—elect a student senate that voted in a jailed Angela Davis as honorary homecoming queen?
 Hadn't . . . ? Didn't . . . ? Wouldn't . . . ?

 So our Ship of Friends set sail in the *Soular System* in a state named after a fictional Black Amazon and warrior queen, *Califia*. (According to Spanish writer Garci Rodríguez de Montalvo who first introduced her in his popular novel *Las sergas de Esplandián* [circa 1500], Califia and her army of amazons inhabited a namesake island off the southwest coast of California.) During the Seventies, Maya and I frequently and vigorously traversed the near-90-miles of Northern California, from Sacramento, where I lived, to the San Francisco Bay Area, where she resided. This swath of flatland, mountains, factories, farms, cities, people and sea was like many US and other world "stages" in the Sixties and Seventies: used both for celebrating human-natural wonders and for "revolutionary" problem-solving of human-natural warts. Be these wonders and warts artistic, cultural, ecological, ethnic, gender, sexual, political or social. For example, we discussed and supported African/Third World liberation movements and witnessed the Independence of dozens of countries. Between 1972 and 1979, the SF Bay Area had one of the most vigorous Africa Liberation (Day) Support Committees in America. Central to our discussions and debates—which were augmented by innumerable rallies, conferences and workshops—were dinners upon parties upon dinners upon book signings at Marcus Books in SF, Maryann Pollar's Rainbow Sign in Berkeley and Elroy Littlefield's Campus Bookstore at California State University-Sacramento (CSUS). At the latter, I was a professor of English and poet-in-residence in Pan African/Ethnic Studies, an appointment that lasted nearly 15 years, beginning in 1970. Maya spoke frequently in my classes and writing workshops and to gatherings at my home and in the community. She also keynoted several of CSUS' Annual Third World Writers and Thinkers Symposiums which featured Jose Montoya, Clyde Taylor, Janice Mirikitani, Simon Ortiz, N. Scott Momaday, Momoko Iko, Ron Takaki, Ishmael Reed, Joy Harjo, Quincy Troupe (with the Watts Writers Workshop), Pinkie Gordon Lane, Ike Paggett (who Maya called "that wonderful looking saxophonist") and scores of others. About my friend Marie Collins, director of Sacramento's Oak Park School of Afro-American Thought and an organizer of the

Third World Symposium, Maya once exclaimed, "What an awesome mental machine!" Lavishing high praise when and where it was due was a consistent trait of my sister for life.

Following the huge success of *I Know Why the Caged Bird Sings* (with its title's nod to "Sympathy" by Dunbar, a favorite poet of Maya's from childhood) and release of the book's made-for-TV movie starring Diahann Carroll, a team of us, including colleagues David Covin, Ted Hornback and Hortense Simmons Thornton, brought Maya to CSUS as a Distinguished Visiting Professor. Then living in Sonoma wine country, she crashed at my crib for a few days each week during her residency. At CSUS, she developed a prototypical pedagogical system that would characterize her classroom ambiance for the next 40-plus years. A combination of raconteur, dramatist and songifier, she meshed the following disciplines: philosophy (ancient Africans/Greeks, African American Folklore and contemporary thinkers like theologian Howard Thurman), literature (a solid cross-cultural/cross-gender sampling with a focus on current issues, consciousness-raising and activism), creative writing (exercises including recitation and group work) and drama—her forte—(including a playlet that she and students co-wrote and produced at the end of the semester). Mingled among all of these were the parties, the dinners, the restaurant (Ming Tree, a favorite) and bar hopping. Meanwhile, her "star" had begun to rise, yes, but it had not reached its full height critically and commercially. So when she was diagnosed with fibroid cancer, her new husband Paul DuFeu, a Welsh-Englishman with a French name, and I taught her CSUS classes during an extended recovery period. In other words, she could not afford to be sick and not have an income at the same time.

(Fact again: Contrast the 1970s, when, if you brought an extra guest to dinner at Maya's home, you might also bring along a bucket of chicken and/or a bottle of wine, with the 1990s through the 2000s when patrons, corporations and friends would spend millions on special occasions honoring her. And when Maya herself hosted annual five-day soirees, including sit-down Thanksgiving dinners for 200-plus relatives and friends—aka "the family." Flash forward: On the eve of her June 7 [2014] memorial service at Wake Chapel on the campus of Wake Forest University in Winston-Salem [NC], Redge Hanes, of "the" Hanes empire, hosted a reception. And the repast after the memorial itself was held at

Graylyn Estate [think Reynolds as in R.J.]).

Into this mix was stirred our own individual or joint poetry readings and lecture tours, with time thrown in for us to get caught up on each other. As "forever"/new friends and artists, we took up the ageless practice of reading out loud—face-to-face or by phone—from our published poems as well as pieces-in-progress. Occasionally included for good "measures" were canonical and newly emerging bards like Shakespeare, Wheatley, James Weldon Johnson, Hughes, Dunbar, Georgia Douglass Johnson, Hayden, Brooks (Gwen), Clifton, Roethke, Mirikitani, Baraka and Brown (Sterling). Maya threaded these poets, along with poems from my books (like *Sentry of the Four Golden Pillars, River of Bones and Flesh and Blood* and, especially, *In a Time of Rain & Desire*) into her touring repertoire. We spoke, ate, laughed and danced to sounds of Satchmo, Duke, Sarah, Bird, Miles, Makeba, Nina (a dear friend of Maya's) and Billie, whose prophetic issuance, "You'll be famous—but not for singing," rang stubbornly true for Maya, once an aspiring singer. And, yes, Maya's own star continually "rose," as she liked to put it, but, as she also said to me, this "rise" created consternation among some of her artistic peers whose stars simultaneously took tailspins or "stagnated." Nevertheless "sister" continued to "cook" creatively, both literarily and culinarily. There were books (*Gather Together in My Name, Singin' and Swingin' and Gettin' Merry Like Christmas*), plays (Oakland Ensemble Theatre's production of "And Still I Rise," in which she included poetry from my third book, *Songs from an Afro/Phone*), film directorships (*Georgia, Georgia* and, decades later, *Down in the Delta*), awards (*Ladies' Home Journal:* "Woman of the Year"), nominations (Pulitzers, Tonys), residencies (CSUS, Wichita State University, The Rockefeller Foundation's Bellagio Center in Italy) and an honorary Ph.D. from Oakland's Mills College (1975), the first of a string ending in a total of 74 before her death in May 2014.

Another brother-friend Alex Haley, in whose made-for-TV movie, *Roots*, Maya played Kunta Kinte's grandmother, said in 1976 that she possessed "at least six women," besting Nina ("Four Women") by two. And like *Amen Corner*, a play by James Baldwin, yet another brother-friend-mentor, had become a staple of black community theater in the Fifties and Sixties, so was Maya's life, fecundity and creative brilliance becoming a staple of new Black/Ethnic and Women's Studies classes and departments across the country. Almost as renowned for her kitchen cookin' as for her virtuosic page and stage performances—"My brother, let me tell ya, I strode on stage carryin' ALL of this 'Black' female equipment"—her multi-personae, cuisinartistic and poetic stance are what I tried to capture in "Maya's Kitchen: Homage to SisterCook," the opening lines of which are:

> *Maya's cookin' again . . . & we,*
>   *epicurious old salts & newly seasoned/newly wrought,*
> *voyage thru her kitchens as words,*
>   *roasting like turkey on her tongue,*
> *roll over lips of her oven & feed our famished minds*
>   *with loaves of poetry,*
> *(purple) onion rings of biography,*
>   *tart salads of song & yeasty yields of drama.*

AISHAH RAHMAN

Aishah Rahman was born on November 4, 1936 and grew up in Harlem, New York. In the late 50s, she moved to Greenwich Village where she hung out with the beatniks and was inspired by the confluence of arts, politics, music and theater. Rahman's work plumbed the experience of Black women but was universal in exploring themes of family, politics and the healing nature of art. And she used humor to draw audiences in and keep them connected to her characters.

Rahman was the author of numerous plays. Her styles range from dramas, such as *Unfinished Women Cry In No Man's Land While a Bird Dies in a Gilded Cage* and *The Mojo and the Sayso*, to musicals, such as *Lady Day: A Musical Tragedy*, and *The Tale of Madame Zora*. Her plays were produced at The Public Theater, The Ensemble Theatre and theaters and universities across the United States. Among her numerous fellowships and awards are a special award from the Rockefeller Foundation of the Arts for dedication to playwriting in the American Theater, The Doris Abramson Playwriting Award for *The Mojo and the Sayso*, and a New York Foundation for the Arts Fellowship. Her memoir *Chewed Water* was published in 2001 to critical acclaim. Rahman was a professor at Brown University from 1992-2011. She passed in 2014 in San Miguel, Mexico.

The Mojo and the Sayso

"On a gloomy morning in April 1973, 10-year old Clifford Glover, a poor Black boy in South Jamaica, Queens, was shot dead by a New York City police officer. The reaction to the 'senseless killing' from both black and white New Yorkers was one of anger as marches and other forms of protests swung into motion."

Amsterdam News, Dec. 24, 1981

This play is dedicated to the family of
Clifford Glover

My torn house
shivers   in the wind

     ragged edges like open nerves.
Hurt and then hurt.
I wrestle with my doubt

     and flailing sorrow.

What can I do? But spin and
then spin
again.
     Out of me, my self, my Jacob's ladder of
     God-loyalty.
     My redemption. My
     Heaven-House.

Angela Jackson

Characters

ACTS BENJAMIN	Late middle age
AWILDA BENJAMIN	Younger than her husband, ACTS
BLOOD	Their son
VIRGINIA	Their daughter
PASTOR DELROY	A man of the cloth

ACT ONE, Scene 1

CURTAIN up on a typically furnished family living room. Stage left is a mantlepiece that has a collection of various colored candles. Center stage on a slight platform is a half built car. Hubcaps, tires, fenders, etc. are scattered around. The rest of the room is neat; it is only this area that is disordered. AWILDA dressed entirely in white is frantically searching for something among the mechanical automotive parts. Her voice is heard over the whirr of an acetylene torch that ACTS, inside the car frame, is using.

AWILDA
Ball joints, tires, shock absorbers, spark plugs, carburetors.

ACTS
Oh! The treasures and dreams that's buried in a junkyard! Damn near tore my paws off trying to get to this baby but I got it. Knowed it was only a few left in the world. Never thought I'd own one but I do now. A Lycomen engine. They used to put it in the only best of machines back in '47. Used to put it in a deluxe car they called The Auburn Cord. It had an electric shift, front wheel drive same as you got today. Car was so advanced, so ahead of its time they took it off the market. Man this engine was so bad they used to put her in aeroplanes. Now I'm gonna put her right in here ... Jim!

AWILDA
Wrenches, hammers,

ACTS
Soon I'll be finished the dream car of my mind.

AWILDA
Batteries, mufflers, spark coils, piston rings, radiator caps, gaskets, fenders, exhaust pipes. White gloves? No white gloves.

ACTS
A chrome plated masterpiece. Brown and gold flecked with a classy body...built with my own hands.

AWILDA
You are not listening to me.

ACTS

(without looking up)
Of course I am.

AWILDA

(she goes over to the candles) *[Throughout the scene Awilda, when not busy elsewhere, will return to the mantlepiece to tend her candles.]*

I'll light an orange candle. It'll help me to concentrate and find my white gloves.

ACTS

One day you're gonna burn us down to the ground with those damn candles of yours.

AWILDA

Shhhh! They can hear you. They won't burn for me if you talk like that. *(lights candle)* There. I've lit the way to my white gloves. I'll have them in time to go to church.

ACTS

I've found a engine for the car.

AWILDA

Pastor Delroy wants all the saints dressed in white. Pure white, from crown to toe.

ACTS

Used to use this engine in an Auburn Cord. They don't come any better.

AWILDA

This Sunday is special. Have you forgotten what today is?

ACTS

A priceless engine. Tossed in the junkyard.

AWILDA

It's the fifth anniversary of the accident. There's even gonna be a special church service for him.

ACTS

I see no need to draw attention to the unfortunate by-products of your womb!

AWILDA

What became of our children?

ACTS

We'll say no more about it.

AWILDA

The girl left us. She speaks several different languages but she's lost the knack for English. Says she doesn't understand a word I say.

ACTS

The boy floats around with a bomb in his heart.

AWILDA

And I dream of Linus every night.

ACTS

I never dream of him. At least not while I am sleeping.

AWILDA

It's always the same dream. Linus is still ten years old but he is older than time. All three of us are strolling down the avenue. You, Linus and me. Suddenly music is all around us. We breathe it in with our bodies. It is like a feeding. Suddenly a mint blue sea jumps in front of us. The boy and I walk naked into the water, leaving our bodies like old clothes upon the shore.

ACTS

(stops working on the car for the first time, completely captivated by her dream)

Yeah? Go on. What do I do?

AWILDA

You...you steal our bodies and run.

ACTS

I do not! I do not!

AWILDA

You run and run and run and run!
(yelling and screaming)
You are such a liar! Look at you with your face twisted like a peach pit. You are such a liar! If lies were brains you'd be Einstein. You are such a liar. If lies were mountain tops you'd be high. As soon as I hear you all cry I rush to your side. I put your bodies in mine. I

keep telling you that.

AWILDA

I know. Maybe I'll get it right tonight.

ACTS

It wouldn't be so hard to deal with if you would say with all your might, "NO" he could never desert his son in danger. He's a man!

AWILDA

But I tell you that all the time. Honest I try not to think about it. What do you care what I think as long as God knows the truth. Isn't God enough for you?

ACTS

NO! I still need people. I still need you. There are nights when I see myself all the way to my bones. Check every corner of my heart and come out so sure that not the slightest doubt is inside of me. But come the morning ... I wake up and look at you and remember the truth. The doubt I see in you makes me guilty!

AWILDA

I'll dream it right. I promise. I'll wake myself up if I dream it wrong again.

ACTS

All of us have a dream world. Get in my lady.

AWILDA

(reluctantly, Awilda climbs in the frame of the car and sits)

ACTS

(in the manner of a king showing his queen the castle)
This is where the radio's gonna be. Soon you'll be able to flick the dial to your favorite music. Not none of them Jesus songs, honey. I mean give me a break. You should learn how to drive. Be good for you. Give you something else to think something soft. Fur maybe. Just for you. Gonna put a bar in the back. You can keep your ginger ale in there. If you want. Hold on. I'll take you for a ride around the neighborhood now. Hold on. Here we go. We're cruising up past Kissena Boulevard, down Sunset past Jamaica Avenue. Mmmmmmm. Smell the air. Someone's barbecuing. Look at those old wooden frame houses next to the tall apartment buildings. See

the churches. See the ladies in they pinks and yellows and whites and blue. See the folks hanging out. See them turn they heads as we go riding by. Whew! Hot isn't it? Let's get a couple of beers and drive out to the beach, take off our clothes and lay in the sun—

AWILDA

(standing up, breaking the spell)

I'm late for church.

ACTS

Shh. Don't be scared. Don't be nervous. You with me now. Sit back down!

AWILDA

(sitting down)

I can't help it.

ACTS

I know. I know. Just get it together. Listen, don't you hear what people are saying? They are saying "There goes the wizard of the automobile world. Acts Benjamin and his wife. See that car he's driving. He only builds them for the leading citizens of the world.

(sees Awilda getting up and tries to pull her back)

Hey, where are you going ... we're almost there. I'll park the car and we can lay in the sun—

AWILDA

I want to get out. I need my white gloves! I'm late for church!

ACTS

It's folks like you that give religion a bad name.
(escaping from the car)

Now you listen to me. I'd rather do what God tells me than listen to you.

(resumes searching for gloves)

All you do is rummage through junkyards, bringing your "buried treasure" in this room, working on that car every hour day or night, winter or summer, snowstorm or heatwave.

ACTS

That's why I want it in the house—so that the weather don't matter.

AWILDA

All the time, whacking, banking, drilling on that ... that ...

ACTS

Car ... it's a car.

AWILDA

All the time working on that car. Tell me. What do you get out of it? What do you see in it?

ACTS

You asked me so I'm telling. When I look at this car I see lots of things.

AWILDA

Like what?

ACTS

Anything I want to see.

AWILDA

What?

ACTS

I see money, no worries, understanding, tittie squeezing and pussy teasing!

AWILDA

It's no wonder that I turned to Christ.

ACTS

No wonder.

AWILDA

Pastor says that you ...

ACTS

If I didn't have first hand personal knowledge that Jesus done locked your thighs and thrown the key away, that religion done stole your natural feelings I'd be 'clined to think that you and that Jack-leg-son-of a bi—

AWILDA

Watch your mouth. Don't you know I'm on my way to church? Imagine being jealous of God. That's why you bad mouth the messenger of God's word every chance. I used to be just like you till I found Pastor. One day when I was listening to him preach, my breath grew short, my throat closed up and I couldn't breathe. It was Pastor Delroy I was looking at but Jesus that I was seeing. "Lord," I said. "Lord, I am in your hands."

ACTS

(going towards her)

I was once into that holiness bag and I know that trick. All them jackleg pastors and deacons and elders laughing at you. Laughing at you and taking your money. All you women jumping up and down yelling "come sweet Jesus" need to stay home and say it to your husbands!

ACTS

(he tweaks her tit and pats her butt)

AWILDA

(backing away from him)

You ain't nothing but the Devil.

ACTS

(laughing)

Forget about the Devil. Forget about the sign of the Cross. It is the sign of Power and the sign of the trick *(holds up her white gloves in hand)* that gets it every time.

(returns to working on car)

AWILDA

You had them all the time.

ACTS

Maybe.

AWILDA

(grabbing them from him)

These white gloves are genuine brushed cotton. The other day

I was downtown window shopping thinking about what I would wear in church today and suddenly I found myself in Bonwits. I don't know how I got there. It was like my feet had grown a mind of they own. I wanted to turn around and run but something made me brazen it out. So I marched to the glove counter and stood there. Four detectives followed me. The salesgirl left the blue haired silver foxed madame she was waiting on and rushed over to me. "Can I help you, miss?" she said. Imagine that. "Miss" to me though I am a married woman and had (at one time) three children. Then I told her "I'm not a Miss, I'm a Mrs. and I'd like a pair of white gloves." "They start at $50.00, Miss." she snapped. And then I took my time and made her show me lace gloves, net gloves, nylon gloves, leather gloves and I didn't like any of them until she showed me these. The most expensive ones and I said "Oh, aren't they lovely. I'll take them. And after all that aggravation I don't see why you would hide them from me unless you wanted to make me late for church an keep me here with you!

ACTS

(absorbed in his car)
I'm hungry. Get me something to eat.

AWILDA

Sure. What would you like? Spark plugs? Machine oil? Gasoline?

(ACTS works on the car ignoring her)

AWILDA

(looking up at him a long time before she says in a pleading voice)
I really can't tell sometimes if you aren't turning into a car.

ACTS

Honk! Honk!

AWILDA

You could come with me if you wanted to. You could get dressed and come with me to church.

ACTS

Don't get started on that again please.

                    AWILDA

(going towards the windows)

I'm opening up all the windows.

                    ACTS

(preoccupied)

Yeah,yeah,yeah,yeah!

                    AWILDA

Every night I lay out your striped blue suit and your Van Heusen shirt with the rolled collar and your diamond stick pin and your patent leather wing tips and your ribbed silk socks and your monogrammed hand embroidered linen pocket handkerchief hoping that you will come to church with me.

                    ACTS

I told you I don't go for that bull.

                    AWILDA

All the trouble that went through was for God but all you think about is that, that, that, thing. That car you building. You can give me a Rolls Royce and say it's mine but it ain't. It's God's car.

(The sound of ACTS hammering away at his car is his only response)

Mr. Benjamin I'm a peaceful loving woman and I'm opening all these windows wide open so that God can come in here and fill you heart.

                (looking up from his car)

Stay away from the windows!

                    AWILDA

(running around opening up windows)

Get him God. Get him God. Come in. Come in. Stab his soul. Pierce his stubborn heart!

                    ACTS

(enraged, runs around slamming windows)

shutupshutupshutup Goddamit.

(he breaks all the windows with a tool)

AWILDA

(singing at the top of her voice)

I knit my world
With strong church yarn
With stitches even and unbroken
for God is my true husband
Who keeps me from harm
He is my only one.

(As she finishes they gaze up at each other silently, the maniacal peal of church bells rushes through the broken windows. They are both ashamed)

AWILDA

(going to her candles)

I'll light a blue candle for us dear. It will soothe us. You'll have to hurry and fix the windows. My candles can't grow in a room with broken windows.

ACTS

(returning to work on his car)

I've got to hurry and finish this.

AWILDA

I'll light a new candle for Linus too. The old one will soon be finished.

Linus is dead. Why must you talk about him all the time? Let the dead remain dead! I'm sick of your foolishness!

AWILDA

(lighting her candles)

The dead live in us. I must light the flame. Linus lives through me. I must light the flame. I depend on his spirit so that I can live. I must light the flame.

ACTS

Only thing I must do is finish this car.

AWILDA

(turning from candles)

We've got to take care of one another. Keep healthy. There'sno one else to look after us. Linus would have if he had liv-

ACTS

But he didn't.

(looking at check)

AWILDA

"Wrongful death" that's what the city called it. Now we got lots of money. Lots of money for the life of our boy.

ACTS

Six figures. Big digits! Wonder how they figger what a 10 year old boy's life is worth to his parents. Think they have a chart or something? Probably feed it into a computer. I tried to protect him that night you know.

AWILDA

Linus is gonna get a memorial ... Something special.

ACTS

I tried to protect him.

AWILDA

You always done that. Protected us, I mean.

ACTS

Let's not talk about it anymore.
It's late Awilda. It's late.

AWILDA

(going toward him)

Then you stop time. I want you to stop it. Turn time back inits track. Make time be five years ago when the girl was still here and the boy wouldn't hurt anybody and Linus was alive. Turn back time! Turn back! Time! Stop Time!

ACTS

There is no more time. Time has melted in our hands.

AWILDA

I thought the boy would have taken over after Linus. Look after things. Look after us. After Linus I put all my hopes on him. He was always making something. Always dreaming.
He was smart! He was kind! He was tender! You remember?

ACTS

(holds her)

AWILDA

Now he wants to set the world on fire. Bombs, guns, Kill, Kill! In his mind he's a killer. Blow the world sky high. Kill all the people. Before the "accident" there wasn't a mean bone in his body. He loved everybody. Everybody loved him.
He used to sing and dance.

ACTS

Go to church. I think a storm is coming.

AWILDA

Let the storm come. Snow is falling on the sun! Trees run blood! Sidewalks grow guns besides dead boy children! But for me there are(*suddenly walking away from him)* no clouds or sign of rain or man made disaster for miles. The sun will light my path all the way to church. When I get there I just pay attention to songs and sermons, music and words, voices and faces and feelings. The things to keep me going. I guess I just believe in spiritual things. Spiritual things is all.

(During AWILDA's monologue, BLOOD has stuck his face through one of the broken windows. While she is still speaking he surreptitiously climbs through the window and bursts in the room.)

BLOOD

(facing the audience and waving a gun at them)
ALRIGHT. WHOEVER YOU ARE I KNOW YOU ARE HIDING IN THIS HOUSE. I KNOW YOU ARE IN HERE SOMEWHERE IN HERE. THROW OUT YOUR WEAPONS AN GIVE YOURSELF UP. CAUSE I CAN BOMB YOU, CUT YOU, SHOOT YOU. I DONE WARNED THIS AINT NO F----- PUNK COPS YOU DEALING WIFFTH! THIS IS ME, BLOOD.

END OF ACT ONE, Scene 1

Henry Dumas

Fiction writer and poet **Henry Dumas** was born in Sweet Home, Arkansas in 1934, but moved to Harlem when he was 10. After attending City College in New York, he joined the Air Force and was stationed on the Arabian Peninsula and in San Antonio, Texas. He identified with the Civil Rights and Black Arts movements and was active on the little magazine circuit. At the age of 33, in 1968, Dumas was shot and killed by a New York City Transit policeman under unclarified circumstances. Eugene B. Redmond, Dumas's colleague at Southern Illinois University-East St. Louis, helped to make Dumas's books available posthumously; they include *Play Ebony, Play Ivory* (1974). *Knees of a Natural Man: The Selected Poetry of Henry Dumas* (1989/2021), which topped SPD's Bestseller List, and *Echo Tree* (fiction, 2021). Dumas's writings are influenced by African American history, blues, jazz, gospel music, and Arabic culture/mythology, as well as Christianity and the supernatural. Many scholars, critics and poets consider him a pioneering voice of "Africanfuturism."

Knees of a Natural Man
for Jay Wright

my ole man took me to the fulton fish market
we walk around in the guts and the scales

my ole man show me a dead fish, eyes like throat spit
he say "you hongry boy?" i say "naw, not yet"

my ole man show me how to pick the leavings
he say people throw away fish that not rotten

we scaling on our knees back uptown on lenox
sold five fish, keepin one for the pot

my ole man copped a bottle of wine
he say, "boy, build me a fire out in the lot"

backyard cat climbin up my leg for fish
i make a fire in the ash can

my ole man come when he smell fish
frank williams is with him, they got wine

my ole man say "the boy cotch the big one"
he tell big lie and slap me on the head

i give the guts to the cat and take me some wine
we walk around the sparks like we in hell

my ole man is laughin and coughin up wine
he say "you hongry boy" i say "naw, not yet"

next time i go to fulton fish market
first thing i do is take a long drink of wine

Love Song

Beloved,
I have to adore the earth:

The wind must have heard
your voice once.
It echoes and sings like you.

The soil must have tasted
you once.
It is laden with your scent.

The trees honor you
in gold
and blush when you pass.

I know why the north country
is frozen.
It has been trying to preserve
your memory.

I know why the desert
burns with fever.
It was wept too long without you.

On hands and knees,
the ocean begs up the beach,
and falls at your feet.

I have to adore
the mirror of the earth.
You have taught her well
how to be beautiful.

Son of Msippi

Up
from Msippi I grew.
(Bare walk and cane stalk
make a hungry belly talk.)
Up
from the river of death.
(Walk bare and stalk cane
make a hungry belly talk.)

Up
from Msippi I grew.
Up
from the river of pain.

Out of the long red earth dipping, rising,
spreading out in deltas and plains,

out of the strong black earth turning
over by the iron plough,

out of the swamp green earth dripping
with moss and snakes,

out of the loins of the leveed lands
muscling its American vein:
the great Father of Waters,
I grew
up,
beside the prickly boll of white,
beside the bone-filled Mississippi
rolling on and on,
breaking over,
cutting off,
ignoring my bleeding fingers.

Bare stalk and sun walk
I hear a boll-weevil talk
cause I grew
up
beside the ox and the bow,
beside the rock church and the shack row,
beside the fox and the crow,
beside the melons and maize,
beside the hound dog,
beside the pink hog,
flea-hunting,
mud-grunting,
cat-fishing,
dog pissing
in the Mississippi
rolling on and on,
ignoring the colored coat I spun
of cotton fibers.

Cane-sweat river-boat
nigger-bone floating.

Up from Msippi
I grew,
wailing a song with every strain.

Woman gone woe man too
baby cry rent-pause daddy flew.

Michael Simanga

Michael Simanga is an activist scholar, artist, educator from Detroit. His work is informed by his study, teachers, mentors, ancestors and life in the Black Liberation Movement. He has written and edited seven books, produced music and more than 200 artistic projects. He lives in Atlanta with his wife, the poet Lita Hooper and their children and grandchildren.

Haiku for Sonia Sanchez

Blues lyrics at dawn
Poetry hums the night mood
Flowers from her song

A Tribute to Amiri Baraka
(October 7, 1934 – January 9, 2014)

Amiri Baraka's death on January 9, 2014, caused the Black ecosystem of institutions, intellectuals, artists and activists committed to our century's long fight for human rights to stagger under the weight of the loss and its possible meanings. Even as we gathered ourselves to publicly mourn and honor him, to write and read our thoughts and feelings, there was a sense that a significant change had occurred in our world of resistance and struggle. In the weeks after his death, when we had not quite found our footing, our brother-Jackson, Mississippi Mayor Chokwe Lumumba-transitioned suddenly, followed by one of our great historians Vincent Harding, our beautiful storyteller Maya Angelou and the relentless advocate for African people Elombe Brath. It was as if Baraka's death was not enough to force us to see we are reaching the end of the era of the Warrior Generation.

Imamu Amiri Baraka was many things to our people, we collectively and us individually. He was an artist with exceptionally deep perception and talent, an educator, a political and spiritual leader, a revolutionary strategist and institution builder, a fearless warrior against all who would diminish black people, an insightful teacher, a scholar of African American history and culture, a determined advocate for Black self-determination, a husband and father, and a prolific writer who created a significant body of work that included poetry, plays, essays, fiction, music and scholarly articles. The many forms in which he came to us were the result of his never ending quest to find a way to give everything he had in service of the people he loved, Black people and humanity. Even his names reminded us of his changes: LeRoi Jones, Ameer Baraka, Imamu Baraka, and Amiri Baraka. We were inspired and sometimes confused by his shape shifting. Sometimes we were angered by it and in opposition to it. But we never doubted it was him. We were never unsure of his voice or that he was our warrior, that all of his prodigious gifts were focused on and fueled by our demand for self-determination and justice.

Amiri Baraka was one of many intellectuals of his generation whose scholarly research and study, writing, teaching and work actually influenced the political struggle of African Americans and called countless young artists, activists and scholars to work on behalf of our people. But Baraka's political influence is extraordinary in his generation of exceptional thinkers and workers because of his direct involvement and leadership of significant historical events in the Black Liberation Movement. That leadership grew from an underlying principle that remained consistent in his activism. Baraka's work has always been based on building institutions that would engage greater numbers of people in an organized effort to advance the struggle. Some of these institutions were local, community-based organizations and some also had national and international scope and impact. He believed that where ever we are it is necessary to build, strengthen or expand structures that will help us wage and sustain our efforts.

Throughout his public life he founded or co-founded newspapers, theatre companies, cultural centers, community organizations, national liberation organizations and numerous coalitions and united fronts. While he is widely acknowledged as the most influential artist of the Black Arts Movement, for the past 50 years he also built cultural institutions including The Black Arts Repertory Theatre, Spirit House,

Kimako's Blues People and Blue Ark as platforms to nurture, engage and organize actors, writers, directors, poets, musicians and cultural workers. The political formations he co-founded and played significant leadership roles in included the Committee for Unified Newark, Congress of African People, National Black Political Convention, National Black Assembly, African Liberation Support Committee and many others. He also formed and supported several publications including *Black NewArk, Unity and Struggle* and *Black Nation Magazine*. In the days preceding his death Baraka was still organizing, supporting and building another political formation, the mayoral campaign of his son, Ras Baraka. Ras won the election and is now the Mayor of Newark 44 years after his father organized the first Black Nationalist led electoral movement in a major city that succeeded in electing Newark's first Black mayor Ken Gibson.

Amiri Baraka left more than forty published works as a record of his research, thought, and constantly developing consciousness. It is evidence of his dedication and seemingly boundless capacity for productivity. It is also evidence of his understanding that we, the writers and artists, the intellectual warriors, the scholars and teachers, have a sacred, crucial role in our people's history and future. There are many pages of his writings that have never been published and hopefully will begin to make their way to us in the near future so we may further benefit from his thought and work and a life of struggle that is worthy of the ancestors who inspired him to give his life and gifts to us.

"When I die, the consciousness I carry I will to black people."
—Amiri Baraka

Ntozake Shange Say

open your mouth
stick out your tongue
unleash the sounds
trapped in your throat
let the deep and frivolous
the curious and profound
explode
into the world
of faces

fix your lips
with kisses
frowns
smirks
and smiles
blow big bubbles of spit
or bubble gum if you got it
make it pop in your molars
on the downbeat
of your walk

squeeze the words
from your head
let them run wildly down your face
and legs
own the flow like the body you claim
grab the hem of your skirt
catch your poems
before they shatter on the sidewalk
stomped on by cheap and expensive shoes

Charlotte "Mama C" O'Neal

Charlotte Hill O'Neal, aka Mama C, aka Iya Osotunde Fasuyi, is an internationally known visual artist, musician, performance artist, ATR priestess, film maker, poet/writer of more than three decades experience.

She was born in Kansas City, KS in 1951 and has lived in Tanzania with her husband Pete O'Neal, founder and former Chairman of the Kansas City Chapter of the Black Panther Party, since 1972. In addition to her decades of community activism, former Black Panther Mama C is co-founder of the United African Alliance Community Center (UAACC) located outside of Arusha, Tanzania.

Her poetry and performing talents have been showcased on stage, television and radio in many cities in Africa, United States, South America and China during the annual UAACC Heal The Community Tour. Mama C has three poetry books including *Warrior Woman of Peace* (2008), *Life Slices* (2016) and *Homage* (2021).

She is presently working on her memoirs and completing her second film titled *Nyatiti Medicine* about a victim of obstetric fistula.

Mama C's love of all things "art" is documented in *Mama C: Urban Warrior in the African Bush* by Dr. Joanne Hershfield. She is also featured in the classic documentary about Pete O'Neal, *A Panther in Africa* by Aaron Matthews in addition to being featured in *Legacy: Spirit of the Black Panthers* by Taishi Thomas and Ni Wakati, a documentary about east African hip hop pioneers by Michael Wanguhu.

Mama C plays *nyatiti* and *obokano*, traditional African eight string lyres from Kenya and *kamalen ngoni*, a 12-string traditional harp originating in Mali. She has four albums of original music and poetry produced at Peace Power Productions and ManduguDigital.

I Almost Lost My SELF!!

It used to amaze me that even though Pre-dreadlocked,
Dressed in *kanga* from head to toe,
Carrying my babies on my back
Basket on my head
Chewing sugar cane sticks
And
pepper sprinkled *muhogo* roasts…
Just like everybody else…

…before I even opened my mouth to speak
They could somehow tell that I was
Someone ELSE…
DIFFERENT…
Other THAN…

I couldn't hide it even though I tried
And
I almost Lost

My SELF!...self...self...self...

In my freshly landed Just-got-off-the-boat enthusiasm
Of living in Africa,
I tried to Blend,
To Melt,
Homogenize,
Disappear,
Erase
The essence of what made me who I WAS and AM...
An African,
Who grew up in and was molded by the 'hoods of America,
And
I almost Lost
My SELF!...Self...Self...Self...

I almost lost that distinctive stride that signals
"She ain't from here!"
(ANATOKA MAHALI INGINE, BWANA!)

I almost lost my fierce, laughing, in yo' face SISTAH tone of voice
And My
Hands-on-hips-finger-wavin'-snake-charmin'-
"You ain't 'BOUT to tell ME I Can't"...
(Neck moves!)

I tucked that 'ME' tightly under my *kanga* wraps
And Demure gaze
And Soft, gentle handshake
And
I almost lost it, in giving it up...
But
I woke up just in time...And place...And attitude

I had to learn to remember that the
"I" that is "ME"
Has a history as rich and as valid as *anyone* born
with the dust of our African Ancestors squished lovingly
between *their* baby toes

I learned to remember that the
Middle Passage memories still twisting in my DNA
(causing frequent bouts of claustrophobic episodes)
are as real as the recollections of those who had never
Been ripped from the reassuring womb of
Family and History and Language and Food
and Religion…Religion…Religion…

I learned to remember that the French etymology of my name
Was just as valid…And honorable…And blessed
As
Habiba's or Amina's or Aishah's
'cause it was given to me in love, by those who loved ME
And marked me as surely as the eternally swollen scarification cuts
Of a Dinka Lady

I learned to reject feelings of embarrassment at having been born
An African in America,
Off-land…Off-shore
Thousands of miles Off-course
From where I *might* have been
Had those captors not had such a pressing need for
Dark rum and Cotton gins

I've learned to remember and bring honor to the fact that
I'm STILL
The *fly in the ointment*
The *Lump in the clotted cream*
The *Wrinkle in the dried cloth*
That *Hard green pea under the stack of mattresses!*

And after having lived in Africa for more than 50 years…
I'm still
DIFFERENT…
SET APART…
MNEGRO!!!!

But It no longer bothers me that folks STILL ask me
(*even after I've explained that I've lived in a village*
In the heart of WaMeru homeland...In Africa...
For years and years and years...
Probably even before they were born)

It no longer bothers me, I tell you...
when they say in response to my explanation...

"...uh huh...Yes...yes...I do understand *that*
But,
(*now watch out...here it comes...here it comes!...*)
But...
WHERE
ARE
YOU **FROM??**"

Margaret Walker

Margaret Walker (1915 – 1998) is best known for her acclaimed novel, *Jubilee* (1966) as well as her richly evocative poetry. Born in Birmingham, Alabama, Walker grew up in New Orleans and eventually settled in Chicago, where she earned a Bachelor's degree in 1935. Growing up, she was particularly taken with the poetry of Langston Hughes. In 1936, Walker joined the Federal Writers' Project and the South Side Writers Group, where she became friends with fellow writer and poet Richard Wright. In 1940, she earned a Master's degree in creative writing from the University of Iowa. She and Wright both participated in the movement called The Chicago Black Renaissance. In 1942, Walker received the Yale Younger Poets Prize for her debut collection of poetry, *For My People*. She was the first African-American person to be awarded this prize. She went on to publish two more collections of poetry, and worked on her only novel, *Jubilee*, based on the true story of her enslaved great-grandmother.

For My People

For my people everywhere singing their slave songs
   repeatedly: their dirges and their ditties and their blues
   and jubilees, praying their prayers nightly to an
   unknown god, bending their knees humbly to an
   unseen power;

For my people lending their strength to the years, to the
   gone years and the now years and the maybe years,
   washing ironing cooking scrubbing sewing mending
   hoeing plowing digging planting pruning patching
   dragging along never gaining never reaping never
   knowing and never understanding;

For my playmates in the clay and dust and sand of Alabama
   backyards playing baptizing and preaching and doctor
   and jail and soldier and school and mama and cooking
   and playhouse and concert and store and hair and
   Miss Choomby and company;

For the cramped bewildered years we went to school to learn
   to know the reasons why and the answers to and the
   people who and the places where and the days when, in
   memory of the bitter hours when we discovered we
   were black and poor and small and different and nobody
   cared and nobody wondered and nobody understood;

For the boys and girls who grew in spite of these things to
   be man and woman, to laugh and dance and sing and
   play and drink their wine and religion and success, to
   marry their playmates and bear children and then die
   of consumption and anemia and lynching;

For my people thronging 47th Street in Chicago and Lenox
   Avenue in New York and Rampart Street in New
   Orleans, lost disinherited dispossessed and happy
   people filling the cabarets and taverns and other
   people's pockets and needing bread and shoes and milk and
   land and money and something—something all our own;

For my people walking blindly spreading joy, losing time
   being lazy, sleeping when hungry, shouting when
   burdened, drinking when hopeless, tied, and shackled
   and tangled among ourselves by the unseen creatures
   who tower over us omnisciently and laugh;

For my people blundering and groping and floundering in
   the dark of churches and schools and clubs
   and societies, associations and councils and committees and
   conventions, distressed and disturbed and deceived and
   devoured by money-hungry glory-craving leeches,
   preyed on by facile force of state and fad and novelty, by
   false prophet and holy believer;

For my people standing staring trying to fashion a better way
   from confusion, from hypocrisy and misunderstanding,
   trying to fashion a world that will hold all the people,
   all the faces, all the adams and eves and their countless generations;

Let a new earth rise. Let another world be born. Let a
   bloody peace be written in the sky. Let a second
   generation full of courage issue forth; let a people
   loving freedom come to growth. Let a beauty full of
   healing and a strength of final clenching be the pulsing
   in our spirits and our blood. Let the martial songs
   be written, let the dirges disappear. Let a race of men now
   rise and take control.

For Gwen—1969
(Gwendolyn Brooks)

The slender, shy, and sensitive young girl
is woman now,
her words a power in the Ebon land.
Outside her window on the street
a mass of life moves by.
Chicago is her city.
Her heart flowers with its flame—

old stock yards, new beaches
all the little store-front churches
and the bar on the corner.
Dreamer and seer of tales
She witnesses rebellion,
struggle and sweat.
The people are her heartbeat—
In their footsteps pulsate daily
all her black words of fire and blood.

Tom Dent

Poet, writer, playwright, and oral historian Thomas Covington Dent was born in New Orleans. He attended Gilbert Academy in New Orleans and Oakwood Friends School in Poughkeepsie, NY. He earned a BA in political science at Morehouse College, completed graduate study at the Syracuse University School of International Relations, and later earned an MFA at Goddard University. After serving in the US Army from 1957 to 1959, Dent moved to New York City, where he worked as a social worker and as public information director for the NAACP Legal Defense Fund, assisting Thurgood Marshall. In New York, he co-founded the Umbra Writer's Workshop. He returned to New Orleans in 1965, where he worked with the Free Southern Theater and, with Bob Costley, founded the FST Writing Workshop, which became BLKARTSOUTH. With Richard Schechner and Gilbert Moses, Dent edited *The Free Southern Theater, by The Free Southern Theater: a documentary of the South's radical Black theater, with journals, letters, poetry, essays, and a play written by those who built it* (1969). With Kalamu ya Salaam, Dent edited the Black Arts literary magazine *Nkombo* and its press Nkombo Publications. Dent was a founder of the Southern Black Cultural Alliance and the Congo Square Writers Union, whose journal, *The Black River Journal*, he edited. In 1969, with Jerry Ward and Charles Rowell, Dent founded *Callaloo: A Quarterly Journal of African and African American Arts and Letters*. Dent's poems offer portraits of daily life in New Orleans, with attention to ordinary cultural and social experiences. Dent published two books of poetry, *Magnolia Street* (1976) and *Blue Lights and River Songs* (1982), and the plays *Negro Study No. 34A* (1970), *Snapshot* (1970), and *Ritual Murder* (1976). His nonfiction book *Southern Journey: A Return to the Civil Rights Movement* (1996) follows his travels in the early 1990s to important sites of civil rights actions in the 1960s.

RITUAL MURDER

a one act play by Tom Dent

CHARACTERS

Narrator
Joe Brown Jr.
Bertha (Joe's wife)
Mrs. Williams (Joe's teacher)
Dr. Brayboy (a black psychiatrist)
Mr. Andrews (Joe's boss)
Mrs. Brown (Joe's mother)
Mr. Brown (Joe's father)
James Roberts (Joe's friend)
Mr. Spaulding (anti-poverty program administrator)
Chief of Police

SETTING: New Orleans, La.
TIME: Now

It is important that the actors make their speeches in rhythm to the background music.

NARRATOR: Last Summer, Joe Brown Jr., black youth of New Orleans, La., committed murder. Play a special *Summertime* for him and play the same *Summertime* for his friend James Roberts who he knifed to death. (WE HEAR *SUMMERTIME* UNDER THE NARRATOR'S VOICE). In every black community of America; in the ghettos and neighborhood clubs where we gather to *hear our music,* we play *Summertime;* and in each community the bands play it differently. In no community does it sound like the *Summertime* of George Gershwin. It is bluesier, darker, with its own beat and logic, its joys unknown to the white world. It is day now. The routine events of life have passed under the bridge. Joe Brown Jr. has been arrested, indicted, and formally charged with murder. It happened ... it happened in a Ninth Ward bar we need not name it for the purposes of this presentation. The stabbing was the culmination of an argument Joe Brown had with his friend. We have learned this, but the *Louisiana Weekly* only reported, "James Roberts is said to have made insulting remarks to Joe Brown, whereupon Brown pulled out a switch blade knife and stabbed Roberts three times in the chest before he could be subdued." The story received front page play in the *Louisiana Weekly,* and a lead in the crime-of-the-day section in the white *Times-Picayune.* After that, it received only minor news play, since there are other crimes to report in New Orleans. Play *Summertime* for Joe Brown Jr., and play the same *Summertime* for his friend James Roberts who he knifed to death. (THE MUSIC DIES OUT). Why did this murder happen? No one really knows. The people who know Joe Brown best have ideas.

(WE SEE BERTHA LOOKING AT T.V. THE SOUND IS OFF, ONLY THE PICTURE SHOWS. BERTHA IS YOUNG, ABOUT 20. SHE IS JOE'S WIFE. SHE IS IRONING WHILE LOOKING AT THE SET IRONING BABY THINGS.)

BERTHA:

Joe just didn't have any sense. He is smart, oh yes, has a good brain, but didn't have good sense. The important thing was to settle down, get a good job, and take care of his three children. We been in the Florida Ave. projects now for almost a year, and we never have enough money. Look at the people on T.V., they make out okay. They fight, but they never let their fights destroy them. Joe didn't have control of his temper. He was a dreamer, he wanted things. But he wouldn't work to get them. Oh, he would take jobs in oyster houses, and he'd worked on boats ever since he was a kid. But he wouldn't come in at night, and sometimes he wouldn't get up in the morning to go to work. Sometimes he would come in and snap off the T.V. and say it was driving him crazy. It's not his T.V.—my father bought it, and besides, I like it, it's the only thing I have. This is just a 17 inch set, but I want a 21 inch set. Now I'll never get one because he had to go out and do something foolish. You ask me why he killed that boy? I don't know. But I think he killed him because he had a bad temper and wouldn't settle down. Joe was a mild person, but he carried knives and guns— that's the way his family is. I used to tell him about it all the time. Once I asked him, "When are you gonna get a better job and make more money?" He said, "When I get rid of you and those snotty kids." He could have done something if he had tried, if he had only tried; but instead, he wanted to take it out on us. I'll go see him, but now look; I have to do everything in this house myself: Iron the clothes, cook the meals, buy the food, apply for relief and get some help from my parents and my father ain't working right now. Joe didn't want to have our last baby, Cynthia, but we couldn't murder her before she was even born and now I got to take care of her too. Joe knifed that boy because he was foolish, wouldn't settle down and accept things as they are, and because he didn't have common sense.

NARRATOR:
Mrs. Williams, could you comment on your former student, Joe Brown Jr.?

MRS. WILLIAMS:
I don't remember Joe Brown Jr. very well. I have so many children to try to remember. I had him three or four years ago just before he dropped out of school. I was his homeroom teacher. Joe was like all the others from the Ninth Ward, not interested in doing anything for themselves. You can't teach them anything. They don't want to learn, they *never* study, they won't sit still and pay attention in class. It's no surprise to me that he's in trouble. I try to do my best here, but I have only so much patience. I tell you you don't know the things a teacher goes through with these kids. They come to class improperly dressed, from homes where they don't get any home training, which is why they are so ill-mannered. We try to teach them about America—about the opportunities America has to offer. We try to prepare them to get the best jobs they can—and you know a Negro child has to work harder. I teach History, Arithmetic, English, and Civics every day, and it goes in one ear and comes out the other. It gives me a terrible gas pain to have to go through it every day, and the noise these kids make is too, too hard on my ears. I've worked for ten years in this school, and I don't get paid much at all. But next month my husband and I will have saved enough money to buy a new Oldsmobile, which I'm happy to say will be the smartest, slickest, smoothest thing McDonough No. 81 has ever seen. Two boys got into a fight in the yard the other day and it was horrible. It pains me to hear the names they call each other—irritates my gas. Some of them even bring knives and guns to school. It's just

terrible. I'm only relieved when I get home, turn on my T.V., take my hair down and face off, drink a nice strong cup of coffee, look out at my lawn in Pontchartrain Park, and forget the day. You ask me why Joe Brown murdered his friend in a Negro bar on a Saturday night and I tell you it is because he was headed that way in the beginning. These kids just won't listen, and don't want to learn, and that's all there is to it.

(LIGHTS ON JOE BROWN JR. HE IS WEARING BLUE JEANS AND A TEE SHIRT. HE IS SEATED. HE FACES THE AUDIENCE. THERE IS A TABLE IN FRONT OF HIM. ON THE TABLE IS A SMALL TRANSISTOR RADIO, BUT THE MUSIC WE HEAR IS GIL EVANS' *BARBARA SONG.*)

NARRATOR:
Here is Joe Brown Jr.
JOE BROWN JR.:
Once I saw a feature about surfing on T.V. Surfing on beautiful waves on a beach in Hawaii, or somewhere....

(THE LIGHTS SHIFT TO ANOTHER MAN WHO IS SEATED ON THE OPPOSITE SIDE OF THE STAGE. HE IS A MUCH OLDER MAN, DRESSED IN A BUSINESS SUIT. HE IS A NEGRO. HE IS DR. BRAYBOY, A PSYCHIATRIST. HIS CHAIR DOES NOT FACE THE AUDIENCE; IT FACES JOE BROWN JR.)

NARRATOR:
A black psychiatrist, Dr. Thomas L. Brayboy.
DR. BRAYBOY:
At the core of Joe Brown's personality is a history of frustrations. Psychological, sociological, economic ...
JOE BROWN JR.:
... and I wanted to do that ... surf. It was a dream I kept to myself. Because it would have been foolish to say it aloud. Nobody wants to be laughed at. And then I thought, I never see black people surfing ...
DR. BRAYBOY:
We might call Joe Brown's homicidal act an act of ritual murder. When murder occurs for no apparent reason but happens all the time, as in our race on Saturday nights, it is ritual murder. When I worked in

Harlem Hospital in the emergency ward, I saw us coming in bleeding, blood seeping from the doors of the taxicabs, ... icepicks and knives ...

(THESE SPEECHES MUST BE SLOW, TO THE RHYTHM OF MUSIC.)

NARRATOR:

Play *Summertime* for Joe Brown Jr., and a very funky *Summetime* for his friend James Roberts, who he knifed to death.

JOE BROWN JR.:

... And then I thought, I don't see any black folks on T.V., ever. Not any real black folks, anyway. There are those so called black shows like *Good Times* and the *Jeffersons,* but they are so far removed from the kind of folks I know that they may as well be white too. I see us playing football, basketball, and baseball, and half the time I miss that because they be on in the afternoon, and I'm usually shelling oysters. "Where am I?", I asked my wife, and she answered, "In the Florida Avenue project where you are doing a poor job of taking care of your wife and children." My boss answered, "On the job, if you would keep your mind on what you are doing ... count the oysters."

DR. BRAYBOY:

...Ice picks and knives and frustration. My tests indicate that Joe Brown Jr. is considerably above average in intelligence. Above average in intelligence. *Above* average. Vocabulary and reading comprehension extraordinary ...

NARRATOR:

(TO AUDIENCE) Our purpose here is to discover why.

DR. BRAYBOY:

... But school achievement extremely low. Dropped out at 18 in the eleventh grade.

JOE BROWN JR.:

I began watching all the T.V. sets I could, looking for my image on every channel, looking for someone who looked like me. I knew I existed, but I didn't see myself in the world of television or movies. Even the black characters were not me. All the black characters were either weak and stupid, or some kind of super man who doesn't really exist in my world. I couldn't define myself, and didn't know where to begin. When I listened to soul music on the radio I understood that, and I knew that was part of me, but that didn't help me much. Something was not right, and it was like ... like I was the only cat in the whole world who knew it. Something began to come loose in me, like my mind would float away from my body and lay suspended on a shelf for hours at a time watching me open oysters. No one ever suspected, but my mind was trying to define me, to tell me who I was the way other people see me, only it couldn't because it didn't know where to begin.

(THE SCENE SHIFTS TO THE DESK OF THE CHIEF OF POLICE. HE MAY BE PLAYED BY A WHITE ACTOR, OR A BLACK ACTOR IN WHITE FACE.)

NARRATOR: The Chief of Police.

CHIEF OF POLICE:
The rate of crime in the streets in New Orleans has risen sharply. We know that most of our colored citizens are wholesome, law abiding, decent citizens. But the fact remains that the crime wave we are witnessing now across the nation is mostly nigger crime. Stop niggers and you will stop crime. The police must have more protection, more rights, and more weapons of all types to deal with the crime wave. We need guns, machine guns, multi-machine guns, gas bombs and reinforced nightsticks. Otherwise America is going to become a nightmare of black crime in the streets.

(LIGHTS UP ON MR. ANDREWS, JOE'S BOSS. HE IS SITTING BEHIND A TERRIBLY MESSY DESK WITH PAPERS STUCK IN DESK HOLDERS. HIS FEET ARE ON THE DESK. HE IS EATING A LARGE MUFFALETTA SANDWICH. HIS IMAGE MUST BE ONE OF A RELAXED, INFORMAL INTERVIEW AT HIS OFFICE DURING LUNCH TIME. IF THERE ARE NO WHITE ACTORS, THE PART CAN BE PLAYED BY A BLACK ACTOR IN WHITEFACE, BUT INSTEAD OF EATING LUNCH, HE SHOULD BE SMOKING A HUGE CIGAR.)

NARRATOR:
Joe Brown's employer, Mr. Andrews.

MR. ANDREWS:
I have trouble with several of my nigra boys, but I likes 'em. (HE ALMOST CHOKES ON HIS SANDWICH). Joe was a little different

from the rest ... what would you say... dreamier ... more absent minded. Joe was always quit ting, but he must have liked it here 'cause he always came back. You can't tell me anything about those people. One time, during lunch hour, they were singing and dancing outside to the radio and I snuck up to watch. If they had seen me they would've stopped. It was amazing. The way them boys danced is fantastic. They shore got rhythm and a sense of style about them. Yes sir ... and guess who got the most style ... ole Joe. (BITES AND EATS). That boy sure can dance. I loves to watch him. (BITES) Recently, he been going to the bathroom a lot and staying a long time. I ask the other boys, "where's that doggone Joe?" They tell me. So one day I go to the john and there he is, sitting on the stool ... readin'. I say, "Boy, I pay you to read or shell oysters?" He comes out all sulky. (SMILING) He could be kind of sensitive at times, you know. I been knowing him since he was a kid ... born around here ... kind of touchy. (ANDREWS HAS FINISHED HIS SANDWICH. HE TAKES HIS FEET OFF THE DESK, THROWS THE WRAPPER INTO THE TRASH, AND WIPES HIS HANDS. A SERIOUS LOOK COMES OVER HIS FACE). As for why he killed that boy, I can't give you any answers. I think it has to do with nigras and the way they get wild on the weekend. Sometimes the good times get a little rough. And them (PAUSE) you don't know what a boy like Joe can get mixed up in, or any of them out there. (WAVES TOWARD THE DOOR) I don't understand it, and I know and likes 'em all, like they was my own family. My job is to keep 'em straight here ... any trouble out of any of 'em and out the door they go.

(THE SCENE SHIFTS TO ANOTHER WHITE MAN. HE IS WELL DRESSED WITH HIS TIE LOOSENED, SITTING BEHIND AN EXTREMELY DISORDERED DESK. BLACK ACTOR CAN PLAY IN WHITE FACE. HE MUST, THROUGHOUT HIS SPEECH, WEAR A PUBLIC RELATIONS SMILE. HE MUST SPEAK WITH A WINNING AIR.)

NARRATOR:
Mr. Richard Spaulding, Director of the Poverty Program in New Orleans.

MR. SPAULDING:
Last year we spent 3.5 million in five culturally deprived areas of

New Orleans. This money has made a tremendous difference in the lives of our fine colored citizens. We have provided jobs, jobs, and more jobs. By creating, for the first time, indigenous community organizations controlled and operated by the people of the five target areas, we have, for the first time, provided a way to close the cultural and economic gap. Social Service Centers are going up in all these areas. We will develop a level of competency on par with American society as a whole. In the Desire area alone, 750 mothers go to our medical center each day. We have, in short, provided hope. Of course, there are still problems.

NARRATOR:

Any insights into the murder of James Roberts last Summer by Joe Brown Jr.?

MR. SPAULDING:

We are building community centers, baseball diamonds, basketball courts, little leagues, golden agers facilities, barbecue pits, swimming pools, badminton nets, and ... if our dreams come true ... well supervised and policed bowling alleys. It is our firm hope that sociology will stay out of neighborhood bars.

NARRATOR:

Thank you, Mr. Spaulding.

(THE SCENE SHIFTS TO A MIDDLE AGED WOMAN SITTING ON A WELL WORN COUCH. SHE IS WEARING A PLAIN DRESS. THERE IS A SMALL TABLE WITH A LAMP AND BIBLE ON IT NEXT TO THE COUCH. SHE IS MRS. BROWN, JOE'S MOTHER. ACROSS THE STAGE, SITTING IN A BIG EASY CHAIR IS A MIDDLE AGED MAN IN WORK CLOTHES. HE IS MR. BROWN, JOE'S FATHER. HE IS DRINKING A LARGE CAN OF BEER WHICH, FROM TIME TO TIME, HE WILL PLACE ON THE FLOOR. HE LISTENS TO WHAT MRS. BROWN SAYS INTENTLY, BUT THERE MUST BE AN AIR OF DISTANCE IN HIS ATTITUDE TOWARD HER AND WHAT SHE SAYS, NEVER AFFECTION. THE AUDIENCE MUST BE MADE TO BELIEVE THEY ARE IN DIFFERENT PLACES.)

NARRATOR:

(Solemnly) This is Joe Brown's mother. (A SPOT FOCUSES ON

MRS. BROWN. THERE IS ENOUGH LIGHT HOWEVER TO SEE MR. BROWN.)

MRS. BROWN:
Joe was always a sweet kind boy, but Joe's problem is that he ... stopped ... going ... to ... church. I told him about that but it didn't make any difference. When we climb out of Christ chariot we liable to run into trouble. I tell the truth about my own children, like I tell it on anyone else. Once, before Joe got married he came home in a temper about his boss and his job. Talking bad about the white folks. Said he wished something from another planet would destroy them all. Said he didn't like the way his boss talked to him, that he should be paid more, and like that. We all get mad at the white people, but there is no point in it. So many colored folks ain't even got a job. I told him, "If you think you can do better, go back and finish school." But no, he didn't finish school, he just complained. "Stay in church," I told him, but he started hanging around with bad friends. Bad friends lead to a bad end. Talking bad about white people is like busting your head against a brick wall.

NARRATOR:
Mrs. Brown, do you feel your son would kill for no reason? There must have been a reason.

MRS. BROWN:
When you hang around a bad crowd on Saturday nights, troubles are always gonna come. I told him to stay out of those bars. I do know what happened or why. A friend told me the other boy was teasing Joe and Joe got mad. He was sensitive, you know, very serious and sensitive. He didn't like to be rubbed the wrong way.

NARRATOR:
Mrs. Brown, the purpose of this program is to discover why your son knifed his friend. No one seems to have answers. We are using the scientific approach. Do *you* have any answers?

MRS. BROWN:
(DESPAIRINGLY) I don't know why. I don't understand. You try to protect your children as best you can. It's just one of those things that happens on Saturday nights in a colored bar; like a disease. You hope you and nobody you know catches it. The Lord is the only protection.

NARRATOR:

And your husband? Would he have any information, any ideas?

MRS. BROWN:

(SHARPLY) I haven't seen that man in four years.

(BOTH MRS. BROWN AND NARRATOR LOOK AT MR. BROWN).

MR. BROWN:

I plan to go see the boy ... I just haven't had a chance yet. I have another family now and I can't find any work. I help him out when I can, but ... (PAUSE) ... I can't understand why he would do a thing like that.

NARRATOR:

If we could hear what James Roberts has to say. (WE RETURN TO THE SUMMERTIME THEME AND THE SCENE OF THE CRIME, THE BARROOM WHERE THE PLAY BEGAN WITH JOE BROWN JR STANDING OVER JAMES ROBERTS' BODY AND ALL OTHER ACTORS FROZEN IN THEIR ORIGINAL POSITIONS AS IN THE OPENING SCENE. AFTER THE NARRATOR SPEAKS THE BODY OF JAMES ROBERTS BEGINS TO SLOWLY ARISE FROM THE FLOOR AIDED BY JOE BROWN. IT IS IMPORTANT THAT BROWN HELPS ROBERTS GET UP.)

JAMES ROBERTS:

(BEGINS TO LAUGH ...) It was all a joke. Nothing happened that hasn't happened between us before. Joe is still my best friend ... if I were alive I would tell anyone that. That Saturday was a terrible one ... not just because the lights went out for me. I heard a ringing in my ears when I woke up that morning. When I went to work at the hotel the first thing I had to do was take out the garbage. Have you ever smelled the stink of shrimp and oyster shells first thing in the morning? I hate that. The sounds of the street and the moan of the cook's voice; that's enough to drive anyone crazy, and I heard it every day. That day I decided to leave my job for real ... one more week at the most.

JOE BROWN JR.:

(GETTING UP FROM THE BUNK INTO A SITTING POSITION) Damn. The same thing happened to me that day. I decided I was going to leave my job.

JAMES ROBERTS:
(LOOKING AT JOE WITH DISGUST) Man, you are disgusting. You all the time talking about leaving your job.

NARRATOR:
(TO ROBERTS, THEN TO JOE). Get to what happened at the cafe please. We don't have all night.

JAMES ROBERTS:
We were both very uptight ... mad at our jobs—everybody ... everything around us.

JOE BROWN JR.:
(EXCITEDLY) I know I was ... I was ready to shoot somebody.

JAMES ROBERTS:
Shut up. This is my scene.

JOE BROWN JR.:
You won't even let anybody *agree* with you.

NARRATOR:
Please.

JAMES ROBERTS:
Joe went on and on all evening and all night. We were getting higher and higher, going from bar to bar. We went to Scotties, then to Shadowland, to the Havana ... we had my sister's car ... Joe getting mad and frustrated and talking 'bout what he was gonna do. By the time we got to the Ninth Ward Cafe, we was both stoned out of our minds. Joe getting dreamier and dreamier. He was talking about all his problems, his wife, his job, his children. I could understand that.

JOE BROWN JR.:
You really couldn't because you don't have those problems.

(WE HEAR OTIS REDDING'S *SATISFACTION* FROM THE ALBUM, "OTIS REDDING LIVE.")

JAMES ROBERTS:
Joe was screaming about the white man. He said he was $1500 in debt ... working like hell for the white man, then turning right around and giving it back to him. He said he couldn't laugh no more.

(FROM THIS POINT ON THERE MUST BE LITTLE CONNECTION BETWEEN JOE'S THOUGHTS AND THOSE OF JAMES ROBERTS.

THE OTIS REDDING RECORDING CONTINUES, BUT MUST NOT DROWN OUT THE SPEECHES.)

JOE BROWN JR.:

I had a dream ... I had a dream ... I dreamed I had 66 million dollars left to me by an unknown relative ...

JAMES ROBERTS:

(SLOW, TO THE MUSIC, AS MUCH PANTOMIME AS POSSIBLE, AS THOUGH HE IS RE-ENACTING THE SCENE). We were in the Ninth Ward Cafe sitting in a booth by ourselves. There was something on the juke box, I believe it was Otis Redding. It was a hot night. Joe was talking about how there was nowhere he could go to relax anymore. Then suddenly, his mind would go off into outer space somewhere and I had to jerk him back. I would ask him what he was thinking about, and he would say he wasn't happy with himself. He didn't know himself or where he was headed to anymore.

JOE BROWN JR.:

... I always get screwed up when I try to figure out the *first* thing I'm going to buy ... a new car ... maybe ... Mark IV ... a new house ... a brick one with wood paneling ... a new suit ... a tailor made three piece ... new shoes ... some high steppers ... a new transistor radio ... a big Sony that plays loud with big sound ... Then I'd give everybody a bill ... but I can't figure out what I'm going to buy *first* ...

JAMES ROBERTS:

I said, man what are you talking about. I don't understand all this blues over what happens everyday. He said he wanted to believe there is hope. I told him there is no hope. You a black mother-fucker and you may as well learn to make the best of it.

JOE BROWN JR.:

... People always tell me I can't make up my mind what I want, or I want things that don't make sense, or I want too much in stead of being satisfied with just a little. People always tell me I ask too many questions ... especially questions that no one can answer ... and I am just frustrating myself because I can never find the answers. The way I figure it you may as well dream 66 million as 66 thousand. The way I figure it, you may as well ask questions you *don't* have answers to; what's the point in asking questions everyone knows the answers to.

Life is just a little thing anyway ... doesn't really amount to much when you think about time and place.

JAMES ROBERTS:
(INTENSELY AND QUICKER) Then he just blew. Screamed nobody calls him a black mother fucker. I just laughed Everybody calls him that cause that's just what he is. There nothing wrong with calling anyone a black motherfucker. We been doing it to each other all our lives, and we did it all evening while we were drinking. I just laughed. He jumps up, pulls out his blade and goes for my heart. I could outfight Joe any day but ...

JOE BROWN JR.:
High steppers ...

JAMES ROBERTS:
... He got the jump on me and I couldn't get to my blade. It was ridiculous. He was like a crazy man ... a wild man ... turning on me for no reason when I done nothing to him at all ... and shouting, "there is no hope."

JOE BROWN JR.:
High steppers ...

JAMES ROBERTS:
Before I knew it I was stunned and weak and there was blood all over the chest of my yellow polo shirt ... I felt the lights darken, and my whole body turned to rubber ...

JOE BROWN JR.:
High steppers on a Saturday night ...

JAMES ROBERTS:
... But I couldn't move anything (PAUSE) Last thing I heard was Booker T. and the M. G.s playing *Groovin'* ... Joe... his eyes blazing ... everything turned red.

NARRATOR:
(TO ROBERTS AFTER PAUSE) You mean this caused such a brutal act? You called him a name?

JAMES ROBERTS:
That's all it takes sometimes.

NARRATOR:
And you think this makes sense? To lose your life at nineteen over

such an insignificant thing?

JAMES ROBERTS:

It happens all the time. I accept it. Joe is still my friend. Friends kill each other all the time ... unless you have an enemy you can both kill.

NARRATOR:

And you Joe?

JOE BROWN JR.:

What is there to say? It happened. It happens all the time. One thing I learned; when you pull a knife or gun don't fool around, use it, or you might not have a chance to. Better him dead than me. He would say the same thing if it was the other way around.

NARRATOR:

(TO JOE BROWN JR.) What did you mean when you said there is no hope?

JOE BROWN JR.:

(EVENLY) I don't know. *There is no hope.* Here in this jail, with my fate, I might be better off dead.

NARRATOR:

One more question. (TO JAMES ROBERTS) Do you feel you died for anything? Is there any meaning in it?

JAMES ROBERTS:

Yes, I died for something. But I don't know what it means.

NARRATOR:

(TO JOE BROWN JR.) And did your act mean anything?

JOE BROWN JR.:

(SOFTLY) I suppose so. But I can't imagine what.

(THE MUSIC OF A BLUESY *SUMMERTIME*. THE NARRATOR COMES OUT TO DOWNSTAGE CENTER, AS IN THE BEGINNING OF THE PLAY. HE ADDRESSES THE AUDIENCE DIRECTLY IN EVEN TONES.)

NARRATOR:

Play *Summertime* for Joe Brown Jr. and play a very funky *Summertime* for his friend James Roberts who he knifed to death.

(*SUMMERTIME* THEME CONTINUES AS NARRATOR SLOWLY SCRUTINIZES THE PEOPLE HE HAS JUST INTERVIEWED.)

Our purpose here is to discover why. No one seems to have answers. Do you have any?

(NARRATOR MOVES TO ACTORS WHO PLAYS BERTHA, MRS. WILLIAMS, MRS. BROWN, JOE BROWN SR., AND DR. BRAYBOY ASKING THE QUESTION "DO YOU HAVE ANSWERS?" TO WHICH THEY RESPOND:)

BERTHA:
Joe knifed that boy because he was foolish, wouldn't settle down and accept things as they are, and because he didn't have common sense.

MRS. WILLIAMS:
You ask me why Joe Brown murdered his friend in a Negro bar on a Saturday night and I tell you it is because he was headed that way in the beginning. These kids just won't listen, and don't want to learn, and that's all there is to it.

MR. BROWN:
I plan to go see the boy ... I just haven't had a chance yet. I help him out when I can but (PAUSE) I can't understand why he would do a thing like that.

MRS. BROWN:
It's just one of those things that happens on a Saturday night in a colored bar ... like a disease. You hope you and nobody you know catches it. The Lord is the only protection.

DR. BRAYBOY:
When murder occurs for no apparent reason but happens all the time as in our race on Saturday nights, it is ritual murder. That is, no apparent reason. There are reasons. The reasons are both personal and common. When a people who have no method of letting off steam against the source of their oppression exploit against each other, homicide, under these conditions, is a form of group suicide. When personal chemistries don't mix just a little spark can bring about the explosion. Icepicks and knives, and whatever happens to be lying around.

NARRATOR:
When murder occurs for no apparent reason, but happens all the time, as in our race on a Saturday night, it is ritual murder.

(THE FOLLOWING LINES SHOULD BE DISTRIBUTED AMONG THE ACTORS AND DELIVERED TO THE AUDIENCE DIRECTLY.)

That is, no apparent reason.

There are reasons.

The reasons are both personal and common.

When a people who have no method of letting off steam against the source of their oppression exploit against each other, homicide, under these conditions, is a form of group suicide.

When personal chemistries don't mix just a little spark can bring about the explosion.

Icepicks Knives

And whatever happens to be lying around.

NARRATOR:

(MOVING DOWNSTAGE FACING AUDIENCE DIRECTLY). We have seen something unpleasant, but the play is over. Yes, we see this thing (GESTURING TO STAGE BEHIND HIM) night after night, weekend after weekend. Only you have the power to stop it. It has to do with something in our minds. (PAUSE. *SUMMERTIME* MUSIC GRADUALLY INCREASES IN VOLUME). Play *Summertime* for Joe Brown Jr., and play a very funky *Summertime* for his friend James Roberts who he knifed to death. (NARRATOR WALKS OVER TO DR. BRAYBOY AND SHAKES HIS HAND AS LIGHTS FADE TO BLACK).

THE END

Lucille Clifton

Lucille Clifton was born in 1936 in DePew, New York and grew up in Buffalo. She studied at Howard University before transferring to SUNY Fredonia. She was discovered as a poet by Langston Hughes (via friend Ishmael Reed, who shared her poems), and Hughes published Clifton's poetry in his highly influential anthology, *The Poetry of the Negro* (1970). A prolific and widely respected poet, Lucille Clifton's work emphasizes endurance and strength through adversity, focusing particularly on African American female experience and family life. Awarding the prestigious Ruth Lilly Poetry Prize to Clifton in 2007, the judges remarked that "One always feels the looming humaneness around Lucille Clifton's poems—it is a moral quality that some poets have and some don't." In addition to the Ruth Lilly prize, Clifton was the first author to have two books of poetry chosen as finalists for the Pulitzer Prize, *Good Woman: Poems and a Memoir, 1969-1980* (1987) and *Next: New Poems* (1987). Her collection *Two-Headed Woman* (1980) was also a Pulitzer nominee and won the Juniper Prize from the University of Massachusetts. She served as the state of Maryland's poet laureate from 1974 until 1985 and won the prestigious National Book Award for *Blessing the Boats: New and Selected Poems, 1988-2000*. In addition to her numerous poetry collections, she wrote many children's books. Clifton was a Distinguished Professor of Humanities at St. Mary's College of Maryland and a Chancellor of the Academy of American Poets.

shapeshifter poems

1

the legend is whispered
in the women's tent
how the moon when she rises
full
follows some men into themselves
and changes them there
the season is short
but dreadful shapeshifters
they wear strange hands
they walk through the houses
at night their daughters
do not know them

2

who is there to protect her
from the hands of the father
not the windows which see and
say nothing not the moon
that awful eye not the woman
she will become with her
scarred tongue who who who the owl
laments into the evening who
will protect her this prettylittlegirl

3

if the little girl lies
still enough
shut enough
hard enough
shapeshifter may not
walk tonight
the full moon may not
find him here
the hair on him
bristling
rising
up

4

the poem at the end of the world
is the poem the little girl breathes
into her pillow the one
she cannot tell the one
there is no one to hear this poem
is a political poem is a war poem is a
universal poem but is not about
these things this poem
is about one human heart this poem
is the poem at the end of the world

fury

for mama

remember this.
she is standing by
the furnace.
the coals
glisten like rubies.
her hand is crying.
her hand is clutching
a sheaf of papers.
poems.
she gives them up.
they burn
jewels into jewels.
her eyes are animals.
each hank of her hair
is a serpent's obedient
wife.
she will never recover.
remember. there is nothing
you will not bear
for this woman's sake.

QUINCY TROUPE

Award-winning poet Quincy Troupe wrote the definitive biography of Miles Davis, *Miles: the Autobiography; The Pursuit of Happyness*, and a memoir, *miles & me*, soon to be a major motion picture. Author of 20 books, he also conducted the last interview with James Baldwin republished most recently in English as *James Baldwin: The Last Interview & Other Conversations* (Melville House, 2014). Troupe's work has been translated into over 30 languages. His most recent book of poetry is *Duende: Poems, 1966 – Now* (Seven Stories Press, 2022).

Duende

for Garcia Lorca and Miles Davis

it's in the bottomless power, magic of duende

climbing stealthily from earth, wrapped inside

secrets, mystery infused in black magic

that enters bodies in the form of music, art,

poetry imbuing language with sovereignty,

in blood spooling back through violent centuries,

voices echoing ancient Africa, rise, thread

from skins of blessed, sacred rituals, people

emerge from drums as heartbeats in time

when memory is revived here now through metaphor

when olden voices find their way vibrating into song,

rhythms stitch forgotten sounds into language

beat out of them by whips on slave ships,

bring back wonder of feet pounding, dance,

the holy ghost lost in bloody homelands,

now souls underneath rise up through bodies,

spool back with talismans, hypnotic, pull ancient

voodoo up in buckets filled with holy water,

evoke memories drinking from whodunit secrets

awakened in poetry of Garcia Lorca,

Andalusian dues heard in Miles Davis' clues

vibrating anew in *Sketches of Spain*, andante blues

DUDLEY RANDALL

Dudley Randall was born in Washington D.C. on January 14, 1914. His family moved to Detroit, Michigan when he was six years old, and he lived there most of his life. He worked in the Ford Foundry and was active in the United Auto Workers Labor Union. After serving in the U.S. Army during World War II, he attended Wayne State University, receiving a degree in English Language and Literature in 1949, and subsequently the University of Michigan, Ann Arbor, where he completed a Master's degree in Library Science in 1951. While he worked as a reference librarian at the University of Detroit, he founded and operated Broadside Press, which was the most productive poetry press of the 1960s and 1970s, publishing 90 titles of books and hundreds of broadsides. The author of six books of poetry and two major anthologies of African American poetry, Randall's poetry has been translated into multiple languages and he received many awards for his poetry and publishing accomplishments. He was named the Poet Laureate of the City of Detroit in 1981 and was awarded a Life Achievement Award from the National Endowment of the Arts in 1984. He passed away on August 5, 2000.

On Getting A Natural
(For Gwendolyn Brooks)

She didn't know she was beautiful,
though her smiles were dawn,
her voice was bells,
and her skin deep velvet Night.

She didn't know she was beautiful,
although her deeds,
kind, generous, unobtrusive,
gave hope to some,
and help to others,
and inspiration to us all. And
beauty is as beauty does,
they say.

Then one day there blossomed
a crown upon her head,
bushy, bouffant, real Afro-down,
Queen Nefertiti again.
And now her regal woolly crown
declares,
I know
I'm black
AND
beautiful.

A Poet Is Not a Jukebox

A poet is not a jukebox, so don't tell me what to write.
I read a dear friend a poem about love, and she said,
"You're in to that bag now, for whatever it's worth,
But why don't you write about the riot in Miami?"

I didn't write about Miami because I didn't know about Miami.
I've been so busy working for the Census, and listening to music all night,
and making new poems
That I've broken my habit of watching TV and reading newspapers.
So it wasn't absence of Black Pride that caused me not to write about Miami,
But simple ignorance.

Telling a Black poet what he ought to write
Is like some Commissar of Culture in Russia telling a poet
He'd better write about the new steel furnaces in the Novobigorsk region,
Or the heroic feats of Soviet labor in digging the trans-Caucausus Canal,

Or the unprecedented achievement of workers in the sugar beet industry
who exceeded their quota by 400 percent (it was later discovered to
be a typist's error).

Maybe the Russian poet is watching his mother die of cancer,
Or is bleeding from an unhappy love affair,
Or is bursting with happiness and wants to sing of wine, roses,
and nightingales.

I'll bet that in a hundred years the poems the Russian people will read, sing
and love
Will be the poems about his mother's death, his unfaithful mistress, or his
wine, roses and nightingales,
Not the poems about steel furnaces, the trans-Caucasus Canal, or the sugar
beet industry.
A poet writes about what he feels, what agitates his heart and sets his pen in
motion.
Not what some apparatchnik dictates, to promote his own career or theories.

Yeah, maybe I'll write about Miami, as I wrote about Birmingham,
But it'll be because I want to write about Miami, not because somebody
says I ought to.

Yeah, I write about love. What's wrong with love?
If we had more loving, we'd have more Black babies to become Black
brothers and
sisters and build the Black family.

When people love, they bathe with sweet-smelling soap, splash their bodies
with perfume or cologne,
Shave, and comb their hair, and put on gleaming silken garments,
Speak softly and kindly and study their beloved to anticipate and satisfy her
every desire.
After loving they're relaxed and happy and friends with all the world.
What's wrong with love, beauty, joy and peace?

If Josephine had given Napoleon more loving, he wouldn't have sown the
meadows of Europe with skulls.
If Hitler had been happy in love, he wouldn't have baked people in ovens.
So don't tell me it's trivial and a cop-out to write about love and not about
Miami.

A poet is not a jukebox.
A poet is not a jukebox.
I repeat, A poet is not a jukebox for someone to shove a quarter in his ear
and get the tune they want to hear,
Or to pat on the head and call "a good little Revolutionary,"
Or to give a Kuumba Liberation Award.

A poet is *not* a jukebox.
A poet is not a *jukebox*.
A *poet* is not a jukebox.

So don't tell me what to write.

Booker T. and W.E.B.

"It seems to me," said Booker T.,
"It shows a mighty lot of cheek
To study chemistry and Greek
When Mister Charlie needs a hand
To hoe the cotton on his land,
And when Miss Ann looks for a cook,
Why stick your nose inside a book?"

"I don't agree," said W.E.B.,
"If I should have the drive to seek
Knowledge of chemistry or Greek,
I'll do it. Charles and Miss can look
Another place for hand or cook.
Some men rejoice in skill of hand,
And some in cultivating land,
But there are others who maintain
The right to cultivate the brain."

"It seems to me," said Booker T.,
"That all you folks have missed the boat

Who shout about the right to vote,
And spend vain days and sleepless nights
In uproar over civil rights.
Just keep your mouths shut, do not grouse,
But work, and save, and buy a house."

"I don't agree," said W.E.B.,
"For what can property avail
If dignity and justice fail.
Unless you help to make the laws,
They'll steal your house with trumped-up clause.
A rope's as tight, a fire as hot,
No matter how much cash you've got.
Speak soft, and try your little plan,
But as for me, I'll be a man."

"It seems to me," said Booker T.—
"I don't agree,"
Said W.E.B.

ANEB KGOSITSILE

The literary works of Aneb Kgositsile (Gloria House, Ph.D.) have sparked imagination and action, articulating passionate and compelling ideas, and honoring the impact, sacrifices, joys, and humanity of those who have dedicated their lives to the path of freedom. Kgositsile's activism has registered people to vote, helped lift the voices of the previously unheard, and awakened people to the hypocrisy and futility of war.

Born in Tampa, Florida, Kgositsile began expressing herself through poetry before her age reached double digits. She published her first books of poetry in the 1980s, including *Blood River* (1983) and *Rainrituals* (1989), both published by Broadside Press. In 2003, her third collection, *Shrines*, was published by Third World Press. *Medicine*, her most recent book, was published in 2017 as a joint endeavor of Broadside Lotus and University of Detroit-Mercy Press.

During the Black Arts/Black Consciousness movement, Kgositsile was among a community of artists that included poet Sonia Sanchez; poet and founder of

Third World Press Haki Madhubuti; South African Poet Laureate Keorapetse Kgositsile; playwright Ron Milner; dancer-choreographer Jackie Hillsman; and poet and founder of Broadside Press Dudley Randall. Kgositsile was also active in the free speech movement while attending UC Berkeley. After leaving university to teach in a freedom school in Selma, Alabama, she worked as a field secretary in the Student Non-Violent Coordinating Committee (SNCC). She drafted SNCC's statement against the Vietnam War, the first public opposition to the war to be issued by a civil rights organization.

In Detroit, she co-founded the Detroit Coalition Against Police Brutality and the Justice for Cuba Coalition, and she participated as a teacher, administrator, and board member in the building of three African-centered schools. Active since the 1970s with Broadside Press, she was lead editor of *A Different Image: The Legacy of Broadside Press,* which won the Michigan Notable Books award in 2005.

For over 40 years, Kgositsile taught at the university level (Wayne State University, University of Michigan-Dearborn, University of Witwatersrand in South Africa), and as a volunteer in classes for elementary and high school students in Detroit's Afrocentric independent schools. She co-chaired Wayne State's Black Caucus and designed UM-Dearborn's curriculum for African American and African Studies (AAAS) and served as the program's director. Upon her retirement, Kgositsile was named Professor Emerita at UM-Dearborn (2014) and Associate Professor Emerita at WSU (1998). Her contributions to future generations of artists and activist extends beyond the classroom, as she has consistently collaborated with and mentored young Detroit writers.

Kgositsile's contributions as a writer and activist continue. She is active in local efforts to end water shutoffs, in the Detroit Independent Freedom Schools Movement's effort to provide classes in African American culture for Detroit students, and as co-editor of the quarterly print publication, *Riverwise.*

FOR DR. RON MILNER
African American playwright
May 29, 1938 – July 9, 2004

You saw despair in the eyes
of a twelve-year old boy
and you filed his face in your memory;
You were moved by the frailty of a little girl
standing on a box to reach the sink, washing dishes,
wearing a too-small overcoat in a cold apartment;
you recalled hungry playmates who snatched fruit
from the Italian vendor's truck and ran away fast;
you remembered the weekend drunk
whose unanswered questions drove him
to wreck his home and his children's hearts
every Saturday night,
and you didn't miss the forgiveness
stretched taut on his wife's face;
and you have never forgotten
your first love,
how the swirl of her polka dot skirt
and the perfection of her saddle oxford shoes
put a spell on you;
nor have you lost the awe evoked by your first baby
and the first swell of fatherhood;
and you still glory in your Baptist preacher mentor,
who showed you our people's elegance, grandeur and protocols,
and whose eloquence wafts through your mind
as a fine cologne, anointing your strivings.

You cherished all these encounters that others call "everyday life."
For you, they were the theater.
You stored them as images in the backstage of your heart,
stacked them like props and provisions for the work to come.
When you were ready
to face the nights alone at your writing table,
you brought them
out of the wings
to center stage.

Animated in your imagination,
they reeled and cavorted like a
merry-go-round of souls waiting for your direction,
and you, not wanting to kill their spirit,
coached them patiently,
a nod of approval here, a hesitant correction there,
all night till the dawn.
You gave them lines that hinted at wisdom.
The lighting you insisted upon
revealed the healing
hidden in their subtle gestures.
You showed them how to walk that walk
and talk the talk
your people could understand.

And we have understood.
In "What the Wine-Sellers Buy,"
"Jazz Set," "Checkmates"—all your stories,
we recognize ourselves—
falling in darkness sometimes,
sometimes rising in possibilities.
We see the answers, too,
floating like auras around the players
in that luminous space of the stage.

Leaving the theater,
we acknowledge you as griot,
marking our journey
in this time and this place,
and we are thankful.
We smile,
return to our lives,
our rhythm restored.

AMIRI BARAKA: A REMEMBRANCE
October 7, 1934 – January 9, 2014

I remember you, when you visited the Berkeley campus,
in the LeRoi days, in crumpled tweed jacket,
your shoulders slouching slightly under the weight
of ennui, alienation, and beat generation swagger.
For us African students in that White world,
you were the genius—poet, writer, our intellectual hero,
the "cat"—whose blaze ignited our reticent anger,
whose rage animated a stage
where for the first time we saw our authentic selves,
not pacified or pastel for the enemy's comfort,
but churning and spitting fire, desperate to be free.
"Twenty-Volume Suicide Note" and "Dutchman"
launched you into the fray of U.S. cultural warfare,
though a clear direction eluded you.
In the time before you believed
in revolution.
I remember Home,
essays of deep reflection and exploration.
You wrote about that revelation in Cuba: Revolution is possible.
It was happening just off the Florida coast.
You understood that ennui and alienation are entirely inappropriate
responses
to the human condition and its immense promise of change.

You recovered your African roots and grounding.
You came home. You changed your name.
Change became the principle by which you lived:
Ready to step off into a churning field of cultural work, issues and
institutions,
conceding there are no guarantees,
that one simply cannot foretell which strategy will meet a given
challenge;
committed to your neighborhood, loyal to peoples' independence fights
around the world;
engaging the enemy with all the resources at your command.
Will revolutionary Black Nationalism engender African rebirth?

Will Marxist-Leninism enlighten? Will Kawaida guide?
You turned all the theories inside out, stretching them against
our turbulent, striving communities,
to see if they fit, to test their efficacy,
all the while facing critics, and moving on.

Your life testified: No single ideological scaffolding will save us—
only our celebration of our beautiful selves,
only our ceaseless, fearless and fierce insistence on freedom
by any means of logic, warfare, imagination, Spirit or magic.
I remember you.

PRAYER CAVE IN BAHIA

Follow those stones
discreetly placed in an arc
up to the cave.
This hollow in the rocky coast
is the Spirit's house.
Walk the saint's ground in bare feet.
Bow to enter this fierce, raw
holiness:
miniature statues, mementoes,
flowers, popcorn, sweets,
secret petitions in tightly folded white notes
left on the altar.
Humble temple—
air inside thick with scent of algae
and incense.
Add a candle to the flames already alight.
Remember the old ones.
Give thanks, give thanks.

Descend the curved path
without turning your back to Spirit.
At the stones' end,
turn, face the sea,
fly away on the breeze.

Melba Joyce Boyd

Dr. Melba Joyce Boyd is a Distinguished University Professor in the Department of African American Studies at Wayne State University in Detroit, and an Adjunct Professor in Afroamerican and African Studies at the University of Michigan-Ann Arbor. An award-winning author of nine books of poetry, two biographies, editor of two poetry anthologies, and over 100 essays, she is also a documentary filmmaker. Boyd's poetry, essays and creative nonfiction have appeared in anthologies, academic journals, cultural periodicals and newspapers in the United States and Europe. Her latest collection, *Death Dance of a Butterfly*, received the 2013 Library of Michigan Notable Books Award for Poetry. She is the poet laureate of the Charles H. Wright Museum of African American History in Detroit and her poem, "This Museum Was Once a Dream," appears on the dedication plague on the museum's wall.

Roses and Revolutions: The Selected Writings of Dudley Randall received the 2010 Independent Publishers Award, the 2010 Library of Michigan Notable Books Award for Poetry, and was a Finalist for the NAACP Image Award for Poetry and the ForeWord Award for Poetry. *Wrestling with the Muse: Dudley Randall and the Broadside Press* received the 2004 Honor for Nonfiction from The Black Caucus of the American Library Association. Boyd's critically acclaimed and widely reviewed, *Discarded Legacy: Politics and Poetics in the Life of Frances E. W. Harper, 1825-1911*, (1994) was the first comprehensive study of Harper. She was a Fulbright Scholar at the University of Bremen in Germany, and a Visiting Professor at Fudan University in Shanghai, China. She has a Doctor of Arts in English from the University of Michigan and M.A. and B.A. degrees in English from Western Michigan University.

To Darnell and Johnny
February 23, 1973

Owen Darnell Winfield, born May 22, 1945 and John Percy Boyd,
Born January 2, 1949 were assassinated on February 23, 1973 by
by the police while fighting for Black Liberation by dismantling heroin
drug dealers in Detroit and Atlanta.
"Africa will rise."

I will always remember
How much life
is you.
your smiles
could cure with bright
stars of laughter.

I will always remember
how much life
is you.
Your strength
could hug and protect
with peace giving arms.

I will always remember
how much love
is your life,
giving them for
tomorrow's children
of the universe.

I will always remember,
and you will always live
in the Spirit of the New World,
you helped to build.

"It Could Have Been Me"
President Obama said in response to the murder of Trayvon Martin

"If I had a son,
Obama said,
he would look
like Trayvon."

He is handsome,
skin the color
of coffee,
cream and
cinnamon.
slight of build,
with a physique
yet to become,
he is shrouded
under hooded
myths and

shadows of
white guilt.

Grasping fists,
armed with a
package of
rainbow-colored
candy,
he is stalked
while striding
across grounds
of a gated
compound;
targeted by
imaginary fears
enforcing
Americanism.

How does Trayvon
stand his ground
when he steps
beyond borders
of the reservation?

What can a
black boy do
when "the man"
with a gun
comes?

How do you
walk away
from death
aimed at
your back?

"It could have
been me,"
the President
said.
"It could have
been me…"

Everett Hoagland

Everett Hoagland was born and raised in Philadelphia, PA, and came of age as a poet at the beginning of the Black Arts Movement. He graduated from Lincoln University and the graduate creative writing program at Brown University. His first nationally distributed collection was the Broadside Press chapbook, *Black Velvet,* and he is mentioned twice on the first page of Broadside Press publisher-poet Dudley Randall's Introduction in the still-in-print 1970 anthology, *The Black Poets.* Since then, Hoagland has been frequently and widely published in anthologies and periodicals as well as in his books, the latest of which is *Ocean Voices*. He has read his poetry to audiences throughout the USA, and in Ghana, Cuba, and China.

Hoagland was New Bedford, Massachusetts' first Poet Laureate and is Emeritus Professor at the University of Massachusetts-Dartmouth, where he created and sustained five black literature courses in addition to poetry workshops. His awards include two Massachusetts Artist Foundation Fellowships, the Gwendolyn Brooks Award and the 2015 Langston Hughes Society Award.

SISTER SAY

Yo, Bro,
the other day,
I visited our local college campus
up the way. To hear what Sister Sonia Sanchez
had to say.

She's my favorite down upbeat poet of my generation,
one of the best & most relevant poets in our nation.
You read her out-of-sight, right-on rally poems, right?
The slamming one she done "…After The…March
For Disarmament"?

Anyway, let me tell you.
You oughta heard what Sister Sonia had to say
during her program's Q-&-A. Sister Sonia told us:
like it or not, we are all tied together by our tongues, knotted,
bound one to another by vocal chords.

Sister say, it's a new day,
say, we need a new & better way to be
in this new century. Sister say, we need
a liberated, liberating language. One still real
enough to deal right when things are tough, things are tight.

But never a man-made dig or quip turned into a word-whip
(even in the name of what some think is hip).
Say, we need words
we do not use to rough up, batter, limit or otherwise
victimize one another.
No, not any human sister, human brother. Sister say,
always be about We,
The People, & free ourselves from mean words & deeds.

Sister say, let's rid ourselves of racist, sexist words. By rite
write hurtful words on recycled paper, cremate or bury them, let
them be

wiped out, in memory of all those African family names forcibly
drowned at sea
during our nation's free market slavery. Sister say, words
like "bitch" & "ho" have got to go. Say, so do those burned in
skin terms —

"octoroon," quadroon," "mulatto," "negro," "nigger."
Sister say,
God knows, anyone is bigger than any one of those.
Say, word-weapons, terms of abuse, don't get nicer behind
in-group-use.
That's no solution. Say, don't call anybody out of his or her
name. Say,
the rivers & our mouths are the same, & pollution poisons both.

So, Bro, in short, here's my report:
at that poetry program up the way the other day,
Sister Sonia say, there is no good bad
word. You heard?

A BIG B.A.M. THEORY OF CREATION
dedicated to poet and organizer Erik Andrade

"We are almost a nation of dancers,
musicians, and poets." — Olaudah Equiano

"...we survive in exact relationship
to the dedication of our poets
(include preachers, musicians and blues singers)."— Maya Angelou

What makes poetry
"Black," with a capital "B"?
It's no mystery:
subject matter, mode,
attitude. You know
our ways. We are

as likely to ritually
recite as write. And when
we do pen a poem about
a who, a what, a where, a why,
or a when, it often "sounds" like speech,
too. And that tends to be
true whether it's about

God, politics, love, family,
or being blue. Or when mining
a motherlode of dozens
with or for Brothers
or Sisters, or when just
improvising with cousins
(something we're not
likely to do with "privileged
others").

We have remained ourselves
while becomingly overcoming,
becoming who and what
we had to be. We the people steeped

in Deep River, risen from Middle Passage
and forced drownings in the main-

stream deep as bloody Old Man
River, daunting as Cape Fear
River, chilly and wide as The
River Jordan of ancestral song; we
who were done dirty, done wrong,
were not, are not bound by "standard"
mainstream English.
We have broken free
of imposed forms, from
the outrages of being bound
in formal and informal cages. Sympathy's
caged broken-winged song
birds now fly more freely than even
Bird's bop. They broke bad
with break-
dancing and hip

hop all over
spoken word's poetry perches
and beyond the lovely, dark, and deep
paper woods and pulp trees some think
they shall never see as lovely
as freed people's
poetry. Free
to be whatever
it wants to be.

What makes a poem Black? History!
It ain't no mystery: ancestry, legacy,
politics, class, culture,
style. Confluence
of the mass mixed
things that come to mind out
of a "consciousness of kind."

Mixed-in out of mouth things
like ring shouts, refrains, signifying, jive,

blues, jazz songs, scat, the dozens, r&b, break-
beats, rap. All that
black mouth evolved
north, east, west,
first hybrid down
south of what
we used to say is
where it's at. Free

poetry, free
of the slave ship's choke hold,
free of the slave-breakers' silencing
iron bit. Freed
from verse cages of poesy.
Free to be what comes out
of its own history.
Be it penned declaration

or improvised oration
as affirmation of its own
nation within
a nation. Recite it,
or write it, or hear it,
or read it like holy writ
because it
is. So
be it.

E. Ethelbert Miller

E. Ethelbert Miller is a writer and literary activist. He is the author of two memoirs and several books of poetry including *The Collected Poems of E. Ethelbert Miller,* a comprehensive collection that represents over 40 years of his work, published by Willow Books. For 17 years Miller served as the editor of *Poet Lore,* the oldest poetry magazine published in the United States. He is host of the weekly WPFW morning radio show *On the Margin with E. Ethelbert Miller* and host and producer of *The Scholars* on UDC-TV which received a 2020 Telly Award. In recent years, Miller has been inducted into the 2015 Washington DC Hall of Fame and awarded the 2016 AWP George Garrett Award for Outstanding Community Service in Literature and the 2016 DC Mayor's Arts Award for Distinguished Honor. He was awarded the 2019 Literary Award for poetry by the Black Caucus of the American Library Association. Miller serves as a board member for the DC Collaborative for Humanities and Education, The Inner Loop, and Folger Shakespeare Poetry. Most recently, he received a grant from the DC Commission on the Arts and Humanities and a congressional award from Congressman Jamie Raskin in recognition of his literary activism. Miller's latest book is *When Your Wife Has Tommy John Surgery and Other Baseball Stories*, published by City Point Press.

1865

After Lincoln's death old people lost their dreams.
There was only emptiness behind their eyes.
There were rumors that spread about Africa and the big river,
places where the land gave birth to food and shelter.
Tired feet left every morning and every day we counted
a loved one among the missing. It was Shonda I tightly held
each night, I buried my face in the center
of her back. I held her tighter than slavery. I was man
and chain. I searched for the softness of her blackness
under her scars and all the false promises of freedom.
I loved her like the North Star I could barely see.

Lost in the Sun

Joyful black fathers
throwing their little ones into the air.

Years later a troubling blue sky
blankets their world

Black fathers at funerals
no longer able to catch their sons.

Black fathers no longer standing
in a field of dreams.

Their black boys gone—
sunglasses unable to hide their

grief.

Love the Ghost in Me Shonda, Hold Me Dear

Do you remember that summer of 1831?
I remember the sky finally confessing its anger.
Stars walking across the sky holding candles.
What did Nat read when he could not write?
What wind told him to take back the night and turn
our lives around as if we were wheels on a wagon.
I learned to fear God more than a white man that night.
But I confess dear Shonda I was a man only by name.
I did not fight or kill—I ran. Nat refused to spare
child or wife. I had known slavery for years but had
only listened to the preacher talk of hell. I could not believe
a man's own flesh could turn against him with fangs that belonged
to dogs. Oh Shonda is this freedom now a terrible
thing? I long for a woman's breasts to know my hands and stop
their tremble. I know no love will stop Nat now.

JERRY W. WARD, JR.

Jerry W. Ward, Jr., is the author of THE KATRINA PAPERS: *A Journal of Trauma and Recovery* (2008), *The China Lectures: African American Literary and Critical Issues* (2014), *FRACTAL SONG: Poems* (2016), and *Blogs and Other Writing* (2018). He lives in New Orleans, LA.

Poem 77
(for birthday July 31, 2020)

I join my ancestors
in knowing virus, our minds
as sturdy as icy fire
to confirm a universe.

I join my ancestors.
Our tears are stones,
wary-wise stones that break no windows
as they whisper to the wind:
enough, enough of death eternal,
enough, enough of defensive failures
which offend the dignity of breathing.

I join my ancestors
in knowing profoundest virus
thriving in icy origins of flame,
surviving in ritual of remembering
an enough, enough for dignity to proclaim.

I join my ancestors
in knowing virus, our minds
as sturdy as icy fire
to confirm this universe, the dignity of breathing.

THE POEM UNDONE
(for Julia Wright)

To be addressed at a beach
she thought most square.
To be called to a window to see
what ought to be heard.
What might sting like a mosquito
infecting one with knowledge.
She thought of Yeats, of Leda, of time,
the coming of a terrifying swan.

Did he say the sea's calm, tamed by moonbeams,
when sound visualized is turbulent?
Is music's allegory of war
no more than conceits of violence
gathering to clash in the death of light?
How violated can a body be?
What's put in pain
by a mosquito's ignorant gift,
by its eternal tweet of sadness,
by retarded misery's ebb and flow
and slow torture of climate changing?
Such faith, such hope, such charity
did Antigone, imitating Isis, sprinkle on a corpse.
Honi soit qui mal y pense
and mea culpa invades the heart.
Tragedy has gone with the breeze
somewhere to fall apart in another country,
to alarm with lack of joy, love, light,
certitude, peace impossible for bloody jewels to restore.
She thought he murmured a snatch of fatal allegory:
"…let us be true/ to one another!"
She thought she was a dream, a dissonance
arising from a mosquito's donation.
She thought of her mind and his
sinking in the quicksand of a beach
as poetic armies clashed that night.

SOMEWHERE NEAR CHARLOTTESVILLE

he tasted the tragedy
of his tongue, in the coffin
of Monticello

for want of imagination
in the mortality of his words,
he shuddered, he quaked, he cringed

thinking no more no less
his properties personified in heirs
wearing his lurid face

should, when God in justice comes,
should make him a slave unique
in an autobiographical noose

no less no more is his story
our comedy of belief.

Opal Palmer Adisa

Opal Palmer Adisa is a Ja-Merican writer who lived in the Oakland Bay area for three decades, and recently returned to her birthland Jamaica, where she is the University Director of The Institute for Gender and Development Studies at The University of the West Indies, Mona, Jamaica. A writer of all genders, Adisa has 20 collected publications and her poetry, stories and essays have been anthologized in close to 500 journals, anthologies and books. She recently completed the authorized children's biography of Portia Simpson Miller, the first female Prime Minister of Jamaica.

They Will Not Take You

April 29 - May 4, 1992 marks the LA riot as a result of the acquittal of four LAPD officers recorded beating and using excessive force on Walter Rodney, an African American man. My son was almost one year old then, and the lynching, police brutality and abuse of African Americans, but specifically African American men, have been institutionalized and normalized. In that moment, I decided that my son would not be a victim to this system. I wrote, "I Will Not Let Them Take You" then as a pledge to him, but now with the wave of protests over the killing of George Floyd and other African American men and women, I've upgraded the poem by reaffirming my commitment to my son, who is now thirty-one years old and living in the LA area. I have also altered the title.

Tell them
Tell them loud and clear
I'm a crazy Jamaican woman

who will wage war for you
I refuse to sacrifice you
to racism

You will breathe
You will breathe
your ancestors breathed for you
to live with dignity
unafraid that your life-breath
will be kneed-out

Tell them
Tell them
I will not surrender you to troubled streets
I will not leave you for dope dealers
I will not abandon you to the police
who targets you—a black man

You will breathe
You will breathe
We all breathe for you

What is the language of tomorrow
that we mothers and sisters
and lovers and wives must speak
words seeped in future years
to raise you
to soar beyond the heavens
to dance in the lap of life
and sleep in the belly of laughter

Tell them
Tell them
you have a mother
who remembers
all she endured
in getting you here
and she will not give you up
will not give you up
to no one

Your breath is filtered
through rosemary water
and eucalyptus oil
so you can leap

You are heir to the next generation
whose path has been cleared
by the blood of your forefathers
who were silenced
humiliated
whose presence were usurped
but still they insisted
on being men so you
could vault

You will breathe
You will live
for all those
massacred
You will live
You will breathe

Tell them
Tell them
Your mother
will not give you up
but to love of
your own dreams

Tell them
your mother
insists that You breathe

Knee on Neck/Race on Hate

on his neck
a knee
presses down
his face on the ground

a knee presses
on his neck
a knee
a neck
a man's knee
a man's neck
a man pinned
to the ground
with a knee on his neck

one man kneeling over another
presses his knee on the
other man's neck
one man pinned on the ground
one with his neck
jammed to the ground
by the other man kneeling
on his neck

why is a man
kneeling on another
man's neck
doesn't the man pressing
his knee on the other man's neck
not hear the man utter
i can't breathe

what is unclear about
i can't breathe
is there a more polite
way to say "let me breathe"
should the man on the ground
with the other man pinning
his neck to the asphalt have begged
pretty please can you please
stop pressing into my neck
i can't breathe
i want to breathe so i can live

i want to breathe so i can tickle
my niece and nephew
hug my brother
high five my son
i want to breathe so i can go
home in time for dinner
let me breathe

but the man who is pressing his knee
on the other man's neck on the ground
ignores that man's plea

a man is pinned to the ground
the man pinning the other man
to the ground
has his knee
on the pinned man's neck
and is being observed by
colleagues who do nothing
to stop him even though they
hear that man that is pinned
to the ground plea
he cannot breathe

why don't they do something
why don't they say to the man
pinning the other man to
the ground with his knee pressed
into the neck of a black man
say
hey man
you've made your point
he isn't going anywhere
we've got your back
he is not a danger
he will not creep
into your house and
sleep with your wife
or seduce your sister

his dick isn't longer or bigger
than yours

but they didn't say anything
because
they were fed the same lies
that they swallowed
a black man aint' worth shit
killing one has never amounted
to anything
they ain't supposed to be
still breathing

damn why are
they still
breathing

8 minutes and 46 seconds
the police pressed his knee
on the neck of
george floyd
who lives
despite the knee
on his neck

Queen Mother to Future I

before your head
rested at my knee
i recognized the mark
on your arm
your eyes twin stars
charting a topography

at council you would sit
by my feet
play with the beads
around my ankle

swallow the words
the other mothers and
i whispered as promised

i am gone now
at least my breath
no longer fogs this world
but your work is not done
go and plant three baobab trees
so their roots will
fashion a river for the
the ships that are coming

you have to erect your own stool
bridging memory
lacing a landscape
spirally infinite in its journey

Charlie R. Braxton

Charlie R. Braxton is a poet, playwright and essayist from McComb, Mississippi. He is the author of three volumes of verse, *Ascension from the Ashes* (Blackwood Press 1991), *Cinder's Rekindled* (Jawara Press 2013), and *Embers Among the Ashes: Poems in a Haiku Manner* (Jawara Press 2018). His poetry has been published in various literary publications such as *African American Review, The Minnesota Review, The Black Nation, Massiffe, Candle, Transnational Literary Magazine, Eyeball, Sepia Poetry Review, Valley Voices, Specter Magazine* and The *San Fernando Poetry Journal*.

Another Mississippi Murder

they kilt that boy
lynched him
just as sho' as my name is
what it is
they did it
cause that what they do in
kokomo mississippi

kill folk
the same way they did
emmit till
in money mississippi
the same way they did
vernon dahamer
in hattiesburg mississippi
the same way they did
medger evers
in jackson mississippi
they same damn way they did
schwerner, goodman and chaney
in philadelphia mississippi
the same way they did
mack charles parker
in popularville mississippi
the same way they killed
andre jones
in a simpson county jail cell
hung him
like he was a skint pig
left to rot
under the watchful eye
of an old pale-faced devil's
moon
down in mississippi
where
raynard ladell johnson
found death's cold hands
draped in swaddling
white sheets
wrapped around his teenage throat
choking the life from his virile black
body
as it swayed
like a lusty whore
flirting in the flushed face
of a history so ugly
only a short ignorant-limp-dick

pot-bellied-beer-guzzling-
rebel-flag-waving-trailer-trash-talking redneck
could love it
mississippi is a slithering seductress
a geographical jezebel
whose whiteness torments me
like an electric ghost in
the industrial machine of
dixicratic politics
I know her well
cause
I love
and
I hate
her so
much
that every now & again
it hurts
it hurts
it hurts
yet we continue to march and sing and pray
for a land soaked in our innocent blood
when war cries
and battle hymns are needed
for this is a new song
for a new day
and a new time
our piece will not be said
in hushed apologetic tones
of slobbering uncle toms seeking reconciliation
naw
this time
we want justice
if not
then
we'll settle for revenge

Babylonian Consequences

a red moon pushed back
against the black sky/ star fire
falls down on green grass

in the far distance
smoke from smoldering sparks rise
the grassy knoll burns

a plague on both the
sinister house and senate
they will rue the day

they ignored us one
time too many, threw too few
crumbs, played us too close

thought we would never
come creeping up on them with
cold steel to their dome

Songs That Are Sacred and Pure
(for Toni Morrison)

we live/
 in a con/strict/
 space/ a place/ where/
 there is/
more love/
 for the wicked/
than/ there is/
 rest/ for the weary
and yet/
we/ do sing/
we/do shout
we/ do chant
and when/

our tongues/ are tied
with the pain/ that is
tethered to/ the
deep souls/ of our ancestors
we/do hum
we/do moan
and groan
our work/songs
that are/
as yet/ untitled
we/ do this
black/magic/music
to ensure/ that
the circle remains/unbroken
and that
the memories/ of
our beloveds' /
remain /sacred
and pure

KARLA BRUNDAGE

Karla Brundage is a Bay Area based poet, activist, and educator with a passion for social justice. Born in Berkeley, California in the summer of love to a Black mother and white father, Karla spent most of her childhood in Hawaii where she developed a deep love of nature. She is the founder of West Oakland to West Africa Poetry Exchange (WO2WA), which has facilitated cross-cultural exchange between Oakland and West African poets. Karla is a board member of the Before Columbus Foundation, which provides recognition and a wider audience for the wealth of cultural and ethnic diversity that constitutes American writing. She curates a monthly reading series called Ugly Beauty. Her editorial experience includes a pan-Africanist WO2WA poetry collection, *Our Spirits Carry Our Voices,* published by Pacific Raven Press in 2020; *Oakland Out Loud* (2007); and *Words Upon the Waters* (2006) both by Jukebox Press. Her poetry book, *Swallowing Watermelons,* was published by Ishmael Reed Publishing Company in 2006. Her poetry, short stories and essays have been widely anthologized and can be found in *Hip Mama, Literary Kitchen, Lotus Press, Bamboo Ridge Press, Vibe* and *Konch Literary Magazine.* She holds an MA in Education from San Francisco State University and an MFA from Mills College. Her most recent project is co-editing a collection called *Colossus:Home with Sara Biel* which features poets from the Bay Area in solidarity with Moms4housing and advocating for housing justice.

Black Arts Movement

To Be Young Gifted and Black
in 1957   marks the first point
of the Black Arts Movement
on the American timeline

meant using the back door
Brown vs. Board of Education
no voting rights
Black Panthers
Kujichagulia   Self-determination,
Umoja   Unity Ujamaa
Cooperative Economics
The 10-point plan
Free school lunches
Taking back our streets from the police
Arming ourselves

Black Arts is
Self love and self liberation
creation of our own literature
calls to action
founding of
Umbra Poet's Workshop
which becomes a magazine
by Ishmael Reed
David Henderson, Calvin and Nora Hicks
and other true New Yorkers who move west

Black Arts is
Barbara Christian chairing
African American Studies at UC Berkeley
LeRoi Jones graduating from
a Beat poet to the School of
Pan Africanism and Black Nationalism
emerging as Amiri Baraka
Poet, Instigator, Novelist
Playwrite, Cultural Critic

Trickster

The country is in turmoil. Do you
Integrate? Do we self separate?

Some BAMs repatriate to Ghana—
who knew why the Caged
Bird Sang, Maya Angelou, founder of the
Association for Women of African
Heritage, member of the
Harlem Writers Guild

Then there were actors—
John O'Neal
Tom Dent—founders
And co-collaborators of Umbra
Of the Free Southern Theater
Members of SNCC who
would influence SF Mime Troupe
And be featured in New Black Voices

Black Arts is
Mary Lovelace O'Neil,
Abstract Artist and professor
At UC Berkeley, but also in New Orleans with
John O'Neal and Tom Dent
Working Writing Witnessing
with SNCC, CORE
the Free Southern Theater
Adrienne Kennedy explored the
Psyche of the black woman in
Funny House of a Negro

Black Arts is
Poet   Intellectual
Eugene Redmond claiming
the most influential schools
In the Black Arts Movement
Were not New York School,

But Merritt College
SFSU, UC Berkeley
UCLA and the HBCU's

Avotcja Jilantro
Bay Area DJ, musician
Poet, producer and celebrity
Starred in Ntozake Shange's
for colored girls who have considered
suicide when the rainbow is enough

Q.R. poem in one Hand
Pen in the other
bops his jazz rhythms at the Elbow room
You pitches words right to the far left

James Baldwin said "Societies never know it,
but the war of an artist with society
is a lover's war,
the artist does, at best,
what lovers do,
which is to reveal the beloved to themselves,
and with that revelation,
make freedom real."

Black is
afros like golden halos
Uplifted fists
Black is   Power   is
Beautiful   is   Black Arts
is a way to reclaim power
Celebrate beauty   discover voice.

Take Her Down

break her arm
touch her breast
encircle her neck

take her down
put your foot behind hers
take your knee behind hers
it fits nicely there
gently push
she will lose balance
hold her face to the floor

if she cries out
release the pressure a bit

after she goes down
put your knee on her back,
but not with all your weight so
you don't crush her spine

You need 2-3 people for a Take down
You have to work together

If your partner does not have Your back
It can quickly become a
Dangerous situation
Report to your higher ups
When you get back to the Office

Come up from behind her
put your arm through hers
like a dance move
arms and legs move
in coordination

Each officer takes one side, one arm and one knee
That when you can ease her gently to the ground
No ones back gets injured and it's easier to cuff her
If she struggles, release the tension, not the grip

                        What happens if her clothes come off

Generally speaking you must proceed
As if this person is a danger to
Herself and you
At this point in time
Clothing does not matter

                                        And if she cries out

Again, women very manipulative
Will say anything to try to gain your trust
But you cannot trust them
They have already done something
To get them into this situation
As it is

And now that they are in trouble
They suddenly want your help

No—all cries for help are false and should be ignored

The Revolution will be Televised
(With apologies to Gil Scott Heron)

The Revolution will be televised
Can't you see it's happening right now
Last night was phase 6
Shock and awe

Phase 1
Destroy the warriors
Define warriors however you want
Every society has always has warriors
Our warriors are being taken down 1 by 1

Phase 2
Cut out our tongues
Change the language

Redefine words to have new meanings
Liberal
Entitlement
Crime
News
Guilty
Apology
Impeach
President
Fake
Real
Footprint
Cloud

Phase 3
Take our religion
Give us icons and devices to worship
Bow you head and text
Bow your head and text
Replace prayer with

Phase 4
Take our land
Displace the people

Phase 5
Destroy the family unit
Undo the matriarchy
Let the women come together for—
No—against
No—for
No—against
No—for
the safety of our children
born and unborn
our bodies
sacred and trampled
Deharmonize love

Phase 6
Shock and Awe
Replay violent deaths
Over and over
For analysis.
Was he really choking
Could he really breathe
Was she really carrying a phone
Was their skirt
Too short
Did they asked for it
Was his back really turned

Tell kids it's okay to dance on the heads of their dead opponents

Introduce the extreme right
I'm right
I'm right
I'm right

Ask the extreme left
Who's left?

The revolution will be televised
Turn off all the lights
Keep them on
Turn them off
Keep them on
Are we running out of water
Are we running out of time
Are we running

Make sure you have a gun
Make sure you have a gun

Lock your doors

Lock them tight

The revolution

Will be televised

Tonight

Amber Butts

Amber Butts is a storyteller, cultural strategist, and grief worker who believes that Black folks are already whole. Her work asks big and small questions about how we move towards actualizing spaces that center tenderness, nuance, and joy, while living in a world reliant on our terror. Amber has been featured in various publications, including *Zora, Essence, NPR, The Black Youth Project, Wakanda Dreamlab* and *Metoo*. Amber is currently at work on a speculative fiction novel that writes elders into our futures.

Ruin

My brother Raheem, who is now dead, once drove his arm through the drywall in our living room nearest the china cabinet that held our mother's most cherished photos. The house didn't shake as that part of the wall crumbled, a composed, white oceaned gap spraying what we never wanted into our lungs. The air never changed, not really. Our house was always damp. We would find small puddles in the corner of rooms, a spring sprung before noticing.

Our mother, Lisa, inherited the china cabinet from her mother Merle who inherited it from her grandmother Lizbet. Every Saturday she was meticulous, giving each frame the attention it deserved before we descended into the chaos of preparing for church. She used the same cloth everytime, bright red and velvet, forever reminding me of cake.

As she dusted, we'd sit on the clear plastic covered couch trying to match names with faces and scars with states, trying not to move, not to scoot, not to inevitably make the sound the owners of plastic covered couches hate most of all. Sometimes I imagined myself melting into that plastic, watching life from a clear, squeaky bubble.

Raheem wanted to keep the fairy he'd found safe and there was nowhere our father's hands couldn't reach. He thought that if he hid the fairy in the wall, and moved the china cabinet over by three feet, our father wouldn't know. But the cabinet was too heavy and when we tried pushing it, the first of mother's things broke: a small picture with a woman sitting on a wicker chair holding flowers. Above and below the hole are little tick marks against the wall for our height, our initials signifying how much we'd grown. The brick house was painted a pale yellow on the inside and always smelled of biscuits, lilac and fried chicken.

When Raheem's ghost first started visiting me, and I came home to tell my parents, my father locked me in my room, terrified that the neighbors would find out.

Earlier that day, I'd gone to the market for some fresh salmon and saw Raheem grinning at me between the cassava and sweet peppers. His body was wrong, pieces of him stuck back together in a rush. Big, jagged scars with thick bandages and thread, sometimes revealing the white of bone. But it was him. As he followed me home, and I did my best to look away, his body healed. He looked like him, intact. Whole. Alive.

I was terrified and excited, playing back the moment when we found his body. When we searched and prayed for any indication that his flesh belonged to some other unfortunate boy, a prayer of distance. Father said I'd lost my mind and forbade me from leaving my cold room until I found it again.

My room became my world. I drew pictures of dead children. I did my homework and read my stories there. I craved sweets all the time. I did everything to avoid ghost Raheem, who'd moved back into the house.

My mother brought food to my door but never came in. She wore a white headwrap for 60 days following his death. Father watched my every move, careful to note any inconsistencies in my recovery. But outside of using the restroom, I was never alone again. Raheem was always there.

Healers visited and were paid extra to keep quiet about what happened. Of course nothing would remain secret. Names might be omitted, but everyone in town will know who it is. The little girl with the dead brother, so touched by his death that she'd begun to conjure him up. A witch. A curse. Someone to be driven out.

Once a thing is spoken, it is made alive. It goes on living, plummeting, weaving, building an arsenal of allies and aliases. It clings to whatever may hold it. I think I was that for ghost Raheem. An anchor. Something to steady the loneliness. But I remained lonely. Even with him there. I barely slept and was terrified at the thought that when I awoke he wouldn't be there, while at the same time remaining fearful that he would be. He was not the same. I didn't know this boy.

On the morning that I was finally allowed to leave my room, after father pronounced that I'd been healed, I woke up early. I went around the house looking for something Raheem might want to help him reach the other side. He told me not to but I did it anyway.

By the time it was midday, I'd searched the entire compound and only found a misshapen blue toy truck. My clothes were dirty and my body sore. I went in to wash and change before lunch and came down once the task had been completed.

At the vision of me sitting still on the couch, without Raheem on my right side, his favorite place, mother calmly broke the newest framed photo in the cabinet across her knee and screamed. Her naked knee bled, and when I jumped up to gather towels and tweezers to remove the glass, she told me to sit down.

"I pray you never know pain like this, Ika. I pray you are never thrown into a world you no longer know, without anything to anchor you here. Pay careful attention, this is how you remove it."

I won't tell you what mother did, just know that I almost lost her too. I want to write that line in such a way that they both become alive again, because mother is half dead now. She sits for hours staring at the earth and weeping, sometimes begging to return to it.

I clean her nails of dirt, we make a ritual of it. Me bringing her the flower printed bowl with warm water, soft cloth and soap. Her imagining that the broken parts of her remain whole.

The china cabinet is covered in dust. The black widows have made a home in the fist sized hole within the wall that is never repaired.

Mother makes one more unsuccessful attempt at ending her life. Father leaves one day and never returns. Mother and I sit in our grief, busying our hands with food and cleaning, expecting some disappeared boy to knock on the door on any given day to make us whole again.

Mother doesn't start seeing ghost Raheem until six years after his death. I have six whole years alone with him and it marks me. His disappointment eating at my skin, his prayers that mother notices he is the one who helps her sleep, his not living taking up the whole of me. I am left with this boy who is and isn't my brother. A new boy angry at his death all the time.

Six years later, and he's just there. Sitting in between mother's knees like he did when we were both still children. She is on the ground, lying on the hot earth, offering it her prayers. She wears an orange dress and her long dreads are pinned in a purple headwrap. Her knees are caked in red-brown dirt. Hakeem smirks at me from one corner of his face and mouths, "watch this." I ignore him. It won't work.

His weightless hand is above mother's right knee, the one that spilled all the blood from breaking. She grows cold and yells, "Ohhhh". Before I know it, she is up on the stairs behind me pointing, "Ika! Ika!
You see that?! What is that? Get away beast!" My shoulders are sore from all the shaking. Raheem hangs his head low, looks up again and then waves bashfully, "Hi, mama."

The curses I've heard and the ones I haven't all come rushing out of mother's mouth at once. Her short soft body buckles together, and she signs the cross, runs to grab the white chalk nearest the door and draws a line with eleven symbols. Then she signals in the air to seal it.

"You shall not enter my home, demon. This is no place for you." Mother locks us in the house, and as we push the plastic covered couch against the door, I see Raheem wipe his forehead and cross the chalk threshold. He is inside now. Mother curses, then faints. Her body spasms. Raheem and I worry now, but only I can carry the ice for her face from the chamber. Mother wakes with a start.

"My son, my son. Is it you? Come."

Raheem goes to her this time, and the face is his. The movements are his. He's a tall boy, but his ghost shape allows him to fit onto mother's lap.

I give them time to be alone. Time for this less weighted me to catch up. Time for six years of no mother-son communication. For the bulk of the world to come back together again. Six years of there being two people in a home when there should be more. An eternity of mourning for someone I see everyday. An unmoving stone.

I run myself a hot bath with lavender, honey and oatmeal. My brother is still dead. My head stays below the water like my mother's lay on the earth, like my brother's the night we find his body torn to shreds, like the bottom of father's cold whiskey glass.

I have never seen the fairies. I hope they find me.

Zakiyyah G.E. Capehart

Zakiyyah G.E. Capehart is a writer, poet, storyteller, performance artist, visual artist, radio producer and host. Zakiyyah's poetry is published in several anthologies. Her radio shows are aired on KPFA 94.1fm. She combines her artistic skills and medical background, producing shows to educate and heal the community. Zakiyyah also performs with her bandleader, jazz vocalist, pianist husband Bryant "Mr. B." Bolling. Born in North Carolina, the family migrated to New York City when Zakiyyah was a child. Oakland, CA is currently where she resides with her husband. Zakiyyah has been granted funds three times from the Akonadi Foundation to write and perform productions to address community awareness in Oakland. Currently she is working on the publication of her book of poems and short stories.

MRI...My Reasonable Imagination

Am I a misfit?
A pop up, propped up mannequin
A muffled woman
A black doll
A silent observer
A speechless participant
An innocent bystander
Or an unenthusiastic gofer

During my confinement in this prison
I imagine how relieving it will be
when I am free
Free to move around
Free to speak
Free to laugh
Free to cry
Free to think of more than escaping from this physical and mental confinement

In my seclusion my reasonable imagination
Keeps me from thoughts I consider unreasonable
Thoughts of me screaming...
Until the volume of my screams
Shatter and crumble the walls
Of this transparent prison
That cripples me
Thoughts I am being transported
To a different place and time

And in this place...
I will be embraced
Not rejected
I will be loved
Not hated
I will have peace
Not war
I will have equality

Not injustice and racism
I will have truth
Not lies
I will have freedom
Not imprisonment
Or the illusion of freedom

Pondering I realized
These are indeed reasonable thoughts
So I embrace all of my thoughts
My reasonable imagination acknowledges and understands
This 6'x12x12 cardboard box
Is symbolic and coincides to the space
I inhabit here on Planet Earth

Fires in Oakland

we always get screwed and that's the drill
the West Oakland apartment building fire
was not on the news
when i heard about it
i got the blues
it touched my heart
and ripped it apart
a tragic fire blazing in the night
causing unimaginable fright
most were asleep
but began to weep

fire burning
smoke filling eyes, clogging throats
babies crying, children screaming
afraid   disoriented   confused
one hundred black people displaced
because of a landlord's greed
property owners, speculators, developers too
all conspiring against me and you

does anybody care?

fire took the lives
of people who lived there
multiple violations, building rundown,
holes in walls
ceilings threading to fall
water leaks causing mold
electrical wires exposed
pipes rusted filled with lead
a drink of water could kill you dead
rats, roaches, bedbugs, running amuck
but the landlord still wants his buck

one hundred black people displaced
driven into the street
no shelter, no clothing, no water, no food
the ghost ship fire
was all over the news
are the deaths and displacement
of black people unimportant news?

elders   disabled people
families with children

those who survived are homeless now

KALAMU CHACHÉ

Born and raised in Brooklyn, New York, Poetess Kalamu Chaché has lived and worked in East Palo Alto, California since the 1960s. Since her residency, Chaché served the East Bayshore community of East Palo Alto and the Belle Haven area of Menlo Park in numerous professional, executive, administrative, advocacy, and artistic areas of employment and volunteer services. The Poet Laureate of East Palo Alto since 1983, she authored three volumes of poetry: *Survival Tactics* (1975), *A Change of Interest* (1983), and *Survival Interest: A Collection Of Revisited Poems* (2013). Her poems appear in several book anthologies, newspapers, calendars, event programs, social media, and a wall exhibit at the East Palo Alto Library. Her Kalamu Productions is dedicated to creative arts works to bring The Arts closer to peoples' hearts.

Mothers Speaking About Their Sons

He was only 22 years old, when he was killed
By a Fruitvale BART Station Police Officer
In Oakland, California
In the early morning hours on January 1, 2009.
Who was he to me? Who was he to me?!
He was my son, and I loved him dearly.
I brought him into the world
On February 27, 1986.
What did I do about this? What did I do about this?!
I cried and almost died myself over knowing
That my son's life had been so wrongfully taken!
My family and I would have to fight a long battle
For justice to be served, which still does not satisfy us.
I am Wanda Johnson, the Mother of Oscar Grant.
My family and I work to no end to stop other families from having
to live this pain. We have established the Oscar Grant Foundation to
benefit grieving families. Remember Oscar Grant. Ashé!
Remember Oscar Grant. Ashé!

He was 28 years old, when he was murdered
On January 3, 2018 by a Bay Area Rapid Transit (BART) Officer. He was
shot and killed at the West Oakland station in California. His back was
turned, and his hands were up, and he was unarmed. He was shot in his
back three times by the BART Officer.
Who was he to me? Who was he to me?!
He was my son, who I loved so deeply.
I gave birth to him on May 14, 1989.
How did I feel about this? How did I feel about this?!
My heart ripped into pieces upon hearing the news!
This was absolutely police brutality waged against my son.
To this day, justice has not been served.
My family and I are still fighting for justice.
I am Yolanda Banks Reed, the Mother of Shaleem Tindle.
My family and I are continuing to call for police accountability. We have
established Mothers Fight Back to stop the killing of men and women.
Remember Shaleem Tindle. Ashé!
Remember Shaleem Tindle. Ashé!

August 17, 2020

He was 21 years old, when he was shot and killed in a robbery attempt
On March 10, 2019 by three men who did not value life.
He was murdered not far from his college campus in Los Angeles, California. He had moved there from Oakland to complete his education and
 graduate with a degree as a Musician.
This was a senseless shooting that we will never, ever be able to comprehend. Who was he to me? Who was he to me?!
He was my son, who I loved through time and space.
I brought him into this world on April 13, 1997.
How did I respond to this news? How did I respond to this news?!
I grieved and continue to grieve in ways that I no Mother should ever have to do! It was so wrong for those young men to take my son's life away from us. My family and I now know the identity of my son's killer, who is now in jail. I am Lynette Gibson McElhaney, the mother of Victor McElhaney.
Since his death, we continue to stand on a street corner
With the Soldiers Against Violence Everywhere
To memorialize the victims of violence and comfort grieving families.
Remember Victor McElhaney. Ashé!
Remember Victor McElhaney. Ashé!

MEILANI CLAY

Meilani Clay is a writer, educator, and mama from Oakland, CA. A graduate of Howard University and the University of San Francisco's Urban Education and Social Justice program, as well as a current student of SF State's Creative Writing program, she strives to be forever in school. Meilani bridges worlds with her words and will one day build a fort out of books written by Black people.

black woman is god, part 1

my fingertips craft spells
weave mythology into coiled strands of hair

my cheekbones be sharp as my tongue
honed against stones piled at my feet

hurled by hands incapable of accepting my divine

they are afraid of me
i know
because sometimes, i am afraid of me too

struggle to accept i not only   contain multitudes
i am, actually, all there is

the edges of the universe are cloaked
in the same inky night as my skin

the sun forever reaches to caress my cheek
just once more

before muddy, fetid shores
swallowed my children whole

my feet stamped legacy into red clay
my body brought the moon close enough

to forever dance with the sea
they are scared i might remember who i am

might remember my smile
can begin and end wars

my magic brings the stars closer to witness miracles
twinkling their excitement

creating celestial arrangements

for me to read before i dream

visions of a world rid
its alabaster parasites

behind closed lids
my pupils contain the unknown depths of the ocean

every tear shed
holy water   flowing freely down my face

black woman is god, part 2

the black woman is god
in a world hellbent on being heathen
betrayed by those at our right hand
hung out to die
knowing streets and temples will teem with parishioners
when it is time to mourn our passing

we show up anyway
to make feasts from scraps
wield righteous rage for a future eons beyond this one
yet
our names are only ever uttered
soft, in prayer
whispered close to clavicle
an exhale on lips before sleep

we call to you
over the roar of the ocean's hush
you don't trust you enough
to meet us in the storm
all our prophets must be false
if our names
can gild the tongues of pretentious pagans
at performative protests
when only black women

can hold the syllables in our mouths
with the reverence they deserve

we have wept
wiped libation from our faces
only to have it replaced with spit
no matter our weary we resist rest
so long as any of you are refused respite

though our bodies blanket this earth
from end-to-end
we continue to offer ourselves to mobs of marauders
though we still the crashing currents
to soothe your worry
we remain
the black woman, a god
rarely granted grace
and still!
how hallowed be
how hallowed be

how holy be

our names

Cole Eubanks

Cole Eubanks is retired as an educator for the Philadelphia (PA) and Atlantic City (NJ) School Districts. He was the featured poet for Atlantic City's Sovereign Avenue Black History Jazz Celebration for eight years. Cole's work can be found in *E. Pluribus Unum, Poet's Against War, Apiary, The Journal of Baha'i Studies, F(r)iction,* and Haiku in Action Gallery.

The Other N- Word

Because of the execution of George Floyd, I am
haunted by the vulnerable ubiquity of necks, it
seems everyone has one… even babies. My father
missed showing me how to shave my neck and I

went to school bleeding. In the backseat of a Buick
at a vampire drive-in Tyra Graham left marks on my
neck like sexual graffiti. I looked like Humphrey
Bogart in The African Queen emerging from the muck

covered in leeches. My wife leaves accessorized
with a choker, she asks why I avert my eyes. When
wolves fight it's not to the death. The vanquished
submit by exposing jugular necks to a killing bite

never taken because wolves be they black,
or white, have no concept of color supremacy.
1880 to 1940 is known as the hanging years when
over five thousand Blacks were strung up by their

necks with picnicking audiences of thousands
cheering Christmas trees decorated in hell. A thick
ten inch scar, like a noose, burns my neck due
to two surgeries where fibulas from both legs

were transplanted to my face to replace a jaw
compromised by a constellation of tumors. Both
times the procedures failed. But, I am grateful.
Unlike George, I can still breathe.

Tanji Gilliam

Tanji Gilliam, Ph.D., M.F.A. is the Founder of Oil House, a neighborhood planning firm. She is the recipient of numerous awards from the Social Science Research Council. She was the Hip-Hop and Media researcher on the Black Youth Project contributing to successful grant proposals for the Ford Foundation and Robert Wood Johnson Foundation. In 2010, she received the Art and Change Grant from the Leeway Foundation for her work on domestic violence. In 2013 her web series, *Scheherazade*, was featured in *Huffington Post* and on Mark Anthony Neal's blog, *New Black Man in Exile*.

Dr. Gilliam served as a development consultant for the Old Bronx County Courthouse and has written the strategic plan and directed curricula for the Universal Hip Hop Museum (UHHM). As the Director of Community Revitalization for Trenton Housing Authority (2013-2015), Gilliam received recognition for her work improving youth literacy by the NAACP, Trenton, founded a workforce development initiative, Rubber Roads, co-funded by the State Department of Labor and Mercer County Improvement Authority. Rubber Roads attracted the attention of the White House My Brothers Keeper initiative, where Gilliam was an invited stakeholder. She also founded the Pulse Public Health program which connected teenage girls with Apple technologies, established the Lartigue (Video and Audio) Lab in Rush Crossing, a 200 unit mixed-income development, developed new database software, integrating Hope VI caseload data and resident admissions info, and founded and co-moderated a resident-led Community Health Task Force.

Gilliam received her Ph.D. in 2009 in History of Culture from The University of Chicago where she edited the first film reel for her dissertation advisor, Melissa Harris-Perry. She also received her M.F.A. in Film, Video and New Media from the School of The Art Institute of Chicago in 2006. In 2002, she graduated Cum Laude from the University of Pennsylvania where she received her B.A. in Afro-American Studies and English. Dr. Gilliam worked as a high school English and film teacher for three years in The District of Columbia Public Schools; she founded the video program at Duke Ellington School of the Arts. Following that, Dr. Gilliam spent four academic years as a postdoctoral fellow at University of Pennsylvania and as an adjunct Assistant Professor at University of Pennsylvania, Columbia University, Monroe College and Lehigh University, at the appointment of Dr. James Braxton Peterson. She currently serves as a Development Consultant for Newark Symphony Hall.

Act Three
Scene One
Time: Middle Passage, Midnight
Place: In the Bowes of a slave ship.
In the middle of a storm.

Sharine, just like my father, was our great-grandmother's child, one of the select few that was raised in the care of the family's matriarch. My mother would explain, "Sharine has lost anyone who ever really cared about her;" my great-grandmother, my cousin Nancy (a beautiful person who we literally watched disappear as Diabetes ripped one extremity after another from her), and my Aunt Cat, one of the sisters. This is not exactly true; however; as I have explicit memories of my cousin Varee, Sharine's sister, adulterized by the sudden role of surrogate mother while still in her teens. There have been other family friends as well that have "taken her in." Sharine's biological mother, my cousin An'ette, has suffered from drug addiction for decades.

Yesterday, I met Sharine's only daughter. Her eyes were closed, her lips were formed in a smile, her hair was "all over her head," and she was lying on a stretcher in Andersons Funeral Home in New Brunswick, where she was brought mysteriously, from an Essex County morgue. Although we know that Sharine's daughter Da'laysia Marie Rhymer, was raped and murdered in her home, and we know that her injuries included broken ribs, a fractured skull and lacerated liver, and we know that she was taken too soon, we have no idea how she ended up at Anderson's, like her great-grandfather and my great-grandmother who are buried just a few minutes away.

On Seamen Street last night, I told my Uncle Benny that my grandmothers willed Da'laysia home, and he corrected that "while that [was] all well and good, we needed to find out who aided in that move on this side of the sky." Sharine, An'nette and Sharine's boyfriend are all currently under investigation by New Jersey Division of Youth and Family Services for Child Abuse. With a family as fractured as hers/ours we just don't know the "whole story." Newark police have arrested Oquan Blake, the boyfriend, and charged him with felony murder, aggravated assault and several counts of aggravated sexual assault. The last thing Sharine remembers about the day is arriving home to find Oquan dousing Da'laysia in the shower and swabbing her vagina and anus with Q-Tips, trying to figure out where the blood was coming from.

On Seamen Street, you are supposed to swing between two houses, one right across the street from the other. The first was my great-grandmother's and is now one of the sisters. It is a four-story converted multi-family house that in its "heyday" was filled with kin and food and song. The second originally belonged to another one of the sisters and is currently owned by her daughter, a way to keep an eye on "Mother," I suppose. Sharine and I spent the hour before arriving at Anderson's in both of these family landmarks.

My one aunt never pulls any punches. As she put it yesterday, "I know this is not what you want to hear, BUT! ..." The "But" included every related thing from "you need Jesus" to "You are a Queen." I learned later that evening that this sister was the fighter growing up, and that she had everybody's back, and that's why you got to walk on over there across the street. There are so many secrets, the most well guarded one is that my great-grandmother's house has become so empty and I fear that my Aunt there is so alone. She told Sharine that she has been hanging with all the wrong people and rhetorically asked, "why don't you ever come visit me."

It was in this house that my father lived separated from his mother and younger siblings. And it was this house, that his little brother Ben, I learned yesterday, coveted from his Harlem project, wondering why "Gerry" got to live in the Big House where he could walk outside with his shoes off.

My Aunt Rachel, who was also at the kitchen table, said that she used to cry, back in the city, over her estranged brother and always wondered as a child why her mother left her brother behind. She also said that she can understand why An'ette could allow her daughter to keep company with Oquan, because that's what drugs do to you, "you don't feel reality when you're high." She remembered her mother saying that she chose not to marry my biological grandfather, that she left him and "started to keep her legs closed." She also heard that my great-grandmother forced her daughter to leave my dad behind. She just did not want to let him go.

Da'laysia, frighteningly, has never met any of this family. She didn't make it to her first annual family picnic, and no one knew at the last picnic that Sharine was even pregnant. We will all see her, for the first time, in a communion dress in her casket, at the viewing Friday morning.

Two days ago I found Sharine in Newark. When she answered the phone I asked her where she was and if she felt safe there. Once she assured me that she did I told her to stay there because I was coming to see her. When I got to her that night, followed soon thereafter by my cousin, we asked her if there was anything she "wasn't telling us," told her that because of the news media, criminal justice and DYFS "attention," "all the stuff was going to come out anyway." In hindsight, I doubt that this statement is even true. There is plenty of shit that gets "swept under the rug" in these kinds of cases. Sharine, like anyone else, may have been entitled to her secrets.

I asked her if her boyfriend was abusive to her. Told her that I would not judge her. Even told her that I had been involved in an abusive relationship before. What I did not tell her was that my son's father raped me, that I knew exactly what it was like to be 21, a single-parent, in an abusive relationship with a man who drank, and used drugs, and didn't have a pot to piss in; I just showed up pretending to be family, alone.

Sharine shared that her mother is using again, and when further probed, that sometimes she gets coke from Sharine's boyfriend. I told my family at the kitchen table that "as a feminist," I thought my grandmother's decision not to marry my father's dad in 1946 was "really dope."

Her would be mother-in-law, Lou McPhatter, once told my father that she fled north to New York City because she murdered her abusive husband. There is no "evidence" to support this, but a man by the name of Henry McPhatter did die in North Carolina at a curiously young age with no specified cause of death. Grandma Lou's advice to my father was that "[she] had better not read about this one day in some book on 125th Street."

I know that all of these stories, though "other sides" of my family, are all related, because no accident of birth can cause this many coincidences. On my mother's side, stories she bravely shared for the purposes of this project (and requested to be identified in) included being knocked unconscious in her first marriage, asking her mother for help, and being told by my grandmother, "the first year is the hardest, have another child." Her stories also include being told by her grandmother that she was the "ugly grandchild." "That kind of stuff leaves scars," she said. "I'll probably take some of these scars to my grave."

By my father's account, all of the trouble with An'ette, Sharine and Da'laysia stems from my great-Uncle Haywood. Someone who my

Uncle Hatim vividly remembers, "shooting up in front of all the kids." Truth is, as I announced yesterday at a rally held in Da'laysia's honor, Da'laysia and Sharine have been impacted by drugs, but they are also victims of the state and federal government.

The decision for where to bury Da'laysia today went down much like I imagine the decision for where to house Sharine went back in the day. She is, according to the funeral home director, long for only 7-months-old, too long, with the additional inches for the casket, for an infant-sized grave, and also too deep to fit in any other relative's single grave. I feel close to how my father feels about what to do with me when I'm gone, "bury me in the backyard for all I care, it's otherwise a waste of space," he says. Despite all of this, I still don't want to pick up the phone and tell Sharine that after her baby was raped and beaten it may now be burned and put God knows where because Aunt Eleanor ain't tryna give up her space next to Mother, and she is not willing to have a third roommate neither. "You can talk all that Jesus stuff but what would Jesus do!," my uncle said.

Sharine fit everything she owned in two bags when we moved her out of her mother's two-bedroom apartment. It was a meticulously clean and organized third-floor walk-up. The walls had exposed brick and in Sharine's room, a collage of pictures. There was no crib and all of her daughter's clothes were reportedly hanging in the closet in her mother's room.

At the funeral, two of An'ette's male friends stood up to "remember" Da'laysia. One of them got under my skin because he told us that he was telling An'ette upon seeing Da'laysia's whole wardrobe, that her clothes were fit for a princess.

In my daughter's room, I have decorated it with a fashion theme. She has two ballet bars with primarily hand-me-downs ranging from her current size of 6-9 months to seven years. I keep thinking not even my husband's closest boys have seen, or cared to see, my daughter's wardrobe. My own brothers and father have paid it no mind.
My homegirl, Giselle, who not only drove Sharine and I to Seamen Street the morning of the funeral, but who also gratuitously styled Sharine's hair the night before, was especially miffed at another of

An'ette's friends who sung a love song to Da'laysia, "his friend," during her funeral. I watched this same friend pace around the periphery of the rally and only walked upstairs with Sharine moments before because he was lingering in front of An'ette's house, along with two other men I didn't know.

I could not bring myself to walk into the bathroom where Sharine found Da'laysia standing in a tub full of cold water, although I could see that tub and everything else from where I stood in Sharine's bedroom, everything except the closet. So I just looked at Sharine's wall of pictures.
At first I only "know" Sharine, but I get to thinking that the little boy smiling with her is her son. There is also a picture of Dale, Da'laysia's father, who looks more youthful then at the funeral. He has an afro in the picture and a small gold Jesus piece and chain, and is standing in the middle of a grocery store smiling pleasantly with two middle fingers up. There is an obituary hanging for an infant boy who Sharine said
was her friend's baby who died." There are a number of liberal-looking white women I suspect are employees in any number of the "programs" that Sharine was put in growing up. There is an erotica graphic of two women pressed up against one another. There are no pictures of Da'laysia. She is nowhere to be found.

According to my Aunt Eleanor, "An'ette is a demon, and [she] moved back into this house in order to get rid of demons ... so Mother could die in peace." Maybe that's why Sharine stood us up for church this morning. I have only been to A.M.E. Mt. Zion once before for my great-grandmother's funeral, though I remember the parking lot quite well from Sunday mornings when my great-grandmother would be picked up and/or dropped off by my dad.

My aunt looks beautiful and dignified as usual, in all white behind the pulpit. This is the first time I have heard her sing in I don't know how long.

It is "name-tag Sunday," and as I write mine I wonder if anyone here knew my great-grandmother. If anyone here will wonder whose child I am.

My aunt told me the reason why An'ette came upstairs is because Mother found her in the basement where she had been left as a young girl for three days, alone. Mother brought them all upstairs, An'ette, and all of her children that "An'ette never wanted, save for a welfare check."

Lucky for me the choir started in the same way they do at my mother's church. The hardest thing about remembering that "God is good, all the time," is keeping in mind that he is not the only spirit at work. My Aunt Eleanor said she also blames her brother because he was living right there and should have been keeping better watch. She was quite clear however, that she expected more from An'ette's mother.
I suspect that if I brought my two boys to this house they would "cut up," just like these two little black boy saints four pews in front of me, beltin' out the lyrics to the song and ghost playing the piano. I wonder if my daughter will eventually rest quietly in between them, perfectly collected.

Almost the entire congregation of mainly black women and children went to the altar when it "opened" for "special prayer." There were so many people praying for themselves and their families that me and my cousins Bobby and Debbie just stayed behind in our seats.

I never like to sit in the front, but I occasionally sit right in the middle. These women are so beautiful. These women and their daughters. "Is Sharine with you?," my cousin Carl asked me, and as she answered hours ago, "Tanj. I'm tired. U can go wit out me. I love U." I wish she could have seen these daughters, in their ponytails and purple liturgical robes. One of them, especially, could have been our daughter. Aunt Eleanor, sitting up there, could be my my great-grandmother, she could be my grandmother. I also see my Aunt Cat, here and there.

I did not mean to cross my Uncle at the rally. I should have known that he would be speaking to the fathers. However, I really feel, despite Pastor Green, that these women, leaning as ushers in all-white at the altar, kneeling as a choir before his feet, are our saviors. And they always have been.

The entire women's cabin pounds simultaneously on the base of the ship. The audience watches as they all fall in unison, fists up, into the sea.

Lisa D. Gray

Lisa opens doors and helps other writers of color claim space in writing and publishing through the reading series she creates, Our Voices Our Stories. This platform allowed her to interview authors Devi Laskar, Natalie Baszile, Renee Swindle, and Tayari Jones in conversations that tackled topics around craft, inspiration, and writing practice. Lisa won the 2018 Edgar Award named for Robert L. Fish and the Henry Joseph Jackson Prize for Distinguished Fiction in 2014. She has attended The Fine Arts Works Center, The Voices of Our Nations Foundation, and the Vermont Studio Center where she completed a residency. She is currently a fellow at The Ruby San Francisco and holds degrees in English and Creative Writing from Spelman College and Mills College. She is a writer and leader who believes that it is necessary for black women and women of color to write and share our stories so that others do not erase or control our narratives. She is completing her first novel, *Stolen Summer*.

No Beats

Disco was dying
as Hip Hop was rising
when House snuck in
on the down beat.

That's the summer I met Chuck
and that Go Go swang
his hip throwing thang,
soundtrack to sticky nights
on DC streets.

Laughing and smoking,
watchin' hard bodied boys
hot and sweaty
b-ballin, shot callin'
cold'n dead by weeks end with

no beats.

Dust Men: A Haiku

Old folks say where wills
live so do ways an I hold
both in my brown hands

Until those days when
when the blue streak hits
An I feel like shit

They tell me be a man
An'at shit fucks with my head cuz
men like me they dead

Blow us away

QUINCY SCOTT JONES

Quincy Scott Jones is the author of the *The T-Bone Series,* published by Whirlwind Press in 2009. His work has appeared in *African American Review, The North American Review, Love Jawns: A Mixtape,* and *The Feminist Wire* as well as anthologies *Resisting Arrest: Poems to Stretch the Sky, COVID Chronicles: A Comics Anthology,* and *Black Lives Have Always Mattered: A Collection of Essays, Poems, and Personal Narratives.* With Nina Sharma he co-curates *Black Shop,* a column that thinks about allyship between BIPOC artists. His graphic narrative, *>BlackNerd<*, is in the works.

All Lines Matter

The New All
A[n] All Love Song
The All Panthers
All Power!
All Art
Let the world be a[n] All Poem
a brief moment / in All History

All and Blue
The All Eyed Peas
Ma Rainy's All Bottom
For All Girls Who Have Considered Suicide // When the Rainbow is Enuf
All Tuxedo
Little All Dress
Heartthrob never, All and ugly as ever / However,
I see a red door and want to paint it all
All Sabbath
The All Album
all-on-all crime

from white hands peeling all skins over / america
the body of one / all man / contains no life
Those four all girls blown up / in that Alabama church
her lynched all boy

The Little All Boy

And I am all, but O! my soul is white
...no lighter / Than an all midnight
So will my page be all that I write? // Being me, it will not be white. /
But it will be / a part of you

you'll sit down and say "The All..."
The all wrestles with the superman.
...the all driver, and in / back the man and the woman, / usually young and always white.
And their allness [becomes] apparent, that one first...
hates, instead, him self / him all self

But
I love you all! // I love all // Because all are me

But all shouldn't be [/] scared of revolution

knives of peace
      for Sonia Sanchez
with apologies to Sonia Sanchez

yeah my sista
where are the knives of peace
the swords of peace
ready to go to war for peace
soldiers of peace
generals of peace
vanguard apache zulu warriors of peace
bloods of peace
crips of peace
got mine with a tech 9 extra clip of peace
napalm of peace
hydro bomb of peace
thermo nuclear multiple warhead of....

sorry?

Oh, you mean knife and fork of peace?
like plate of peace?
like the slice of pizza I just ate for dinner
                                          for peace?

why are you trying to do that?
why are you trying to feed the world
when half of America's overweight
and the other half can't feed ourselves?

why are you trying to cure our cancer?
why you trying to heal our heads?
why you talking all peace?
don't you know all that peace talk spreads?

get peace in the streets
get peace in the schools
then all the kids start thinking peace is cool
start putting peace all on Youtube

then it spreads to TV
hour-long special brought to you by drug companies
whose side effects include mild heart disease
wobbly knees
and massive migraines every time you sneeze
and you want us to swallow this pill called peace?
sista, please

peace ain't buying no car
peace ain't paying no bills
peace ain't supply those knockoff thrills
we crave in the cry of the night
and when we try to holiday from everyday plight
peace gets stopped at security
       makes us miss our flight
that ain't right.

this ain't no time for peace
or peace marches
or protests in the park
by old heads to throw all these army recruiters off their mark
or talk to have men in dark suits knocking on the door

asking whatcha writing?
who you teaching?
who's talking this peace
we want names

nah, this is end game
end days
time to pull down the shades
blow a little haze
and watch ourselves kill ourselves on TV

no peace for you no peace for me

time to cut the throats of killers and victims alike
and we might not get our peace
by at least we'll have
our silence.

Venus Jones

Venus Jones is the founder of SHE ROSE™, an acclaimed author, performance poet, TEDx speaker and mentor. She continues to help emerging leaders go from page to stage and become more poetic, poised, and powerful under pressure. Her Kwanzaa iPhone app, full of poetic affirmations, has been downloaded in 90 countries. She's the author of three poetry books and four spoken word albums. Her work has been endorsed by the legendary Langston Hughes family. Her one-woman-show, Poetic Soldier, was dubbed "Most Inspiring Solo Performance" at the Los Angeles Women's Theatre Festival. Her one act play *Race and War: an awkward conversation* was featured at the Tampa Bay Theatre Festival. Venus graduated from Mills College with honors and earned her MFA in Creative Writing. She loves hugs from her best friend and husband Steve of 20 plus years. She also likes to make funny faces while dancing to funk and soul music. Visit venusjones.com

PLIGHT

       we're protectors of truth,
       of infinite love and light
       shape shifters in transit
       this is our plight.

connect those who seek understanding
to those who believe they're alone in the wind.

       this is our plight,
       we mend.

i'm a lonely mender, who's moving again.
moving where my ancient friend leads me
today, i'm a pretender and my role, complexity

but i'm really as simple as *one* can get.
capturing every fish in the sea in my invisible net
tomorrow we travel light years through black holes

we're the sacred spirit   a total sum   of creative souls
what does humanity like most about me?

my invisibility
i hide inside of folds, i'm sprinkles that show up
on the tongues of freckled five-year-olds
opening the hearts of wrinkled women,
who taste kiwi for the first time.

showing up in a glass of sweet lemonade,
i'm freshly squeezed lime.
the essence of reason, rebellion, and rhyme.

i appreciate open invitations. it's been way too long.
where are the poets, teachers, and writers of classic song?
let's hitchhike with some musicians who want to drive us home.
where's the café. our next stop: cappuccino foam.

> we're protectors of truth,
> of infinite love and light
> shape shifters in transit
> this is our plight.

connect those who seek understanding
to those who believe they're alone in the wind.

> this is our plight,
> we pretend.

Margaret Porter Troupe

Margaret Porter Troupe is a writer and editor. She is the founding director of the Harlem Arts Salon and The Gloster Arts Project, bringing the arts to children in rural Mississippi or wherever they may be. www.theglosterproject.org

Mourning the dead

    For my siblings

When Betty died

it was the first time

I'd spoken to a person

who was leaving this earth.

Her voice was garbled.

She could barely articulate her words,

but she understood perfectly

what I was saying

when I said, "I love you"

I didn't really know what to say

To her as she lay dying.

When Harry died

it was the first time

I'd held the hand of someone

who was leaving from this earth.

His hand was cold

in a way that stone is cold.

Yet it was the hand of a human person,

the hand of my brother

with whom I'd grown up

playing in the dirt underneath the house

suffered his teasing

I turned my back

when he refused to fight

not for his job

not for his health

not for his life

couldn't stand up

his cold hand

a vise on my heart.

Then Wash died and I just couldn't

Stand up.

JUDY JUANITA

At SFSU in the 1960s, Judy Juanita joined fellow student protesters to revolutionize American higher education and create the nation's first black studies department. Her semi-autobiographical debut novel, *Virgin Soul* (Viking, 2013), features a young woman in the 60s who joins the Black Panther Party. Her stories appear in *Oakland Noir, Crab Orchard Review, The Female Complaint, Imagination & Place: an anthology, Tartt Six* and *Tartt Seven*. Her writing focuses on black politics, culture and art. *De Facto Feminism: Essays Straight Outta Oakland* (EquiDistance, 2016) explores key shifts and contradictions in her own artistic development as it explores black and female empowerment. In her play, *Life is a Carousel*, featured at Beyond Baroque in Venice in 2019, a black woman academic argues with the forgotten founder of Black Studies about the academy, Black Studies and the struggle. This play is included in Juanita's book *Homage to the Black Arts Movement: A Handbook* (EquiDistance, 2018). Juanita's twenty-odd plays have been produced in the Bay Area, L.A. and NYC.

Bruno was from Brazil: a prose poem

"I'm from Oakland and I'm not a statistic. Yet. But New Year's Eve I left the Bank of America at 2:30 pm; the news that night flashed on my bank. It was the scene of the last homicide of the year, at 3:20 pm. – which meant I dodged a bullet by 45 minutes. Witnesses say two Latino males and two African- American males had a parking lot altercation. The Latino driver used an ethnic slur and one of the black guys pulled out a gun and shot him. The two blacks drove off, witnesses say, and Bruno who was from Brazil and delivered pizza, for god's sake, died on the spot... now you know the last word in the guidebook for new arrivals is nigger. And I know poor, poor Bruno heard the word a thousand times delivering those pizzas. 'Some nigguz on 90th Ave. want mushroom/salami/chicken... only nigguz want combos like that... you my nigga... when you get money from nigguz, check for counterfeit... nigguz, Bruno, watch out...' Poor Bruno, the word probably came off his tongue like spit. And he didn't know you could call a black person a nigger and get utter scorn and contempt. Like down South where they just ignored it and kept their inner dignity. But Bruno, you don't call a real nigga a nigga. That's like a death wish. Are you crazy? Suicidal? Certain words are like gods. They command respect. Nigger is a god. I'm so sorry for Bruno. He was a sacrificial lamb-that's what you have to do with gods. You have to appease them, give em a lil' somepin somepin. And I know Richard Pryor went to Africa after he made $50 million off the word and came back with religion. Stopped using the word and used crack instead. But he didn't stop folks from using it. He just made the word an academic issue: shall we nigger; shall we not nigger? Forget Dick Gregory's autobiography called Nigger. No, a Harvard law professor writes a book called Nigger: The Strange Career of a Troublesome Word. Nigger is a God, nigger made millions, now it has a career. And the country's leading black intellectual, a guy named Skippy, finds one of the first novels written by a black, titled, what else, Our Nig. So I'm proposing a constitutional amendment on the use of the word. There are simply days when it is dangerous to use the word. And one of those days is Friday night. And another of those days is Saturday night. Ok? On MLK's birthday, abstain. Christmas, it goes without saying. The season is the reason. And proceed with caution on the Fourth of July. Fireworks, drinking and the use of the word by the wrong people don't mix."

I first see LeRoi Jones in the flesh

I first see LeRoi Jones in the flesh, at his vociferous best, at the student body funding debate. I am stone-ass surprised that he is even here. I thought of him as a Big Important Writer From The East Coast In A Tweed Coat With Books Under His Arm squirreled away from us except for class. I knew he was due to teach a class; I was assigned by the BSU to find him and his wife Sylvia an apartment at which task I failed after two weeks of walking up and down the hills of the Fillmore and the Haight with $250 in cash in my purse. They end up having to stay at the Travel-lodge on Market St. until someone else, more on the ball, finds them a pad, some other soul.

And here he is, not in his book-lined study, not surrounded by Balzac, Genet, Ionesco, or Brecht, not hunched over a Smith-Corona portable as inspiration pours from his fingertips, not on the phone long distance with some big bubba tubba negotiating another run of "Dutchman." Nope, he has left beat nihilism for black nationalism, He's with us, giving much lip to the punk-ass white boys who control the student body budget and who want, for some perverse reason that I'm sure would never have occurred to them in Stanislaus or Siskiyou counties, to pick a fight with the BSU over our altogether legitimate and defensible hiring of LeRoi. We pack the classroom for the meeting with black, white, Hispanic, Asian students and community people, all black and formidable. Academia's cherubs, goodbye. We drown them, wash over them in a wave of derision. Every time they try business as usual, we up-against-the-wall-motherfucker them. The white boys get tired real quick of beating their heads against a united front and they grudgingly agree to give it up. Yea-us.

Yea-me. Financing LeRoi means I get financed too. LeRoi immediately sets us to rehearsing and performing his play "Black Mass." We are the Black Arts and Culture Troupe, we get a van, we run up costumes at the pad, we put on shows within a matter of days. I'm the warm-up act, reading poetry. Chandro-Imi writes a play, "Night-time is the Right Time," and we're gone, black train down the black track, LeRoi the engine. An array of BSU talent, actors, singers, modern dancers, supply motive force, the cars, if you will, and I am the caboose. Chandro-Imi, saying I am the quintessential naysayer, even gives me a part in the play, the last line which I deliver and even changed if I chose, since the clapping and the right-ons start just before it and nobody can hear me say squat. We take the show to colleges, centers and anyplace they let us in East Palo Alto, West Oakland, Western Addition, South Berkeley, Marin City, Seaside, Hunter's Point. I am a little star. Maybe not a Betelgeuse or a Procyon, but one of the white dwarfs like Sirius B.

The play is big fun to perform. No Romeo and Juliet here; no boy gets girl, boy loses girl, boy gets her back stuff here. We improvise a riot, more like man gets mad, man gets Molotov, woman throws it. The play, as written, is a one-page set of instructions like this:

PROLOGUE
    A single light shines on a man off to the side mad, making a Molotov cocktail. Across the stage, dancers rise from the floor, reaching upward; lighting goes from shadowy to bright. A voice projects:

> Night time is the right time
> for riot, for love
> for surprising the man
>
> Evening is our spring
> If all we got is one day
> Then we only have one night
> Not a winter night
> lonely bleak
> desolate
> Spring in the night
> Wake up
> Bloom into blackness
> brothers and sisters
> Burst wide open
> Be/come
> be/come
> Yeah come hard
> and then come out
> Come out
> Into the streets
> Dance in the streets (Play "Dancing in the Streets" here)
> in the streets
> Fight in the streets

> Run in the streets
> Throw a Molotov cocktail
> in the streets
> Die in the streets
> Live and Die in the streets
> Bring this society
> to its knees
> in the streets
> Bring LBJ to his texas
> cracker barrel knees
> in the streets
> Bring all the traitors
> in the ivory towers
> into the streets
> Move into the streets
> Reclaim society
> in the streets

Scene One
Fat mama and a sister carrying sorrow like a ball and chain beg their brethren not to throw his Molotov cocktail.
Scene Two
A younger brother watches as he throws it. The police came looking for him, He hides, and the mother deliberates on whether to turn her son in.
Scene Three
The police get vicious and kill him. The younger brother announces he's going to join the army. The mother approves until she finds out it's the Black Militia.
Scene Four
The mother decides she has nothing left to lose. She joins up too. A neighbor comes as she's leaving and says (my line):
"Some people join church, I see you joined the world."

Sometimes I throw in Goosey's old favorite, "Don't let no man drag you down," changing it, if people hear me, to "Don't let the man drag you down," or the old standby, "You can do bad by yourself." But the point of the naysayer, as LeRoi explains to us in class, is to show that quality of self-doubt in blacks that will always accompany liberating actions, but which will be drowned out by the exulting of the people at the moment of liberation.

Once, driving back from a show, I stand in the back of the van towering over LeRoi; I hold onto the rail and observe him. He has a nice funny cackle of a laugh; he is a little guy who hunches; even standing here in my head, he's hunched in his little finely embroidered dashiki. A compact man. A nice man. Even a gentle man. He banters, for heavens' sake. I like him and not at all in a sexual way. Thank goodness, he doesn't give off that vibe. He's short, anyway. His vibe is Let's get going, Let's do business, Let's put on a really good show. Onstage, on podium, he becomes ferocious, shrill, harsh, demanding, killer-scary.

The one time I see him mix the two personas is his last night in town, our crowning performance at the Black House in the Fillmore district. LeRoi rants, raves, screams; he also talks soft and tender about his wife and the baby on the way. I get the shock of my life when he points her out. LeRoi Jones' wife! She has foreboding eyes and is taller than I am! I force myself not to gape. He married up not down! But I can't help staring. She's pregnant, nearly due. Her belly blooms out so perfectly pregnant you can see her enlarged belly button sticking out through the African cotton like a pacifier. I feel bad I was the cause of her and the unborn child staying in a motel. Her hair surrounds her proudness like so many twisted branches of a tree. Even with the baby blooming, she retains a feminine slim curve to her dancer's figure. And she talks about California like it has a tail. She doesn't dig California, San Francisco, the Bay Area, and by extension, us. California niggers are out to lunch, I hear her say loudly several times that night. She insists on dancing a solo bit. We give each other the elbows. So supple she looks boneless, she rolls on her bloomy stomach as if it's a bag of raked leaves. When she finishes, she gets up and goes upstairs. I hear her say, These San Francisco niggers are trifling-ass. Zora Neale says language is like money. Goosey's old rose-jumping, hide and seek rhyme comes to mind:

honey in the bee ball/I can't see y'all /all ain't hid/caint hide over

No hiding from Sylvia Jones. The applause at the end of "Night Time's the Right Time" is prolonged.

While they're clapping, I mimic Sylvia Jones:
don't wanna struggle, don't wanna work, don't wanna make real change
humph, California humph
a place with a whole lotta people who wanna do nothing
white folk here cuz they made it

niggers, what's your excuse?

Of course, people see my grumble-face but all they hear are the last few words.

Dillard's come, watching everything with a slit-eyed demeanor. I tried to get him to give a few hours at the Tutorial Center; he laughed me down to the ground. I reminded him he could get credits toward his degree. It's all a get over Geniece, Don't you see that? Niggers getting-over. Tutorial, BSU, the movement. It's all Get Over City. He has upset me so that I write something for him. I guess I write it at him. It isn't a poem, like one by Mali. I have taken to reading it like filler over the din of the stage crew. I read it right at him. I don't even know I memorized it until I start saying it and it pops out of me, a few kernels at a time:
I hear you

brothers are original even when they're being unoriginal, charade in black, imitation men and women bending in the wind like trees or like ridiculous parodies of trees bending in the wind, one of you brothers told me this great mass movement of people in the cities—what the man calls uprising, what we know is revolution-looks like a murph. rip-off. rip-off, get over, take the money and run. same brother said college could never teach me what I learned in the game, I already got a Ph.D. in gaming. I hear you talking but you can't come in. I hear you talking but you won't come in. said brother has a beautiful con, you know, as in can't read but can outcon a bank, smooth, he could con fur off a bear if he had to. his name in card games, is 'big white' —there he's all con and B.S. and front and lie and whatever way he can to get a guy to go along. his specialty is conning Jewish guys. he'll even dress down sometimes, on a friday night, when they get the sucker trade, you know, come across as an old country slick guy, big coveralls, big cigar, talk with a drawl, only his hands and eyes look like a con. he told me he looks at a man's hands and eyes for the tells, the signals that he has a hand or he's bluffing, if he bets one way, talking a lot and later bets another way and he's stopped talking, then his hand has changed, said brother says it's very hard for a man to keep from disclosing his hand one way or another, said brother said, if you're going to beat a game, you have to control a game, said brother sounds like he knows how to win, said brother sounds like he thinks, if he could feel as hard as he thinks, as hard as he probably bangs his ole ladeez, said brother could rule the world. said brother is the people personified.

Dillard doesn't bat an eyelash. Maybe he's high, ethereally out there; he looks like raw meat that I ate out of sheer hunger. He seems to float in a galaxy out of my sphere of need. We go outside to talk. The icy riffs in the San Francisco air run up my nostrils and into my ears, carried on little knives.

"Did my poetry insult you tonight?"

"You call that poetry? Shit, Sound like somebody babbling on and on. Telling all their business. Putting somebody else's in the streets." He's putting me down.

"I think you're an interesting sociological specimen."

"I think you're full of shit. Naive, innocent shit, but shit just the same."

"At least, Dillard, I'm trying."

"Yeah, you're trying all right. My patience." Every time I almost decide to stop seeing him something changes my mind and we spend the night. But now the thought of his hard rubbery dick turns me off.

"I'm trying to help people," I say. His ridicule brings up stuff I left behind.

"My people, my people, as de monkey said."

"You must need something you can only get here, Or else you would be someplace else." My aunt talked once about somebody's divorce. Her comment stuck in my brain: When a woman loses her taste for a man, it's gone.

If you're so cynical, then why are you even here?"

"I came to see you. To be insulted by the great Geniece."

"It wasn't an insult. It was a kind of praise."

He shakes his head. "I know what you're trying to do. You want to convert me. This is your church."

"It's not."

I have lost my taste for him.

"Yes, it is, and I'm the unrepentant sinner."

It is gone.

"Dillard, I think we should stop seeing each other."

There, I said it, and it silences him, He looks at me like I told him his house burnt down.

"I'm into this," I say, pointing toward the Black House. "You're not."

He starts coughing, the smoke from his burning house caught in his throat. "Don't want to be."

"We can still be friends," I say.
"That's what your girlfriends are for."
"It's not going to work. We're different."

Why was he making this hard for me? He had never even said I love you, not even in the heat of passion. He didn't love me, didn't like the things I was doing, had just belittled me. Why?

"Why is this difficult?" I say.

"Ah, difficult. That's what my teachers always called me in grade school, difficult."

He shrugs his shoulders, looks me dead in the eyes, good riddance-to-bad-rubbish high on his shoulders and walks off. I walk back in feeling just this way: I'm so alive.

devorah major

devorah major is a California-born "granddaughter of immigrants, documented and undocumented who works as a writer, editor, writing coach, spoken word performer, recording artist, and poetry professor." The Poet-in-Residence of the Fine Arts Museums of San Francisco, major has toured internationally in places such as Northern and Southern Italy, Bosnia, Jamaica, Venezuela, Belgium, England and Wales, and throughout the United States both performing her poetry and serving on panels speaking on African-American poetry, Beat Poetry, and poetry of resistance. In 2015, major premiered her play, *Classic Black: Voices of 19th Century African-Americans* at the S.F. International Arts Festival. Her most recent poetry collection is *califia's daughter* (Willow Books, 2020).

downpressors

Woe to the downpressors:
They'll eat the bread of sorrow! Bob Marley

you walked on our bones for centuries
turned them to sand
poured into sandboxes
for your children to build sandcastles

and when the sand became translucent
filled with the sunlight
burning your eyes
you found more to sacrifice

sent vultures to strip away our skins
and built ladders formed
from our ribs, limbs and skulls
on which you climbed
to get a better view of the lands
you planned to conquer

and now we rise
joined by
some of your children
and grandchildren
who have eaten of shame
and refuse to travel
on the rails you laid
with our bones

and each of you
who blocks our path
tries to press us back
will be blinded by our brilliance
blinded
blinded
blinded by our brilliance

city values

for Kenneth Harding

two dollars
in the city of san francisco
is not quite enough
for a sunday newspaper

but you could get a liter of generic
soda pop and have a bit of change
maybe two large organic apples
or a medium order of fast food fries

one tin of quality black shoe polish
or one condom from a club vending machine
or one thigh with a side at church's chicken

or the life of one cocoa skinned
nineteen year old roughly
trying to become a man-

who for want
of a two dollar bus transfer
was shot in the back of the head

writing love

all i want to write are love poems

in this season of rotting flesh
and hollow bellies
in this year of hidden corpses
and shrapnel graveyards

all i want to write are love poems
to the one whose breath
mixes with mine

for the lips i taste
for the hips i encircle
for the sap i share

all i want to write are love poems

about shining eyes
and sweat's perfume
about promises made and kept
about secrets and fears
shared and revealed

in this year of the buried city
this decade of the hunger crop
this century newly begun yet already
with thousands upon thousands
of limbs torn off
eyes burnt out
hearts eviscerated

all i want to write are love poems

i don't want this job of
recording the children's despair
the mothers' grieving the fathers'
misery the sons' brutalization
the planet's storms and fires

it's all too much for me
my eyes fill with salt and become blurred
and only love poems will make it better
will clear the way

but all around me
these others who i love
in knowing and as strangers
are being murdered or enslaved
starved or tortured
imprisoned or forsaken

and the poems i want to write
evade me until i am left
with nothing but this howl
wedged between my teeth

all i want to write are love poems

about blue kissing my morning
lemons tart and fresh flavoring
my afternoons crescent moons
arching away from venus' sparkle
in a star hungry sky

all i want to write
are love poems

all i want to write
is love

LENARD D. MOORE

Lenard D. Moore is a poet, fiction writer, essayist, book reviewer, public speaker, photographer, and the author and/or editor or co-editor of several books, including *All The Songs We Sing* (Blair, 2020), *The Geography Of Jazz* (Blair, 2020), *One Window's Light* (Unicorn Press, 2017), and *A Temple Looming* (WordTech Editions, 2008). His literary works have appeared in *African American Review, Agni, Callaloo, Colorado Review, North American Review, North Dakota Quarterly, Obsidian, Prairie Schooner* and *Valley Voices*. He is the founder and executive director of the Carolina African American Writers' Collective and co-founder of the Washington Street Writers Group. He is the recipient of several awards, including the North Carolina Award for Literature (2014); Haiku Museum of Tokyo Award (2003, 1994, and 1983); and Margaret Walker Creative Writing Award (1997).

SUMMER BLUES FOR GEORGE FLOYD

I wish you were here for your children
Tall, treelike to guide them
Say I wish you were here for your children
Way up treelike to guide them
You don't know how bad we just hurt
Our nerves sting above the hem

Checked the neighborhood for you
Walked up and down the street
Say I checked the neighborhood for you
Walked up and down the street
But I only found the wind
And summer sun to greet

How must you cope everyday
When your feet are heavy?
Can I still proceed now
Just when your feet are heavy?
You pray for strength and stamp away
Hold the tears like a levee.

Say I wish you were here for your children
Tall, treelike to guide right
Say I wish you were here for your children
Tall, treelike to guide right
You dig how my coping now
Has nerves to sting above all might

Now you dig how my coping
Has nerves to sting above all night

8 Haiku

for Amiri Baraka

first month of the year—
you transform
into Transbluesency

winter recliner—
you bend language
across borders

snow-glazed night
your words flare
off the page

all the voices
rising from Yugen…
the heater hums

close reading...
I recall your voice
amid the chill

falling temperature...
a student's research paper
on your riffs

frigid shadows—
black pupils stare
from Home

the cold deepens...
the conjuring
of Blues People

HAIKU SEQUENCE
for Sonia Sanchez

your whole notes
wake the dormant trees
the wind's breath

drums thump
pulsing of the heartsong
the opening sky

jazz and haiku
shake loose my skin*
a dusting of pollen

insistent running
of the long river
you're a cappella

my black hands
cupping the sunlight
jacuzzi bubbles

orange lilies bow
your noontime strut
up the sidewalk

rain long gone
I recite the syllables
of your language

evening walk
I catch your riff
in my voice

shake loose my skin is the title of Sonia Sanchez's poetry book.

DENISE NICHOLAS

Denise Nicholas is an actor and writer who has starred in numerous films and TV shows, including *Room 222,* for which she earned three Golden Globe nominations, and *In the Heat of the Night,* for which she also wrote several episodes. She lives in Southern California.

Freshwater Road

Chapter 3

A hard something landed in Celeste's lap, waking her from a doze. Behind the continuous murmur of voices in the office, typewriter carriages banged, bells sounded, and a radio played. "Sign that. I'll take you to the apartment in a minute. I'm Margo." Celeste grasped the clipboard, frowning up at the short, pretty, blue-eyed white girl with edge-straight blonde hair cut just above her shoulders. By the time she got "hi" to her lips, Margo had pivoted into a small army of coverall-wearing Negro and white young people moving around the airless office/storefront picking up papers, diagramming patterns on a blackboard, sticking pins in a map of Mississippi. Celeste wondered if the pins marked the locations of dead bodies, burned buildings, or some other horrendous occurrence. On the walls, pictures of Martin Luther King, Rosa Parks, Medgar Evers. Through the front windows, she saw that the police cars hadn't moved.

Margo huddled over a mimeograph machine near the back wall with a young dark-skinned guy, she cranking the handle of the old inky cylinder while he caught the copies. Celeste eyed them through slits. The last thing she'd expected in this office was a white girl telling *her* what to do, even if it was only signing some form. Mississippi *and* the civil rights movement meant pushing two years of Ann Arbor's surrounds of white people to the rear.

Here, both Negro and white student-types were working and talking together in easy familiarity. Hard to tell who was in charge. Serious faces, cigarette smoke spiraling up to the white-tiled ceiling, and music coming from a small radio in the corner, Wolfman Jack's gravel-choked voice punctuating the melodies. It had the feeling of a campus gathering, without the food and alcohol.

Celeste walked to the bulletin board to see the photos of rural-looking Negro people grinning with their arms around overall-wearing student-types. Everyone seemed to be old and young at the same time. And, photo after photo of burned down buildings. She went back to her folding chair.

A ballpoint pen dangled at the end of a thin string attached to the clipboard. A typed page and a carbon under it, the word "release" in caps across the top.

> *In the event of your injury or death, neither you nor your family or heirs to your family have a legal right to sue or to otherwise seek compensation from One Man, One Vote.*

This whole trip was going to break Shuck's heart. Beneath the fine suits, the stingy-brimmed hats, the sleek cars, and the smooth demeanor, Shuck was a race man. But Mississippi was a different story. He'd want to come down here and snatch her back to sanity. She'd better call him soon. He'd need to hear her voice to know that she was OK. Wilamena would more than likely hiss and fume and blame it all on Shuck being a race man, constantly talking about Negro this and Negro that, filling Billy and Celeste's heads with all that Negro-ness. She'd have preferred to have them less anchored in things Negro. More classical music, less jazz, more London and Paris, less Harlem and Chicago. And for sure, less Detroit.

A line of typed dashes stretched across the bottom of the page. Celeste's full name was typed under the line and the dates of her stay in Mississippi. A note at the bottom: *Be sure to send one copy home to a parent or guardian before leaving for your project city.*

Celeste's departure date, the end of Freedom Summer, August 21, was two months away. She might be dead by then—or a hero, a northern agitator hero who'd managed to register an entire town of disenfranchised Negroes. She saw herself as a cross between Joan of Arc and Harriet Tubman, the fires of righteousness flaming in her heart stoked by the news reports that had been coming out of the south for the last three years. Her departure date floated on the paper as if the ink had run out, as if there'd be no leaving Mississippi. She signed on the line and pulled the copy from under the carbon, then slipped it into her book bag. Shuck said your decisions were your own when you crossed from teen to adulthood. Age eighteen marked the beginning of adulthood, but the years between eighteen and twenty-one were a kind of nebulous grace period you were given if you appeared not to have good sense. She'd be twenty in November.

The clatter in the office scaled down as the volunteers filtered out in groups of two and three. When Margo led her out to a 1960 Ford and told her to get into the back seat, the police started their engines, too. Had police cars, lurking around midnight corners, followed the other volunteers when they left? She'd seen enough squad cars on the way from the train station to handle it. Was this the routine or was special attention given to new arrivals? Her suitcase gave her away.

Margo's car stank of decomposing cigarettes and sweaty armpits. Celeste added her own train-funk to the haze of odors. From the dark of the car's backseat she watched the back of Margo's head as they rode through the deserted streets of downtown Jackson. The two police cars followed half a block behind them. More than likely, the police knew when she'd arrived at the train station, knew the volunteers' every move. Already Mississippi felt like a moldy hole, a long dark tunnel without enough fresh air, too much moisture, and no light at the end. This interminable night ranked as one of the longest of Celeste's life. When she checked behind them again, the police cars had disappeared. She wanted to relax, but something told her the effort would be a foolish waste of time.

"If you're with a white person and you get stopped by the police, let the white person do the talking." Margo's pure New York City accent leaned against the slow southern night as she drove well under the speed limit, checking to the right and the left and eyeing the rearview mirror at every intersection. Perspiration slicked her face to a moony shine. A dark bandana covered her blonde hair. "Act like you're the maid getting a ride home from work."

"Are you *serious*?" Celeste rolled her eyes at the back of Margo's head. "Nobody's that dumb, even in the movies." Then, she remembered the porter at the train station. Was he acting servile to survive? To get paid, for sure. Now she wished she hadn't looked at him so harshly. She might find herself bobbing and weaving, shuffling to save her own life before this summer was over. Could she do that? What would it do to her? She tried to follow the thought to its conclusion. And what in God's name would Shuck think about her riding around in the backseat pretending to be somebody's maid? He'd want her to survive, pure and simple. Pride could get her a one-way ticket to a tongue lashing, or a beating—or worse, get her tossed into a fast-moving river.

"You'd be amazed." Margo double-checked her rearview mirror, then accelerated. "Another car fell in behind us when the police cars turned around. He's gone."

Maybe it was still the police but in an unmarked car, Celeste thought.

At the next intersection, Margo slowed. "When it comes to the movement, every white person in the south is the police. They all follow us. There's no real distinction between regular white people and the police down here."

Celeste sank deeper into the backseat, her heart skipping through its beats like a drummer on smack. Margo knew what she was thinking before she'd opened her mouth. She dug her fingers into the crack where the seat meets the seat back and brought her hands out with dirt and lint pieces sticking to her fingers. "So what do I do if I get stopped with all Negro people in the car? Jump out and start tap dancing?"

"You might have to." Margo turned into a residential section of wood-framed houses set back beyond night-black lawns. "It's already happened. Some volunteers were stopped and the cops made them dance in the middle of the highway. Guns drawn."

Celeste's neck tensed as though her vertebrae were fusing. What to say now? Nothing. Just listen. Pay attention. She caught Margo's eyes in the rearview mirror.

"Be respectful and pray. Sing freedom songs in your head. By the end of orientation, you'll know the words to a lot of 'em." Margo let her eyes go back to scanning as they moved quietly through the streets.

No lamps lit the windows, no porch lights were on, and the shrubs and hedges were just dark shapes in the night. Not even the trees moved, just the car gliding in slow motion over the black tar. Celeste ducked her head well below the back window, gasping for air, legs sprawled across the bump, peering out like a child. She tasted again the train coffee and that mayonnaisy ham sandwich from the shop in Memphis.

Margo turned into what looked like a housing project of low, dark-brick buildings. "Try to get the name of the officer stopping you. The patrol car number, details that can be reported to the FBI. Try to stay calm. Try to stay alive."

Celeste bucked herself up a bit, and pushed aside her bristling self-consciousness at being a trainee with a white-girl boss who obviously knew more about staying alive in Mississippi than she did.

"Remember names and squad car numbers. Sing the words to freedom songs," Margo repeated. "As soon as I get you ready for Pineyville and the other straggler ready for the Delta, I'm going to Aberdeen." Margo put her arm on the car window ledge, the warm air fluttering her bandana. She looked so in control, she made it sound like they were off to be camp counselors.

Celeste strained to sense Margo's fear. Maybe she was so afraid herself, no one else's fear had a chance. She glared beyond the car's front lights. "Pineyville? Where's that?" She checked the map of Mississippi in her mind. Greenwood, Vicksburg, Natchez, Yazoo City. Names like dreams that pillowed nightmares.

"Down below Hattiesburg, a few miles from the Louisiana border." Margo stopped the car in front of an apartment building with windows across the front, then turned off the engine and the lights. The engine ticked down to nothing. "Used to be the Piney Woods before the loggers cut down all the trees." She sat low in her seat but alert, head turning like a radar scanner. "The Gulf coast is nice, but it's still Mississippi, and when it's not, it's Louisiana or Alabama or Florida. Same goddamned thing."

How much farther *down below* could they go? Where did Mississippi end? Celeste stopped a moan that formed in her throat, and said, "Aren't you afraid?" She didn't want to be the only one afraid.

"Yeah." Margo turned a little in the car seat and looked directly at her, and Celeste saw a wide-eyed girl very much like herself. They were about the same age. They had come to Mississippi for the same reason. "Only a nut wouldn't be afraid in this place."

Celeste sighed, thanked God she wasn't alone. "That helps."

The shrieking of cicadas and mole crickets swelled, aroused by the sound of the car, the low-talking voices. Nothing romantic about it. No harking back to benign nighttime stories of the sounds of the south, no animated crickets and puffy-haired Negroes with smiles and songs on their lips. This was a tunnel of death. Her mouth tasted like sandpaper. Then, suddenly, the quiet mushroomed around them. Celeste heard her own heart beating. All she could see were dark trees, hedges near windowpanes lit only by the reflected moon. She sat up a bit to see the surrounding area.

"Stay low." Margo's voice was sharp. "There's a car under the trees across the street. It's always there." Margo turned to Celeste and smiled a creepy smile in the soupy darkness. "The Klan shot out the street lights when they found out we were housing volunteers here. We think that's one of their cars."

Celeste glared at the car, caught between wanting to thump Margo on the back of the head for scolding her like she was a child and being thankful that Margo had warned her about the lurking danger. Nothing moved inside the dark car. Just black windows and no heads.

"How long've you been here?" Celeste's voice crackled between her true voice and the hoarse whisper of fear.

Margo pulled a single key out of her bag and held it up in the streak of moonlight coming through the front windshield. "Six months." She sounded proud. Celeste didn't want to look up to a white girl, but she had sense enough to know that Margo had already passed tests that she hadn't even studied for. She had to give Margo her due, relax inside for a moment, and listen to her as she would her teacher.

"For the next few days, you go through nonviolence training with the stragglers. Y'all are the last group. We need to get you going to your projects so you'll have time to do what we're here to do." Firm-voiced, Margo laid it out, though the "ya'll" was a tight fit with her New York accent. "You'll be running your freedom school and your voting project at the same time. The voter education classes take priority. That's pretty much it. Oh, and try not to get killed." Straight faced and no nonsense. She handed the single key to Celeste and indicated with a nod that it was time for Celeste to get out of the car.

Fear approaching terror hurtled through Celeste. She opened the door and hunched over to climb out of the backseat. The civil rights demonstrations on campus seemed so harmless. That was another world. This was the real deal. Run a freedom school and try not to get killed. She'd read it in her packet of materials, knew the school was a part of the summer project, couldn't remember precisely what she was supposed to do. She needed to sleep, to bathe, to eat a meal that had a green vegetable on the plate. Negro people were *her* people. She didn't want a white girl from New York to be more courageous on their behalf than she was. She had to submit, though, because it might be the difference between life and death. Mississippi wasn't Ann Arbor or Detroit, and she needed to keep that foremost in her mind.

"Your contact's Reverend Singleton." Margo never stopped scoping the darkness, even as she leaned across the front seat and talked to Celeste out of the car window. A real soldier. "He's the point man in Pineyville. I'll fill you in over the next few days."

Celeste tried to gather up some mettle for her cracking, slipping voice. She leaned down, head in the window, wanting to crawl through the window back into the car. "When do I go?"

"As soon as I see you're ready. Stay low to the floor at night. That apartment's been shot into. Grab the empty mattress. There's another volunteer in there."

Celeste hefted her suitcase and book bag out of the back seat, wondering how long it would take her to get ready. Ready for what? Nonviolence training, of course. Practice being oppressed, practice not getting killed. Taking low to keep the peace, removing chips from shoulders, anger from lips, history from heart. She lingered by the side of the car, afraid to walk through open space. Afraid she'd end up like Medgar Evers, shot dead a few feet from his front door. Across the street, the dark car waited. "What about the police?" Celeste heard her own dumb question too late to pull it back. They'd just been followed by the police. The police were all over Jackson waiting.

"Forget the police." Margo sighed on the verge of impatience. "I'll pick y'all up in the morning. White volunteers have to sleep in another unit. No integrating. Not yet anyway." She started the car, staying low, her parchment-white face surrounded by her dark bandana and the night. "I'll wait 'til you're in the door. Go on."

Celeste hunched over and scurried for the door as Margo started the engine. Her suitcase and book bag scraped along the walkway. She might've crawled on her hands and knees, anything to not be a walking target. She found the door knob and felt around for the keyhole, then finally got the door open. When she turned around, Margo gave her a quick wave and headed, it seemed, almost directly for the dark car across the street, going so slowly it seemed to be a taunt.

A miniature lamp sat on the floor next to the mattress but barely lit the dark corner of the living room. Two folded sheets and a flat pillow with no case lay on top. In Ann Arbor, Celeste's mattress was on the floor, too, but not because it had to be, not because someone might shoot at her through the windows. She positioned her suitcase and book bag at the end of the mattress to form a footboard, or at least a blockade, then undressed down to her underwear before pulling a light cotton nightgown over her dirty body, keeping low the whole time. The jumper and the blouse were going in the bottom of her suitcase, never to be seen again until she got home. No, better to air out the sweaty clothes before putting them into her suitcase. She laid them on the wood floor. To take a bath or even to just wash up in the face bowl meant turning on lights, which would locate her for the mystery men across the street in the dark car.

She sat on the mattress and leaned against the wall staring at the small, bare living room. Always she had a sense of waiting. It went way back. Waiting for Wilamena to shower her with the hugs and kisses she saw other children receive from their mothers, waiting for Shuck to pick her and her brother up from some relative's house, waiting for Shuck's numbers to fall. Waiting for her life to begin. Now she'd begin her own journey with no clue as to how it would end.

"Your name better be Celeste." The voice wavered, followed by the padding of bare feet on wood. "Otherwise, I'm going out the bedroom window."

"It is," Celeste called in a whisper. She had hoped the other volunteer would be sleeping, giving her time to just sit there and mull over the possibilities of what lay ahead.

"Good." A door closed and in seconds there was the sound of a flushing toilet. A young woman crept into the living room, walking squatted down. "Ramona Clark."

Ramona sat down on the floor and leaned back against the door frame. Her hair was a mass of wooly kinks, round like an upside down bowl. Celeste could make out a small brown face, big oval eyes. "Haven't slept since I got here."

"Celeste Tyree." She felt her dirty, frizzled, humidity-inflated curls and waves, every strand symbolic of a contorted family tree. "That car across the street might keep anybody from sleeping."

"Amen to that." Ramona said. "Where're you from?"

"Michigan. Detroit. Actually, I'm in school in Ann Arbor." She tried to see more of Ramona's face in the dim light.

Ramona's head moved back and forth, her big bowl of kinky hair swaying. "Ooo wee. Not many black folks up there."

"Not many." Celeste heard the "black." Speakers from the movement who came to campus said it too. She hoped Ramona wasn't excluding her, tossing her in the "other" pile—the "good hair" pile, the light-eyed Negro pile. Negroes used to be "colored." Kids used to fight over being called black. It was the new title, the new calling. Black folks. She wanted to be in it. Shuck would be. Wilamena wouldn't. Celeste herself hadn't gotten comfortable saying "black."

"I'm at Howard with the black intelligentsia, the so called 'high-yellow first line of defense,' no offense intended." Ramona's voice eased out, consonants hit then released very quickly, sliding softly off the edges of the words.

Celeste bristled and lied. "None taken." Shuck was in her head telling her there was no high yellow, no low yellow, or anything else. There was just Negroes. Now, just black folks. Period. Celeste gave herself a point. Shuck was always ahead of the pack, in the vanguard. And she always trying to catch up.

"Where're they sending you?" Ramona stretched her legs out on the wood floor.

"Someplace called Pineyville." All she could see was the bowl of hair and flashes of the whites of Ramona's eyes. "I never even *heard* of it."

"Boy, you hit the jackpot." Ramona's eyes flared wide. "That's where they lynched Leroy Boyd James."

"Jesus." Celeste's train-weary mouth dried like dusty bones. She'd never heard of Leroy Boyd James, either.

"It was in the fifties. I did a paper on lynching in three deep-south states since World War II. I'm a sociology major." Ramona leaned her head back against the door jamb.

Every Negro in America was a sociology major, like it or not, college or not. You had to be. "What happened to him?" Celeste knew before Ramona said a word.

"They say he raped a white woman. Never got to court. Got kidnapped from the jail down there, beaten, shot, and dumped into the Pearl River. The sheriff said it never happened. A fisherman pulled him out. Body got caught on some tree roots or something. Otherwise, he'd have been swept down to the Gulf by the currents. Disappeared. A prisoner told the FBI that the sheriff there opened the door to some men. Nobody was charged with his murder."

All the air sighed out of Celeste's body. This wanting to know could definitely give you nightmares. Maybe Ramona exaggerated. Maybe there was more to the story, but she couldn't fathom what that might be. She'd seen the photos of Emmett Till. She'd seen the range of horror when it came to white women and Negro men. She'd tried to stir up enough saliva in her mouth to swallow. Where're they sending you?"

"Indianola. In the Delta." Ramona sighed. "Plantation country."

Wasn't Mississippi *all* plantation country? And what was Pineyville? A lot more than the Piney Woods, evidently. Leroy Boyd James. A new wrench of fear cranked her stomach, sent the acids churning and the ghost of that ham sandwich flying.

"You running your project by yourself?"

"Unless some more volunteers show up. They've got a pretty active bunch of black folks in the town." Ramona got into her squat-walk position. "Oh, the lady across the way brings biscuits and jelly in the morning. We've got coffee. The phone in the hall is for emergencies. They said we can call collect anywhere. The FBI numbers are right next to the phone there." Ramona disappeared around the corner. "I hope *you* can sleep. I sure can't. Don't forget to stay low."

"Goodnight." Celeste shriveled down the wall, legs spread out on the mattress. She felt like she'd been awake for days. Too many thoughts swirled in her head.

Sporadic dog barks, crickets, the creaking of trees. No low music in the background. No laughing voices with conversation riffs in between. It had to be three in the morning by now. A thickness in the air that made you think you were hearing things, but when you really pressed your ears to it, there was nothing there.

Celeste squat-walked to the open front windows, sat down on the hard-wood floor, and pushed on the screens. They were locked in place. Light-colored curtains waited for a breeze, any slight shuffle of air. The car across the street glimmered in a sliver of moonlight. Ghosts with guns. Sweat bubbled out on her forehead, under her arms, between her legs. She smelled her own body, the dampness curdling into a pungent aroma.

She crawled back to the mattress. The heavy air weighted her down on the thin bed, the hardness of the floor rising into her spine. What had Leroy Boyd James really done? Was it like Emmett Till? A whistle, a nothing whistle? She knew there were white girls in Ann Arbor who loved the easy grace of long dark arms and lips that felt like pillows in heaven. But this wasn't Ann Arbor. Margo standing at the mimeo machine with that guy? What was that about? Maybe nothing. Margo was from New York. No big deal. But where was he from? He's the one who'd pay the price. Down here, death came hunting when you reached across the lines of demarcation. In Ann Arbor, maybe just a hateful look, a bad name slung across some busy street. She and J.D. turned heads. Here, crossed love got dropped in the cracks of old storm shelters, locked away with warning signs marked Danger. People died for flirting. She'd read enough to know this was the real deal. Mary Evans's voice in her head, *You be careful, girl, you hear? Miss'sippi ain't nothing to play with.*

ALDON L. NIELSEN

Aldon Lynn Nielsen, poet and scholar, is the George and Barbara Kelly Professor of American Literature at the Pennsylvania State University. He was the first recipient of the Larry Neal Award for Poetry, and has since received the SAMLA Studies Prize, the Josephine Miles Award, the Darwin Turner Award, The Kayden Prize, the Gustavus Myers Citation, The Gertrude Stein Award and a Sigma Tau Delta Outstanding Professor Award. His edition of Lorenzo Thomas's *Don't Deny My Name* received the American Book Award. In the past he has taught at The George Washington University, Howard University, San Jose State University, UCLA, Loyola Marymount University and Central China Normal University.

NOTE TO "IN A CLASS WITH BARAKA"

In 1978, I was a beginning graduate student at George Washington University, earning my tuition by working full time as, of all things, a campus police officer. One of my frustrations early on was that there were no faculty in the English Department with whom I could continue the studies in African American literature I had begun as an undergraduate at the University of the District of Columbia, where my professors had included Gil Scott-Heron and C.L.R. James. Then word came from my poetry professor that the next year's writer in residence was to be Amiri Baraka. That brightened the outlook considerably.

The first book of poetry I had ever purchased with my own money had been *The Dead Lecturer* by LeRoi Jones. From that start, I had moved back to his earlier writings, in *Preface to a Twenty Volume Suicide Note . . .*" and to the subsequent large collection *Black Magic*. Baraka had been my major introduction to the radically alternative poetries of the twentieth century's second half, to the conjoining of Olson's "projective verse" to the jazz and blues inflected aesthetics of Jean Toomer, Langston Hughes, Margaret Walker. In Baraka's poems I came to know of an Ed Dorn, a Robert Duncan, but also a Robert Williams, and a Willie Best.

By the time Baraka arrived at George Washington University he had made the difficult and controversial move to what most critics have termed his third world Marxism, a move that had stunned such former comrades as Haki Madhubuti. As a former student of C.L.R. James, I was well versed in Marxism and the writings of Lenin, and while I was more of a post-Marxist than anything, I was prepared for the shifts in Baraka's work that had come by the time he came to my university.

But here's the kicker; also in Washington, D.C. at the time was Larry Neal, who had accepted the leadership position at the D.C. Council on the Arts and Humanities. So here were both editors of the landmark anthology

Black Fire working for a time in the same city. Neal even did a stint as substitute teacher for Baraka when Amiri was out of town for readings. I'm sure the other students in Baraka's Afro-American Literature course were sometimes annoyed by my constant asking of questions about, say, The Society of Umbra. Most of my fellow students were coming to African American Studies for the first time. But I was already headed in the direction of the work I intended to do in the future, and Baraka was more than willing to point me in the right paths. We may never have agreed entirely on ideology, but we were both committed to the same objectives, whether in poetry or in politics.

This poem grows out of those experiences and out of that classroom. And oh, by the way, a bit later I had the honor of receiving the first Larry Neal Award for poetry. I had not the advantages of an Ivy League education, but there in D.C. I had the benefit of working with the greatest of educators.

IN A CLASS WITH BARAKA
(1978)

In the end then to a room
Half hangs outside
The hall trashed overheated
Pupils smart
Squirm in dust
Ashes add up under chairs
Motes streaming
Cling to blinking lids
An odor of investment accrues
To this room

English beats against the glass
Shadowing through the panes
Upon the table obstructing
Paths of passing planes the capital's
Accumulation of images in the mute
Wavering grain is something we dissect
Practicing between ourselves the
Removal of harmful forms

Head at the window
Scarring the glass
Meaning glazes over
The watching White House
Beating back American
Artist in residence in the new
Department
Of corrections
Planes the blades
Of our speech
Asks examples

Mine is of a piece
With a room at an end
That hangs outside
In essential
Popular air

Mine is of a flight that exclaims

Fingers against the glass
I check my watch
Prepare to give examples

Halima J. Olufemi

Halima J. Olufemi was born and raised in Jackson, MS. She is a member of the Malcolm X Grassroots Movement, JXN People's Assembly and work with the People's Advocacy Institute around their Participatory Defense Program. "My work is deeply rooted in the total liberation of Black people."

POWER

I have too much power in me
To stay behind a desk
Or pray for some man to give me his last name
I have my own

Oya changed it to Olufemi
Which means the Lord loves me enough
To protect me from the King's misogyny

God has spoken and She sick of y'all shit

I don't really care how you feel about me
I know who I am; Say her name is affirmation for both the living and the dead;

Least we forget

Black women are killed by many and protected by few....even though we are present both behind and on the frontlines; our wombs and minds have been beaten reticent with the expectation of resilience in an abundance of silence

See...

Before our dear sister BREONNA TAYLOR was killed, AIYANA STANLEY-JONES was shot dead at the age of 7…Women in Black show up at the age of 7

ELEANOR BUMPERS was killed because she was behind on her rent and SANDRA BLAND was killed for driving while Black and MIRIAM CAREY was killed at the White House gate and TANISHA ANDERSON was killed because of a mental break and MICHELLE CUSSEAX was too, and PEARLIE GOLDEN and KAYLA MOORE and SHEREESE FRANCIS was too...

KATHRYN JOHNSTON was killed during a drug raid at the menacing age of 92;

TYISHA MILLER was killed while unconscious

DANETTE DANIELS and her unborn baby were killed in the back of a squad car

REKIA BOYD was killed for standing with her friends and

TARIKA WILSON was killed because they were looking for her boyfriend

IT'S SICKENING

Emaciated minds live behind badges, guns and riot gear attacking black bodies seeking asylum from years of false democracy and isms that hold our emancipation in red tape and rhetoric guided by ELEPHANTS and ASSES draped in robes, holding gavels and deadly pens intent on making black people live in carceral spaces so much so that they place surveillance cameras in communities and call them real time crime centers or operation green light to further intimidate people of color who they already target and terrorize daily under the guise of working to eliminate crime that could really be addressed if they divest funding from murderers and invest in communities and stop monitoring our every gotdamn move, we are treated like lab rats, injected with tests and monitored for our reaction to shit that may or may not work—- on display for the world full of critics, in lieu of scientists reporting and analyzing the results-- we are the ant being killed slowly with a magnifying glass by some lil bad ass red-head sociopath.

When I say we can't
You say stop…We can't STOP
We can't STOP

Even though it's fucking exhausting
And seems bleak at times
It's our absolute duty to win...

With uprisings and continuously uplifting the beauty of black skin; and political education grounding our emotions; and voting our conscious in the next election(s) and organizing communities against oppression; and promoting the act of governing ourselves and encouraging the thought of sovereignty by purchasing our own land; and protecting ourselves with more than our mouths and our hands; and with healing circles called BLACK yard barbecues and grandmama like hugs that say

I love you…

Even when no one else will

We must build
We must fight
We must educate
We must organize

Black Power in Black spaces
Revolutionary greetings to those who can dig it

When I say we can't
You say stop…We can't STOP
We can't STOP

When I say we won't
You say stop….We won't STOP
We won't STOP

I said

You can't stop the REVOLUTIOOONNN!
You can't stop the REVOLUTIOOONNN!
You can't stop the REVOLUTIOOONNN!
You can't stop the REVOLUTIOOONNN!

The End

Tired of Running

Hurt and berated should not be a stronghold and if you're Black, that first sentence is weighted
It could mean a number of things and take you a lot of places but always ends up in healing circles with weed and wet faces

A beating is still a beating if you do it with your tongue; your medicine looks like cane fields and burns like ashes that smell like sex from running to make children to plow the field..they will not quit

Hey Jim, "Would you hang Black Jesus in your living room?" I mean the painting, not the evening news

If Barbie's name was Kalesha
And Ken's name was Khalil
Would you still buy them for Karen?

Would biased education be the key if your history was taught in a month, that used to be a week—where you give speeches on the last day draped in Kente cloth your momma bought from Wal-Mart the night before because you forgot to tell her you had a program the next day and you were playing Nat Turner?

Would you be cool as a hyphenated-race, or if someone decided it was ok to dress in Black-Face for Halloween (the only day that god-fearing people openly celebrate spooks)
OR wearing nooses everyday wit suits
OR wearing someone else's hair because that's the only way they see you

They... co-opt the black experience and start groups That theorize about how we should feel; then instruct us on how we should treat them in reference to how they feel; and then march in solidarity with us so we can feel ok about them continually taking lives that are not theirs, in a delusional system that then makes us responsible for educating them on how to rearrange our feelings to better deal with their racism

It's really fucked up—let me say it again

Another black man was killed today

at the hands of an officer that couldn't deescalate the situation before they both ran and needed a gun because HE was scared.

Niggas on soapboxes and ignorance say:

"The shooting was justified, why burn down a building—to which I reply

Why the fuck you care, they can build another Wendys"

I mean, don't it kinda hurt your feelings that a dog fighting is considered more serious then Black killing?"

I mean, it started because a man was asleep in the drive thru—and I'm not saying I agree

But of course he failed a field sobriety test and if we lived in a world where life made sense, they could have just let Rayshard use his cell phone to call his ex and say bae come get me..."where you at"
—Because, theoretically it would have taken the same amount of time for them to spare his life

But compassion never leads the discussion because indifference is loud and undisciplined when used as weapon and not understood as the result of a social construct intent on slaughtering black men, black women and black children

We are sick of this shit

Hey, Sis
We going to the protest?

Can you ask that young lady to make me a shirt that says no justice no peace and another one that says, I woke up dead and another one that says, I still can't breathe and another one that says, I'm tired of running and another one that says I like Skitttles and Arizona Sweet Tea and another one that says WILL sell cigarettes for food and another that says I didn't hang myself and another one that says I didn't hang myself again and another that says I'm completely innocent and another one that says, Emmett didn't do nothing and another one that says, It was a fucking toy gun and another one that says but I was handcuffed and another that says you shot me in the back and another that says you shot me in the back again and another one that says BUT YOU KNEW IT WAS A TASER...

Stop blaming other people for your incompetence

I mean
You woke the brotha up dead in the middle of a lane

And If he was drunk he couldn't have got that far running and how exactly was he a threat if you shot him in the back and did you ever consider he took the taser so you wouldn't tase him

Did you ever consider that he was scared
Or that he felt threatened
Or that he thought he was about to die trying to save his life In 30 seconds

I mean, that's what you want us to do

"Remember Officer so and so
he has a family too"
but What we really seem to forget is that—two of them might not make it home from a job that only one of them trained to do and the families hurt the same

Ohhh mercy, mercy me
Things still what they used to be

We in the street with bloody poems and political education in a pseudo democracy called "Birth of a Nation"
Featuring criminals in black face

But like Playing a game a spades where the cards was set and uncle Bobbie caught em trying to cheat …

We push back from the table—stand in a rage and say:

Deal this shit again
I swear to God y'all won't play us again
Either do it right or catch these hands

We are not playing

All Power to the People
Revolutionary greetings to those who can dig it

We carry tennis shoes and picket signs in our trunk just in case the revolution pop off from another night ride in the parking lot

The End

Mozel Zeke Nealy

Mozel Zeke Nealy was an active participant in the protest movement and the struggle for Black liberation since his late teens. Mr. Nealy spent three years in federal prison for opposing the Vietnam War, racism, injustice and inequality in America.

EXULANSIS

        n. the tendency to give up talking about an experience people are unable to relate to or understand.

They…deaf of mind
Blind of ears
Unkind first degree
Never registered
Blinked eyeless
Slashed the whip
Ripped flesh wound
Scars of salt
Rain on black
Skin of fire
History moaned
In grotesque keys
Human oaks
Dangled bitterly
Jeering crowds of everyone
And no one
Nothing said.

Marching Papers

Marching the barricades
Bumper crops of insanity
Toting AR-15's
Traditional khaki Dockers
Surreal twisted faces
Grotesque scarlet fear
Hate inflamed nostrils
Arrogance on the trigger…
What in the Karen??!!

Unhinged panic sighted
No knock assassins
In golden camouflage
Ammunition bible store
Rubber pellet chaos
An unsympathetic flag
Handcuffs peacefully gathered
Fellowship of teargas
Marching the barricades.

Non-descript popup army
Moonstruck mannequins
Bobble head obedience
Beer-bellied unicorns
Evade Justice's knees
Invades Parliament
Terrorizes State Michigan
Nothing done Was done.
Marching the barricades.

Outrage at front doors
Had Enough's on wake
Democracy in backrooms
Waiting for elevation
Defrost the masquerade
The consequence of lies
GMO anthems and bacon

Resistance grows legs, grows traction
Marching against barricades.

Dr. V.S. Chochezi

Dr. V.S. Chochezi is the daughter member of the mother/daughter spoken word poetry duo known as Straight Out Scribes. Now in their 30th year of collaborating, the Scribes have produced two cds, seven anthologies of their poetry and published an anthology of womynistic, afrofuturistic sci-fi short-short stories by Staajabu. Chochezi's poems have been included in numerous publications including *Voices 2020* published by Cold River Press, *Cosumnes River Review, Late Peaches, Drum Voices Revue* published by Southern Illinois University Edwardsville and many others. By day, Chochezi is a college professor.

Black Girls Bop
For Shannon and her girls

Black girls hope
Black girls dream
Black girls cry
Black girls scream

Black girls laugh
Black girls play
Black girls dance
Black girls pray

Black girls think
Black girls do
Black girls matter
Just like you

Black girls jump
Black girls run
Black girls achieve
Black girls have fun

Black girls read

Black girls write
Black girls work
Black girls fight

Black girls live
Black girls love
Black girls do
Just like you

Black is beautiful

Black is beautiful
Is not a battle cry

It is not an attempt
To diminish or overshadow
Other types of beauty

It is not a boast
Or used with an overabundance
Of pride to be interpreted as
Black is the only beauty in the world
Or even the source of all beauty
Though that can't really
Be ruled out

Black is beautiful
Is not spoken in haste
A waste of breath
Like stating the obvious
Though perhaps it should be
Since in fact
Black IS beautiful!

And of course
Black is complex
So beautiful is not
The only thing that

Black is
Black is more than beautiful

Black is beautiful
Is a slogan
To help those who
Have been taught
Openly or indirectly
That Black is anything
But beautiful

And if you are not Black
Saying Black is beautiful
Does not negate your own
Beauty to be perfectly
And poetically clear

So when you hear
Black is beautiful
You don't need to fear
Black is beautiful is not
A battle cry

It is a slogan to be chanted
And used to greet each other

Open your heart to it
Feel and believe it
Reinforce it and let it
Sink in waaay deep
To counteract the negative
Stereotypes, subjugation
Micro-aggressions, drama and pain
That can too often accompany
This skin we're in

Because in the end
The simple truth is
Black is beautiful

Fabric of the Universe Pledge

What I do reflects upon those who raised me
I will strive to appreciate their sacrifices
And their investment in me
I will work hard, do good deeds,
and make thoughtful choices

What I do now affects my community
In addition to my family and friends
I will recognize opportunities for them
To support me and for me to give back
In service with love and patience

What I do today impacts my future
I will love myself, forgive my mistakes
Learn from the past and the pain
Push forward and excel
Building upon a foundation of strength
And self care

Setting goals, attaining dreams
Overcoming hardships and difficulties
Giving thanks, cherishing love
Growing and blossoming
I will prepare myself because
What I do tomorrow, whatever I do tomorrow
All that I do tomorrow will be important
Will matter, and will be as I am,
A significant thread in the fabric of the universe.

ALLISON E. FRANCIS

Dr. Allison E. Francis has been a Professor of English for sixteen years at Chaminade University of Honolulu in Hawaii. She teaches and publishes academic papers on a range of topics, which include Victorian and Scottish Literature, Theatre and Poetry, Vodou in Haiti, 19th century African American and Caribbean women's Literature and Women's Literature, with a focus on science fiction and fantasy. Dr. Francis is an accomplished performance poet who was been featured at venues in London, Edinburgh, New York and on Zoom.

She co-edited *South Sea Encounters: Nineteenth-Century Oceania, Britain, and America* published with Routledge in 2018, which includes her chapter "Ernest Hogan's Colored All-Stars Minstrel Show: A Case of Racial Discrimination in the Republic of Hawai'i." Also, Dr. Francis recently published a chapter, "Complicating Escape in the Neo-Slave Narratives of Sherley Anne Williams' Dessa Rose and Octavia Butler's Kindred" in *Human Contradictions in Octavia E. Butler's Work* (Springer 2020) and her poetry will be featured in Bamboo Ridge Press' *Kipuka: Finding Refuge in Times of Change* in 2021. Currently, she is drafting a book manuscript on Afrofuturism in popular media cultures—music, television, and film.

Dr. Francis is also an actor, director and playwright, who has written several plays, including *Chocolate Cake* (8:46), archived in thebreathproject2020) and a theatrical adaptation of James Weldon Johnson's novella, *The Autobiography of an Ex-Colored Man*, which will be staged in California and Hawaii.

We are

1850
Running running!

between starlight through open ravines deep
woods cane cotton tobacco

fleeing spitfire homemade bullets his caress dogs
almost rabid for our dark tails.

Crouching with water moccasins green leeches
hollow reeds Dare you breathe? Dare you breathe? our heartbeats so numb.

We are

1956
Running running!

On your left! Watch the German Shepard! Turn right! Right!
to Montgomery! Mobile! Missi- Missi- Oh Lord, whose missing?

The twitchy man in blue displays his toys:
power hose gun metal baton baton batter up! and niggers be gone.

We are

1966
Sitting Standing Holding ground.

Formica countertops little bridges revival tents chapels
on six wheels rocked us away from Jim Crow rants.

Fruits! Preachers! Men in cassocks! Beanies of all nation! Raise your fists!
Where are all de wommin at? Right here in the front machine guns in hand.

We are

1991
Protesting Rioting!

Not one not two but four batons rain down a fury on black flesh
recorded on shaky cameras in the dead of an L.A. night.

Why can't we all just get along? he cried bruised eyes ignite urban fires.
Another man named King, but this is the one who somehow survives.

We are

2012 Trayvon Martin Sanford Florida
2012 Jordan Davis Jacksonville Florida
2014 Michael Brown Ferguson Missouri
2014 Tamir Rice Cleveland Ohio
2015 Sandra Bland Waller County Texas
2015 Freddie Carlos Gray Jr. Baltimore Maryland
2016 Keith Lamont Scott Charlotte North Carolina
2016 Sylville Smith Milwaukee Wisconsin
2019 Botham Jean Dallas Texas
2019 Atatiana Jefferson Forth Worth Texas
2020 Ahmaud Arbery Glynn County Georgia

2020 Breonna Taylor Louisville Kentucky
2020 George Floyd Minneapolis Minnesota
2021 YOU NEXT

We are
Running running— Not again?

Candlelight vigils light up summer skies sweet boys & girls dead on city streets.
petals of mourning trampled by prejudice fear   sweat   heat

please everybody just   stop

stop   stop

stop

because   we   are

going   nowhere.

Night Hawks

In Tennessee they did
declare that cheap white
cloth layer known
identities
And every Spook in southern
lands would suffer
The Wrath
 of God's chosen Dixie Man.

Twice Twice! Five miles of fertile ground
with barbed ethnic wire girdled
round and round and round
where bloomed many a flesh-charred
fruit tree under which

amused families picnicked on
cold meats and raw whiskey.

And did not the nights burn:
"A savage place! As holy and enchanted"
as ever was beneath blood   circles of moon
waves of skin   fear   crosses of
fire   lighting
their path   their Way
to their single race desire.

In Tennessee they did
Decree their Specialness their
Singularity

They believed themselves
Miracles of pure rare device
Robed Night Hawks in scarlet flight.

Chocolate cake (8:46)
A Short Drama

Setting:	1910, in and around a Ford Model T automobile, at the Kentucky state border, late evening
Characters:	JACK, African American male, 32 OFFICER 1, white male, early 40s OFFICER 2, white male, late 20s
At Rise:	JACK is driving the Model T, and speaking to his unseen passenger.

JACK
Baby, I already done told you. De best Angel Food cake is at Terry's Diner. (beat) Yes, dat's what I want, and dat's where we goin'. (beat) Uh-huh. Yes, Sugga. Daddy always knows best (laughs). Ain't dat right?

(Police bell rings loudly, so JACK stops driving)

JACK
Sheeet! Not again.

(OFFICER 1 saunters to driver's side. Officer 2 whistles appreciatively while slowly circling Model T)

OFFICER 1
Looky, looky. What do we have here?

OFFICER 2
That's a nice automobile (continues to circle Model T).

OFFICER 1
Where you think you headed this time of night, son? (turns on flashlight and looks inside) What in the tarnation! (steps back with hand on baton) Is this why you tearing through the Bluegrass State? (smiles coldly) Is this a kidnapping, boy?

JACK
Oh no, officer. We was just on our way to eat. And…and…she's with me.

OFFICER 2
Oooh weee! Look at dem wheels. And those fancy headlights. Must've cost a mint! I bet you riding a sweet little chassis in there too, yessir (laughs rudely).

OFFICER 1
(Ignores JACK) Ma'am, has this man hurt you in anyway?

JACK
Officer, I said she's with me.

OFFICER 1
Boy, best you don't interrupt me (strokes his Billy club menacingly). It's a quiet night, and ain't nobody around except us. You hear me?

JACK
Uh-huh.

OFFICER 1
What you say, boy?

JACK
(Grips steering wheel) Yes sir, Officer, sir.

OFFICER 1
Now that's better. We all gonna get along real nice, ain't we?

OFFICER 2
Hey, lemme have a look (leans in). Hey! Hey! I know you…you that boxer, ain't you? The Galveston Giant! (turns to OFFICER 1) He's the one, you know, who knocked out—

OFFICER 1
I don't care if he's the Pope's mammy, Officer. This here nigger looks like he fixing to carry a white woman across—

OFFICER 2
(Excitedly) You knocked out that Canadian fella in '08, right? I heard it on the radio. That was quite a fight.

JACK
Thank you, Officer. Thank you.

OFFICER 2
And you just knocked out Jeffries too, right?

OFFICER 1
You done licking his balls yet?

JACK
Yes, I shore did. "The Great White Hope, y'all called him (chuckles). You heard dat one too?

OFFICER 2
Yeah. Yeah, of course I did. Who didn't? Hey, can I shake your hand?

(JACK extends his hand to OFFICER 2 who roughly pulls him out of the car, then kicks JACK to his knees.)

JACK
What the f—?

OFFICER 2
I lost a lot of money in both them fights, you goddamn nigger! (backhands JACK hard in the face). And now here you go, in your fancy Model T with some two-bit floozy. (yells into the automobile's interior) No! Don't you move, ma'am. Don't you move.

(OFFICER 1 slaps his thighs and laughs loudly.)

OFFICER 1
I guess the missus yonder likes her meat dark. Real dark. (sharply) Best you also keep your pretty little mouth shut, missy.

OFFICER 2
You think you better than Tommy Burns? Jimmy Jeffries?

(OFFICER 2 backhands JACK again, then knees him in the groin. JACK crumbles slightly from the unexpected pain)

OFFICER 2 (cont)
They is white men, boy. You hear? White men! You don't best white men. We will always be better than you, no matter what you darkies do. (smashes a headlight) Or own.

OFFICER 1
Now, now, Officer. That Ford might become state property. Don't damage it too much. (to JACK) You doing okay, boy?

(OFFICER 1 has been circling JACK, casually kicking him as the OFFICER speaks in a relaxed manner)

OFFICER 1
Operating a motor vehicle without a proper license. Assaulting an

officer of the law. Resisting arrest. Transporting a woman…a white lady! Across state lines for immoral purposes—

(OFFICER 2 crouches close to JACK and punches him)

OFFICER 2
You like that? How it feel to be knocked out?

(OFFICER 1 stops circling, then leans over JACK whose head is hanging down)

OFFICER 1
So, is it true what they say about you big, black bucks? You built like stallions? (squeezes JACK's groin). Oh. Oh. (laughs) I guess it is true! (squeezes JACK again then straightens up). My, my.

JACK lifts his head slowly, and stares at each OFFICER, defiantly. Shaken, OFFICER 2 lifts his hand to strike JACK once more)

JACK
(slowly) Don't you touch me agin, you cheap, little peckerwood.

OFFICER 2
Or what? What you gonna do, you damn crybaby (pulls out handcuffs).

(In slow motion, so that the action resembles a dance, and/or a RADIO ANNOUNCER can call out each move to recreate a boxing match: JACK kicks out his left leg, toppling OFFICER 1, who throws his baton in the air as he falls. JACK gracefully jumps to his feet, catching the baton which he uses to knock OFFICER 2 to the ground. JACK then roundhouse kicks OFFICER 1 when the OFFICER tries to stand up. Both OFFICERS end up face down, next to each other, facing the audience. JACK puts a knee on each man's back, then hooks the baton across their necks, raising their heads.)

(OFFICERS 1 and 2 speak slowly in pain)

OFFICER 1
I CAN'T

OFFICER 2
BREATHE!

OFFICER 2
I CAN'T

OFFICER 1
BREATHE!

(JACK pulls on the baton even harder. OFFICERS 1 and 2 struggle to speak.)

OFFICER 2
PLEASE…PLEASE…PLEASE…

OFFICER 1
CAN'T…CAN'T…CAN'T… Please…please…please…

OFFICER 2
Can't…can't…can't…

JACK
Breathe? (beat) Breathe? Can't catch a breath, muthafuckas? Do it just like dis… (takes a deep, slow inhalation and releases).

(JACK makes a final pull on the baton. OFFICERS fall forward hard.)

JACK
(Stands and faces audience) I ain't your Mandingo, Stepin Fetchit, a nigga, a darky, your jigaboo, your stallion, your tap dancer, your plantation fantasy, your worst nightmare. I ain't no hooded gangbanger, a street thug, a deadbeat dad, another black statistic.

I am a man. I am a man. I AM A MAN.

(JACK stares at the audience for two beats, then moves the OFFICERS into a sitting position, or leaves them face down as he handcuffs them together. He walks to front of Model T to inspects the damage.)

JACK
Sheet. That's gonna cost me.

(JACK looks back at the moaning OFFICERS as he straightens his tie and readjusts his jacket. After another beat, JACK circles the OFFICERS, then plants sloppy kisses on each OFFICER's face. JACK then grimaces, and spits. He walks upstage to his Model T.)

JACK
No sir. Vanilla just aint gonna cut it tonight (wipes his mouth). (to car) No not you, Sugga. Not you. But I really do want me some chocolate cake now. Maybe two thick slices.

(JACK smiles before jumping back into the Model T.)

JACK
Baby, you okay? Well, alrighty then. Evansville, here we come!

JACK turns to the audience, holds up his gloved fist, then puts the automobile in gear. Lights fade.)

the end.

Bryant B. Bolling

Bryant B. Bolling has a Masters of Art in Musicology and a Bachelor of Science degree in Music Education from Morgan State University in Baltimore, MD. While at MSU, Bolling was part of a three week European tour with the Morgan State University Choir, under the direction of Dr. Nathan M. Carter. The choir toured England, Finland, Denmark and Russia and recorded with the Helsinki Philharmonic Orchestra and the London Royal Symphonic under the baton of Dr. Paul Freeman. While completing his Masters degree at MSU, Bolling was commissioned by the Baltimore City Health Department and the State of Maryland AIDS Administration to write and direct a rap musical entitled "It's a Time for Life, We're Protecting Ourselves Against AIDS." Bolling received Proclamations from the Governor of Maryland, the Mayor of Baltimore and the City Council. At the present, Bolling is the founder and bandleader of the Bryant Bolling Quartet. He has received several grants from the Akonadi Foundation to create programs that address social conditions in the Oakland communities, "Love Will Find A Way" and "Stop The Violence." Numerous publications have been written on Bolling's musical career.

What it is to Be a Man

What it is to Be a Man, in this World that We Live in
Would you give a Helping hand, to the Life that You're Living
Do you Seek to Understand, What it is to Be a Man
To have Wisdom and Honor and Truth
Without Love, Nothing But Love Can Do
With Two Hearts, Will let the Sun Shine Through
Without Love, Nothing But Love Can Do
So if You Seek then You Will Find
A True Loving State of Mind
To have Wisdom and Honor and Truth

STAAJABU

Staajabu is a writer, editor, producer, poet, health advocate, graphic artist, Air Force veteran and UC Davis retiree. She volunteers at the Crocker Art Museum and serves on the Sacramento Housing and Redevelopment Commission and is the mother in the mother/daughter poetry team, "Straight Out Scribes." Originally from Camden, NJ, she now calls Sacramento her home.
www.straightoutscribes.com

The Tude

I don't know about you
but I got a big attitude
about my people being enslaved
I got an attitude about
the lies that were told and
the bill of goods we were sold
about us being inferior
and them being superior and
I'm madder than a big dog
about the rapes and lynchings
they did especially to a kid
named Emmett Till
Yeah, I'm still mad about that
AND Fred Hampton, Malcolm X
Martin Luther King, Medgar Evers,
George and Jonathan Jackson
Bobby Hutton, THE MOVE FAMILY AFRICA
And nothing makes my jaws tight
like when I remember the night
they beat Rodney King and another thing
They never apologized to us publicly
Never made good for all
the years we cried bitter tears
for our lost children, husbands, wives
brothers, sisters, mothers, fathers
they sold or the gold they stole

My blood starts to rise when I realize
We have yet to have our day in court
For the wrongs that were done we ought
to be able to make a good case
about the injustices done to our Black race
We need to negotiate a settlement
Like in every other disagreement
I could represent myself
and when the jury is chosen
on it would be a dozen former

slave's great, great, grandchildren
I know we'd win without a doubt 'cause
even before the jury went out
once they've checked out the evidence
they would surely sentence the defendants
to 500 years of hard labor and restitution of
400 trillion dollars of back pay. Okay?
Yeah! I'm running hot and am plenty vexed
and want some satisfaction
now you can act like everything's cool
and la dee da all that action
but from what I can see and I ain't blind
Their payments are lagging way behind and
I'll chill out with a smile on my face when
those overdue payments pick up the pace
until then better give me plenty of space
'cause I got a BIG ATTITUDE!

The Message

When our enslaved ancestors were
Granted freedom with no money and no place to go
What message could be clearer?
When Black people were refused education
Jobs housing medication or
A seat on public transportation
What message could be clearer?
With the shameful treatment of the
Black and poor after hurricane Katrina
What message could be clearer?
With high unemployment and infant mortality rates,
Plus innocent people killed by police
What message could be clearer?
When they cut back public assistance
Dismantle affirmative action
Reduce food stamps and deny us reparations
What message could be clearer?

When they bombed the MOVE Family in
Philly killing 6 adults, five children and burned down
Sixty-one homes on Osage Avenue
What message could be clearer?
When Black communities are flooded
With drugs and guns causing all kinds of
Chaos, mayhem, self-annihilation, incarcerations
A profitable increase in prison populations
Followed by amazing upscale gentrification
What message could be clearer?
Rosewood Florida, Birmingham Alabama
Greenwood Oklahoma, Soweto, South Africa
Did they get the message?
Strange fruit, Emmett Till, Bobby Hutton, Fred Hampton,
Amadou Diallo, Trayvon Martin
Malcolm X, Dr. King, George Floyd.
Get the message?
The death penalty is legal lynching
Racism is still prevalent and unflinching
We must be diligent, be strong, be brave
For our children and grandchildren
We've got a planet to save
What message could be clearer?

Tongo Eisen-Martin

Born and raised in San Francisco, Eisen-Martin is the founder of Black Freighter Press. He is also San Francisco's 8th poet laureate. His 2017 book *Heaven Is All Goodbyes* (City Lights) received the 2018 California Book Award for poetry, a 2018 American Book Award, and was shortlisted for the Griffin Poetry Prize. His curriculum on the extrajudicial killing of Black people, *We Charge Genocide Again!* at the Institute for Research in African American Studies at Columbia University, has been taught across the nation, and he has taught at various detention centers throughout the United States. In his time as Poet Laureate, Eisen-Martin intends to organize poetry reading circles in Sunnydale, Bayview-Hunters Point, and the Tenderloin, as well as seek out and foster San Francisco artists from marginalized communities. Eisen-Martin's as-yet-titled second book in the City Lights Pocket Poet series was released in the fall of 2021.

A Good Earth

I talk facing away from the dead
They replace me with the change in my pocket
A penny that has yet to be invented

They say, "You have to know how to cut a throat on the way to cutting a throat"

After sleeping on a mattress made from two garbage bags of clothes
I became content with the small gestures of plantation fires

Playing with couch ashes, I realized how weird the universe was. It exists in so many places. So many random things. It interrupts me when I am trying to dream. Like your clay correspondence, Lord

To be transparent
I have twenty books next to a bullet
Like an old man giving advice at the beginning of a revolution

I've really done it, Lord. Explored the mumbles of my mind. Explored what's naturally there. And I found no brainwashing. I found Africa, Lord.

I have a future
It takes place in the diasporic South
I have morning possessions
Modern militancy
I mean windows to the South
I will walk on a missile for food

I guess you will not want flowers for a few years, Lord

Will I be tied face to face with the country I murder

Merge with us, Lord

our old metal vs. the new metal
our old metal vs. a pool of meandering imperialist faces

A multiculturalism of sorts

The dead replace me with a comedian's chest cavity
Instead of a chest cavity held tight

It takes a violent middle man for me to talk to myself
Stories that travel through other people's stories
A song about a song
A hemisphere about a hemisphere
Stories that travel through a conquered poet

My mother remembers Africa, Lord
She killed on behalf of you, Lord

I wore a machete all winter and no one asked me what it meant
I read one thousand books in front of the world

What I do is fight poems

And sleep through decadent San Francisco prayer circles

Watch people play for post-working class associative surfaces
Or Recreations of a governor's desk

ruling class art of utility
Playing find the sociopathic bureaucrat

A day white people scare even easier
Tv in a basket next to a ceramic baby
Wearing ceramic armor
Musket progeny fantasizing through the art of the poor
Their trendy latches locked before God
Black art hunted down like a dog

Hand over my friends, Lord

Lord, I think that I am going to die in a war

Unelected white people in my small house

Like A blues song of no spiritual affect
or dollhouse H-bomb
A pony show near dead bodies
Apartheid weddings that go right
Apartheid white people who give birth to mathematicians
The spiritual continuity of barracks and police stations
The chemical interpretation of a Sunday trip to church
Church smells in their pockets
A river mistaken for a talking river
No autobiography outside of small personal victories of violence and
drug use
Made in the image of God's trinkets
What white abolitionists confided in their children about
Chemical assurances that
They will switch from Black artist to white artist
Black God to white God
Black worker to white worker

I think about you cautiously, Lord
In the same way I think about my childhood, Lord

Foxhole Friday nights
Most of life is mute

Comedian points out the planter's field to the priest

King sugar cane
King cotton
King revolutionary

The bottle is central
Containing all modes of shallow introduction
Introducing an unlisted planter class
Speaking about fever and balance sheets
And reassuring the masses
That we can figure out our fathers later

A priest took my mother lightly, Lord
Stood in front of the parishioners re-raveling

Fantasies about black art
Priest reading confidently
Before I broke him
And broke his parallel

After today, I have never been a poet before

A little brother watches his big brother's friends
They lean rifles on shelter walls
They agree with me and call it literature

It's a simple matter this revolution thing
To really lie to no one
To keep nothing godlike

To write a poem for God

I Imitate You

Picture, 1960s newspaper clippings and teeth hang on a string—
Like a book of life

I'm in the kitchen with my would-be killer
Picking their canines out of a mouth harp
Cigarette-ing a pen
Calling Black Fire to prayer

unscrewing the blues
I am played down

The aim to only die for money once

mouth harp prepared:
Ladies and gentlemen: we know what you all are not doing. Mainly you all are not leaving the universe to its childhood.

A church signals another church with mirrors and nose-drips
The spirit-world up and starts murdering city trees

Our psychic re-break
sleeping-in-my-car Sunday chores
allegory of new hard R's
Or folk tale about a wolf's tongue in the cartons of cheap milk

Trace amounts of white sheet on a politician's teleprompter
A glass case grows in Brooklyn
lower ninth ward houses play hop scotch and leap frog like white children
while cops wave their bills at the world

The news cameras follow
a teenager's descent into hell

I have grown up a little bit lately
Almost becoming inanimate will do that for you

activist peril and new millennium jug music
or the bottle you'd rather throw at your head than drink

no going to regular-people jail/no being hunted by regular-people cops"
"Believe In the Street" is my first thought
Is my parallel first name

A feat in spiritual equilibrium, I am waiting for God in front of a container factory

Put another way:
Yawning after a night in jail feels like keeping busy
Feels like imitating yourself severely
a bar code no more
nor new junkie's angst
one step ahead of every plantation owner in your pocket

The Lord's blues

I am eating every imagination in the room
looking through Camden windows with perfect Zen concentration
I understand the constitution and all the drugs it promised

Looking at shapes martyred by an imperialist state
Jail barges on a grandmother's table
couple poems away from your class suicide

"May the white citizens council steady your hand."
artists ordered to embroider "Enemy of the people" onto millions of
pillow cases.

Aiyana Jones sown into body temperatures
A cue to cook Brooklyn
Children watching and identifying with people
The man you made out of a face card
The most uncooperative object in a cell

Police state only a few inches from your address
I talked to a class'less people today
They were not essentially overworked nor military captains
They were not wage-washed nor inbred in a Victorian series

Maybe I am the last white man on earth

All I dream is physical death
Thinking about God/and God empty

In clumps of prison, my poem
my cubist-remade scar
      my Saturn for adults
      my junkie industrialism

I knew my father as much as I want to be known

Ewuare X. Osayande

Ewuare X. Osayande is a poet, essayist and publisher. The author of several books, his latest collection of poetry is entitled *Black Phoenix Uprising* (Africa World Press). His other books include *Blood Luxury* with an introduction by Amiri Baraka and *Whose America?* with an introduction by Haki R. Madhubuti.

Our Afros Are Us

our afros are astral antennae
attuned to the ancestors
a drumbeat bop greased thick
and textured as our history

our afros are black sunrays
hieroglyphs reaching back to the heavens
with Dogon eyes
peering into a million midnights

our afros are coiled compasses
charting freedom dreams
by the light of stars

our afros are bouquets of consciousness
radiant rainbow bushes
hush harbors where secrets are kept
hidden

our afros are not empty slogans
are not costumed curls
are not wigged expletives
mounted on dumbstruck mannequins
blaxploitating Hollywood never not
shown us past their type caste

our afros are natural
like our love

like grass growing in the backyard
like the way we walk in this world

our afros are perfectly unkempt

our afros are defiant halos
God's cloud climbing gravity
a clenched fist of nappyness
picked tight and towering

our afros are dangerous
only to those whose eyes been blinded
by paranoid pale-faced fragilities

our afros are ours
shapeshifting like our movements
like our hips swaying to good music

our afros are our truths
washed in the waters of many tongues

our afros are us as we are
walking down the runway of destiny
daring you to look

saying go 'head
but don't touch.

Black Phoenix Uprising

They call us magic
when it's just us being who we are
scarred and black

We resilient as sunrays
no way to comprehend it
so we name it as God

Yet we are the holy without the ghost
the evidence of things unseen
the spirit within us has no need to haunt

Black vortex of the inexplicable
the word made flesh
enchantments of the divine

We speak in tongues
native and colonized
still conjure the force of creation
like volcanoes erupting
we enunciate new worlds into being
and name them all freedom

Ancient as the pyramids

When we congregate
we come together not just to remember
but to resurrect the dead

We the progeny of those that dared be free
who been to hell and came back
smiling through bloodied teeth

Black phoenix uprising

We are an insurrection of fire
reborn from the bone embers of our ancestors
A righteous indignation igniting revolt
in the minds of the assassinated
dynamite exploding from our mouths
heat hollering past hotness
burning like the north star

Though some of us were once
tarred and feathered
we been known to fly
our wings span centuries

Talk to me of love personified
of a million Black souls reincarnated
into the backbones of our sons and daughters
their freedom dreams etched into our genes
forged from centuries of revolt
a cauldron of liquid fire
poured like a shaman's rum into these charmed skins
epidermis of steel
melaninated mutations
trauma alchemized to genius

Our badassness been long archived
no need for every episode to be televised
our revolution be satellite beamed from our eyes
bright as liberation yearning
smoldering a beauty that would leave the world blind

We are root connected
by the solder of Ogun
beating life from his blacksmith's hammer
on the anvil of our hearts conjoined
bleeding like lava
no matter where in this world
our blackness is common cause
is kin that goes deeper than this skin
mood vicarious
maybe that's the reason
we often cry without knowing why
or when we deja vu in blue
every step taken in kind
this the collective conscious of the wretched
the damnation of the yet vexed

Whatever justice there is in this world
comes from the kerosene flame burning within us
comes from our conviction
like the match that strikes
the match that lights

the match that ignites
our will to remake this world
like we remake ourselves
African again
before the English, the Spanish, the Dutch, the German, the French and the Portuguese
before we were chained in those ships
before Leo Africanus
when what we knew ourselves to be
was the genesis of humanity
that indigenous spark
that will remake this world

They say we are magic
but that is just us being ourselves
scarred and black
we resilient as the sun rising
no way to comprehend it
so we name it God.

DARLENE ROY

Darlene Roy has served as President of the Eugene B. Redmond Writers Club for 35 years and is associate editor of *Drunvoices Revue: A Confluence of Literary, Cultural & Vision Arts*. She is widely published in journals and anthologies and has performed in readings, on radio and television throughout the United States and Paris, France. She has published one chapbook, *Soon One Morning and other Poems* in 2001, and one book, *Afrosynthesis: A Feast of Poetry & Folklore* in 2015.

BAMtized

Speedin' on blues cruise motha wit, words
flowed like lava from pens of born/e
again scribes. Refusin' to bow heads or
step back, BAM bards rose in black
lights' glow to blow and show/case.
They over threw jailers of conch us
thought; dropped verbs into our real-nest.

Considering the artistic and cultural impact of the Black Arts Movement.

Pen Felt Around the World

BAM!! Like a tommy gun, Baraka's caustic
 pen pumped toothy verses or jones-scripts
into a deprav'd world's decayin' heart to
trauma-ties war wooers & neo-klan's
men, then bull's-eyed off shore book
makers' fat bucks. He pulled quick draws
on, *the devil what do d evil.*

In celebration of Amiri Baraka's 70th Birthday in 2005.

Black Arts Movement Warrior

In stealth drive, Redmond snared multi-tiered
laurels; stalked urban-fried tales across globe
scapes. He out-fitted word-souljas with
BAM-jammin' kwansabas, haikus, ballads for honin'
& drummin' into kente-dressed lit mags.
W/riters-in-arms, Amiri, Maya, Quincy, Toni,
relayed tactics from the Literati War Room.

For Eugene B. Redmond, editor, publisher, poet and professor emeritus; upon his being awarded an honorary Doctorate of Humane Letters from Southern Illinois University Edwardsville on May 10, 2008.

Wanda Sabir

Wanda Sabir is a poet, essayist, arts editor and senior writer at the *San Francisco Bay View* newspaper. *Wanda's Picks* column & radio show are a local and national staple. Her interest is in Art for Social Change. A depth psychologist, Sabir's area of research is historic and persistent trauma and its impact on memory. Sabir also serves as board member for Legal Services for Prisoners with Children and is a member of CA Coalition for Women Prisoners. An advocate of Diaspora Citizenship for descendants of formerly enslaved Africans, Sabir is co-founder and CEO of the Maafa SF Bay Area. She also co-founded the International Coalition for the Commemoration of African Ancestors of the Middle Passage and is a recipient of the inaugural Distinguished 400 Award, 400 Years of African American History Commission (2019) She is a Transformative Justice (TJ) or Community Accountability facilitator and believes the true revolution starts at home.

Night Rain
for Brianna

I
We are the girls who get up when pushed down
Shake off the pain and keep walking ignoring the blood dripping from ripped shirt
Taking off the offensive item
Our shame in the dirt where we drop it
In the dust
The clouds a place to hide until we can re-member where we placed our hearts
II
We are the girls who grit our teeth to keep our tongues from jumping out of our mouths
We are so full of ourselves we have to open channels so that we don't explode
We levitate
Fly and try to remember boundaries
Human boundaries
Limitations and rules adults press like gravity
When we're into grace and gratitude and escape
III
We are the girls who don't have addresses
Girls you can't find

Girls you'd better appreciate now, 'cause ya blink and it might be forever
We are that impossible to grasp
Hold
Destroy
IV
Destruction
That is a problem
We are the girls who abhor reformation
We like flying instead of walking
Leaping and singing instead of sleeping
We lay me down to sleep when we die and not a second before
We too busy thinking and plotting and planning our future to doze off
V
We the girls who get sent to the office
Learn to smoke cigars with the principal
And blow smoke and laughter in teacher's faces
We are the smart girls
We are the girls who figure it out long before the answer is discovered
We only ask for a small royalty cut
We are the girls who know her worth and make a world pay and pay and pay
We not taking any checks
Nope
Gold, silver and . . . pearls
We like the trade
VI
We are the mean girls
We are the girls that will cut your throat before you think about cutting ours
It's easier that way, 'cause we are the kind of girls you either love or hate
The binary is hella clear
We step over the dead,
Burying our secrets with the slain
We travel light and don't allow hitchhikers
We are not into charity and well, if we have enough to share—
We probably won't
Yeah, we that girl!
VII
We hard 'cause we learned drinking formula, the formula
Even family is unreliable
Family can hurt you worse that an enemy
Something about the blood

The way family organs are stitched together along a seam
Carry a seam ripper and amputate it before it atrophies
A prosthesis is better than gangrene
Cut your loses
Talk mean
'Cause the world ain't feeling no pussy cat
Wear your armor, cause the armor gets respect and respect spends a lot further than

kindness
Fear is an even better deal, but fear is hard to sustain
Ammunition is expensive
And then you need a firing range and ducks

VIII
We are the girls who give birth to themselves
Who never had a mama
Who don't miss what they never had

IX
Mean girls make it rain, so carry an umbrella.

X
We are the girls who live in cars
Who walk the streets
Who ride BART all night
Whose looks will rip your heart out
We are the girls wishing for a bit of peace
But all we find is trouble
We are the girls who call home and hang up before there is an answer
We are the girls who erase memories
And feel so alone
We are the girls who can't forget and can't forgive
We are the mean girls
Tough and strong and invincible
Between layers insecurely latched
We admit
"Mean girl" is a persona that can't last

Kalamu ya Salaam

Kalamu ya Salaam is the founder of NOMMO Literary Society. NOMMO is a New Orleans-based creative writing workshop whose members are published in national anthologies such as *Dark Eros, Kente Cloth, Catch the Fire* and *360° A Revolution of Black Poets.* He is also a founder of Runagate Press, which focuses on New Orleans and African heritage cultures worldwide.

THE MAN WHO WROTE I AM

I think art has always been political and has served political ends more graciously than those of the muses. I consider myself to be a political novelist and writer to the extent that I am always aware of the social insufficiencies which are a result of political manipulation. The greatest art has always been social-political, and in that sense I could be considered striving along traditional paths.
—John A. Williams

August Wilson was insistently whacking the dinner table. He had been at it for 47 times and still had eleven more thrashings to go. John A. Williams, sitting to Wilson's left and beaming a small, self-effacing smile was obviously honored by Wilson's animated response to Williams telling all of us sitting around the small table that he had submitted his new novel, *Clifford's Blues,* fifty-eight times before finding a publisher.

"Fifty-eight!" an incredulous August Wilson echoed, not sure that he had correctly heard Williams. When Williams confirmed that he had submitted the novel about a gay, black jazz musician interred in Dachau Nazi concentration camp to fifty-eight different publishers over a number of years before finally receiving an assenting nod, August Wilson stopped all conversation as he patiently began ticking off the repetitions while intoning the count in his resounding baritone voice: one, two, three, and so on, not stopping until the final hit, Fifty-Eight!

We were attending the Gwen Brooks Writers Conference at Chicago State organized by Haki Madhubuti and staff. August Wilson, born April 27, 1945, was only two years older than me. But John A. Williams was a master from an earlier era. Williams was born December 5, 1925 in Jackson, Mississippi.

Williams was the first novelist whose work fully engaged me in terms of my life experiences and aspirations. Indeed, while I was in high school, just when my interest in jazz was deepening, I encountered Williams' 1961 novel, *Night Song*, which subsequently was made into a 1967 movie, *Sweet Love, Bitter* starring Dick Gregory as jazz musician Richie 'Eagle' Stokes, a character based on Charlie 'Bird' Parker.

Like many writers of my generation, jazz was the artform that moved me the most. I wanted to be able to write with the innovation, intensity and impact of jazz musicians who were for me the leading artists of the sixties and seventies. While *Night Song* got my full attention, what really got all inside me was Williams' 1967 novel, *The Man Who Cried I Am*. Black cultural twists on the existential questions of being and identity were deeper than simple reflections on racial bigotry. Williams wrote about the complex humanity of the black condition and not just the topical politics of African-American life and struggles.

While what it means to be black in America is a general preoccupation of 20th century black writing, male novelists seem almost compelled to deal with the difficulties of self definition. Initially published anonymously, in 1912 James Weldon Johnson dropped *The Autobiography of an Ex-Colored Man*; in 1952 Ralph Ellison kept us wondering as we tried to identify and identify with the nameless protagonist of *The Invisible Man*; in 1953 Richard Wright confounded many a reader with *The Outsider* after having enraptured millions with *Native Son*; Baldwin notably entered the fray with 1962's *Another Country*, providing a veritable Rubik's Cube of inter-racial/inter-gender juxtapositions in which everyone seeks to find theirself in the wake of the suicide of a black man. That's just a quick handful of examples, but that search for manhood and self identity is a long, winding, and too often lonely road.

I read *The Man Who Cried I Am* as a young man, full of all the certainty about existential questions that only the young possess. I can not speak for everyone, but most of the black writers who are males and specialize in fiction whom I know of or whose work I have read, most all of them are swinging their pens at this elusive target. It is almost like we are blindfolded celebrants at a sixteenth birthday party trying our best to swat—indeed trying to bust, to destroy—the perpetual pinata as though it were a wasp nest that we could bat away and thus rid ourselves of the deadly stings of a vicious and racist society within which we were born, sort of like coming of age in a sacred circle of hell—it's sacred because it's not only our birthplace but belonging to this peculiar society is also our birthright, and it's hell, well, because it is, our very own personal and public place of persecution.

I did not have to read anything more than the title to understand the profoundness of *The Man Who Cried I Am*; especially to grasp the multifaceted import of the verb in the title. Cry has so many meanings, so very many meanings, not the least of which is the paradoxical injunction commonly said to us, shouted to us, extorted, pleaded, you name it, constantly ringing in our ears: "a man ain't suppose to cry." And yet every African American man I knew, at some point or another must cry "I am"—or die.

Asserting one's existence can easily get your ass killed if you are black and male. (Our sisters are also killed and imprisoned, but the routine with them is that they are exploited and sexually traumatized with the rapist and exploiters too often being men of color.) Making it in America, how soever one defines "making it" does nothing to alter that deadly equation of brutality and lynchings—ask President Obama, how come there are so many, publicized ritual murders happening now that a black man is president. Could it be that the police and others are engaging in a ritual slaughter of the "nigger in the white house"?

Williams novel includes the controversial idea that the government has prepared concentration camps for African Americans. What the mainstream dismissed as fantasy seemed to me a realistic possibility. In 1965 when I was in the Army one of my platoon buddies was a young soldier of Japanese ancestry. He had been born in a California interment camp during World War 2. After so many long, hot summers and the conflagrations that arose following the assassination of Martin Luther King in 1968, the possibility of concentration camps for blacks seemed not only possible but probable to me.

Michelle Alexander's 2010 publication *The New Jim Crow* struck a resonant chord. America leads the world in incarceration. Louisiana leads America in per capita incarceration. New Orleans leads Louisiana. Could it be that the prisons are America's concentration camps? Is America's penal system the fulfillment of Williams dystopian prophecy?

Most young men in this new millennium have never heard of, not to mention have not read, John A. Williams startling and perpetually relevant novel. Significantly the protagonist of the book is a writer. We writers spend a lot time, expend a ton of words, trying to explain ourselves to our audiences but actually to ourselves. We writers are trying to make understandable our very existence whether for the race in general or as an individual in particular.

It is said that on one of the ancient temples of Egypt an injunction is inscripted: know thy self. The graffiti scrawled on the soul houses of black males in America is the simple, confounding question: Who Am I?

When I met John A. Williams I was in my fifties. I had a biological father whom I revered and a close friend and mentor whom I sometimes refer to as a father-friend. Both of my grandfathers had been preachers: on my father's side was what was called a jack-leg preacher, a man without church or congregation, and on my mother's side, he was a pastor who founded two churches, one in the country side and one in the city. I did not lack for role models. I left the church at fifteen (or thereabouts) and never looked backed. I peeped myself in John A. Williams. Actually, at the time I met him, I saw him as a grandfather figure. One of countless older black men whom the weathering of time and social battles had mellowed but never defeated. I never told him how much I admired his work nor did I attempt to stay in touch with him. But when I was in Munich, Germany in 1998, I was compelled to sojourn to Dachau concentration camp, the same camp John A. Williams described in his last novel *Clifford's Blues*, which I enjoyed immensely.

John A. Williams has written both fiction and nonfiction; has published over 20 books both here and abroad. I try to avoid cliches, but in this case the cliche is correct: if John A. Williams were white, he would be celebrated and widely taught in high school and colleges, as are writers of far, far less accomplishments. The more I learned about Williams, the more I admired him. I should have bowed when I met him. He was a quiet, dignified elder/warrior. He had never wavered in the struggle, nor had he attempted to simplify or reduce our struggle to obvious, albeit wrong-headed, dichotomies of right and wrong, black and white.

John A. Williams was not only a socially conscious craftsperson, he was a meticulous and extensive researcher, and an elegant wordsmith. His deeply researched, historically accurate fiction and non-fiction holds up well because it is both factually accurate as well as artfully scripted. What we have in John A. Williams is a success at communication, if we would but read and reflect on what he was attempting to tell us. In America success is too often measured by popularity. Williams wrote fiction, journalism, essays, biographies, as well as edited anthologies.

He now serves as a model of who and what a writer should be. My three early influences were Langston Hughes, LeRoi Jones (bka Amiri Baraka—like him I too had changed my name), and James Baldwin in that order. Currently, although I still very much admire my personal triumvirate, in my elder years I have come to respect and treasure the work of John A. Williams. He not only stayed the course, but although he won a bevy of awards as well as authored numerous publications and related projects, unfortunately Williams remains relatively unknown and seldom celebrated. Regardless of how the world treats him/treats us, we should never forget. We should never forget who he is, never forget who we are. Indeed, to the degree that we do not know John A. Williams, to that same degree we men and women who are writers do not know the fullest reach of ourselves as voices who are crying in the wilderness; crying out both for self recognition as well as for the recognition of our people.

But regardless of how well he is or is not known, is or is not lauded, regardless, even in his obscurity John A. Williams is a resplendent example of a writer who confronted and answered that eternally perplexing question of "who am I?" While endeavoring to describe the enormous complexity of our being, Williams gave a profoundly simple, existential response to the ultimate query. Like god and nature, our existence is its own explanation: I am/we are. Being is definition. Our struggle as writers is to adequately give voice to the complexity of our simple response. Thank you brother John A. Williams.

NINA SIMONE

Nina is song. Not just a vocalist or singer, but actual song. The physical vibration and the meaning too. A reflection and projection of a certain segment of our mesmerizing ethos. Culturally specific in attitude, in rhythm, in what she harmonizes with and what she clashes against, merges snugly into and hotly confronts in rage. All that she is. Especially the contradictions and contrarinesses. And why not. If Nina is song. Our song. She would have to be all that.

Nina is not her name. Nina is our name. Nina is how we call ourselves remade into an uprising. Eunice Waymon started out life as a precocious child prodigy -- amazingly gifted at piano. She went to church, sang, prayed and absorbed all the sweat of the saints: the sisters dropping like flies and rising like angels all around her. Big bosoms clad in white. Tambourine-playing, cotton-chopping, tobacco-picking, corn-shucking, floor-mopping, child-birthing, man-loving hands. The spray of sweat and other body secretions falling on young Eunice's face informing her music for decades to come with the fluid fire of quintessential Black musicking. But there was also the conservatory and the proper way to approach the high art of music. The curve of the hands above the keyboard. The ear to hear and mind to understand the modulations in and out of various keys. The notes contained in each chord. She aspired to be a concert pianist. But at root she was an obeah woman. With voice and drum she could hold court for days, dazzle multitudes, regale us with the splendor, enrapture us with the serpentine serendipity of her black magic womanistness articulated in improvised, conjured incantations. "My daughter said, mama, sometimes I don't understand these people. I told her I don't understand them either but I'm born of them, and I like it." Nina picked up Moses' writhing rod, swallowed it and now hisses back into us the stories of our souls on fire. Hear me now, on fire.

My first memory of Nina is twofold. One that music critics considered her ugly and openly said so. And two that she was on the Tonight show back in the late fifties/very early sixties singing "I Love You Porgy." Both those memories go hand in hand. Both those memories speak volumes about what a Black woman could and could not do in the Eisenhower era. They called her ugly because she was Black. Literally. Dark skinned. In the late fifties, somewhat like it is now, only a tad more adamant, couldn't no dark skinned woman be pretty. In commercial terms, the darker the uglier. Nina was dark. She sang "Porgy" darkly. Made you know that the love she sang about was the real sound of music, and that Julie Andrews didn't have a clue. Was something so deep, so strong that I as a teenager intuitively realized that Nina's sound was both way over my head and was also the water within which my soul was baptized. Which is probably why I liked it, and is certainly why my then just developing moth wings sent me shooting toward the brilliant flashes of diamond bright lightening which shot sparking cobalt blue and ferrous red out of the black well of her mouth. This was some elemental love. Some of the kind of stuff I would first read about in James Baldwin's Another Country, a book that America is still not ready to understand. Love like that is what Nina's sound is.

Her piano was always percussive. It hit you. Moved you. Socked it to you. She could hit one note and make you sit up straight. Do things to your anatomy. That was Nina. Made a lot of men wish their name was Porgy. That's the way she sang that song. I wanted to grow up and be Porgy. Really. Wanted to grow up and get loved like Nina was loving Porgy. For a long time, I never knew nobody else sang that song. Who else could possibly invest that song with such a serious message, serious meaning? Porgy was Nina's man. Nina's song. She loved him. And he was well loved.

In my youth, I didn't think she was ugly. Nor did I didn't think she was beautiful. She just looked like a dark Black woman. With a bunch of make-up on in the early days. Later, I realized what she really looked like was an African mask. Something to shock you into a realization that no matter how hard you tried, you would never ever master white beauty because that is not what you were. Fundamental Blackness. Severe lines. Severe, you hear me. I mean, you hear Nina. Dogonic, chiseled features. Bold eyes. Ancient eyes. Done seen and survived slavery eyes. A countenance so serious that only hand carved mahogany or ebony could convey the features.

The hip-notism of her. The powerful peer. Percussive piano. Pounding pelvis. The slow, unhurried sureness. An orgasm that starts in the toes and ends up zillions of long seconds later emanating as a wide-mouthed silent scream uttered in some sonic range between a sigh and a whimper. A coming so deep, you don't tremble, you quake. I feel Nina's song and think of snakes. Damballa undulations. Congolesian contractions. She is an ancient religion renewed. The starkness of resistance. And nothing Eurocentric civilization can totally contain. Dark scream. Be both the scream and the dark. A crusty fist shot straight up in the air, upraised head. Maroon. Runaway. No more auction block. The one who did not blink when their foot was cut off to keep them from running away. And they just left anyway. Could stand before the overseer and not be there. Could answer drunken requests to sing this or that love song and create a seance so strong you sobered up and afterwards reeled backward, pawing the air cause you needed a drink. You could not confuse Nina Simone with some moon/june, puritan love song. Nina was the sound that sent slave masters slipping out of four posted beds and roaming through slave quartered nights. Yes, Nina was. And was too the sound that sent them staggering back with faces and backs scratched, teeth marked cheeks, kneed groins, and other signs of resistance momentarily tattooed on their pale bodies. And despite her fighting spirit, or perhaps because of her fighting spirit, the strength and ultra high standard of femininity she established with her every breath, these men who would be her master would not sell her. Might whip her a little, but not maim her. Well, nothing beyond cutting the foot so she would stay. With Nina it could get ugly if you came at her wrong, and something in her song said any White man approaching with intentions of possessing me is wrong. Nina sounded like that. Which is why this anti-fascist German team wrote "Pirate Jenny" and it was a long, long time before I realized that the song wasn't even about Black people.

Nina Simone was/is something so potent, so fascinating. A fertile flame. A cobra stare. Once you heard her, you could not avoid her, avoid the implications of her sound, be ye Black, White or whatever. Her blackness embraced the humanity in all who heard her, who experienced being touched by her, whose eyes welled up with tears sometimes, feeling the panorama of sensations she routinely but not rotely evoked wherever, whenever she sat at the altar of her piano and proceeded to unfurl the spiritual history of her people. When Nina sang, sings, if you are alive, and hear her, really hear her, you become umbilicaled into the cosmic and primal soul of suffering and resurrection, despair and hope, slavery and freedom that all humans have, at one level or another, both individually and ethnically, experienced, even if only vicariously. After all, who knows better the range of reactions to the blade, than does the executioner who swings the axe?

Nina hit you in the head, in the heart, in the gut and in the groin. But she hit you with music, and thus her sonorous fusillades, even at their most furious, did you no harm. In fact, the resulting outpouring of passions was a healing. A lancing of sentimental sacs which held the poisons of oppressive tendencies, the biles of woe-filled self-pity. A draining from the body of those social toxicants which embitter one's soul. A removal of the excrescent warts of prejudice and chauvinism that blight one's civil make-up.

Sangoma Simone sang and her sound was salving and salubrious. Her concerts were healing circles. Her recordings medicinal potions. She gave so much. Partaking of her drained you of cloying mundanities. Poured loaded essentials into the life cup. You left her presence, filled to your capacity and aware of how much there was to achieve by being a communicative human being.

Nina Simone. Supper clubs could not hold her. Folk songs were not strong enough. Popular standards too inane. Even though she did them. Did them to death. Took plain soup, and when she finished adding her aural herbs, there you had gumbo. Nina hit her stride with the rebellious uprises of the sixties, and the fierce pride of the seventies. Became a Black queen, an African queen. Became beautiful. Remember, I am talking about a time when we really believed Black was beautiful. Not just ok, acceptable, nothing to be ashamed of, but beautiful. Proud. And out there. Not subdued. Not refined. Not well mannered. But out there. Way out. Like Four Women. Like Mississippi Goddamn. Like Young, Gifted And Black. Like Revolution. Like: "And I Mean Every Word Of It". This was Nina who did an album with only herself. Voice. Piano. And some songs that commented on the human condition in terms bolder than had ever been recorded in popular music before. Are we The Desperate Ones? Have We Lost The Human Touch?

My other memories of Nina have to do with the aftermath. I recall the aridness of counterrevolutionary America clamping down and shuttering the leading lights of the seventies. Nina's radiance was celestial, but oh my, how costly the burning. Seeking fuel she fled into exile. Who would be her well, where could she find a cool drink of water before she died?

Then, like indiscreet body odors, the rumors and gossip began floating back. The tempest. The turning in on the self. What happens when they catch you and bring you back. Reify and commodify you, relegate you back into slavery. You are forced to fight in little and sometimes strange ways. But the thrill is gone. Cause only freedom is thrilling, and ain't no thrill in being contained on anybody's plantation, chained to anybody's farm. Anybody's, be they man, woman or child. Nobody's. Nothing thrilling about not being liberated.

Nina, like most of us, went crazy so that she could stay sane. Just did it hard. Was a more purer crazy. Cause she had so much to be sane about. So much that leeches wanted to siphon, sip, suck.

How do you stay sane in America? You go crazy. In order to be.

To be proud. And beautiful. And woman. And dark. Black skinned. You have to go crazy to stay sane. You have to scream, just to make room for your whispers. You have to cry and cuss, so that you can kiss and love. You have to fight. Fight. Fight. Lord. Fight. I gets. Fight. So tired. Fight. Of. Fight. Fighting all the time. But ooohhh child things are gonna get easier.

Don't tell me about her deficiencies, or her screwed up business affairs, her temper tantrums, her lack of understanding, her bad luck with men, her walking off the stage on the audience. Don't tell me about nothing. None of that. Because all of that ain't Nina. Nina Simone is song. And all of that is just whatever she got to do. Like she said: Do What You Got To Do. Oh Lord, Please Don't Let Me Be Misunderstood.

I play Nina Simone. Yesterday. Today. Tomorrow. This morning. Tonight at noon. Under the hot sun of Amerikkka, merrily, merrily, merrily denigrating us. In those terrible midnights. I play Nina Simone. Just to stay sane. Stay Black. To remember that Black is beautiful, not pretty. Beautiful is more than pretty. Beautiful is deep. I play beautiful Nina Simone. Nina Song. I play Nina Simone. And whether Nina's song turns you off or Nina's song turns you on, whose problem, whose opportunity is that?

No. Let me correct the English. I don't play Nina Simone. I serious Nina Simone. Serious. Simone. Put on her recordings and Nzinga strut all night long. And even that is not long enough.

To be young, or ancient. Gifted, or ordinary. But definitely Black, definitely the terrible beauty of Blackness. Nina Simone. Nina Song. Nina. Nina. Nina.

Oh my god. I give thanx for Nina Simone.

my father is dead. again.
(for my father-friend tom dent)

1.
i was thousands of miles away
when tom's tree fell

the weight of missing him
answers the age old question

because
his aftershock's tremble

reverberates within
the chamber of my skull

at all
the oddest moments

like discovering a special person
within the skin of a child of mine

and discerning at the same time
a lady i used to love

a lady whose love
shaped me

there are periods
when our ability to perceive

presence and potential
is predicated

on having been groomed
by those who have gone before

on having been shown

how to see beyond

what is now
what is known, how

(continued)
to appreciate the shape
of things to come

all this prescience a product
of learning the living wisdom

some come from a brusque old man
whose gruffness was so tender

so touching
in its honest intimacy

as he suggested that
there was something beyond

what ever was
and is, and yes, even will be

there is always
something more

something better
to be/come

2.
english words were never meant
to adequately articulate
the anguish in our mouths, our hearts
when we lose the stretching part
of our selves - the stairs we climb
to see further, to descend deeper

as we look out and over
past the limits of horizon line

our vision is improved when we stand
on the shoulders of elders
whose height hoists us higher
than we could ever grow
if we remained flat-footed
married to the ground
the view from these human
balconies enables us to eye
not just near and far
but also back and down
into the wells
of our own personalities

if we are fortunate
we have fathers
who help us
clearly see
depths
as well as distances

3.
perhaps a moan
is the most profound
sound one can make
when a father is gone

when my first father died
i cried publicly
this death time my tears
for tom are silent
words on paper

the two times
a man is most
alone

are when

he loses
a father and when he
loses his own
life - his
beginning his end

4.
in the new orleans
that tom knew
old griots die singing

(continued)
they do not go silently
into some lonely night

in his new orleans
we do not kill our fathers
to prove that we have arrived

but rather we learn
from them that we can
crack open the kernel
of our own becoming
only by completing
the final maneuver
of life's ultimate passage rite

the step of accepting the torch
and making of ourselves a light

volunteering
to lift the father spirit
to shoulder the responsibility
of becoming beacon
for those newly born
and those yet to come

in our new orleans we do not stop
at simply burying aged bodies
we also dance forward
from funeral line
and accept the awesome
task of filling father shoes

if i really come from
a house of the rising sun,
if i really believe
in resurrection
if i am really
my father's son
then i must be reborn

be his life
after life

5.
in earth ways
my father is dead. again.

but yet again
he lives

the older i become
the more people i contain

another of my fathers
is dead

long live
my father

long live my father
in me

long live
my many fathers

long live
long live

all the fathers
i am

and all the fathers
i will ever be

Landon Smith

Landon Smith lives in Oakland, CA, but was born in L.A. and grew up in San Jose, CA. He received his B.A. in English from the University of Michigan-Ann Arbor, and his M.A. from Mills College in Oakland, CA. He has performed poetry in Oakland, New York, Detroit, Berkeley, Bowery Poetry's virtual No Desk Concert, and the Santa Clara Poet Laureate Inaugural Poetry Reading. His work has been published in *Silver Pinion Magazine, Cathexis Northwest Press,* and *Eris and Eros Journal.* His work seeks to disrupt institutions, poetry's elitism, and express raw social critiques while drawing audiences into how he processes the world. He hones his craft weekly with the Patrice Lumumba Writing Group based out of the East Side Arts Alliance in Oakland, and is currently a full-time faculty member at Chabot College.

Oxymorons in Margins

The margins
                              seem to be filled with people cast aside
                                        to confined spaces
                              being told to be the bigger person.
Oxymoronic decrees declared from the smell
        of paranoia paint lacquered onto policies passed
                      under the cover of midnight flag-pins in
hallways.
    Feet shuffling across tile,
    gripping sweaty palms,
pushing buttons in fear of what retaliation looks like.

Oxymorons in Margins

Eugenics formalized into government policy
and state line   fractures in search of the hairline atop a compound.
    Turner Diaries distribution to terrorists taking up arms
       against imaginary pyromaniacs;
           empowered by poisoned police pyramids.
Not sure if we'll make it out of this future case study
       with lungs intact.
    Pandemic poisoning working class human sacrifices
breathing toxic emissions from capitalistic debilitating decimation
inhaling tear gas
       paid for by city budgets and tech company slush funds
        through backdoor donations propping up genocide
           for stock options and public
offering;
Not sure if we'll make it out
with lungs intact.
    Not sure on what spirit to call
since white Jesus was clasped onto wrists in a shack church
glowing from a burning cross and a church bomb—
   essence stolen like wombs in concentration camps while U.N. hands
stay tied.
Down bottom death camps recycling rises to power
for fear mongers and IQ destitution.
    Echoing in hallways from shuffling feet drowning out
      screams from
margins.
Oxymoronic existence of minimized grandiosity ripping
apart insides and tearing apart families like barbed wire on flesh—
           we have no
body left.
All we are is an idea.
      An idea within a theory.
A theory with a flag and a constitution baked in blood, tobacco,
sugar, and cotton fibers
    rewritten to be large in   margins resembling burial
plots.
Not sure if eugenics' precedent can be pulled from tiled hallways
and step n' fetch tap dance shoes.
    Fatigue filling the lungs of an oxymoron

fighting for freedom,
    basking in air unsafe to breathe
    and tear gas blankets.

Kathryn Takara

Born in Tuskegee, AL, and a Hawaii resident since 1968, Kathryn Takara possesses a M.A. in French and a Ph.D. in Political Science. She studied at the University of Bordeaux and was a summer lecturer at the University of Qingdao, China. A retired Professor of Black Studies at University of Hawaii at Manoa and a French Instructor, Takara is an Afrofuturist, eco-poet and the author of nine books and scholarly articles. She is the owner and publisher of Pacific Raven Press since 2008. Takara is traveler, spiritual teacher, healer, community activist, gardener, mother and wife. Awards include: Life Time Achievement (NAACP), The History Makers (national award), Black Futures Award and the Knighted Orthodox Order of St. John.

Takara has been interviewed nationally and locally on Blacks in Hawaii and about inventor Alice Augusta Ball. She co-produced a jazz night in Honolulu featuring the music of Thelonius Monk and given presentations at the UN/NGO (Cry Children of the World on the Black Arts Movement for the Honolulu Museum, and performed in several poetry readings in California, Alabama, Honolulu, and online poetry readings including *Black Fire—This Time* and *Wake Up America*. She is a consultant for several projects and a film on Martin Luther King, Jr.'s early visit to Hawaii.

STOLEN JEWELS

Who stole the jewels from Africa?
They missed the essence of what they took.
Chasms of misunderstanding and misinterpretation.

For in Africa
Sharing was like sunlight
Abundant as sky is blue.
Gold was for beauty and celebration of

The people,
Adorning anyone's body.
Rubies and pearl-dust of Brotherhood,
Sapphire skies,
Amethyst halos of Consciousness,
Emerald clusters of Community,
Abundant in ebony and copper
Drum Rhythms.
Presence in opal harmony
Like planets to sun.

Who stole the jewels from Africa?
They missed the essence of what they took.

There were no banks
No uniformed law and order
Of separate we's and they's.

And those who introduced
And perpetuated we-they,
Abounded like hail-stones

Collected stolen jewels for elite and noble
Kings and queens
Popes and churches
Of "Civilized" lands
In imagined devotion to those who sat
Pretentiously
Puppets of pride
On paper-maché thrones.

Who stole the jewels from Africa?
They missed the essence of what they took.
Who stole the jewels from the people?
And gave in mirages of generosity
Imitation jewels,
Turned holy expectation of honesty
Into dingy imagination

And gaudy hopes of betrayed receivers watched
As drabness settled in
Like drearsome fog.

Who?
Did you say who it was?
That with graceless wishes from lecherous fantasy
Who it was that turned purity of being
Into ego safety deposit boxes
Of threatened, stolen jewels?

Who stole the jewels from Africa?

Whoever it was,
You missed the point.

SWEET HONEY IN THE ROCK

O mio Yemanja
Ha!
Alo- ha!!
Ha-a-a-aaa,
The breath, sacred to Hawaiians
Treasured by other people
But westerners   sometimes forget.

This breath of communication
Expands as the wind travels
To family, friends, clan, communities, nations.
Listen,   listen,   feel.

Sweet Honey chants
"I'm gonna stand!
We will not obey wrong."
Celebrate the breath
Like Sweet Honey, flowing out of the rock
Like black women

Strengthened by inner revolution
Outward absolution
"Ain't gonna study war no more."

Women gathering
Things, people,
Women making music, creativity
Women birthing
Nurturing with our breasts and pussies
Healing,   letting go.

Sweet Honey sings
Repeats, renders, rescues
Transforms legends, myths, folklore,
History, jazz, blues.

Songs of love, war,
and life itself spreading...
Staining the listener
Like moon's blood.

Listen to their breaths
Haunting in spirituals
Meandering through life's currents and passages
Crevices and dungeons, gardens and oceans.

Listen to the voices
Colored blues and greens like sea glass,
Rough as coral
Smooth as the Pacific ocean
On a blazing summer day,
Varied as each breaking wave.

Voices textured as the sand
Mysterious as rustling windsong
Whispered in tall coconut trees
Messages of the ancestors

Inspiration of Esu.

Voices, illusive as the clouds
Yet real as the sturdy Koolaus.
Whispering, driving, clapping, laughing
Thumping, shouting
hollering their inspiration.
Listen to their rhythms
Weaving the African trickster tradition:
Use of counterpoint wisdom
Juxtapositions and contrasts
Serendipitous tones, improvised jazz riffs.

Voices skip rope
Call and response
Call and response jumps
Jump and escape worry, in space and time.

Listen to their message
Freedom, physical and spiritual
The upper room
Church on Sunday
Bourgeois blues on Monday
Martyrs like Biko inspire
But hell of poverty undermines hope
In our undervalued black communities
All over the world.
Heaven sings, "Don't you see me comin' to you?"

Listen to the voices, our voices,
Through Sweet Honey in the Rock.
Echoes of the ancestors
Of the sons and the daughters
Echoes of racism, anger and rage
Echoes of peace, of a survival tradition
Affirming
"We will not bow down to oppression."

Wake up!
Listen as Sweet Honey in the Rock
Lifts up nature's sanctification.
Be glad
In the resurrection
And the power
Of the word in music.

Michael Warr

Poet Michael Warr's literary honors include a 2021 San Francisco Arts Commission Artist Award and the 2020 Berkeley Poetry Festival Lifetime Achievement Award. His books include *Of Poetry & Protest: From Emmett Till to Trayvon Martin* (W.W. Norton), *The Armageddon of Funk, We Are All The Black Boy*, and *Power Lines: A Decade of Poetry From Chicago's Guild Complex* (Tia Chucha Press). He is a San Francisco Library Laureate and recipient of a Creative Work Fund Award for his multimedia project Tracing Poetic Memory, PEN Oakland Josephine Miles Award for Excellence in Literature, Black Caucus of the American Library Association Award, Gwendolyn Brooks Significant Illinois Poets Award, and a National Endowment for the Arts Fellowship. His poetry is translated into Chinese as part of "Two Languages / One Community" a collaborative project with poet and translator Chun Yu. Michael is the former Deputy Director of the Museum of the African Diaspora and a board member of the Friends of the San Francisco Public Library.

What Not To Do (an unfinished poem)

Breathe: **Eric Garner** (choked)
Sell (loosies)
Resist (to death)
Stare: **Lamont Hunt** (shot.)
(in back)
Make: **Akai Gurley** (a jarring sound) (shot.) ("accidentally")
Stand: **Amadou Diallo** (in vestibule)
Carry (wallet)
Loiter (while walking)
Look (out of place)
Act (suspicious) (forty-one. fired.) (nineteen. bullets. kill.)
Walk: **Terence Crutcher** (hands in air)

Appear (intoxicated)
Have (a "very hollow look") (shot.)
(in back)
Drive: **Samuel DuBose** (without) (license plate) (shot.) (in head)
Drive: **Walter Scott** (with broken taillight) (shot.)
(in back)
Move: **Kendra James** (into driver seat)
(after driver arrested) (shot.) (in head)
Sit: **Jordan Edwards** (unarmed in car) (shot.) (with rifle)
Reverse: **Diante Yarber** (too suddenly)
(thirty. bullets. fired. ten. kill.)
Park: **Tanya Haggerthy** (on side of road)
Talk (on cell) (on side of road) (shot.) (on side of road)
Drive: **Philando Castile** (with broken brake lights)
Carry (legal firearm)
Announce (you have a gun)
Shout (not reaching for gun) (shot.) (five. bullets. two. to. heart.)
Crawl: **Daniel Shaver** (toward officers) (as instructed)
Pull (loose gym shorts) (too suddenly)
Beg (not to be shot) (shot.) (anyway)
Approach: **Oscar Grant** (the police)
Beg (not to shoot)
Kneel (shot.) (anyway)
(in back)
Fail: **Sandra Bland** (to signal)
Act (too uppity) (found hanging in cell)
Carry: **Anthony Lamar Smith** (planted weapon) (shot.) (five. bullets.)
Carry: **Tamir Rice** (toy gun) (shot.) (with. real. bullets.)
Carry: **Cameron Tillma**n (BB gun) (shot.)
Carry: **Rumain Brisbon** (prescription bottle) (shot.)
(two. bullets. to. torso.)
Carry: **Laquan McDonald** (knife in road) (shot.) (sixteen. bullets.)
Carry: **Miles Hall** (gardening rod)
Have (schizoaffective disorder) (shot.)
Carry: **Steven Demarco Taylor** (baseball bat) (at Walmart)
Have (a manic episode) (shot.)
Not carry: **Keith Lamont Scott** (a gun) (when told to drop it) (shot.)
"Drop": **Kajuan Raye** (a gun) ("found" later) (shot.)
(in back.)

Be: **Natasha McKenna** (schizophrenic)
Be ("superhuman")
(stunned while shackled) (50,000-volts) (to death)
Be: **Tanisha Anderson** (bipolar) (head slammed to pavement)
Be: **Michelle Shirley** (bipolar) (while driving)
(thirty. bullets. eight. to. chest. back. arms.)
Be: **Shereese Francis** (off) (meds) (four police bodies suffocate) (on bed)
Be: **Aaron Campbell** (suicidal)
Be (unarmed) (shot.)
Be: **Yvette Smith** ("armed") (when not armed) (shot.) (on front porch)
Be: **Mike Brown** ("too large")
Be (same height as shooter) (shot.) (six. bullets.) (two. to. head.)
Be: **John Crawford** (an "imminent threat")
Shop (for Walmart air rifle)
Carry (Walmart air rifle) (at Walmart)
Talk (on cell phone) (at Walmart) (shot.)
(with. real. bullets.) (at Walmart)
Be: **Terrance Franklin** (a suspect) (shot.) (five. bullets. to. head)
Be: **George Floyd** (a suspect)
Be (a 6-foot-7 Black man)
Be (claustrophobic)
(asphyxiated) (knee on neck) (while handcuffed)
Be: **Tony McDade** (trans)
Move ("consistent with using a firearm") (shot.)
Pose: **Ezell Ford** (an "immediate threat") (shot.)
(while schizophrenic)
"Display:" **Manuel Loggins Jr.** (a "mean expression") (shot.)
(in front of daughters)
Call: **Charleena Lyles** (police) (while mentally ill) (shot.) (seven. bullets.)
Fit: **Jordan Baker** ("the description") (shot.)
Flee: **Freddie Gray** ("unprovoked") (spine severed) (in custody)
Run: **Stephon Clark** (through grandmother's yard)
Carry (cell phone) (shot.)
(twenty. bullets. fired.) (eight. hit.) ("primarily")
(in back)
Run: **Chinedu Okobi** (unarmed in traffic) (tased) (to death)
Run: **Walter Scott** (shot.)
(in back)
Jog: **Ahmaud Arbery** (shot.) (two. bullets. kill.) (while hunted)
Play: **Atatiana Jefferson** (Call of Duty) (in bedroom)

(little Zion watching) (shot.)
Sleep: **Alyana Jones** (on couch) (shot.) (one. bullet.)
(to. seven-year. old. head.)
Sleep: **Breonna Taylor** (in bed) (shot.) (eight. bullets. kill.)
Sleep: **Rayshard Brooks** (at Wendy's)
Flee (for daughter's birthday)
Point (dead taser over shoulder) (shot. two. bullets.)
(in back)
Walk: **Elijah McClain** (home)
Look (sketchy)
Play (music)
Wave (hands)
Wear (ski mask)
Buy (iced tea)
Carry (iced tea)
Resist (contact)
Act ("crazy")
Cry (can't breathe)
Beg (to go home)
Be ("superhuman")
Be (anemic)
Be (an introvert)
Be (suspicious)
Be (agitated)
Be ("tense")
Be ("on something")
Be (medicated)
Be (undetermined)
(choked) (to death)

Breathe…

(Since 2018 I have continued to add the names of a fraction of black people unjustly killed by the police to this serial poem.)

Back to the Ark (Axum, Ethiopia) 1978-2020

On my return I will leave my dogma at the doors of the Church of Our Lady Mary of Zion.

I will surrender to my once virginal curiosity of all the things I do not know.

I will revel at the rarity of an outsider inside this ancient kingdom's presence now knowing where I walk.

I will respect the grey-haired guardian of the Ark of the Covenant despite his frail frame and seemingly antiquated weaponry.

I will recognize the sacred tablet replicas in Lalibela's rock-hewn wonders as 3000-year-old tethered nodes serving a mystical Mainframe.

I will interpret accounts of angels carving red rock megaliths at night as sightings of sculpting Afronauts.

I will believe that the wisest place to hide an acacia tree is in a forest of 20,000 houses of worship.

I will read the Geez liturgical symbols on the King Ezana Stone as codes for our African origins.

I will stand before the Crowns of Menelik in awe this time feeling their power under past and coming revolutions around the sun.

I will blaspheme for a moment against historical materialism while traversing back through time.

I will speculate.

The Armageddon of Funk
In Memory of James Brown (1965-2006)

If I ruled the world, every day would be the first day of Spring.
—The Godfather of Soul

Watts rebels. A tethered cosmonaut "walks" in space.
T.S. Elliot, Nat King Cole, and Sir Winston Churchill die.
Malcolm is murdered. The "Grateful Dead" is born.
Sekou Sese Mobuto steals and sells the Congo.
Che crosses Lake Tanganyika as "Tatu" to take it back.
Ginsberg Howls and speaks "flower power" in the city
where I first imagine. The entire Northeastern United States
blacks out. The Voting Rights Act is passed. US troops
deploy at Da Nang, Vietnam. Gang of Four ascends.

My only worry, at ten years old, is what will happen to
the world if James Brown dies?

Monks rebel. Pluto is no longer a planet. The sun eclipses.
Robert Creeley, Coretta Scott King, and the King of Tonga
die. Monks are murdered in Myanmar. The Dead still
play live. Congo holds its first "true" elections since Patrice
Lumumba's assassination. Howl turns fifty. Jack Hirschman,
communist, is Poet Laureate of the city where I first imagined.
Deadliest heat wave since Dust Bowl plagues Midwest.
Voting Rights are extended another inadequate quarter.
Saddam Hussein hanged. Forbidden City evicts Starbucks.

KATRINA WASHINGTON

Katrina Washington is a poet and prose writer from the south side of Chicago. She holds a BA in English with a concentration in Poetry as well as Masters in Higher Education Administration and Organizational Leadership. She is currently pursuing a PhD in English with concentrations in Poetry, Prose, and Black Studies from the University of Illinois at Chicago. Katrina has published work in online journals such as *Kissing Dynamite* and will be featured in the upcoming anthology *Selkie Noticia*. Outside of teaching and writing, Katrina enjoys cooking, being black, and rebelling against gender and racial oppression.

Queen

For black women it is always winter and magic
don't mean that we ain't real.
They buried souls bred to rise like seeds
but not from water.
Then all the roadmaps home sunk when our
mothers jumped.
We shoulder wings crafted of anguish and
fear of flying.
Mad and black ain't the words to describe
flowers forced to burn for sun.

Myth

The body structure of a bee
renders it incapable of flying
but because it doesn't know
it soars
I am afraid my child will know
so he will never fly
I imagine him
as black as Jesus
as smart as Nelson
as the hate in a nation
will know pain
and mothers
will desperately try
to absorb every bit of it
but fail
As he falls in love
with my womb
I hate that he will soon
lose that comfort
That his first sign of life
will be tears
dependency and
vulnerability

If I had anticipated him more intently
I would have built him a sanctuary
saved my tears
and presented them to him
as enough proof that life is hard
Without him having
to see it for himself
I pretend to protect him
while we're still one
Like we all originally were
Two hearts four arms
four legs
his face and mine
too powerful for even
the gods

LOLITA STEWART-WHITE

Lolita Stewart-White is a poet who lives and works in Miami. Her work has appeared in the *Iowa Review, Callaloo, Kweli* and *Beloit Poetry Journal*. She was a finalist for the 2020 Center of African-American Poetry & Poetics first book prize. She has received fellowships from Cave Canem, The Atlantic Center for the Arts and the Betsy Hotel's Writers Room. Most recently she was the winner of the Paris-American Readers Series where she was invited to New York City to read at Poets House with Mark Doty and Tomas Q. Morin.

the only black woman she can think to compare me to

The white woman tells me
I look like Michelle Obama.
A compliment that was pre-naps,
 before I set the African loose,
before I divorced Dark &
Lovely, before I stopped
setting my woolly curls on fire.
It was when my locks lay limp
and they were swept to the side
and each perfect strand dared

not talk back. It was 2008
and the White House was chocolate.
But even then, I ached for teeth,
dreamed of a pick with a fist
to rake the natural Earth
beneath the artificial terrain
that held me and Michelle
hostage.

Dear Miss Jeantel:

And I hate how she sings acapella,

how notes ring out of her chest
and blast through the courtroom
like buckshot.

And I hate that she won't be quiet.
And I wish the words written in cursive
that she can't read will loop
around her throat and tighten
until she chokes.

And I hate the way she recounts
how Trayvon called his killer
"creepy ass cracka."

And it hurts when her startled eyes
flit up because she can't follow the questions.
And it hurts when the almost all-white
jury looks away.

And I want to be her in this moment
wearing a white, cotton dress
with white pearls and white teeth
answering the defense attorney's questions
white and clean.

And I hate myself for loathing her.
And I hate that my house in the suburbs changes
nothing about what white folks think about us.

Camille T. Dungy

Camille T. Dungy is the author of four collections of poetry, most recently *Trophic Cascade*, and the essays *Guidebook to Relative Strangers*. She's edited three anthologies, including *Black Nature: Four Centuries of African American Nature Poetry*. Her honors include a Guggenheim Fellowship, NEA Fellowships in poetry and prose, and an American Book Award.

This'll hurt me more

Don't make me send you outside to find a switch,
my grandmother used to say. It was years before
I had the nerve to ask her why switch was the word
her anger reached for when she needed me to act
a different way. Still, when I see some branches—
wispy ones, like willows, like lilacs, like the tan-yellow
forsythia before the brighter yellow buds— I think,
these would make perfect switches for a whipping.
America, there is not a place I can wander inside you
and not feel a little afraid. Did I ever tell you about that
time I was seven, buckled into the backseat of the Volvo,
before buckles were a thing America required.
My parents tried, despite everything, to keep us
safe. It's funny. I remember the brown hills sloping
toward the valley. A soft brown welcome I looked for
other places but found only there and in my grandmother's
skin. Yes, I have just compared my grandmother's body
to my childhood's hills, America. I loved them both,
and they taught me, each, things I needed to learn.
You have witnessed, America, how pleasant hillsides
can quickly catch fire. My grandmother could be like that.
But she protected me, too. There were strawberry fields,
wind guarded in that valley, tarped against the cold.
America, you are good at taking care of what you value.

Those silver-gray tarps made the fields look like a pond
I could skate on. As the policeman questioned my dad,
I concentrated on the view outside the back window.
America, have you ever noticed how well you stretch
the imagination? This was Southern California. I'd lived
there all my life and never even seen a frozen pond.
But there I was, in 70 degree weather, imagining
my skates carving figure eights on a strawberry field.
Of course my father fit the description. The imagination
can accommodate whoever might happen along.
America, if you've seen a hillside quickly catch fire
you have also seen a river freeze over, the surface
looking placid though you know the water deep down,
dark as my father, is pushing and pushing, still trying
to get ahead. We were driving home, my father said.
My wife and my daughters, we were just on our way
home. I know you want to know what happened next,
America. Did my dad make it safely home or not?
Outside this window, lilac blooms show up like a rash
decision the bush makes each spring. I haven't lived
in Southern California for decades. A pond here
killed a child we all knew. For years after that accident,
as spring bloomed and ice thinned, my daughter
remembered the child from her preschool. And now,
it's not so much that she's forgotten. It's more that
it seems she's never known that child as anything other
than drowned. My grandmother didn't have an answer.
A switch is what her mother called it and her grandmother
before her. She'd been gone from that part of America
for over half a century, but still that southern soil
sprang up along the contours of her tongue. America,
I'll tell you this much, I cannot understand this mind,
where it reaches. Even when she was threatening
to beat me, I liked to imagine the swishing sound
a branch would make as it whipped toward my body
through the resisting air. She'd say, this is hurting me
more than it's hurting you. I didn't understand her then,
but now I think I do. America, go find me a switch.

Metaphor of America as this homegrown painted lady chrysalis

        My head has come off
and by a string of my own creation
        is dragged what remains
of my last meal. Here, too, you see
my waste, and my brothers' and sisters'.
        You can take this literally or not.
Whatever I might have been has dissolved.
        When you moved me, I shook
        like a leaf preparing for autumn.
The child panicked. But soon, I returned
        to my patience. Call it potential
if you're feeling optimistic. There will be wings.
Bright, brown, black. With just a little
        white to set things off.

Jamestown 2019

> *Poem written on the imminent quadricentennial*
> *of the White Lion's arrival at Point Comfort,*
> *Virginia—which ship carried the first 20-some people*
> *—mostly young—who would begin to build*
> *this nation with their bodies—black—and blood*

rock the other mother's babies down
slowly slowly slowly—maybe for four—yes
—for four hundred years —slowly slowly
—slowly rock the gone now babies down—
you know how a boat rocks on a calm

what rhymes with water rhymes with dry
your eyes—what rhymes with mothers
waiting at the corner—mothers waiting
at the coroner—these babies—their bodies
—they've kept them—hundreds of tears—

what rhymes with ocean rhymes with empty—
tell me—what rhymes with keep crying
I'll give you something—today too
someone's earth brown body baby discovered
who thought them no better than dirt

what rhymes with snatch a life and name it
building—this burden—don't end there—
what rhymes with help the mothers love
these babies—help them help them help them
—help them rock their stolen babies down

QR Hand, Jr.

QR Hand, Jr. was born in Brooklyn, New York in 1937. He is the author of three poetry books, *i speak to the poet in man* (jukebox press, 1985), *how sweet it is* (Zeitgeist Press, 1996), and *whose really blues, new & selected poems* (Taurean Horn Press, 2007). He is a member of the poetry and jazz ensemble Word Wind, and worked as a community mental health worker in San Francisco, where he has lived for more than four decades. Most notably his work was published in the 1968 *Black Fire: an anthology of Afro-American Writing*.

dopey poetry in the rhetoric of blood

I don't know no poem I can write that's legal
that'll get you a high called love and stamina
more habit forming than ice and crack combined

there is no poem for this occasion any way
poetry is a lost language gone south
     don't bother to look in the war colleges   and
attendant CIA telegrams to and from
the embassy's most private chambers
     or so they think

this here's killers   aint no metaphor   not

a mother fuckin thriller diller   it's all ready
on video tapes you can't buy or won't

the poetry that was here is on a night flight
to hell   sent in place of bodies to be
converted   like sounds into poetry into medicines
and machines   escape routes   a march of trimphs
like the peoples did in managua enough to
fill a vacuum the nation states create in lands
like el salvador

you won't have to smoke it
or get a guvmint stamp

Defense Offense Back Fence

defense   offense   back fence   and   the one around the gold yard
barkin' like a devil dog   keeps some on the plantation of things   that

don't care for you no matter how good the bass is   and stealin' home's
more den gospel no matter where you are this sound happens   don't

make no matter   other sounds loud as can be dis   rhythmic riff is
happening   and   you could still hear it when armies off others

to establish deaf zones where it was loudest   and   people(s)
were observed dancing   which   when out lawed even public fidgets

6 months   and   humming   or   whistling in public 2 years of hard labor
and   drummers had their hands broken as did piano players   and

music news from out side was for bidden   it was rumored many were
dis appeared   and   cleff and   staff marks left on side walks   or

sand dunes hinted that some thing was wrong   but   futures like this were
officially denied   and   who knows   weren't there divine signs every
night

and   horses too   like a stampede of dust   and   no sounds   if it wasn't here
you'd think it was weird swingin' a way   or   taking every thing you can   you

wanna get a good con duct in wars against the homies   and   roll
your owns in those alleys the lucky make time in   make love in   and   no

bodies can hide from the truth   being on public tv provided by cops   who
never need to leave their station house   and   send holograms to courts   and

make testimonies with those hip hop stances authorities had legally co opted
to further blur lines   and   furrow brows   unless you were really in the know

about what few knew   and   were more hungry   and   stodgid (sic)
what went on be for(e) only more dogged   surprise   could get in the way(s)   of

these cogs   and   their mobiles   as impossible as this thing you say   you
want free dom   justice   and   equality   in this process   you're so fast   you

can't participate except in vague dusky hotels   in obscure   obsolete cities   where
the help seemed to say none here   jack   and   negotiators had just started   with

out you again easily since they lived there   and   you had trouble getting in
the door till the boss sent a picture of you   and   a quick finger prick   check

your dna be in the right places   as   one of your teams is winning   and   other
losing every bag out of tricks   the trick of bags got you   and there's alotta

alligators who can't see in the dark and   bump in to you   if   you don't pay
attention to rules from a bag   dad   trickle trickle about the jewels in that

ring of fire   gold running down your leg   in the book where it was some
body's gold getting beau coup attention in the fillipines where this was

goin" on at   planting an other preposition at the end of a sentence   tho'
you can be tricked   'cause   it didn't stop there   a relic aspiced in deep

acting   thirsting   still nothing but all brazen bad   not adrift but no go here

don't care for soul   no matter how good the bass is   and   stealin' homes'
more den gospel   no matter   where you are this sound happen's

Gruencjipersnoots

Up dating alice's wonder land   bleeding hearts   and
Lines of credits flooding drenched plains
Generations stoopified   bent in famines
It's a not to night darling all the times
Ghastly at high noon   shutting off streams

What's a place like this supposed to be like any how
How any   how many a trumpet note grabs mind
In its wander   no wonder to this   and   then there's
Games   and   tournaments   and   competitions
You can listen to musics with   you   concertedly

Hoping the song is there   a swing freeer   and   a sling gunner
All of this while the boss is on a vacation   yatching
Around a changing world   a whirl   a whirl wind   a plenty
Coming down the pikes after them   revolt no body talk 'bout
'cept in dis satisfactions   and   other tomes   or   is it tombs

Like dat   more immediate persons in my dreams   even
The dead (ones)   still   just goin' back   and   forth   in the swing
Of things   and   their orbits   and   momenta   ta ta   and
There was a very strange   enchanted   boys   and   girls
And   clubs   and   diamonds   and   called it class less

The chickens are dying   and   I'm not   so far
When it was bennies   the speed of the times   all
The druggists in harlem   the black ones any how   knew
What that drummer Blakey comin' 'round   lookin' in   and   i
Heard he's good too   my father told me about art   when

You hit it   smokin'   but   right at some body   and   thinkin'
About a game of inches   for your mama   the bright

Side of things   bright   and   shining   lies   neil
Wrote about   and   some   we knew were off the chart
Smarter than the law allowed   yet   out laws of course

Reluctantly accepting the change in season   as
October is the day after tomorrow   and   a breeze
To come with it   harvest moon gone   garden turning
Dried out   crispy like   waiting for the rainy season   we think
Is coming this year of no Indian summer at all

Hate winter's coming on   knowing thank fully it ain't like
The apple   or   the 'cuse   or   philly too   as I realize
Snow   and   storm go from fun   to   hassle   to   persecution
By natural forces making poems from lines blown about
The hood hiding from the hawk in door

Ways   and   tunnels through the archeologies about to be
Launched under the hinter lands   cables
Fine   or   thick with fibrous tentacles sliding in
To plug in devices   and   phone attacks   ring-a-bling
Ding   ding   dong   and   don't ask whose number is

Being hacked   a future   or   dead ending spaced
Out of a loop waiting for the real deal at the foot
Of a cantankerous hill some Sisyphus gotta push you
Up   and   down   and   of course all around town   they
Knew what time you'd roll back hopin' to retrieve

Some of the box lunch they made for you for the trip
Up   and   of course they can't blame you for tryin'
Again tho' some think you need a better pusher
Man   or   woman   no room for sexism in serious
Matters   no tellin' what it takes between the legs

Threatening skys   to whom   just 'cause it's chilly   and   grey
All of 'em as good as new   like in a new porn shop
All buy his tone   some ness   who missed their x's   and   o's
So gates is that open   and   a kick offensives again
Where's the news here   just another line backer   !!

Tony Bolden

Tony Bolden is Professor of African and African-American Studies at the University of Kansas. His teaching and research interests include African American music, African American literature, cultural studies, African literature, and ethnic American literature. He has published extensively on funk and blues.

Blues People

(For Amiri, Billie & Ella Nem)

1.

blues is black folks' literature

memory stored on a pentatonic

scale. cultural philosophy distilled

in songs. the low end theory

black thought embodied in body

talk like james brown's camel walk

the cakewalk & crip walk

slow drag rhythm & holy profane

the shimmy shake whipped to a jelly

cold duck & hucklebuck; the dog

catcher. or take the moonwalk

black down memory lane: bill bailey

bopped the backslide in dope stage exits—

a decade before the king of pop

was born & vertamae grosvenor

space walked into the future

of a three-sided dream

astral traveling through galaxies

on a sun ship w/ sun ra

when michael jackson played bongos

on a oatmeal box in gary

2.

blues lingo: a tale told in pitch

swivel hips & harmonies

historiography composed in vamps

runs in e flat; lexicon like dogon

the funky frequencies of falsetto

imagine five generations crammed

into a bassline. tone colors like bright

mississippi encircled inside golden bells

of a horn; talkbox or the kansas city

two-step. roughneck rhythms in a riff

jumping at the woodside

like jitterbugs & confirmation

configurations of black soundscapes

sampled from half-notes & 5/4 themes

fine & mellow as billie holiday's white gardenia

yet tragic as a heroin needle

holiday's life was a broken blues record

her voice scarred like six strings

of a bottleneck guitar; twelve bars

of pain—picked & strummed

over misogyny & bruises

in the land of jim crow

3.

blues sang,

good morning heartache

here we go again

at the savoy ballroom

battle of the bands in 1937

the lindy hoppers spinning like tops

jamming in mid-air

like a ella fitzgerald scat solo

she's singing to beat the band

a blues chorus of staccato swing

vocal percussion of old school

freestyle straight, no chaser

right off the top of the dome

a rhyme scheme of dance moves

written inside a drum

like a wang dang doodle

all night long.

brian g. gilmore

brian g. gilmore is a native of Washington, D.C. A Senior Lecturer in the Law and Society Program at the University of Maryland College Park, gilmore is the author of four collections of poetry, the latest, *come see about me, marvin,* (Wayne State University Press, 2019), a Michigan Notable Book Recipient for 2020. A Cave Canem and Kimbilio Fellow, gilmore is a contributing writer for the *Progressive Magazine*.

amiri baraka, d.c. space, 1989

> "space is the place…"
> sun ra

leroi eats too much pork. he's sweating a lake
in the lights. he was drinking light beer on the train
down from city brick, i bet. in his element like always
but the space got him all shook up. he look a little like
otis blackwell anyway but don't write tunes for presley or
jerry lee. he got a gap in his fronts &
a northern chant, the south is never too far away.

they are closing this place, we have been told. leroi has come
for one of the last of his shouts. not many dives in this town
will risk being molotoved. coffee beans & wi fi will
replace the rage just like every lttle tavern it seems sells
chinese cuisine now. that is a long way off from this beatnik
black banjo. is that sonny murray slobbering on
the snare barely clutching his mallets?

leroi keeps it apocalyptically short.
he's grace jones in paris, sun ra with hand grenades,
ronald reagan is a junkie. george bush a
ghoul.

once they had poets read in here all night. once they
had poets read here all day. once they had poets
reading here…

buy some starbucks.

enjoy your chai mocha latte
& some vanilla scones.

but space is the place.

space is the place.

space is the place.

now, somebody turn off that goddamned
       wi fi & watch america get blown up.

come back charleston blue (for larry neal)

for church shooters
& other misguided

persons. do come

quickly. we are more

fed up than monks
over vietnam.

something bad might
happen if you don't

show, brother. not that
race war some pray

for. something complex
& hard to under-

stand. like the word
deontonlogical.

so, hurry now
charleston blue

don't forget your
straight razor. your

lady still has it
i've been told.

sharpened &
still shining, like

a star at night in
a place called harlem

it is there waiting for
your delicate hands.

right where you left it
last time you were here.

amadou (for breonna t, george f., etc. etc.)

here we
are still

as
always

standing
in the
vestibule

KEISHA-GAYE ANDERSON

Keisha-Gaye Anderson is a Jamaican-born poet, writer, visual artist, and communications and marketing strategist based in Brooklyn, NY. Her debut poetry collection *Gathering the Waters* (Jamii Publishing 2014) was accepted into the Poets House Library and the National Library of Jamaica. She is the author of two other poetry collections: *Everything Is Necessary* (Willow Books 2019) and *A Spell for Living* (Agape 2020), which received the Editors' Choice recognition for the Numinous Orisons, Luminous Origin Literary Award. The multimedia e-book includes her audio poems set to music and original artwork. Her poetry, fiction, and essays have been widely published in national literary journals, magazines, and anthologies that include *Kweli Literary Journal, Small Axe Salon, Interviewing the Caribbean, Renaissance Noire, The Caribbean Writer, The Killens Review of Arts and Letters, Mosaic Literary Magazine, African Voices Magazine, The Langston Hughes Review, Streetnotes: Cross-Cultural Poetics, Caribbean in Transit Arts Journal, The Mom Egg Review*, and others. She is a past participant of the VONA Voices and Callaloo writing workshops, a former fellow of the North Country Institute for Writers of Color, and was short-listed for the Small Axe Literary Competition. In 2018, Anderson was selected as a Brooklyn Public Library Artist in Residence. Her visual art has been featured in numerous exhibitions in the tri-state area and in such literary journals as *The Adirondack Review, Joint Literary Magazine, MER VOX, Culture Push*, and *No, Dear Magazine*. Anderson began her career as a journalist, having written for national consumer magazines like *Psychology Today, Teen People, Black Enterprise*, and *Honey*, and working as a producer or associate producer on documentary programming for networks like CBS, PBS, and NHK (Japanese television). Anderson currently works as a senior communications and marketing director at The Jed Foundation, a nonprofit dedicated to protecting emotional health and preventing suicide for our nation's teens and young adults. She teaches English courses across The City University of New York and also leads writing workshops for nonprofits and other organizations. Anderson is a graduate of the Syracuse University Newhouse School and College of Arts and Sciences and holds an M.F.A. in creative writing from The City College, CUNY.

Black is Not Enough

Black
is not enough
to go by
is too narrow a
space
too clumsy a way
to reveal
you

Don't you see
your place
up high
along the winding trail
of lights
resting on
Mother's neck?

Can you name
all the shapes
of your
intelligence,
that sometimes,
when it feels like,
splashes over the brim
of infinity
to condense as jazz
a dance of colors
at 5Pointz
Denzel's deep sea eyes
and our snaking hips

to the dancehall riddim's
dip
dip dip
dip
dip dip
dip—

Unleash your
ecstatic laughter
for this joyous walk
through time
and mirrors
where you can love
you as
us,
as all of this
salt foam under a lavender sun
the jubilant tail of your familiar
a warm kiss of wind
in a glade
exploding with new life
that sweet sacrifice
of guiding
the next navigator
of your blood

Black is not enough
is too dim an idea
too minuscule
a name
for us

Curtis L. Crisler

Curtis L. Crisler was born and raised in Gary, Indiana. Crisler has five full-length poetry books, two YA books, and five poetry chapbooks. He's been published in a variety of magazines, journals, and anthologies. He's been an editor and contributing poetry editor. Also, he created the Indiana Chitlin Circuit. Crisler is a Professor of English at Purdue University Fort Wayne (PFW).

What Mamie Till Gave the World

1) Her son tattooed by fist and fury of gnarled souls.

    2) A perfect binding so history books can lower their heads in shame.

3) Overkill. Overkill. Overkill. Overkill, and then some.

    4) Transformation of beauty into the ethereal likeness of man.

5) A chance to grab hold to the elusive flower of benevolence.

    6) Burial means to live, so we don't hinder the grave.

7) Her son—a boy. Her son—a soul. Her *son.* *Her* son. Her *baby.*

    8) In total circumference to the end of all time—Whys?

9) A voice stuck in groove of record: *Take care Mama, I'll see you soon.*

Before the (Re)showing of Medgar Evers, His Son Sits Alone

I search for the birthmark a fueled man
with rifle gave you, a bullet that mistook
you as lifeless, magnified your name through
the dense tunnel of America without asking

for permission, and your chest took him in
like an old secret hidden in mattress. The bullet
threw his hands up, gave conspirator away in
interrogation, made my baby-boy-hate bury
love, long before I would get to the real of
life, the magic of the sun—now we resume.

I never bought that yellow odious lie from
their tongues, claiming you dislodged. Lost
to your cause. *Daddy, they don't know you.*
Don't know I've become your twin, will kill ill
words for justice, wish to handle your ears with
homonyms, and squeeze you into man-laughter,
as you sit next to me now, *Dressed to the tee,*

man. I'm still coughing up cotton in throat,
still craving, still seeking like a prophet, looking
for sanctuary. *I got my stripes honest.* It took Mama
two life-times to get one grain of justice, so I know
your blood matters, coagulates into a crazy head-
spell within me. *Daddy...before you go back...*
I lost my mind for thirty years, blind forever,
until today, until this moment. *Now let me help
you back into casket. There's still resurrection.*

Amoja Sumler

Recognized by Poetry Slam Inc as a "Legend of the South," Amoja Sumler author of *Fables, Foibles, & Other 'Merican Sins* (Willow Books, 2020) is a nationally celebrated poet and essayist. His poetry appears in the *Pierian Literary Journal, Muddy Ford Press, Swimming With Elephants, FreezeRay Poetry* and the *Antigonish Review* as well as other journals.

Peace Be? (For Nikki)

That fine forebear say
peace be still
                                           looking.

Be blindboy in dead
alley on pitch night.

Peace be advertised
like xanax and war. Be
that sleep where the blood spill.

Peace be that thing
the boom brings

that bap on Brown backs.

Peace be missing
be deliberate as run aways marveling
at found food.
Be gone like girl
gone like desert rain
Gone like a past tense Felicia.

Peace be like AK spray,
like angry toddler
be mouthful of spit

Peace be compliance
and "get on the ground"
and" hands up."

Like DJ's and porkchops.

Forebear said Peace
was the beginning
and a whole word.
And we heard her.

We just still
        waiting
                for our piece.

We be looking for peace

like kind sounds from a Trump-
et, quiet as the death of a bomb-dropping
hater of unbent Saigonese.

Peace be that mellow to masculine.
    A detox and salve to smear
        upon bruised butted head.

Peace be that shame satiation that
    in similar situations
        we might sneer at.

I'm guilty too
    but I ain't the great "They"
so I'm that witness.
        Witness
            WITNESS.

Its not like we can't see.

Peace be locked up liquor store
    a crime to even get to
        a dirty job in and of itself.

Something we gotta want anyway. Still.

ALAN KING

Alan King is an author, poet, journalist and videographer. He is a communications specialist for a national nonprofit and a senior editor at Words Beats & Life's global hip hop journal. As a staff writer for the *Baltimore Afro-American Newspaper*, King often out-scooped the *Baltimore Sun* when covering housing and the Baltimore City Council. His three-part series on East Baltimore's redevelopment and the displaced residents brought together stakeholders (community leaders, elected officials and developers) to work out a plan that gave vulnerable residents a role in helping to build up the city's blighted neighborhoods.

During a trip to Kingston, Jamaica, King introduced AFRO readers to the island's rich history by highlighting its national heroes such as Marcus Garvey and Bob Marley. Additionally, his historic pieces from slavery to emancipation helped his readers understand the significance of the island's 47th Independence Day celebration.

King is the author of *POINT BLANK* (Silver Birch Press, 2016) and *DRIFT* (Aquarius Press, 2012). As a visiting author for Pen Faulkner's Writers-in-Schools program, he's inspiring the next generation of readers and writers. King's honors include fellowships from Cave Canem and Voices of Our Nations Arts (VONA) Foundation, three Pushcart Prize nominations as well as three nominations for Best of the Net.

King is a graduate of the Stonecoast MFA Low-Residency Program at the University of Southern Maine. His poems and short stories appear in various literary journals, magazines and are featured on public radio. He lives in Bowie, Maryland with his family.

The Land of Innocence
for Jade and George Floyd

A YouTube clip shows a protest
ignited after police killed George Floyd—

torched SUVs, overturned cop cars,
armored officers retreating—

all of that sinks my wife
into a deeper postpartum,
having made it through
our personal crisis.
We watch the python of despair
coil itself around America, blowing out
glass storefronts and colliding angry bodies
as the tension constricts and crushes.

We're miles from the mayhem,
but a different kind of danger finds us
in the maternity ward—

a decreasing heartbeat, frenzied nurses
rushing my wife to the OR, surgeons scrambling
to save our daughter.

Watching the news, I'm reminded of slogans
on chaos as necessity: "real discoveries come
from chaos," "chaos is beautiful
and full of fertility."

But when it's a violent pattern
of reactions, what's the real discovery,
where's the beauty in things shattered and tagged
if the same pattern of injustice
ripples our lives?

Maybe "chaos" isn't the right word.
Let's try, instead, "challenge."

And since it means refuting the truth
or validity of, isn't a protest a public dispute
of someone else's truth

like the one about the fear of dark bodies,
how it justifies them being mangled
or discredited in news cycles?

Wouldn't the beauty then
be new laws that get us closer
to becoming the people
the constitution claims it protects?

Let me begin again.

When my wife told me several months ago
she was pregnant, we knew the challenge
of this birth could take her life

just as the challenge in the hospital
threatened our daughter's.

And isn't it an act of faith to go blindfolded
into the future and be delighted
by the light there?

Now, we're lit by a dancing star named Jade,
short for Jadesola (Jah-de-sho-lah), which in Yoruba
means "come into wealth."

She's Jade like the green stone
said to emit wisdom and clarity.

I'm feeding her while watching
the YouTube video.

Someone onscreen yells,
"We're better than this,"
and she squeals—mouth dripping
with her mother's milk, smiling
while dreaming her baby dreams—
that land of innocence, where it all starts
before we lose our way back
rationalizing our destruction.

RON MILNER

Ron Milner (1938–2004) was a playwright, writer, editor, critic and director. Born in Detroit, Michigan, Milner attended the Detroit Institute of Technology and Columbia University in New York. In the early 1960s, Milner received two prestigious literary fellowships, the John Hay Whitney Fellowship (1962) and a Rockefeller Fellowship (1965), to work on a novel, *The Life of the Brothers Brown*. Milner is affectionately known as the "people's playwright" for his use of Black theater for the advancement of Black people. Milner taught widely and was a Writer-in-Residence at Lincoln University from 1966 to 1967, where his friendship with Langston Hughes, who urged him to use a personal voice in his writing, matured.

Milner's first major play, *Who's Got His Own*, premiered in Harlem in 1967. Milner, along with friend and producer-director Woodie King, Jr. were part of a touring production of three plays by Malcolm Boyd in 1964, where they joined the American Place Theatre, where *Who's Got His Own* and *The Warning: A Theme for Linda* (1969/1970) were conceived and performed. Other published plays include *The Monster* (1968), *(M)Ego and the Green Ball of Freedom* (1968), and *What the Wine-Sellers Buy* (1974).

Milner lived in California in the late 1970s to early 1980s and taught creative writing at the University of Southern California and carried out community work. Milner later returned to Detroit—he felt his creative energy fed on the unique experience of life in his hometown.

Milner's critical writing includes "Black Magic, Black Art" (*Negro Digest*, 1967) and "Black Poets and Prophets" (1972). Milner declared that Black Art must affirm, inspire, and touch the souls of Black people. Milner's *Roads of the Mountaintops* (1986) deals with the internal struggle of Martin Luther King, Jr., following his receipt of the Nobel Peace Prize in 1964. The million dollar-earning *What the Wine-Sellers Buy* (1974) dealt with a young Black man choosing between good and evil while also addressing the issue of Black male responsibility. *Checkmates* (1987) starred Denzel Washington and portrayed the potential strength of Black love. *Don't Get God Started* (1988) was a Gospel musical play featuring the famous family singing group the Winans.

A lesser-known work from Milner's career is his short story "Junkie Joe Had Some Money," anthologized in Langston Hughes's *Best Short Stories by Negro Writers* (1967). Milner's crucial contribution to the field of Black drama collections, *Black Drama Anthology* (1972), was co-edited with Woodie King and documented important works by Milner, Amiri Baraka, Ed Bullins and Langston Hughes, among others.

Black Theater—Go Home!

If a new black theater is to be born, sustain itself and justify its own being, it must go home. Go home psychically, mentally, esthetically, and, I think, physically.

Now what does all that mean? First off, what do I, myself, mean by a new *black* theater? I mean the ritualized reflection and projection of a unique and particular way of being, born of the unique and particular conditioning of black people leasing time on this planet controlled by white men; and having something to do with the breaking of that "leasing-syndrome." A theater emerging from artists who realize that, for black people of this world, and specifically, this country, every quote "universal" human malady, dilemma, desire, or wonder, is, by the heat of the pressure of white-racism, compounded and enlarged, agitated and aggravated, accented and distilled to make that omni-suffusing, grinding sense of being we once called the blues but might now just term: *blackness*. From this peculiar and particular extra-dimension of being, of experiences, of conditioning, will come the kind of theater I'm looking for.

Out of the fact that something as "universal" as the inner-drive and desire for success takes on a different shade, another prick-point, when it is beneath a black skin; there are some strange hi-level goals, some other, further obstacle considerations involved. Out of the fact that even Love vibrates to these ultra-earthy subterranean accents. Love for family, for woman, for friend, for self, are all touched somehow, somewhere, by this infra-shadow. And it is from this deep shadow that will come this new theater I am seeing; come in many brilliant new forms of enlightenment, illumination.

It will be a theater having to do with love of one's self, and one's personal, national, and international family with wariness and hatred of one's personal, national, and international enemies; with, ideally, points as to how to break their grip and splatter their power.

Now, let me stay right in here a minute. I want to make sure I get across at least some hint of all the levels I see *here*; try a couple more parables, examples, similes, or whatever. All-right? So, let's take the French Film, *Black Orpheus*. A sweet, bright, touching thing. (Just good to see a woman like that in full color.) But to make it Afro-American Orpheus there would have to be some extending and deepening of dimensions. Understand me? A writer in the new black theater might want to make the Hell, the Death, the girl's going into the White-World, rejecting not only Orpheus but all other cats and things black. That would be the Hell. And Orpheus going to get her back with just courage and con and a song would really be something, wouldn't it? And how could he not look back at the past, at the promises of the Devil? Yeh, deep stuff. Tragic. And neither Shaw, O'Neill, nor any of those other great ones, could write it. Not within this level of blackness I'm talking about. I can almost feel some of you thinking: Racism, pure racism. Well, I don't know, now. All the universal implications, messages, of the tale are still there. What this imaginary writer has done is to put Hell up on Earth where it belongs; and say that it has something to do with rejecting. And if there is racism in it, it only makes it more validly of your own people and images for other people and images, of this time and of this world; Your fire driving others' fires out of your brain.

Now that little adaptation points at just one level of what I'm visualizing. But there will be so many other levels coming simultaneously. Levels of love and joy and strength and courage. Like, how did bighearted, big-bellied George Jones, this elevator-operator, Pullman-porter, foundry-flunky, keep that deep clean laughter going?— Raise all those kids and keep that strong groovy woman swept all those years on it? How did he do it? How come everybody in the barbershop, poolroom, work-house, and everywhere is glad to see him coming?

Turning to him to warm their psychic and spiritual hands? How? Why? Who? What? Can't you see him, in a blue-light, sitting up on the side of the bed, plotting next week's bill-dodging and bill-paying, with all of them asleep, except maybe her lying there touching his back now and then, telling him to get some rest? But in the morning, with still no answers in sight, he's got the right glowing laugh of confidence to send those kids on out ready to run through those prejudiced teachers and all that other crap—to look for something he never saw. Now how does he do that? He knows what's happening.

He's been through a thousand hunky overseers on a thousand poisonous jobs. He's had to dodge and stall the buzzards so long he can smell 'em a month away. Now—how? He's some huge, terrific soul stretching his low-ceilinged cage all out of shape—defeating it even while it kills him. A peculiar and particularly tragic-hero; made both tragic and heroic by his way with a particularly peculiar poisonous situation. Getting George Jones, and that deep resilient lady of his and their indigo moments, on stage, is being in another level of the new black theater. So many levels. All levels.

Because there is no personal style, or hang-up, or revelation, that can't be worked out within and through the stances and situations of black people; through the questions and answers in the Right-Now relevance frequency we must tune ourselves and our audiences into in order to nurture race, self, and art. A writer coming this way won't lack in his work any of those universals everyone screams about—not if he has any in him; (if you look for 'em you'll find 'em even in the comic strips but he ill become involved in the projection of a certain uniqueness that is his hard-earned birthright.

Now, any of you who know about writing, or about speech-making, probably realized that there was the return of the bridge back there: that stanza ending in that riff of—race, self, art. That brings me back to where I started. Where I said that if this theater is to be it must—psychically, mentally, aesthetically, and I feel, even physically—go home. I'm sure you know now what I mean by going home psychically and mentally. But, just in case, let me try to run a short, quick summary. By *psychically*, I mean coming away from your dues-paying to all those "outside influences" and going into the real, black, YOU, by way of those places, people, and experiences which began and had the most to do with the shaping of what is now yourself—mean, making works, theater, out of that and, in doing it, extending and validating that particular psychic. By mentally, I mean understanding that you and the experiences of you are in time and history collective repetitions, have been repeated and multiplied many times; so, as artists, you are to try to find the terms, and the pictures, which will most simply clarify those experiences and that knowledge for the *you's* who do not, or could not, understand what is, or was, happening to you, and to future you's who will need to be warned and directed in terms from inside that level we call: *blackness*—for it is within that level that most of the added, making or breaking, weight comes.

Going home aesthetically will follow naturally after those first two steps—since your aesthetics come out of your mental and psychic environment. So I won't go into the demand for new dynamics, for a new intensity of language and form, that the material and the desired atmosphere will make on you; except to say that the further you go home, the more startlingly new and black the techniques become: Musicians are pointing that out to us.

Now, going home physically with the new theater means just that. Probably, I should have started here. For this new theater must be housed in, sustained and judged by, and be a useable projections of, and to, a black community! The community itself will be the theater, and the black artist's house of drama like a weirdly fixed and pointed looking-glass, a light-prism casting warnings, directions, fruitful memories and marvelous imaginings on the walls of the doomed, or soon to be recreated, buildings. Right there in the community are your materials, your situations and conflicts—relevant and powerful.

When you stand on those streets feeling the human whimpering going on under the beast's muzzle, when the myriad poisons are part of your natural everyday elements, the needs will either come bursting out off your pens onto your stages, or they'll drive you sick with your own f----- cowardice.

The need to displace and replace pale and dark villains and heroes, ideas and concepts, images and symbols; the need for defined and dramatized, hugely-drawn, clearly shown, walking and talking details as to how to organize community, county, nation, world for a shattering attack against the most voracious power-machine the world has ever known. Details! Not stunning poetic generalities. Details! Details should be moving around those stages in all kinds of explicit images; huffing and puffing and working themselves out of the killing situations—or showing why they cannot! Pictures of who and what was the past; how it was called and who answered, and why it all went down. Who were those heroes the kids have got to know of and believe in before they can believe that you, or any other black man, has anything to tell them? What were the betrayals? How does Judas look when he's black? Detailed pictures of who and what is doing the killing now. And how it—awesome as it might seem—can be maneuvered into deathtraps. All the while you're singing about that woman, that buddy, those personal art-promises you made to yourself. All and any of it placed right in the context in which you found it, and from which you can only free it through direct confrontation—that is, America's ball-cutting racist vise.

You've grabbed every piece of beauty, thought, insight and style you've ever achieved in your life while dodging that crap. And to put it out of your work before it is out of your life is making a lie of your art—which is nothing but your life (thoughts, feelings, seeings, imaginings, doings sent out to others with an imposed re-order. You will never have a theater, an art, a life really representative of the soul-beats and desire-lines of you and your kind until you and your kind have come together and pooled desires, plans, resources and capabilities to throw off the jailers.

The people, the communities, are trapped in both unconscious suicide and subtle, dedicated genocide. You have a tool that might be able to help. What're you going to do? Go out on a bridge hallway between realities and blow to yourself? Or serenade the downtown people and catch the pennies they throw at your feet? I hope not.

Speaking of pennies—and we have to—there is also a definite practical, economical, reason for the new theater going physically to the black communities. That is that Broadway doesn't want your blackness, wasn't designed or intended for it; definitely doesn't want any strange new forms inspire by that very blackness. She is a contented fat white cow. If you can slip in and milk her or a minute—well, then, more blackpower to you brother. But, I'm telling you—it's a weird price she's asking: She wants you to be a singing hyena, dancing on the graves of yourself and everyone you know. (Serious things, dramas, are things to come from some other country, some other century, and even then are best set in a mad-house. And (quote) black-comedy has nothing to do with Afro-Americans!) Broadway cannot support you, brothers and sisters; it would be against *their* interests.

If you're thinking that Off-Broadway is a haven, think again. It is, finally, as a perfect example of what America would have its artists involved in: a zoo, with a carnival, where the animals and the freaks play delightfully, curiously, shockingly, with lights, colors, words, forms, gestures, always with some ingrown aspect of themselves, never with anything in the outer-world should any relevance be uttered or implied it is usually done so with the utmost obscurity. Now and again, I have to admit, something disturbs that tranquil scene down there, something real and relevant—related to other peoples' lives—seeps in; then everybody does a double-take and goes back wondering if maybe something could really be starting down there after all. But it's usually just something or someone healthy getting ready to break-out of there; nothing to be alarmed about; won't happen often. To round off my thinking on Off-Broadway, I tell you that art for art's sake is: incest! And the offsprings of that are usually strange and feeble.

We, black people, desperately need a healthy natural art-form: art coming from an intercourse with life! Our lives! As we have, and must, live them. In order for our art, theater, to provide this for us, it must become an organic, functioning part of our communities. As black artists we must go home in every way; go wherever it is we most feel indigenous and organic and, therefore, a natural observer and commentor. It is there that our talents must pay dues and spend dividends. The communities, the people, can sustain, assist, and inspire us to essential and brilliant levels in our new black theater, our new visions. But only if we assist and inspire them to the same levels in the new black theater of their living, to new visions of their lives.

CONNIE OWENS PATTON

Connie Owens Patton graduated from California State University, Stanislaus with a Bachelor of Arts in English. She has previously been published in *African Voices* and *Writing For Our Lives*. In 2020, her poem "Lie to Me" was featured on Heard/Word Galleyway, an online audio series. Connie has also performed spoken word in various cities throughout the Central Valley. She resides in California where she is working on a book of poetry entitled *Through a Tightly Coiled Lens*.

Kindling

Centuries of indignities
Become internal kindling
Carried by black bodies
That defy gravity
Remain upright
Much to the wonderment
Of those who
Attempt to oppress us
As we carve out spaces
Among relics still

Clinging to supremacy
By their fingertips
Affirmations of blackness
Elicits fear
They know
A change has come
We will no longer "cautiously be"
As not to trigger the inexplicably afraid
It is an impossible task
We are murdered, anyway
So
When internal kindling is set aflame
And the streets swell
With our bodies in protest
Recognize that our flesh
Can be compromised
But nothing can murder
Historical DNA
It's as futile as trying to extinguish the sun

Charlois Lumpkin

Charlois Lumpkin, aka Mali Newman, is a native of St. Louis, Missouri and a member of the Eugene B. Redmond Writers Club and its performance troupe, the Soular Systems Ensemble. Her work has appeared in *Drumvoices Revue, Valley Voices—A Literary Review, Crossing the Divide from the Poets of St. Louis* and *The Hoot and Holler of the Owls,* an anthology published by the Zora Neale Hurston/Richard Wright Foundation. New work will appear in the forthcoming anthology *400 years: stories of black people in poems written from love,* published by Broadside/Lotus Press.

Neo Kwansaba in Barakan Verse

Poetree grown from stanzas tongue my ears
Don't play Dough Ray Me Vaso Latte
Unless Dada Doowop Dadaism is dead, unless
Trans(it) Blues in C, major or minor
Died by volumes twenty one times, don't
Play scale up/scale down, while Baraka
Breaks off a piece of his mind.

Atomic Remedy, Or Jayne's the Bomb
For Jayne Cortez (1934 – 2012)

Jazz lingo's fusion artist goes nuclear. Fission
with mike in hand. Jayne the reactor
splits atoms and fire lines in equal
measure. Cortez's atomic Yari Yari are remedy
for a power strafed world where polar
blue inmates house grey cells of reason.
Mush-Room-Boom, Jayne clears the air.

Kwansaba for Maya (1928 – 2014)

Acrid world that calls her outta her
Name also reminds her who she is:
Grace giving rise to courage. So Walk
Eyes say WALK AKIMBO with adelphi heart
Living a poem nakedly true as haiku
Of kinship among women who die hungry,
Unloved and unsaved. Maya knew them all.

DARRELL STOVER

Darrell Stover is a poet, cultural historian, performance artist, and science communicator with a Masters degree in writing from Johns Hopkins University. His most recent volume of poetry is *Somewhere Deep Down When*. His work has appeared most recently in the 25th Anniversary celebratory anthology of the Carolina African American Writers Collective, *All the Songs We Sing*. He lectures in Africana Studies with a focus on Afrofuturism more broadly known as the Black Speculative Arts Movement.

Look Back: Amiri, the Blues God Lives

A book looked back at me as it sat in various places around the Landover, Maryland residence of my middle youth. Two pairs of eyes, two dark faces peeked out from the image on the cover through a door or a wall that could be anywhere in urban America, maybe DC where I was born and we moved from in 1967. The book was being read by my mother at different times in different spaces of the house. She would say she read it because she liked him, the author, Leroi Jones, whose name would be changed several years after the assassination of Malcolm X in 1965 to Amiri Baraka. The book, *Home*, a 7th printing edition collection of his early 60s essays, would embrace and intrigue me in 1971 as I immersed and nourished my black teen into black manhood intellect. I picked it up, scanned the content pages, turned to page 9 and initiated a decades long relationship with that powerful mind, global comrade, steadfast cultural worker, purposeful political strategist, masterful griot, jazz daddy, Amiri Baraka – mentor and friend.

Those essays as personal narrative, as reportage, as analysis and invitation to the real, not the science fictions that I was so accustomed to reading in my youth and still today, brought me to a place in the world that my parents were determined to not let my siblings and I ignore. We should know who we are, where we came from, question everything, and fight ignorance with studied insight and practical politics. That ignorance included an America deep in the throes of denying that a shift was amidst in the 60s and 70s—Black folks in DC, Prince George's County, Maryland and elsewhere were getting politically organized and involved. DC wanted and would get home rule. People in other countries wanted to be self-determined and free from present and former colonizers. "Cuba Libre," the first and most revealing essay in *Home*, related a personal homecoming and identity redefining moment for Amiri (one of several to come), and as I read it, for me.

The exchanges and encouragements of the many "revolutionaries" he encountered and presented in that essay on his early 60s trip to Cuba had a major player and hero, Robert Williams, 50s and 60s era Monroe, North Carolina NAACP president who was a vocal advocate and practitioner of an armed self-defense that challenged the KKK and eventually the nation. I suggest *Radio Free Dixie* by Timothy Tyson for the fuller exploits of Robert Williams, although Amiri would tell of him many times over the years, because he was so inspired and impressed. He was jettisoned on that trip into global political realities in ways that caused him to question his role as a writer in times of unforgiveable oppression and disenfranchisement. "Cuba Libre" and the other essays in *Home* empowered and expanded my resolve as an active agent for change through bringing the arts and historical analysis to the table in service to the community where ever I have found myself. The name Leroi Jones was at the forefront of my mind's eye and literary tastes from that point on.

The next intellectual encounter with Amiri would come in 1972 not too long after engaging those social essays. It was the habitual and free outlet of release that presented itself on many Saturday mornings when I and Donald Barber, a teen, fellow science-focused buddy of mine, journeyed on the streets of downtown DC from Chinatown (5th and H streets NW) to Georgetown University (37th and O streets NW) stopping at museums, comic shops, and used book stores along the way. We witnessed and participated in many a protest as our stroll would many times take us past the National Mall and the Nixon White House. Parental trust was a thankful blessing in what amounted to 10 full hours of exploration each time, if not in the direction of Georgetown then it was to the Library of Congress. We caught rides into town in the morning with his father who worked on the weekend at the Government Accounting Office (5th street NW) and would be picked up by my father after attending late afternoon Washington Junior Academy of Sciences meetings on the campus or chess playing and reading on Capitol Hill.

The journey into my cultural identity was struck by lightning one Saturday when that day's bookstore visit revealed a jewel of a tome, a thick book that bore the "Leroi Jones" imprimatur. It was *Black Fire: An Anthology of Afro-American Writing*, co-edited with Larry Neal. BAM! Yes, Black Art Movement bounty bounced between my left and right lobes for months immersing me in cultural calculations and constructions by John Henrik Clarke, Stokely Carmichael (not too far from the change in name to Kwame Ture), Harold Cruse, Sonia Sanchez, A.B. Spellman, Lorenzo Thomas, Stanley Crouch, Henry Dumas, Roland Snellings (now Askia Toure, born in Raleigh, NC), and Sun Ra among so many others. Amiri appears as "Ameer" in this signed edition, which I still own, but it is his conspirator in Black Art, Larry Neal, who now shared central intellectual focus for me, because I came to view them both as primary jazz poets, scholars, and activists.

Sterling Brown, blues poet, literary scholar and close associate of Langston Hughes taught Amiri and others at Howard University that black music was our history, a vast archive to reap untold insights into our past and present cultural practices, thoughts, spirit, emotions, and creative genius. Amiri's *Blues People* and *Black Music* would be informed by this thinking and buttress my embrace of he and his kindred spirit, Larry Neal who passed into ancestorhood in 1981. I personally experienced for the first time the atomic, physical performance presence of Amiri and the spiritual manifestation of Larry Neal in 1984 in the Senate Office Building on Capitol Hill in DC as Amiri gave the keynote speech at the

2nd Annual Larry Neal Writer's Conference. This is where I purchased my still cherished copy of Neal's *Hoodoo Hollerin' Bebop Ghosts* published by Howard University Press in hardcover for $6.95. Baraka would say of his friend in his truly classic performance poet, "griotic" manner that Larry was "one of the hot lipped hip bebop poetry warriors trying to take the language someplace else, just as King and Malcolm were trying to take the whole society someplace else."

Baraka opened his presentation at the conference with "Wailers," the tribute/praise poem for Larry Neal and Bob Marley, who also ascended in 1981. His keynote speech followed and included when Larry and he first met at the UN to protest the assassination of Patrice Lumumba with Maya Angelou, Max Roach, and Abbey Lincoln among others, the revelation to him of Larry as activist, artist, poet, and writer, their ensuing collaborations in establishing the Black Arts Repertory Theatre School with Askia Toure, Cricket magazine with A.B. Spellman, and co-editing of *Black Fire*. He included the Larry Neal poems, "Ghost Poem #1," "Poppa Stoppa Speaks from His Grave," and "Don't Say Goodbye to the Porkpie Hat for Mingus, Bird, Prez, Langston, and them." It's the last of the three poems that I consider the quintessential jazz poem with its roll call, Afro-spiritual migration history lesson soundscape of jazz, what many including Amiri call African American Classical Music. Neal lays it out in his professorial fashion, "Dinah knows/Richie knows/that Bud is Buddha/that Jelly Roll dug juju/and Lester lives/in Ornette's leapings/the Blues God lives…"

"Bones beat/Blues Gods Arise!" I utilized the "Blues God" motif in my signature poem, "Bonesongs" as Neal raises it three times in his homage to jazz, the jazz aesthetic, Lester Young, and as a response to the Charles Mingus' tribute to Lester Young in the classic tune, "Goodbye Porkpie Hat." I have performed Neal's poem many times with two other voices (primarily Lasana Mack and Kenneth Carroll) and musicians, most significantly at the Folger Shakespeare Library for an award program of the Larry Neal Writers Competition and a gathering of DC's Jazz Listening Group. This group was founded in part and led by Amiri's friend and fellow poet/activist Gaston Neal (His saga is a grand one, too). Periodically Amiri would be a presenter at some of the monthly meetings of the Jazz Listening Group which I became a member of after that Larry Neal poem performance provided the ticket into those august gatherings.

I am a hard bop aficionado with a strong attachment to the avant-garde of the 50s and 60s, but I don't deny the essentialism of Armstrong,

Ellington, Basie, Holiday, Vaughan and their peers of the 20s, 30s, and 40s. Granted my true introduction to the music was in the late 60s when the young naturalist "me" placed one of those "not to be touched" albums of my father's on the turntable. What I thought would be birds, since the cover was speckled with them and the title was "Ornithology," turned out to be Charlie "Bird" Parker making the alto sax do dazzling things. My neighborhood pal Marty Williams called me around to his house in the mid-70s to listen to an album his mother had brought home for him. He had dreamed about Sun Ra, so she hooked him up. It was another mind-blowing invitation to the music and I continued down the path offered by live concerts and DC's jazz stations – WPFW (on which I started reading my poetry in 1981) and WDCU. I spent a lot of time perusing the bins and purchasing jazz albums from a little record store around the corner from my grandmother's apartment on the DC/Takoma Park, Maryland line and another in Georgetown.

There were the joyful times Pharoah Sanders, Phyllis Hyman, Roy Ayers, and Plunky and the Oneness of JuJu played on campus at the University of Maryland at College Park in the late 70s. While in college there I established a close friendship and was mentored by Otis Williams, son of Jackson, Mississippi and then a Baltimore resident, Director of the Nyumburu Cultural Center where he taught classes on jazz and blues as cultural art forms and history. He used Amiri's works in those classes. I grew to value most the poetry in *Wise, Why's, Y's, Funk Lore*, and he and his wife Amina's *The Music: Reflections on Jazz and Blues*. They collectively point to some serious sound scientists and conjure critical thinking necessary for these and all time. Oh and I must not leave out of the jazz poetry aesthetic canon the Amiri Baraka recording "New Music-New Poetry," featuring Steve McCall on drums and David Murray on tenor sax and bass clarinet. The photo on the back cover provided me the signature "cool pose" posture of a poet in performance and the attitude I took on is reflected in Amiri's liner notes where he states, "The poetry I want to write is oral by tradition, mass aimed as its fundamental functional motive."

The emphasis I placed and passion I had for social activism and jazz music—its performance, recording, contextualization, writing, scholarship, and performance poetry in jazz mode, especially Larry's work—drew Amiri and I into a long friendship. It was a shared empowerment by the Blues Gods. I, like so many of us, would not miss him whenever he came to DC. Accompanied by musicians or not, he was always explosive, conscious-raising and challenging, encouraging "unity and struggle," using the music as exclamation and indictment. His poem of highest literary jazz aesthetic poignancy would be "In the Tradition for Black Arthur Blythe." It lays down a gauntlet of fact fortified argument and debate, a black lineage of bad battlers, and 10 doctoral degrees worth of vital cultural history, "come out of europe if you can/cancel on the english depts this is america/north, this is america/where's yr american music/gwashington won the war/where's yr american culture southernagrarians…"

Approachable, yet able to talk a charging elephant into an about-face, I remember many times witnessing fools on the wrong side of experiencing his verbal combat legerdemain. I tried to give him my first chapbook in 1988, *Record of the Green Hat Chronicles*, a reference to my green hat wearing days in college and around DC in the 70s and 80s, even signing my poems "THE MAN-IN-THE-GREEN-HAT." He handed it back and asked what I was doing, reached in his pocket, pulled his wallet out and said, "Let me show you how this is done. Now, how much is it? As many books of mine you done bought." Those books bear his signature along with encouragement, a long standing battle cry, or a personal note – "Keep writing," "Unity & Struggle," "To the Man in the Green Hat," "To the Man in the Green Sky," "Darrell Stover My Man," and "Be as Wise as All Us Together!"

I invited him twice to the Hayti Heritage Center, the former St. Joseph's A.M.E. Church in Durham, North Carolina. The first time he gave a fist-pounding reminder of the significance of Robert Williams, Kwame Ture, and W.E.B. Dubois' greatest work *Black Reconstruction* in October 1999 as we celebrated his 65th birthday in a full sanctuary as the last performance previous to the renovation of the 100 plus year-old structure. How he enjoyed afterward hanging out in Raleigh at the CYPHER organized by Tracey Evora, Matt Sherman, R.C. Glenn and a host of other young cultural workers. Amiri spoke of how his son Ras would have truly been into the "happenin" scene – live music, spoken word, good food, cultural vendors, and a Pan African spirit. The second time was in March 2012 when he came down from Newark to specifically celebrate the release of *Somewhere Deep Down When*, my compilation in response to his demand for a book from me when I saw him at "1968 and Beyond: A Symposium on the Impact of the Black Power Movement on America" presented by the Smithsonian National Museum of African American History and Culture in 2009. "You owe us a book," he said in a voice that carried the weight of a million villages. He even gave me an added nudge in 2010 when all of us were at Shaw University to hold up in bold relief the significance of the Student Nonviolent Coordinating Committee (SNCC) in a 50th Anniversary spirited revisitation and celebration. I got busy and got it done, inviting in some of my staunchest cultural performance allies to be a part of the celebration.

A month later after my book release I saw him at Duke University where he was invited to give a reading by a literary society on the campus. He greeted me and introduced me to Nathaniel Mackey, another great jazz poet. Amiri also asked how the book and the family were doing. It would be my last time seeing him, although I hear him still, blaring, still kickin' science for social change. "The Blues God Lives!"

The announcement of his ascendance in January 2014 traveled via social media with a "quickness" that matched his stature as our reigning intellectual king, true Black Cultural Royalty. I posted many photos of carefully selected collations of his books I own and have read in groups of 3 or 4 to signify the abundant inheritance we have before us through his scholarship and extensive literary productivity. It was a prelude to catching the Carolinian train from Cary, North Carolina to Newark, New Jersey for his home going celebration. I was able to share the trip with a young man migrating to New York from Raleigh after graduating from Shaw University. I told him of Amiri and he purchased one of my books. He was honored to share in Amiri's legacy and a few days later I received an e-mail thanking me for the book and the cultural immersion it provided him. I handed down the tradition further as I told him to seek out Amiri's *Digging, Razor,* and *Home.*

Be We We?
For Amiri and Larry

"One Nation and We're on the Move…"
Yes One
Yes one more spirit raised
Every time you sprayed deep traditions
A syllable, simile, metaphor or solar plexus punch
The World became the holiest place
Ka'ba
Heaven
Boom bad for the good of us
Yes One

Fist pounded on the podium
Reconstruction Blues Jazz Incantations Abounded
Ba Daa Du Dit Ba Daa Du Dit Ba Daaaa Du Dit Dit Du Daaaa*
Stretched Gullah from South Carolina to New Ark
Stretched the meaning of Nation
Across pages and pages
Our faces and minds
We became WE
In your tears for Malcolm
    Your calls to struggle
        To sing fight
          Sing Fight
            WRITE FIGHT
            Sting
              Fall down
                Get back up
                  SING FIGHT

BRING FORTH OUR NEW

    NATION!!!

"Nothin' Can Stop Us Now…"

NOTHIN'

    *[The Benny Golson, Blue Mitchell & Art Blakey versions of "Blues March"]

Another Trane
    For Alice and John Coltrane

Love interludes between play
Preacherly their piano and sax
Raised in notes of the spirit
Pews and pulpits
People full of grace to survive this place
Swirled in their dreams

Prepared for each other
A Detroit High Point organ blessed singularity
Coordinated North and South
Churchical immersions
Humble miles and years
Hard bop approaches to sound
Calculated in silence
His silence churning inside
Silence she listened to
Her harp admired in its own way
His peace and perfection
Inspired in a booth in Birdland
Back tight by the bandstand
He played something just for her
Turned the planet cosmically out
Turned us spiritually in
Now they play blues forever together for God.

JAMES E CHERRY

James E Cherry's latest collection of poems, *Loose Change,* was published by Stephen F Austin State University Press. He has been nominated for an NAACP Image Award for his first collection of poetry, *Honoring the Ancestors,* from Third World Press. The first of two editions of his collection of short fiction, *Still A Man and Other Stories* (Willow Books), was nominated for a Lilllian Smith Book Award and a Next Generation Indie Book Award. His latest novel, *Edge of the Wind*, was re-released in 2022 from Stephen F. Austin State University Press. Cherry is an adjunct professor of English at the University of Memphis-Lambuth and resides in Tennessee.

MISSISSIPPI: A HISTORY

The road from Jackson winds south, cuts

through cotton fields of west Tennessee

over hills rolling with soybeans

across the Mississippi state line.

Its two lanes push through low hanging clouds

on a January afternoon towards Oxford. I want

to shake hands with William Faulkner, take

a photograph with Eudora Welty, sip

corn liquor at the feet of Robert Johnson, sit

on the Square on a Saturday afternoon.

But, just past Rust College, the body

of Emmit Till floats past my windshield,

Goodman, Schwerner and Chaney rise

in my rearview mirror, the engine

of a passing pickup explodes like the report

from de la Beckwith's rifle. On campus,

the smell of gunpowder from Kennedy's troops

and Confederate reinforcements still singe

the air. Governor Barnett walks the grounds

with papers in his hand. James Meredith

has been chiseled out of 1962. The gray

of afternoon drifts to dusk and somewhere

the roar of a crowd hoists Archie Manning

upon its shoulders. The road from Oxford

plows north, a two hour drive before me

the Mississippi night behind me and a history

that catches me somewhere in between,

awaits all the places I'll ever know.

ELIZA WOOD

Jackson Tennessee

(08/18/1886)

Most nights, you can find Eliza Wood downtown,

sitting on the base of our monument to the Confederate Dead,

digging into the dirt under the moonlight, excavating

for a relic of justice. Speak her name,

she'll raise her head, scan the horizon that swallows

your voice with echoes of curses, rebel yells,

shotgun blasts that leave exit wounds in the sky.

Sheriff Person could not protect you, Eliza.

White men with torches, blood lust in their eyes

ripped the clothes off your back and drove you

from a jail cell into the August night. The carnival

had come to town: White kids cartwheeled the stars,

white women jostled babies on hips and reminisced

about the last time, their men slobbered a flask between them

and music square danced from HC Bryant's Hardware.

Did you recognize the faces, Eliza--black faces

made to assemble and bow to a history of degradation and fear,

lessons taught from a crumbled Constitution in the hands of Jim Crow?

Forced to confess poisoning Mrs. Jesse, you spoke silence,

would not be the last to be slapped, spat upon, driven

from one judgment place to another. Your sex would not save you.

The color of blackness unforgiveable. Your flesh

bruised along cobblestones, scrapped raw on Jackson streets,

strangled in a noose and nailed to a tree where gunshots

found your body. The mob roared. The night sighed.

In the morning, makeshift grave clothes entombed you.

Shafts of sunlight filtered your remains, cast shadows

on a silver crucifix, trampled in the broken earth.

NOCTURNAL POETICS

Amiri Baraka burst all the windows out of my dream.

I sat in a circle of poets where he towered

in the midst of us; Randall Horton was there.

Baraka advised that we read, practice, make certain

our words lindy-hop across the page. He admonished

against over revision, to not limit our minds

to what we think and to never imitate anyone,

not even ourselves. He reminded us

to consider the world, construct form

to compliment content and that poetry is

the bastard of politics. Baraka touched

my shoulder, encouraged me to seek

that smile at the bottom of the world

and with a wink of the eye boarded daybreak

as if it were the A-Train headed uptown, going home.

Raymond Nat Turner

"The Town Crier," Raymond Nat Turner, is a NYC poet privileged to have read at the Harriet Tubman Centennial Symposium. He is Artistic Director of the stalwart JazzPoetry Ensemble UpSurge!NYC and has appeared at numerous festivals and venues including the Monterey Jazz Festival and Panafest in Ghana West Africa. He currently is Poet-in-Residence at Black Agenda Report. He's also Co-Chair of the New York Chapter of the National Writers Union (NWU).

Essential Work

We'll always need Race car drivers roaring
down streets where children chase balls; like
We'll always need peaceful protesters pepper
sprayed like cockroaches; And
We'll always need sleeping seven year-olds shot
while dreaming of dolls, sleepovers, tooth fairies;
We'll always need children playing with toy guns
in parks executed before becoming "Hulk Hogans"

We'll always need doors kicked in and our daughters
and sons slaughtered in wee hours—even if it is the
Wrong address…
We'll always need elderly parents whacked for
Accidentally pressing emergency alerts; like
We'll always need mentally ill loved ones massacred
in our homes…

We'll always need men rushing pregnant wives to
Hospitals shot for speeding; And fathers of six
Hustling too hard chokehold lynched;
We'll always need young women who drive and
smoke, stopped and suicided; And mothers wearing
masks wrong wrestled down in subway stations—as
their 4 year-olds watch…

We'll always need wallets mistaken for guns—Glocks
for Tasers; fleeing Black men shot in their backs; And
bridegrooms butchered, night before their weddings…

We'll always need Tasered hearts skanking
in Reggae rhythms; And broken broomsticks
rammed up mens' rectums for fun…
We'll always need bruised, bloodied, disfigured
Faces—eyeballs dangling from sockets;
We'll always need drugs and guns planted—
Growing into cases, concertina wire, COVID-19…

We'll always need right hooves raised Testi-lying
To judges and juries of peers on the need for knees
on necks—56 licks or 41 shots—Served to Protect
Property…

It's capitalism, baby…

Gravediggers feed hungry Hart
Island trenches plain pine boxes;
stacked three-high, they rest side
by side in solidarity.
For now, they share island real
estate with AIDS and 1918 Flu fallen.
New York is not new to this.
Ask African Burial Ground
Ancestors—it's capitalism, baby…

799 died today.
Tasered with temperatures of 103.5
and shortness of breath—
A bus driver, track-worker and a couple
of conductors I know on sight and speak
to, came down with chills. They've breathed
welding manganese, steel dust and diesel
fumes decades for New Yorkers—Yet, they
couldn't be tested—it's capitalism, baby…

What if they'd whispered Three Little Words?
Pleaded 12 times—instead of 11—like

Eric Garner as the long, white, tatted
arm of the law crushed his windpipe?
What if they'd pleaded, "I can't Breathe…"
12—or even 13 times—would they've been
Tested, treated and alive today?
That's not MTA's concern. Bottom line,
liability, lawsuits are—it's capitalism, baby…

Nurses slash garbage bags open—using them
as PPE/Personal Protection Equipment.
Docs reuse gloves and masks—multiple patients—
in the world's 'richest' country—it's capitalism, baby…

Hand sanitizer was $15 a bottle yesterday—
$50 today—if you can find it. Ventilators were
$25,000 yesterday—$45,000 today and climbing—
It's capitalism, baby…

If water is life, hand-washing's a lifesaver.
Unelected 'emergency' management cut
Detroit water off and poisoned pennywise
Flint's—oh, please—it's capitalism, baby…
San Francisco hotel rooms sit empty.
The unhoused "shelter in place" below
freeways; in overcrowded shelters and
on cold convention center floors; oh well—
it's capitalism, baby…

Parasites "self-isolate" on swanky
Yachts, toasting tax-breaks looting
Labor's fruits; sucking up shares,
senators, congress members and
Blood.
Leeches storm the Hamptons—hoarding—
greedily buying meat, frozen foods—filling
Extra McMansion freezers; While working-
class shoppers tussle over
Toilet tissue; or stand their ground in long
lines buying guns—it's capitalism, baby…

Cars sob in food bank lines stamped 'Insufficient
Funds' a mile-long... While farmers plow perfect
cabbage heads and green beans back into black
soil. And ivory rivers swell from dairy farmers
dumping millions of gallons of milk in manure
pits. And chicken 'processors' smash 750,000
eggs a week—for Profit Omelet-obscene food fights—
it's capitalism, baby...

"Return To Normal?" That Titanic sailed months ago—
it does seem, however, that it left ashore capitalism's
grave-
diggers...

THURMAN WATTS

Thurman Watts (Tee Watts) is a founding member of The Nairobi Poets. His work has been seen in *The Pan Africanist, Black Creation, Holloway House Publications (Players Magazine and Sweet Lucy), The San Francisco Examiner, The San Francisco Chronicle,* and many other outlets. Currently, he writes for *Cadence Jazz Magazine* and *Blues Blast Magazine.* He is also co-writing *Time Has Come; The Memoirs of Lester Chambers.*

Mbombe's Glass

It was a time of extreme seasons. High Priestess of Soul, Nina Simone was my rib of existence, even then until now. Her fervent anthems of counter-slave elevation accompanied me through my post psychedelic Cointelpro coincidences, however real or imagined.

I was in Salem, Oregon again, after flunking out a couple of years earlier at the University. I'd originally arrived on campus back in '68 at the apex of the Democratic National Convention. There were twelve of us at the time; nine guys and three women out of a total student body of fifteen hundred. Lessening the sting of being dark sojourners in a land of snowy winters, we called ourselves the dirty dozen, like the Jim Brown film of that era, and imbued our presence with brazen Bay Area and South Central cool. We wore black leather and "Free Huey" posters adorned our dorm room walls.

My cool however, left me bereft of survival skill in classes like *The History of Western Civilization*. The discourses of modifiers like Descartes and Voltaire all but bum-rushed me back to the comforting solace of my dorm room where I wrote poetry, consumed Baraka and hungered for the Funk that was sure to come. I also smoked a lot of Portland pot which wasn't very good.

The one time I raised my hand in class to answer a question occurred in freshman English class. My peers were allegedly the scholarly cream of the Pacific Northwest. They seem to exist in an academic realm wholly foreign to my mode of understanding. But on this day, the professor asked a question that perplexed the whole class; except for me.

"Whose philosophy of non-violence did Martin Luther King study and apply as a leader of the Civil Rights Movement?" Her question was met with blank stares by everyone except me. I raised my gravity defying hand with all the strength I could muster. She called on me.

"Gandhi," I sang and proclaimed, rising above the cream. It was the loftiest perch of my University experience.

After flunking out, I'd returned to the Bay and joined a group. We patterned ourselves after The Last Poets and called ourselves The Village Griots. We were gigging on the West Coast, and now, two years later, had a date at the school where I'd been deemed academically unworthy. This is how we met Dr. Mbombe. Life is a helluva drug.

We stayed at Lumumba House while there. It was a rented house that offered solace to the Black populace in and around campus. It was named after fallen freedom fighter Patrice Lumumba, the first legally elected prime minister of the Democratic Republic of Congo. (Another hero that was killed or betrayed, like Gil sang in *Winter In America*.) There, students could decompress from the rigors of minority academic life and the young African-American locals could also comfortably socially mingle. The young locals were the offspring of Black migratory farm workers who followed the crops from Arizona to Oregon.

There was a wino by the name of Leroy who hung around Lumumba House, enjoying the energy of the young folks there. One day, out of earshot of Leroy, a brother whispered to me, "That cat can eat glass!"

At the next opportunity I asked Leroy about it. He shined me on, focusing instead on the feminine apparition in front of him.

On our last night there, a small crowd assembled at Lumumba House. The Village Griots, having earlier slain the University community at large with our performance, now gave a private, intimate reprise for the Lumumba House audience. Again, we got up to get down and the spirit was high. So high in fact, that Leroy, the elder, commandeered the scene as we finished our set

In booming elocution he said to one of the sisters, "Baby, would you brang me some salt and pepper from the kitchen?"

Seasonings procured, Leroy stood on the coffee table and unscrewed a light bulb from the ceiling. He stepped down and ceremoniously wrapped the bulb in his handkerchief. Suddenly he smashed the bulb on the coffee table and opened the hanky. With the flourish of a seasoned shaman, he sprinkled the shards of glass with salt and pepper. To our astonishment, Leroy ingested the sharp pieces, in between swills of his favorite beverage, Tingle Pink. He continued until only metal remained. Then he looked at me and spoke.

"Youngblood, run your finger 'round my mouth and see if there's any glass left."

I respectfully declined, already thoroughly convinced. "How do you do that," I asked. He then told me the story.

"When I was a young man, as a Merchant Marine, I became stranded in North Africa. I studied with a tribe of people who awakened the power of my mind. I was shown how to walk on hot coals and eat glass. *All you have to do is believe!* When I had a full set of teeth, I could eat soda pop bottles. When I came back to America, I worked in the circus as *Dr. Mbombe, Witchdoctor from Africa.*"

****

The Village Griots flew back to SFO the next morning. We stayed together as a group for about another year. We individually morphed into other pursuits and as relationships sometimes famously do, broke up. We have remained in contact and sometimes reminisce about the Black Arts Movement or the art of being Black. For us, the beginning and the end remain one. We also have stayed in contact with the thread of African-American students that we came to know through our Salem experience. No one seems to know though, what happened to Leroy.

Recently, I took my 34 year old son on a road trip up through Salem. He had asked me how I ended up going to school in Salem for a season and I thought the trip might provide the answer that I didn't readily have.

Salem, though a tad more diverse, still only has about a 1.5% Black population. As my son Marley and I drove the streets near the University, I was reminded how starved for Soul music we were as students all those years ago. Even in the frosty snow of winter, we would go out to the student parking lot late at night when the radio signal from XERB, near Tijuana was strongest. It would reach even Salem, with the Legendary Wolfman Jack pumpin' the latest Dyke & The Blazers, The Flamingos, Sam "Mr.Soul" Cooke, or Mr. Excitement, Jackie Wilson. Yeah, we loved the old Wolfman. Baby!

When we pulled up to the old Lumumba House, I was only half-surprised to note that though the structure was still there, it was no longer designated in remembrance of Patrice. It was still student housing, but most traces of Africa had been removed. There was one left. Someone, not so very long ago, had scrawled in a square of replaced cement, *Mbombe Lives!*

C. Liegh McInnis

C. Liegh McInnis is a poet, short story writer, instructor of English at Jackson State University, the former publisher and editor of *Black Magnolias Literary Journal*, and the author of eight books, including four collections of poetry, one collection of short fiction (Scripts: *Sketches and Tales of Urban Mississippi*), one work of literary criticism (*The Lyrics of Prince: A Literary Look at a Creative, Musical Poet, Philosopher, and Storyteller*), and one co-authored work, *Brother Hollis: The Sankofa of a Movement Man*, which discusses the life of a legendary Mississippi Civil Rights icon. He is also a former First Runner-Up of the Amiri Baraka/Sonia Sanchez Poetry Award sponsored by North Carolina State A&T and edited the *Black Magnolias* Special Prince Issue. He has presented papers at national conferences, such as College Language Association, the National Council of Black Studies, the Neo-Griot Conference, and the Black Arts Movement Festival, and his work has appeared in numerous journals and anthologies, including *The Southern Quarterly, Konch Magazine, Bum Rush the Page: A Def Poetry Jam, Journal of Popular Music and Society, Down to the Dark River: An Anthology of Poems on the Mississippi River, Black Hollywood Unchained: Essays about Hollywood's Portrayal of African Americans, Black*

Panther: Paradigm Shift or Not? A Collection of Reviews and Essays on the Blockbuster Film, Asymptote, The Pierian, Black Gold: An Anthology of Black Poetry, Sable, New Delta Review, The Black World Today, In Motion Magazine, MultiCultural Review, A Deeper Shade, New Laurel Review, ChickenBones, Oxford American, Journal of Ethnic American Literature, B. K. Nation, Red Ochre Lit, and *Brick Street Press Anthology.* In January of 2009, C. Liegh, along with eight other poets, was invited by the NAACP to read poetry in Washington, DC, for their Inaugural Poetry Reading celebrating the election of President Barack Obama. He has also been invited by colleges and libraries all over the country to read his poetry and fiction and to lecture on various topics, such as creative writing and various aspects of African American literature, music, and history.

"What Good Are Poems?"
from *Da Black Book of Linguistic Liberation*

Can a poem be as effective as a .357?
Can the images of a poem spray buck shot holes
into the body of a greenback stuffed sheet wearing shoat?
Can a poem be thrown as a brick through the window
of a grocery store so that we may pillage and plunder
its shelves for food for the hungry?
Can a poem be laid on top of a poem,
be laid on top of a poem, be laid on top of a poem
until we have built a shelter for the homeless?
Does a poem need a million dollar war chest
or a foundation grant to be mightier than the sword?
What good does a poem do a spoiled, bloated belly?
Can a poem lay hands on the sick and clothed the naked?
Can a poem work hoodoo on an ACT score?
Can a poem pull the rent payment from a magician's hat?
Can poems assassinate Negro turncoats
who have sold their souls to racist rags?
Can poems cut short the lives of serpentine superintendents
who slyly suffocate African babies in Euro-excrement
disguised as Caucasian curriculums?

Poets are the African bees of political pollination.
Poems are the sperm of revolution.
We need poets to stop adding extra syrup and saccharin

to their sonnets so as to appease the pale palates of people
who have not the stomach for the straight-no-chaser truth.
We need poets to stop mindlessly masturbating away
their talents into the mental napkins of oversexed audiences.
We need poets to start impregnating thoughts of
Black magnolias bursting through white cement
into the minds of Raven virgin souls who without it
toil in the reproductive process of self-aversion.

Poems are the sperms of revolution.
Are you making love to your people,
or are you merely fornicating away your existence?

> "The more black folks transitioned from farming, the
> less independent and sovereign black folks became."
> Hollis Watkins, Mississippi Civil Rights Icon

> "I can't leave my PhD to my children, but
> I can leave my raggedy farm to them."
> Thomas Boyd

> "Nora said you lost your track.
> Can't plow straight when you lookin' back.
> Keep your hand on the plow and hold on.
> If you wanna get to Heaven, let me tell you how;
> just keep your hand on the Gospel plow.
> Keep your hand on that plow and hold on"
> "Hold On" (Negro Spiritual)

Us from Dirt
(for John Boyd, Jr., and Black Farmers Everywhere)

Who knew that Moses could wear a size 7.5
coal-coated Stetson and well-worked blue jeans,
tame a tractor like a bull,
plow fields watered with sweat and blood[2],
plant kernels fertilized with determination

so that justice can be harvested one yield at a time—
45 bushels needed to turn a profit
sometime 55 because snowy scales
can't calculate moon-kissed crops
as weighing-up with white gauges don't ever
seem to balance the bottom-line of black pockets
even though onyx farmers were all-knowing before the almanac
as Alkebulan is the womb that gave birth to husbandry
from the Nile to the Mississippi; still, blue-eyed bleached bankers
deny ebony hands that forever pulled life from obsidian soil.

An ocean of 949,889 black farmers evaporated
under the heat of white supremacy to a puddle of 45,508
as a reenactment of the Berlin Conference that
dismembered and divided eighty percent of their acreage.
Yet, they still seed the hope that "the land don't know no color"[3]
so they cast down more than a bucket
pulling themselves up from slavery
even when they had boots devoid of straps
while they were lynched by regimental red tape
or beaten brutally by bureaucratic bullwhips
because the FHA[4] forcefully withheld fertilizer
to erode the economic ecology of blues people
as the bank be using the wrong formula
so that white weeds can colonize black soil
as afro-applications just be invitations to agri-gentrification
because they never share in the profits of the products
but always be bearing the lion's share of the struggle
for chalky charlatans get to be enshrined as homesteaders
while bronze bodies are perpetually redlined into squatters.

It took Big John unloading his six-shooter
before the USDA tumbled like the wall of Jericho
as Boyd and 400 midnight plowmen
weaved and welded individual strings of courage
into a well-wrought web of Pigford v Glickman
to snare the silver snakes blocking the dam, allowing
a river of greenbacks to finally flow to R&B fields
that created a garden where goodness could be grown

with the help of a sable knight from Chicago whose pen
became a sword carving the 2008 Farm Bill into stone.
Daring to do damage in Dixieland,
they dig through dastardly difficult terrain
like the Union Soldiers sliced through the South.
Rebel flags be damned because losers
don't get no parade nor no respect.
For this Moses, guided by the star of Madam Moses,
crossed the Jim Crow Sea more than once,
to ensure that not one planter be left behind
in Pharaoh's sharecropping cell.
That spirit blossomed into the First Lady's Movement Initiative[5],
sparking a ferocious financier[6] to trade her high-fashion heels
for some soil-stomping boots to create a new Foot Print[7]
of revolutionary farming to slay the dragon of diabetes.

And even though they try to treat them like Jacks and Jennys[8],
these stallions and mares could not be broken by backroom horseplay,
their faith in the land stronger than the heat of hatred
as they were able to fatten up the farmhouse
'cause they pay tithes to the Most High
cultivating commodities that overflow their cups
from the wellspring of their bountiful brains
to flower the fruit of freedom
as they produce some produce for the production of power.
Rainbow children from
Purple Braves to Blue Bengals to an Electric Eagle Queen
reap the benefits of tilling tough turf for tomorrow's treasures
as mission men like Michael Coleman
continue to spread the Good News of living off the land
while Ben Burkett harnesses that Petal power
to battle the ever-present pack of white wolves
constantly shape-shifting the rules and sheering the sheep
while fleecing the noble cowhands of their cash cattle
or poets turned planters like Jeff Gibson weave seeds like words
into a poetic pollination of each-one-teach-one so that fields never fade
or agronomic activists like Carlton Turner play
the black-bottom blues in the sharp key of sovereignty so that
the art of agriculture continues to be a psalm of liberation.

Us from dirt rise like mustard seeds and acorns
into a full forest of freedom fighters fending and feeding,
becoming militant magnolias, obstinate oaks, and Nigra flowers
unwilling to bend to the will of wicked winds.
Planted in righteous soil, they are the tree that shall not be moved,
providing fruit to those hungry for independence.

[1] Title inspired by Jackson, MS, Hip Hop group Us from Dirrt (Undefinable Sounds from Divine Inspiration of Rhyme and Rhythmic Thought)
[2] Reference to Fields Watered with Blood: Critical Essays on Margaret Walker edited by Dr. Maryemma Graham
[3] Quote by Thomas Boyd, John Boyd, Jr.'s grandfather
[4] Farmers Home Administration
[5] Michelle Obama's Let's Move! Healthy Foods Initiative
[6] Dr. Cindy Ayers Elliot
[7] Foot Print Farms of Jackson, Mississippi, founded by Dr. Cindy Ayers Elliot
[8] Male and Female Donkey

Dr. Liseli A. Fitzpatrick

Liseli A. Fitzpatrick, Ph.D. is a Trinidadian poet and professor of African Cosmologies and Sacred Ontologies in the Africana Studies Department at Wellesley College, MA. Her penchant for poetry is driven by her deep-rooted desire to effect emancipatory change in the co-creation of an equitable, compassionate, just, and breathable world. Love, ancestral reverence, embodied wisdom, nature and liberation are central themes in her work. In 2018, Fitzpatrick made history as the first Ph.D. in African American and African Studies at The Ohio State University. She is a 2019 Furious Flower Poetry Center fellow, and a member of the Wintergreen Women Writers' Collective. Fitzpatrick's writings, which she dubs "poetry for the people's sake" is fueled by her resolute spirit and unshakable love for life.

Her most recent publications appear in the *About Place Journal* and *Chicken Soup for the Soul®* special issue *I'm Speaking Now*. Fitzpatrick currently has forthcoming publications in the *A (Re)Turn to the African Girl—(Re)Defining African Girlhood Studies* edited collection, *Feminists Speak Whiteness* anthology and *Black Love* special issue of *Women's Studies Quarterly*.

Amazing Grace
(For the children of John Newton)

a-maze-ing grace,
how could you
press against the necks
of my brothers
with your crooked knees
and murderous soles
and not expect your buildings
to go up in flames
black blood, and bodies
cannot breathe
    because of the
    nauseating odor
    of injustice and
    ulcerated ozones

a-maze-ing grace, how
bitter the sound of bullets...
and sirens and black male bodies
crying out for their mommies
because 46-year-old black men
    know that life is ordained in the womb
    and not the rib cage
    and mother and God
    are the same

a-maze-ing grace, how
could you kneel before God
and demand that the world
saves your skin from its own cancers
and paper-thin fragility
    see, the God we serve lives in us
    and commands the Sun, and orders
    lightning to strike without warning
    because salvation has no afterlife

see, freedom deferred
is never good

it festers and erupts
like a corpse in the sun

       oya and shango know this
       nanny, nat, cudjoe, harriet,
       malcolm, martin, toni, jimmy
       angela, assata, stokely,
       garvey, fannie, butler,
       knew this,
              we know this.

a-maze-ing grace,
how sweet the sound
of swift justice, oh Lorde,
how sweet the sound
      of justice!

seen and heard
(for little black girls)

in my world

little black girls

are born

to be seen

and heard

to defy docility

to look up

and see themselves

in the face of the Moon

in the mystery, magic and

mysticism of night

to climb trees and

break glass ceilings
to open doors and
walk in light
and not shadows
because little black girls
are l i g h t
little black girls
are l i g h t
black girls
are l i g h t
girls are l i g h t
are l i g h t
l i g h t

"reach the reacher"
(For Val Gray Ward, Queenola Valeria)

she is an altar
a gathering of
offerings and
sacred sacrifice
    the sweet sweat
    of our harvest
    a fruit basket
she quilts us
into the rhapsody
of her breathing
into the syncopated
patterned pieces
and patches
of her textured memories
hues of Langston, Jimmy,

Jimmy's mother, her mother,
my mother, our fathers,
Gwendolyn, Mari, Sonia,
Aminah, Toni, Endesha,
Margaret Walker, Margaret Burroughs,
Mu'Kai, Kenneth, Rhonda,
Akintola, Sheree, Cheryl, Terry, Nora,
Inonge, Yumekia, Soyini, Kimya, Frannie,
Doris, Marva, Harold, Tyrone, Kanya,
Marilyn, Paulette, Barbara, Hoyt,
Useni, Haki, Fahamisha, Pemon, Maséqua,
Julie, Ron, Nguvu, Fannie and Nikki
Norma, Alice, Joanne, Ginney,
Wintergreen Sisters,
Daddy Francis, Babatu
    Mound Bayou's Sunshine
    Queenola Valeria
    Syracuse, Harlem,
    Chicago, Ohio
she is Kuumba
Black theatre
FESTAC
flowing through the veins
of Black Folk
— a prayer, a spark
"Black art is Black Life"
fish call her Mother/sister
Oshun/Yemonja
    we ascend upon her tongue
    like an ancient melody
memory — an island, a continent, a spark
"My Soul is a Witness"
portal/prophet/ sister/daughter
creator/creation
we have loved each other, deeply, always, all ways... interwoven
we never knew yet we have always known
that we were one
    God ...

Paulette Pennington Jones

Paulette Pennington Jones, Professor Emerita at Olive Harvey College, one of the City Colleges of Chicago, was born in Bronzeville on the Southside of Chicago. She was an undergraduate and graduate student of English and Rhetoric at the University of Illinois Champaign-Urbana during the Black Power on campus movement 1962-1972. Pennington Jones also studied at the University of Pittsburgh and the University of Chicago.

Her poetry, performance, and literary output have always been inextricably associated with our people, our places, our global African diaspora. Professor Pennington Jones' research involves the entire spectrum of the Chicago, national, and international Black Arts Movement, particularly spotlighting Amiri Baraka. Her work is published in several magazines, anthologies, and she is the author of *Checklist for Theatre Quarterly: No. 18 Amiri Baraka, London 1978*.

Flying African Survival Song for Roi
flying african survival song for baba j. roi jones

part i
big baba roi rocking

this
this is
this is a
this is a flying
this is a flying african
this is a flying african survival
this is a flying african survival song
this is a flying african survival song for roi

in the beginning
was the word
and the word was love
and the word was life
and we became the word
in nommo spirit
we rise
in nommo spirit

we fly
the energies are coalesced
the manifestation of love, of life

we be
in our blues
the sky became
effervescent rare essence
the sky became
the vehicle
upon which
the mauve winds whisper
decided to fly
soaring, sailing
winding a midnight calm
the greens
of ourselves as sustenance
we nurture and nourish our own
power/force rises
on blinking butterfly wings
the greening of ourselves
became the raffia grasses
that we dance upon
our mauve winds
and water waves
with caribbean rhythms
reggae 'long nommo way
zooming
transforming
ringing
winding
zinging
yeah, red
the lips of our mothers
the red red lips of our mother's mouth
on malcolm's strong neck
on roi's strong neck
on our men
me and my sisters smile

and the survival
became easier
got a new rhythm
decided to go out on friday night
and thought we would
we could stretch out on faith
magnanimous clarinet playing

big baba roi rocking
magnanimous trumpet mouth playing
classroom text
the guerrilla teacher learning
the guerrilla student teaching
deep in the bush
high on the mountain
all across the continent
close to the delivery of instruction
keep the sacred lip
unbruised yet blushed with
the sunsets of fire
in qunu flaming hope
spear of the nation
at the golden close of day

shooting star griot
the lover roi
wailing the blues of baraka
in his own kind of way

wailing the theme of xhosa
wailing the theme of soweto
wailing the theme of the transkei
singing a thembu royal song
singing nkosi si kelele
marching through the whole of south africa

marching from robben island
on the long long walk to freedom
on the finite road to johannesburg
on the long road to guinea
in his own kind of way
the sway sashay
of a black man's sartorial splendor
flying no jet stream to pollute the land
up, up, and away
over oceans, returning to waters warm
filled with bones and no mystery

no misery striding to the boat
body waters in rhythm,
in synch, in the pocket
in king's horseman's style
big bold brave
hathaway body sway way
languid lagoon hurricane man j. roi
his motion fluffs the tall prairie grasses
heads toward the horizon of open sea
transforms into rushing oceans

being tilted on the axis of the
african world
you represent yourself
your parents
miss rosalie brown, mr robert carwell
your family, your daughters, eboni and indigo
your brothers sonny, bob, michael, jonathan,
your sisters carol, deedee, lisa,
your cousins, especially lucky, your crew,
the low end, your loves, your lovers, your haters,
your entire gorgeous race
africans all
bringing the good news
good god news

speaking the language
the pentacostal language
talking loud and saying something
speaking tongues that people understand
understanding his people

after marching,
after protesting,
after voting,
after surviving,
speaking after death,
speaking through life,
through living,
through being
through being black,
over oceans
speaking after being lynched
after being kneed,
after being shot,
after war,
speaking police knowledge
defining racism
speaking good news
of the ancestors
speaking in tongues
talking loud saying something

big baba roi rocking
fela's mice elf through low
through high
through low law
roars soars home

talking about survival
talking about a rainbow
talking about a nommo

a rainbow nommo
a rainbow nommo brother
the colors of our people
as in our brownness
as in our blackness
and in the blackness of our nommo spirit
the candle flame flickers
the afro cuban heart beats
the levitation
rushes to the rise
and baba j. roi jones has survived
in   us   all
singing roi's flying
singing roi's flying african
singing roi's flying african survival
singing roi's flying african survival song

Flying African Survival Song for Roi
flying african survival song for baba j. roi jones

part ii
state of grace segment

when the day is bronze and the sorrow is full
the moon always follows the sun
contemplate family, heritage, and faith
o comfort and the moon always follows the sun
forever we shall mount up with wings
as eagles singing and flying
from the black pool of genius
when the day is bronze and the sorrow is full
this is our lineage, our legacy
sing our favorite song

our
kush king ancestor from centuries ago
pharoah roi draped in cowrie shells
wings moving fast
when the day is bronze and the sorrow is full
this is our lineage, our legacy
your favorite song
our yes

yes,
as the world, the whirl spins around
keep your self respect
your manly amen pride
assentient stride a tall rah walk
(you better)
build your dreams to the sky

mauve winds sway
in issy-les-moulineau,
april breeze rains
at haynes in paris eating and singing soul food
in gustavia on saint barts lobster
yes, taino and arawak people frequent
marigot harbor on saint martin
yeah,
panama and the black builder's canal
un huh,
cozumel where trees grow through buildings
greens and blues
chillin' in chicago
boppin' in acapulco and in baby'o's
where in the world? is la perla?
yup,
the magnifique markets in dakar
marché artisanal de soumbédioune
even genuine marché kermel

you bet,
on goree isle and its young basketball players
winning the game seizing the day concurring in life
sure,
in elevators high in
banjul agreeing to the affirmative
positively free from doubt in serrekunda
hearing indubitable black men
readers of the koran on latenight tv

true that at
swanson's villa in mobay
swimmin' pool dippin' and slippin'
to harmonious homes back up in the hill
big baba roi rocking
without question
leaping on the stage with the dancers in brooklyn
resolute in raffia ribbon grass
sweet basil
on pullen keyboards and skirts afire
baraka at the bar cools the play down
village vanguard drinking milk in the back room
slugs and pharoah doesn't sleep
shep plays while floyd nods
la famille in harlem stepping to the last dance
st. nicholas' pub be definitely good
an uncaged lion's song and donald's absolutely unchained piano
s.o.b.'s and gil shows on time, victor and brian ready
already rollin' blue note sarah's mike is swiped
in eileen's zebra room a traveling revolution
by all means
this uprising on tour

  crawford's grill no recording not at the bar
  velvet lounge drinking/ordering tea and   sunrise
  chez george yassa chicken, puree vegetable soup
  and the jukebox spinning in puerto vallarta

ipso facto jammin' to stevie's ngiculela-es una historia- i am singing
roi you became this melody
20/20 solid rhythm in the pocket in the apple
in santiago in the iris jazz club
in the mountains of the sierra madre
frolicking in banderas bay
remain in havana expecting the best
around the corner and down the steps to la zorra y el cuervo
roi you became this melody
this uprising on tour
magnanimous digeridoo playing while walking
wishing wooden flute playing piping
soprano saxophone while parading
digeridoo, wooden flute, soprano saxophone
certain solemn parade
god is blessing you
mama lottie it's all true

hang onto the world
the floodgates are open
as it spins around
water water all around
things are moving fast
waves abound
tall pyramid water water all around
encircling   crashing   waves abound
from which   we we will we'll arise and go in peace
soaring flying sailing singing
someday we'll all be free

because donny hathaway
and you will come with sound
seizing winning life as
some, not all, sum of life
turning.point.life
arise
arise and go

in peace
flying singing
bursting
the floodgates are open
water water all around
waves abound
tall sky scraper pyramid
water water all around
kush king from centuries ago
black blueblack blue safe harbor
ebb and flowing deep consistency
we you us weusi
with serious abundance of assurance
in water and words ebb and flow indigo
recessional/processional percussion
o prodigious storm
through the storm
through the night
leading on to the eboni light

thank you for building ritual…
pharoah roi draped in cowrie shells
tall spirit warrior man
sing unto the lord
for he has triumphed gloriously
horse and rider thrown into the sea
we expand our minds
with a sankofa coltrane testimony
roi you are the opening act
baba j. roi jones you are the headliner
j. roi you are the after party

surviving in us all
singing in a state of grace
a flying
a flying african
a flying african survival

a flying african survival song

for us all
for us all
for us all

emmett till saga

the assassination of emmett till
              part I: to assassinate the assassination
              superheroes revenge by hebru brantley

know your heritage
shape your future

the sun was shining in blood bright money, mississippi
the clouds were not summer, but ominous grey in chicago, illinois

two adults attacked one child
came into his cousins' house
his southern summertime camp
vamped a horror unspeakable unknown
on a child used to kid's games used to fun running and eating the day long
with a song children's marbles checkers cracking jokes don't prevent a homicide
or stop a murder
only we grown folks can

a train ride that crosses the mason-dixon line
from mccosh elementary to a resting space in burr oak cemetery we share
this experience with his mother our mother
his father our father who art in heaven
lynched on a tree on calvary

acquitted of admitted crime
recanted lightening white courtroom lie
a nine year old girl remembers the remains
an eight year old boy studies the decades old case
and interviews our community
tallahatchie is a choctaw name meaning rock of waters meaning river of sharp rocks barbed wire
discarded cotton gin fan
the natives knew before the sin
there is a darkened casket filled room for him in our national african american museum
of culture and history in a home church way

extrajudicial violence
enforcement of jim crow mores evident green pickup truck
black bayou bridge
chicago boy, three days later
a body abhorrent
the incident a yellow lynching
a red mississippi trying to maintain white supremacy through murder

images of till's boy body
prints in the chicago defender
views jet magazine at a. a. rayner funeral home
attends thousands at roberts temple church of god in christ
free death in the free state of tallahatchie

to assassinate the assassination
history present
unspeakable, but not untold

from emmett till road
west 71st street
south side chicago

the assassination of emmett till
>
> part II: history present
> for franklin ward
> eight years old
> who innocently asked "could this happen now?"

it's 1955 i'm back in chicago from korea discharged from the army been through fort sheridan through camp polk in louisiana it's news on the radio, the sunday sun-times, news, news, news whispering through the streets of the southside
i'm brother emanuel bell
history present

it's 1955 i'm a new graduate of the wonderful wendell phillips senior high school when his mother bravely decided on an open casket i'm totally devastated this hot august watching the reports on television i decide to go see him i'm not married yet, not a travel agent yet, standing in a line because he's younger than me
my sister winifred, we call her winnie, knew his mother mamie
mamie till bradley in 1960 when she graduates from chicago teacher's college after her son was tortured by terrorists mutilated in 1955 now she's in graduation photos
cap and gown grown
cruel hot august still on her mind and mine
i'm sister glenda hunter
history present

it's 1955 i'm no longer living at 638 east 38th place in the newly constructed ida b. wells homes projects first negroes belonging 39th street kids me and my sister-girl phyllis bracy james, but i'm married three years now when we hear the whispers, negroes got the news first, gossip then radio words, it happened down south, way down south in money, mississippi but the whole world was at his services on 40th street under the el robert's temple church of god in christ casket open to see a crying living shame
i'm sister mary johnson
history present

it's 1955 i'm getting off from the evening shift at r.r. donnelly's at midnight my co-worker and i decide to go down to a.a. rayner on 43rd and cottage grove

to see, lines as far as you could see, to view the body 24 hour lines, to
see terrible, terrible to see, sorry to see, as far as you could see shocking
to everybody everywhere real hatred real prejudice they didn't like no
niggers none he was an african american boy killed for nothing, his
uncle's trauma for nothing, his mother's agony for nothing, his cousins'
shock and our misery for nought karma will catch up she was a white
woman unbelievable, said he was a black man like james baldwin i
never wanted to be white
i'm mother frankie davis
history present

it's 1955 i'm with my family, my brother and my sister, all alive and
well, in the city of chicago, illinois straight out of the city of houston,
mississippi there where the blood bright mississippi delta leads the
nation in lynchings, tallachatchie is a choctaw name meaning rock of
waters meaning river of sharp rocks barbed wire & discarded cotton gin
fan near the old natchez trace 62 years ago they assassinated a young
black man emmett till yes, i remember his name yes i'm gonna make it
i'm mother bessie edmondson
history present

hear now
here now emmett till
history present

circa 2017
blackwell israel samuel african methodist episcopal zion church

hello as much as goodbye

for val's daughter mukai

the tenor saxophone player
is a girl
a woman
is femme
with a grand piano soul
sound massive

big band strong still
out of the strong south amazing
migrating throng this world wide volume
house of music monk epistrophy
house band gallops
playing her smile up
riffing her laugh gallop up
sixteen teen age mukai
all hands clap and scat
transition to another rhythm
au revoir city sounds brass strutting
stepping chi style

blue light dawns and a hand full of stars
scatter for mukai's smile alive and well
her laughter rings planets
comets called
come by her laugh more hello
than goodbye
as much then as now
as much uber as jitney
criss cross as much as joe turner's come and gone
more bonjour than au revoir

women do the heavy lifting
in ancient and modern african grace
as now just change the rhythm
justice evidence of harmonica sirens
turn off the cops with emts
gabriel's trombone duet right and left
horns blare blown galaxy sound
monk turning turning bringing it
all back
as much hola as alto
as much ciao as ciao
as much hello as goodbye

circa winter 2018

VAL GRAY WARD AND FRANCIS WARD

Val Gray Ward and Francis Ward are an iconic husband-and-wife team and indefatigable activists in the Black Arts Movement, in Chicago, nationally, and internationally.

Val Gray Ward is an internationally acclaimed dramatist-historian, producer, director, educator, and cultural activist who is known throughout the world as "The Voice of the Black Writer." Ward was born Queenola Valeria Ward in the oldest all-Black town in the U.S., Mound Bayou, Mississippi. She is famously recognized for her ritual and staged theatre productions; one-woman shows, *Harriet Tubman* and *My Soul is a Witness*; and popularizing the works of celebrated and lesser-known prolific black writers through her sensitive interpretations. In 1968, Ward founded Chicago's pioneering Black theatre, Kuumba Theatre, with the active support of her husband Francis Ward, their children, and the community. In 1969, Ward opened the door as the inaugural director of the Afro-American Cultural Center at the University of Illinois Champaign-Urbana. Ward is the recipient of over 200 awards including several lifetime-achievement awards, 21 Emmys® for her edu-tainment film *Precious Memories: Strolling 47th Street*, and a Grammy® nomination for her tribute CD *rhapsody in Hughes 101* honoring the life and legacy of Langston Hughes. The soon-to-be nonagenarian is still giving edifying lectures and electrifying virtual performances.

Francis Ward is a veteran journalist and professor emeritus of journalism at Syracuse University. Ward was born Usher Francis Ward in Atlanta, Georgia. He is an alum of Morehouse College and Syracuse University, where he earned his B.A. in English and M.A in Journalism, respectively. Ward is a former associate editor of *Jet* and assistant editor of *Ebony*, and co-founder of the National Association of Black Journalists (NABJ). In 1968, he joined the staff of the *Chicago Sun-Times* and later became the Midwest correspondent in Chicago bureau of the *Los Angeles Times*. In 1978, Ward went over to the *Miami Herald* and, in 1980, WHUT-TV at Howard University. In 1984, Ward entered the mayor's press corps, in Chicago, as an Assistant Press Secretary, working through the Harold Washington and Eugene Sawyer administrations. After a brief teaching stint at the Medill School of Journalism at Northwestern, he was hired, in 1990, by the Newhouse School of Journalism at his alma mater Syracuse University. Ward has been a pillar of support for his wife, Val, whom he met, in 1965. Ward is now happily enjoying his retirement.

THE BLACK ARTIST—HIS ROLE IN THE STRUGGLE

The current phase of the black liberation struggle, this newest Black Power-Black Consciousness stage, successor to the old civil rights movement, is, without a doubt, the most profound and meaningful period of this century for black Americans. No period has produced such sustained political and social militancy among blacks; no period has been such a significant break with the old, stereotyped, white-oriented past; no period has so emphatically validated our glorious African past, as well as our cultural and racial beauty and life-styles. And no previous period has held such uncertainty for the black future. In fact, never in the Afro-American past has it ever been so convincingly uncertain whether we do in fact have a future in the white Western world.

If black Americans decide they do have a future in the white world, the wise prognostication will attempt to forecast no further than the next ten years. These will be pivotal, climactic years, for it will be decided in this decade of the 1970s whether blacks will cease to exist as a people in this country, whether they will discover real freedom and dignity, achieve a cordial accommodation with white people. Whether a state of permanent hostility shall exist between white and non-white peoples in the Western hemisphere. Whenever I talk about the future, it will be this decade I'm referring to. It isn't safe to venture a prediction beyond that.

One fact of that future has already been settled. This concerns the leadership, planning and execution of the liberation struggle, particularly in this century, has centered around one man or a group of men who were vested with charisma, strong abilities and minds, and dedication to the cause which propelled them out front as either the spokesmen for black people or the embodiment of their struggle.

This was true up to April 4, 1968. The shot in Memphis ended all that. In fact, the period of the "noble Negro leader" was headed for extinction anyway, for Martin Luther King, Jr., even if he had lived, would have been the last of the so-called "responsible Negro leaders and spokesmen," titles bestowed on us by white people. The period of sustained militancy and heightened struggle in which blacks have engaged the past five years has lessened the role of the old, familiar "leaders" such as King or Roy Wilkins, and increased the stature and importance of previously lesser known, but strategically placed, men and women whose major contributions to the history of the period and struggle was that they happened to be at the right place at the right time. If there is one lesson that the post-civil rights period has taught us, it is that those most likely to shape the destiny of black

Americans in the next decade are activists and artists, who may possess additional skills as organizers.

When discussing the black artist and his role, we must begin by dispelling the false notion that an artist is an artist, no matter what his color, and that being black imposes no special responsibility on him. Though some black performers deny it, being black does have a particular meaning to the life and work of all black people, artists included, despite instances in which black people have overcome the barriers imposed by racism and achieved a measure of personal success.

Some black artists may have adopted purely Euro-American ways, may have the greatest appreciation for Western culture and values, or have been thoroughly inculcated (brainwashed, in other words) with the white, Western viewpoint. Even so, his Western inculcation cannot wipe away the subjective sense of rhythm, timing, speech and movement that his black culture environment instilled within him. The black artist may not even be aware of the extent to which blackness has influenced him, but in critical situations, the influence will inevitably surface. To the extent that any black artist hides from or denies his African or African-American roots, his courage, honesty and dignity as an artist suffer.

How, then, does the artist react if he does admit to influences of being black? Does blackness impose special responsibilities or limitations?

If the black artist is special by virtue of color, does he have to "act black" or "think black" or somehow express his blackness in his every utterance, movement or work? The simple answer to these questions is no; his blackness will express itself, consciously or unconsciously. The crucial issue underlying these and related questions is the artist's own definition of himself and his work. The issue has been debated by black and white artists for decades, maybe longer; whether art exists for its own sake, or is there a related, higher purpose to one's art. If the artist accepts the first definition, art for art's sake, then he believes his work is its own justification and cannot be subject to any external considerations, or variations other than what he himself chooses to impose.

A second school of thought argues that art, like any other aspect of life, is influenced by the artist's own culture and background, and the current conditions of his expression of life as he sees and feels it. Therefore, a Jewish painter reared in Czarist Russia, for example, cannot help but bring the influences of his life to his canvasses. The same is true of a black American, living under the lash of white racism. What else should he be expected to reflect in his art but the feelings of a victim of racist oppression?

This realization seems logical, but did not become a distinct fact of life for black artists until the Harlem Renaissance, from 1919 to about 1931. There were good and great black artists before then but few, if any, distinguished themselves as "black" or "race" artists, preferring instead to be guided by the prevailing standards of art for art's sake.

With the coming of Harlem Renaissance, the volume, quality and nature of black arts changed—from "mainstream American" to distinctly black art, with obvious, conscious emphasis on racial themes and pride, and with a new fusion of art with the political and social struggles of the day.

This NEW conceptualization of the role and responsibility of the black artist has tremendous import for the black present and future. It was no accident that Garvey-type black nationalism developed during the 1920s as the handmaiden of the Harlem Renaissance. Similarly, it is no accident that, in the late 1960s the cry for black liberation, black culture and identity are inseparable, products of the same source: an intense pride in being black. Black pride and black power are based on the same premise:

- All of America's institutions are racist to the core;
- The political powerlessness of black people – best symbolized by their colonization in big city ghettoes – is directly related to the racism of the white power structure;
- That powerlessness, a political phenomenon, has been rationalized by a set of theories of black inferiority, black laziness, black ugliness, black docility. In other words, a people with no sense of pride, heritage or value in being themselves;
- These theories have been validated by a white man's history and social science which justify and glorify white Western economic and political hegemony world-wide;
- Black economic and political power – its theory, if not the fact – rest on a broad amalgam of ideas which reject the entire white Western interpretation of history, thereby providing the basis for a new politics, a new culture, a new economics and a new psychology of black consciousness and pride;
- A rejection of the old history and standards which would redefine the meaning of black existence, past and present.

With the advent of the black power movement, the black artist assumed a new role. The artist became the re-interpreter of the black past, the redefiner of the black present, and the analyst of the black future. He became the creator of a new blackness which has made the most significant break with the past of any generation of Afro-Americans. Since the black artist is central to the re-interpretation of the past, he must be central to the building of a new future.

In the future, I can see the black artist fulfilling six major roles:
1. creator;
2. critic (social and artistic);
3. propagandist;
4. activist;
5. hero figure to young blacks;
6. fund-raiser.

Let's discuss each one of these.

<u>The Black Artist as Creator</u>—The artist will "do his thang" to the best of his ability and commitment. He'll continue to write, paint, act, sing, dance, photograph, play and compose. The crucial difference will be that his reasons for engaging in his art—the standards governing his involvement and the kind of art he seeks to create—will be radically different from the old ones. As has been indicated before, black art of the future won't be art for art's sake, but will be based on a new fusion with the lives and times of black people.

If an artist or writer seriously probes the lives and varying moods of black people, the material he would find would be endless. He would not have worry about variety and being "caught in the stereotyped bag," as some critics of black artists have charged. While on the point of black artists being "stereotyped," we can't go further without laying to rest that most ancient—and preposterous criticism of black artists: that they aren't "universal." Briefly, the argument goes that black artists can't be black and universal at the same time; that, to conform to "universal" standards, black artists cannot treat black subjects exclusively but must move beyond race in their work to some mythical human (non-black) understanding.

Those who argue this point of view miss two obvious, but very essential points. First, their definition of "universal" is not that at all. It is a white, Western standard they are talking about—not one which derives its essence from a collection of thought from all over the world. Their universality is not so cosmopolitan that, say, students and critics in Japan, or Korea, India, or Ghana, Brazil or China would accept its verdicts the same as students in France, England or the United States. When the white critic talks of "universality," he means those forms, subjects and habits common to the white Western world, the United States, Great Britain,

Western Europe and Australia.

What the critics ought to realize is that it is they—white Westerners—who are not universal, if we take the meaning of the word literally. The world is three-fourths non-white. How, then, do white critics and students of the arts assume the arrogance, the pure gall, to presuppose that themes drawn from the lives, culture and traditions of the world's majority are somehow not universal?

Secondly, if an artist draws his inspiration only from black people on the South Side of Chicago, is it not possible that South Side blacks are just as human and have just as much to add to the totality of the human condition as the Jews in the works of Philip Roth or Saul Bellow or the Irishmen in the works of James Joyce and Sean O'Casey? The experience portrayed is both limited and universal, if one understands it—as with any other nation's expression.

The new fusion of black art with the politics of black life does not demand that the black artist consistently, without fail, every time he creates, argue the moral superiority of anything, blackness included; nor flail away at the white man in every poem, novel, play, song or picture. There may not even have to always be conflict between "the honky" and black people. In short, blackness demands from the artist, a consistent honesty, a truth to his being, and the fulfillment to his obligation of being black. If these standards are obeyed, his range of subjects and themes will be limitless, and his universality never in question.

The Black Artist as Critic—This role naturally follows from being an honest, truthful creator. Black artists dealing with the realities of the black condition, and white condition, are strong, forceful critics, indeed. One could argue that their criticism need go no further. However, it must go further. The artist must be a self-critic. The artist must be certain that his visions of life, as it is and as he would like to see it, are so accurately and clearly defined that those who view or listen to his work can share his vision. If the artist is to be crucial to the building of a new future, he has the responsibility to outline and advocate those laws, standards and values he feels are necessary to that future. The artist must a visionary, a social analyst, the guardian of sacred morals and traditions, the teacher, the questioner and/or foe of those people, practices or habits which do not belong to the new, revitalized blackness.

The Artist as Propagandist—This function can engage us in discussion for a lifetime. It goes right to the heart of what academic purists call non-ideological art and scholarship. Their argument is that art and scholarship must be pursued without the imposition of ideological considerations, which, if felt, will prejudice their results and jeopardize their integrity.

The non-ideological argument has essentials which, I agree, are useful to blacks. However, its application doesn't prevent black artists from fulfilling their roles of propagandists. That role comes naturally if the artist is true to his subjects as he honestly sees and feels them. Any good writer, for example, who lays bare the sickness of Western society, or the brutality of white Western man, is a good propagandist for the liberation struggle, perhaps unconsciously or unintentionally. There are legitimate limitations to this role and the artist must define his own line of demarcation between artistic fulfillment and the obligation as propagandist. Let me point out that the liberation struggle does not demand that every single principle of Western society be jettisoned, but that it be revalued in terms of its usefulness to the struggle, and to the new black future. The crucial idea to remember is that the current status of the black condition demands the obligation be met in some way by the artist.

The artist is morally bound to take up the cause of black liberation in his work, some perhaps more than others, but all to some degree. This assumption rests on two arguments: (1) That no black artist can be true to himself, having been born, reared and shaped by white Western (racist) institutions, without dealing with racism and, at least, by implication, the black liberation struggle. If he is to reflect those forces and values which gave him his being, his vision of the world, how can he avoid dealing with that world from his point of view and remain honest? (2) Although artistic freedom allows the artist a choice of subjects, moods and themes to treat, that freedom does not permit him to skirt the responsibility to black people and, in a larger sense, of all mankind. If there is any limitation on the artist's right to choose his medium, subjects and level of work, it is the overriding imperative of his own freedom as a person, his manhood, and the sacredness of his life as well as the lives of those he purports to explore and influence.

<u>The Black Artist as Activist</u>—The activist role has a practical as well as creative side. Practically, the black artist, like other black people, may one day have to engage himself in the struggle for sheer physical survival. He may have to pick up the gun and use it. If not that, he may be thrust into the position, at any moment in time, of being the chief planner or theorist for a particular phase of the revolutionary warfare. Even if these eventualities don't occur, the artist, from time to time, needs the exhilaration, the warmth, the education of personal contact with things happening in the street.

Creatively, if the artist is to capture the feeling and spirit of those critical movements among black people, he must be there. He must be a part of them, among and of the people doing the shooting, the burning, the dying, whatever and wherever the action is. The black artist must sometimes become a reporter, not merely a statistical recorder of deeds, but an accurate reporter and interpreter of those deeds for the sake of an accurate historical record. He may record them as part of his art. Whatever his level of commitment and methods, the black artist must be involved. For activism is a critical part of that black life which he must live, know and explore and interpret. However, it should be added that being in touch with brothers and sisters everywhere, whether they are on the corner, in the bars, in the park or directly acting in the struggle, is a critical phase of the artist's preparation for creation, and of his "re-creation" (spiritually) for further creation (artistically).

The Black Artist as Hero-figure to Young Blacks—The role, relatively minor now, but which will grow in importance, has not been thrust upon some black artists. Perhaps it never will be. But it is important to discuss, however, because of the value of the artist's place in the building and shaping of the black future, and the uniqueness of the hero-figure in black life in America, especially the cities.

Outside of those image-figures young people find within their own families, the most popular hero-figures to young blacks have been athletes. Though their value to black children and as black hero-figures is grossly and dishonestly inflated by white people—particularly newsmen—the hero-figure, nevertheless, does have a place in the life of black people, if only to serve as a symbol of healthy adulthood. Black athletes, for the most part, were never the clean livers, and good Christians they were pictured to be. In real life, they were most frequently the opposite.

The black artist, because of the increasing importance of his place in the emerging black communities across the land, may find himself thrust into the position of being one of the most popular, respected hero-figures by young blacks. If one examines the popularity of Ameer Baraka, or Don L. Lee, leader of a new school of militant young black poets; or of James Baldwin, Gwendolyn Brooks, Larry Neal in New York, or Gaston Neal in Washington, D.C., one would find elements of the black artist already emerging as a hero-figure. The artist, through his work and personal example of discipline, will assuredly have its positive effect on young people.

The Black Artist as Fund-raiser—Most black artists have already been doing this for some time and shall continue to do it with increasing regularity. It is also part of the artist's life and commitment to black people and their struggle. The amount of time devoted to causes will vary from artist to artist. Their activities will vary, depending on their talents and time. While some painters may find themselves selling some of their works and donating the proceeds to the community museum that sponsored the art show, black poets, or actors or singers may find themselves performing, without charge, at rallies in behalf of a worthwhile cause.

The artist as fund-raiser again raises the question of whether artistic freedom is somehow threatened and/or lessened by the demands of a rising social consciousness. To those harboring such fears or doubts, a short, but timely reminder: The burgeoning social consciousness which black artists express through their efforts to sustain worthy causes through find-raising, should not be seen as a burden on their creativity, but as an opportunity to expand their understanding of people and things via increased contacts.

What kind of future can black people expect? The uncertainty of the black future is created by the uncertainty of the white response to black demands for liberation. In the interplay of demands and response, these facts are clear: black people will settle for nothing less than total liberation, white people will concede nothing without a demand. White people, given the options of black liberation or black extermination, may choose the latter, if they are led to believe that extermination of blacks will cause them no great sacrifice, and that this is the only way to handle "the problem".

The timing of the black future will be determined by the degree to which demands for liberation are met. However, which of the two options white people choose to exercise and how soon will be left up to the black people, for the choice and exercise of either option will depend ultimately on the intensity of the black struggle, how much is demanded from whites and how soon. In this sense we blacks will ultimately determine our own future—or if we'll have one.

With the conflict clearly drawn, the future of black people in America seems to be limited to either repressions, genocide, continued hostility, radical separatism as a form of tenuous co-existence, migration to a motherland, or simply social and political stagnation—where we do little or nothing and just hope for a solution to the problems of race and class, in other words, Moynihan's "benign neglect".

Is there reason to hope for a just solution? Does a just solution seem imminent? Both answers are no, for an affirmative answer to either must be based on an honest assessment that the white power structure is changing fundamentally and accepting the inevitability of sharing power, wealth and freedom with non-whites. No such assumption can be made now, and yet it is this very change—in white people, white people with power—that must be essence of a just, orderly and free society for blacks and whites.

If the black artist has a dilemma, it is that, despite his realization of the black burden and white responsibility, he must address himself primarily to black people at the present time. He cannot talk to the white power structure because it won't listen to him and because his primary responsibility is to black people and their plight.

The task of educating the white power structure of this country to morality and reason rests with white people, particularly white artists and teachers. For them and all well-meaning whites (whoever and wherever they are): their job is not to seek work, or understanding or chances for study among black people, but to exert their energies changing the minds and hearts of white people. Changes inside the hearts and heads of the power elite at Chase Manhattan Bank, General Motors, the Pentagon or the White House are worth far more to black people than all the changes that white missionaries could ever dream of making in Harlem, Chicago, Watts, Africa or anywhere else in the Third World.

MEGHA SOOD

Megha Sood is a Pushcart-nominated award winning poet, editor, author, and literary activist based in New Jersey, USA. She is an Associate Poetry Editor at MookyChick (UK), Life and Legends (USA), and Literary Partner in the project "Life in Quarantine" with Stanford University. Works featured in journals include Poetry Society of New York, NPR, PBS American Portrait, WNYC Studios, *American Writers Review, Kissing Dynamite, Rising Phoenix Review*, and many more. Sood is the author of a chapbook, *My Body is Not an Apology* (Finishing Line Press, 2021) and a full length collection, *My Body Lives Like a Threat* (FlowerSongPress, 2021). She is the Co-Editor of anthologies *The Medusa Project* (Mookychick) and *The Kali Project* (Indie Blu(e) Press). Sood is the recipient of a 2021 MVICW fellowship (Martha's Vineyard Institute of Creative Writing) and a 2020 National Level Winner Spring Mahogany Lit Prize. She is the recipient of a "Certificate of Excellence" from the Mayor of Jersey City and is a three-time state-level winner of the NJ Poetry Contest.

Asphyxiated

Inspired by the death of Gambian British photographer Khadija Mohammadou Saye who was killed in the Grenfell Tower Fire in 2017. The survivors of Grenfell are still awaiting justice, while the official inquiry refuses to recognize the systemic racism of social inequality and institutional response as contributing to the disaster

They say *"Eyes are the window to the soul"*
yet yours are shut tight,
saturated with injustice and discrimination
birthing around you in every passing moment
the raging flames engulfing the last sliver
of hope;
of light,
of love
sucking out from every single soul
holding onto their dear loved ones
in that fateful tower that day.

They say, *"An artist takes in the beauty
through their eyes"*
and yet yours are closed
overwhelmed with the injustice
the raging inequality;
hoping of the day, the perfect utopia,
where everyone is blessed with the
basic privilege
to live;
to love,
to breathe.

They say, *"Eyes are the embodiment
of the soul"*
a metaphor for the muted language;
spoken between the souls
and yet yours are closed shut
averting the view from
all the hunger and greed
burning & leaving
the stench of devouring flames
a putrid stench of indifference
towards your life
They say, *"Take in the world through all your senses"*
and yet you devoid yourself

from this ethereal experience
as your world burns down from inside
screaming and whelping,
the injustice leaves welts and blisters
on your suppurating skin

When the empty words shower like
the scarring acid rain
on your open wounds
you scream,
you wail in the hollow nights
hoping for a single soul
to lend their ear
to hear you,
hear you screaming
I can't breathe!!!

Lamont Lilly

Lamont Lilly is an independent journalist, Black radical activist, poet, and community organizer based in Durham, North Carolina. His time and experiences in the ongoing Movement for Black Lives spans over a decade. From Occupy Wall Street to the Ferguson Uprising—from Standing Rock to the Baltimore Rebellion, Brother Lamont has been tirelessly engaged on the front lines. His poetry, journalism, and collective writings echo the struggles for justice and Black Liberation for this generation.

all natural

i like the kind of hair
that will stand up for its rights
the kind that kicks
screams and protests
the kind that resists
and boycotts with every coil
the kind that fights
riots and rebels

the kind that won't
be quiet for nobody
the kind that won't
be anything but black
the kind that refuses
to relax

assata: general shakur

they would like us
to forget
the likes of her sacrifices
one dark woman
well-dressed
in plaid shadows
called afro-freedom

fighting yelling teaching
staying alive
on the frontline
imprisoned exiled wounded
still living
loving her people
from the outer edges

etched within our hearts
tucked safely
within our minds
one dark woman
well-dressed
in plaid shadows
called afro-freedom

clawing scratching scraping
staying alive

on the frontline
wow what a warrior
wow what a woman
what a wonderful general
she's been

in baltimore

in baltimore
if you're black
they'll just
sprinkle some crack on you
and call it a day

call it legal
call it justice
and call an arrest

and then
when they're taking
your black ass in
to the county jail
they'll call the media
call the press

call the newspapers
so they can
call you crazy
call you guilty
and call you ghetto

what they *won't* do
is call you a minor
call your parents

call the community
so we can call you innocent
and call for your
release

nah
the police won't do that

in baltimore
if you're black
they'll just
sprinkle some crack on you
and call it a day

a full day's pay
and tomorrow?

on to somebody else's
child
and they'll be calling it
good police
work

JOANNE V. GABBIN

English professor Joanne V. Gabbin was born on February 2, 1946. She earned her B.A. degree in English from Morgan State College in Baltimore, Maryland in 1967. Gabbin then received her M.A. degree in English in 1970 and her Ph.D. degree in English and literature from the University of Chicago in Chicago, Illinois in 1980.

Gabbin began her career as an instructor of English at Roosevelt University in Chicago, Illinois in 1971. She was then hired as an assistant professor of English at Chicago State University in Chicago, Illinois in 1972, where she remained until 1974. Gabbin served as program director and instructor of Catalyst for Youth, Inc. in Chicago, Illinois from 1973 to 1975. In 1977, Gabbin became an assistant professor of English at Lincoln University. She was promoted to the position of associate professor of English in 1982. Gabbin remained in that position until 1985, when she was hired as an associate professor of English at

James Madison University in Harrisonburg, Virginia. In 1987, she helped form the Wintergreen Women Writers' Collective. Gabbin also became the director of the honors program at James Madison University in 1986 and was promoted to the position of professor of English in 1989. Gabbin organized the first academic conference on African American poetry, entitled "Furious Flower: A Revolution in African American Poetry," in 1994. She established the Furious Flower Poetry Center at James Madison University in 2005.

In addition to her work as an English professor, Gabbin also published a variety of works that included *Sterling A. Brown: Building the Black Aesthetic Tradition*, *The Furious Flowering of African American Poetry*, and *Furious Flower: African American Poetry from the Black Arts Movement to the Present*.

Gabbin was awarded the Creative Scholarship Award by the College Language Association in 1986 and, in 1988, received the Award for Scholarship from the James Madison University Faculty Women's Caucus and Women's Resource Network. She was the recipient of the Virginia State Council of Higher Education's Outstanding Faculty Award in 1993, as well as James Madison University's Provost Award for Excellence in 2004. Gabbin was given the Distinguished Faculty Award in 2005, and the Woman of Distinction Award in 2007, each from James Madison University.

In addition to her career as a professor, Gabbin served as a board member of several organizations that included the WVPT Community Board, Shenandoah Shakespeare, the Virginia Foundation for the Humanities, and Cave Canem (A Home for Black Poetry). An avid art collector, she is also the owner of the 150 Franklin Street Gallery in Harrisonburg.

Excerpt from "Introduction," Furious Flower: African American Poetry from the Black Arts Movement to the Present

Gwendolyn Brooks's literary career serves as the inspiration, the touchstone, and the genesis of the idea for this anthology. Not only did lines from her poem "The Second Sermon on the Warpland" inspire the naming of the Furious Flower Poetry Conference held in 1994 on the campus of James Madison University, the poem has provided a striking metaphor for defining and understanding African American poetry.

> The time
> cracks into furious flower. Lifts its face
> all unashamed. And sways in wicked grace.

The metaphor Gwendolyn Brooks intended to describe a tumultuous time in America during the late 1960s serves well as a trope for African American poetry. We can read into these lines the urge toward a liberating identity crowded back in the language of Phillis Wheatley, or Countee Cullen's conundrum in "Yet Do I Marvel," or Amiri Baraka's call for a black poem that "All Black People Speak Silently or LOUD." We can read into these lines a literature that mirrors the beautiful and rageful struggle of African Americans toward expression.

Until her death in December 2000, Gwendolyn Brooks was the *furious flower,* whose heroic and eloquent portraiture of the lives of black people seeded and pollinated poetic expression throughout the second half of the twentieth century. Her winning the Pulitzer Prize in 1950 opened the gates for American writers of African descent to win other major literary awards. In 1968, when the Black Arts movement was gaining strength and followers, Brooks succeeded Carl Sandburg as poet laureate of Illinois. From this position she conducted writers' workshops for the Blackstone Rangers, inspired the activities of the Organization of Black American Culture, and became a major proponent of black publishers, namely Dudley Randall's Broadside Press and Haki R. Madhubuti's Third World Press. In the 1970s, when those in the feminist-womanist movement were looking for models, Brooks had a gallery of portraits of women that were anything but monolithic. Brooks became the twenty-ninth, and final, consultant in poetry to the Library of Congress in 1985. As the first black woman to be appointed to this position, she, in Sonia Sanchez's words, "demystified the Library." In the second part of Brooks's two-part autobiography, *Report from Part Two,* she delighted in the fact that all kinds of writers, once intimidated by its "cool magnificence, had felt free to come past marble and gold to see [her]" (84).

In 1994 the author of nearly thirty books, including poetry for adults and children, *Maud Martha* (her novel), and part one of her autobiography, Brooks was showered with numerous awards: Jefferson Lecturer from the National Endowment for the Humanities, National Book Award for Distinguished Contribution to American Letters, and the Furious Flower Lifetime Achievement Award. When more than thirteen hundred people gathered in Wilson Hall on the James Madison University campus to celebrate her distinguished career and her legendary generosity, two generations had grown up nurtured and nourished by her poetry. Michael S. Harper called Brooks a pioneer who had written beautiful sonnets and ballads and after carving out that territory had used the creative process to work against the tradition to create poems such as "A Bronzeville Mother Loiters in Mississippi. Meanwhile, a Mississippi Mother Burns Bacon." Dolores Kendrick, who sees poetry as a way to move people into a finer and truer recognition of themselves, said of Brooks's poems that they "Take you into yourself and bring you out whole again." Eugene B. Redmond acknowledges the continuing contribution of Gwendolyn Brooks and other poets who began writing in the 1940s and 1950s. He said in conversation at the 1994 conference, "You can never fill their steps, you can never take their place, but you stand there because you want their light."

In significant ways, Brooks's fifty-five-year literary has mirrored the commitment of contemporary African American poets who stand in the light. With a legacy of liberation dating back to the eighteenth century, African Americans have been creators of social values as they envisioned a world of justice and equality and eyed the prizes intended for every individual in America. They railed against the status quo and protested attitudes and institutions that stood to impede the human rights movement that changed the nature of American society. These poets have given voice to the civil rights struggle of the 1960s and 1970s and continue to cry in the wilderness of America today. Sometimes quietly and sometimes stridently, they have transformed society and reflected that transformation in their lines. These poets not only cultivated their agonizing and beautiful rage, they also created their lines with intense beauty and truth in the service of universal humanism. They have imaged stokes of grace and heroism; they have celebrated the perennials: life, death, love, and music. History, myth, and prophecy flourish in their poems. And justice delicate as a lotus flower withers but for their constant tending.

With the lines from the poem "The Second Sermon on the Warpland," Gwendolyn Brooks thus created a metaphor that encapsulates the literary and cultural strivings of these poets as well as captures her own spirit.

As the embodiment of the furious flower, Brooks was responsive to the dynamism, complexity, and richness that compose African American culture. Her fierce dedication to craft; her close examination of the stylistic, linguistic, and imagistic qualities of language; her reverence of the expressive originality of the black masses and their folk traditions; and her embracing the black aesthetic and a newly energized black audience make her poetic career a touchstone for the exploration of poetry during the second half of the twentieth century. As Maria K. Mootry suggest in the introduction to the book *A Life Distilled*, there is a dual commitment everywhere in Brooks's work: "In terms of art, she has never been wary of 'the fascination of what's difficult'; but in terms of social justice, she has always addressed a range of America's social problems. In short, at the nexus of Brooks's art lies a fundamental commitment to both the modernist aesthetics of art and the common ideal of social justice" (1).

From her earliest poems, Gwendolyn Brooks conveyed a spirit of militancy that she delivered sometimes with razor-sharp precision and at other times with indirection and irony. She exposed racism so virulent in the nation's armed services that the narrator in "Negro Hero" "had to kick their law into their teeth in order to save them." She laid bare intricate horrors of lynching emanating from intimacy and innocence in "Ballad of Pearl May Lee" and "A Bronzeville Mother Loiters in Mississippi. Meanwhile, a Mississippi Mother Burns Bacon." She attacked the inanities of self-loathing and color consciousness in "Jessie Mitchell's Mother" and the insidious enslavement of Satin-Legs Smith whose "hats/Like bright umbrellas; and hysterical ties" are perverse antidotes for his oppression. It is not surprising then that these concerns merge in "The Second Sermon on the Warpland," a poem rooted in the black folk traditions we see in James Weldon Johnson's poetic sermons, Langston Hughes's urban blues and jazz riffs, and Sterling Brown's heroic folk characters animated by acts of struggle and survival.

Brooks made the poem an exhortation. Like the preacher who is a master of metaphor, she filled her call with language that commands a response. It is a language stunning in its understatement and ellipses; it is a language that depends on the audience to perform the creative act.

> Whose half-black hands assemble oranges
> is tom-tom hearted
> (goes in bearing oranges and boom).

> And there are bells for orphans-
> and red and shriek and sheen.
> A garbageman is dignified
> as any diplomat.
> Big Bessie's feet hurt like nobody's business,
> but she stands-bigly-under the unruly scrutiny, stands in the wild weed.
>
> In the wild weed
> she is a citizen,
> and is a moment of highest quality; admirable.
>
> It is lonesome, yes. For we are the last of the loud.
> Nevertheless, live.
>
> Conduct your blooming in the noise and whip of the whirlwind.

It is significant that the poem is a sermon, for the sermon is at the heart of the sacred traditions of black people. The sermon demonstrates the striking communication of the preacher-poet, using language that is creative, experimental, prophetic, and lyrical. It carries the communal knowledge, like that from the lips of the ancient griot; the preacher dispenses the history, knowledge of rituals, and signs the community holds dear. It is part of a larger tradition that represents the source of much of Brooks's creativity. According to D.H. Melhem in *Heroism in the New Black Poetry*, "That center was, as Brooks put it in "The Second Sermon on the Warpland,' 'tom-tom hearted,' African and African American, infused with the jazz and blues of Black music and with the sermonic power that varyingly touches all the poets in this study" (3). In "The Second Sermon on the Warpland" Brooks's message is redemptive. Her prophetic voice is urgent, unashamed, graceful, and radical. She tells us that, even amid the loneliness and the fear, we must live and "conduct [our] blooming in the noise and whip of the whirlwind."

In these "preachments" as Brooks was fond of calling them, she succeeds in defining an age of struggle and giving a prescription for health. Her poetic voice suggests a highly-charged time that calls upon the "tall-walkers," the "almost firm" to ride the whirlwind (*Report from Part One* 85).

In 1968, the year she published *In the Mecca* (the volume in which "The Second Sermon" appears), Gwendolyn Brooks reflected the maelstrom of social and political change that was reshaping the nation. The Civil Rights movement had scored some major victories. The Montgomery Bus Boycott, which brought Rosa Parks and Martin Luther King Jr. to national prominence, was the beginning of the end of discrimination in in-state transportation. The courage of the Freedom Riders opened interstate travel by bringing national attention to the violence against blacks. The Civil Rights Act of 1964 made discrimination illegal. The losses, however, were many. The senseless violence that had bloodied the history of black people in this country from the time of slavery was symbolized by the lynching of Emmett Till, a 14-year-old boy snared by Jim Crow in Mississippi. The assassination of NAACP organizer Medgar Evers in Jackson, Mississippi, and the bombing of the Sixteenth Street Baptist Church in Birmingham, where four girls were killed, would tragically foreshadow the assassination of Martin Luther King Jr. In *The Bean Eaters*, published in 1960, Brooks immortalized the tragic drama surrounding the drama surrounding the death of Emmett Till, recorded in almost journalistic precision the violence encountered by blacks who dared to integrate a white neighborhood, and made us see the storm of hatred hurled at the children who integrated in the high school in Little Rock, Arkansas. Later, in her poem "Malcolm X," Brooks captured the magnetism of the martyred leader with "hawk-man's eyes" who beguiled a black nation into being.

Malcolm's ideas provided the radical and philosophical framework for the Black Power and Black Arts movements. According to Larry Neal in *Visions of Liberated Future* (1989), he "touched all aspects of contemporary black nationalism." In Brooks's words, "Original. / Ragged-round. / Rich-robust," Malcolm X sounded the tough urban street style and inspired a revolutionary world vision. With his image resonating in their consciousness, several of the voices in this anthology began writing in the 1960s and became moving spirits and visionaries of the Black Arts movement. Amiri Baraka absorbs the power of the spirit force that was Malcolm and saw the movement as a necessary means to create a literature that would fight for black people's liberation. This revolutionary fervor and commitment led Baraka, Larry Neal, and Askia M. Touré to create the Black Arts Repertory Theater School in Harlem and that led to Baraka's collaboration with Neal in publishing *Black Fire*

(1968), the seminal anthology of the period.

Before 1968, Brooks had already experienced the palpable energy of a radical black activism that was present at the Second Fisk University Writers' Conference in April 1967. In *Report from Part One*, she recalls the incident:

> Coming from white white white white South Dakota State College I arrived in Nashville, Tennessee, to give one more "reading." But blood-boiling surprise was in store for me. First, I was aware of a general energy, an electricity, in look, walk, speech, *gesture* of the young blackness I saw all about me. I had been "loved" at South Dakota State College. Here, I was coldly Respected. Here, the heroes included the novelist-director John Killens, editors David Llorens and Hoyt Fuller, playwright Ron Milner, historians John Henrik Clarke and Lerone Bennett (and even poor Lerone was taken to task, by irate members of a no-nonsense young audience, for affiliating himself with *Ebony Magazine*, considered at that time a traitor for allowing skin-bleach advertisements in its pages, and for over-featuring light skinned women). Imamu Amiri Baraka, then "LeRoi Jones," was expected. He arrived in the middle of my offering, and when I called attention to his presence there was jubilee in Jubilee Hall. (84)

By Brooks's admission, she "had never been, before, in the general presence of such insouciance, such live firmness, such confident vigor, such determination to mold or carve something DEFINITE" (*Report from Part One* 85). In *A Life of Gwendolyn Brooks*, George Kent describes what she experienced as a "rebirth" at the Fisk University conference in 1967. The two historians opened the conference, which had its theme "The Black Writer and Human Rights." According to Kent, Clarke in a manner reminiscent of the southern folk preacher said, "It is singularly the mission of the black writer to tell his people what they have been, in order for them to understand what they are. And from this the people will clearly understand what they still must be" (197). After Clarke presented the history of blacks from the precolonial period through the abolitionist era to the age of protest, Bennett gave an impassioned call for a revolution that would remove "the last elements of white supremacy from the 'minds and hearts of black writers, themselves'" (198).

...

Gwendolyn Brooks was riding her own whirlwind of a generational shift from cultural integration into the American mainstream to the wild weed of the black aesthetic, a shift evident at the Fisk conference. She became aware of a growing urgency among the young black community being given voice by poets such as Baraka, Haki R. Madhubuti (Don L. Lee), Sonia Sanchez, Etheridge Knight, Walter Bradford, Nikki Giovanni, Askia M. Touré, Mari Evans, and Carolyn M. Rodgers. With their iconoclastic attacks on all aspects of white middle-class values, it is not surprising that they rejected unequivocally Western poetic conventions. Their poetic techniques emphasized free verse; typographical stylistics; irreverent, often scatological diction; and experimentation. In Sonia Sanchez's "For Sweet Honey in the Rock," she has reinvented this fervor as she extends her techniques: "i had come into the city carrying life in my eyes." In her "Under a Soprano Sky," we hear the lyricism of her sustained committed voice, often rendered in her deeply spiritual chanting-singing style. Eugene Redmond, Jayne Cortez, Kalamu ya Salaam, and Sterling D. Plumpp are representative of those poets in this anthology who incorporate rap, blues, jazz, and soul music in their poetry, making it move with the rhythm of contemporary beats. Nikki Giovanni, who achieved national popularity when she wedded her visionary, truth-telling poetry with gospel music, captures perhaps as well as anyone the sassiness and pride that are hallmarks of this generation in her classic poem "Nikki-Rosa." Haki Madhubuti sounds the notes in "The B Network" that remind us that many of his early poems established a cadence and hip style so familiar to us now in hip-hop. With his explosive, annunciatory rap, he has been one of the most imitated poets among younger artists seeking to establish their own performance style. These poets expanded a world that had as its center the sound of African rhythms. It is alive with boldness and beauty, and old patterns are inverted.

Despite this shifting terrain, Gwendolyn Brooks's work is rooted firmly in a disciplined adherence to the essential task of transporting feelings and ideas into poetic language. Her voice provides the touchstones for excellence I have used to select and organize the poems in this anthology. Those that are most apparent include mastery of craft, exploration of forms found in a rich vernacular tradition, chronicling history through poetic portraiture, and implementing poetry as an agent of social change.

...

In the first years of this new century, African American poetry is again experiencing an expansive renewal. The emerging poets, some fresh from poetry incubators such as the Dark Room Collective and Cave Canem, find their voices. Their poetry is rich, organic, and authentic, affirming the regeneration of the black poetic tradition in America. This sense of renewal was dramatically evident at the watershed Furious Flower Poetry Conference in 1994 held on the campus of James Madison University in Virginia. Not since the historic black writers conference at Fisk University in 1967 had so many writers gathered around one purpose. And never had a conference of this magnitude been devoted solely to African American poetry. The conference, dedicated to Gwendolyn Brooks, brought together three generations of poets. It was a singular idea—to come together to celebrate poetry, to celebrate the phenomenal development it had achieved over the past fifty years, and to celebrate a woman whose literary career had been emblematic of that development.

TUREEDA MIKELL

Named "Story Medicine Woman," Tureeda Mikell has published 72 at-risk classroom student anthologies. She was featured at Soul of a Nation at de Young Museum, Afrofuturism, Wall and Response, and was a poet/storytelling delegate in Beijing, China. Recent books include *Synchronicity*, *The Oracle of Sun Medicine*, 2/2020 and she is Co-curator of the *Patrice Lumumba Anthology*.

IF I HADN'T

If I hadn't run in circles when 3-years-old on fields of grass with Black Bird chasing me or me chasing it,
If I hadn't remembered recurring dream at 7 years of age, swallowing small stones, choking under bright lit sky in front of a long dark tunnel, holding pinpoint light; if an Ethiopian woman hadn't interpreted my dream recognizing an old saying from her culture,

If my body hadn't heaved and cried that day in 1989, recalling what happened 17 years prior with a chemistry professor who said I could not use the problem solving methods of Africans with whom I studied because they were going back to Africa; I was not,

If I hadn't learned PTSD & PTSS are body's cognitive ability to record and remember pain,

If I hadn't experienced migraines while studying for three exams, looking for subject-connectedness within a circle, reading a book given to me, titled *Muntu*, and find a quote that read, "For the African, to disengage one subject from life's circle would paralyze the rest," and have migraines disappear shortly thereafter,

If I hadn't been haunted by small globular lights, Van Allen's belts solid gold, lime, purple spheres amassing iridescent lights that would suddenly appear, and learn inter-dimensional beings do exist,

If I hadn't been awakened by a tiger watching me calmly in dream, heard a spirit come down the roof through the ceiling, and feel its weighted impression beside me,

If I hadn't called and talked to a Zen Buddhist priest for 2 hours, who assured me I was not going mad or crazy, nor had I committed a sin, but was merely entering my enlightenment,

If I hadn't commissioned my astrology chart to be calculated 5 times, aligning on earth as it is in heaven, as an active noun verb agreement system,

If I hadn't recognized, while studying organic and inorganic chemistry, that iron is not only a common element found in the body but throughout the universe, causing life to be pulled or repelled in some way,

If I hadn't attended the Berkeley Psychic Institute, learned how one can absorb another's programming, been invited to Stanford's Parapsychology Department with BPI, and discovered a trans-medium who allowed a spirit to share her body, then discover another at my job,

If I hadn't seen a slug-sized, lip-suctioning leech, undulating around a relative's head as though looking for a place to land; and when it did, weeks later, said relative could not lift her head,

If I hadn't suggested she go to a Chinese acupuncturist, who told her at the end of the examination, "It's as though something has sucked the life force from her head," which left me questioning, what did I see?

If I hadn't read, in *The Archeology of Knowledge,* "We must also ascribe to the institutional sites from which the doctor makes his discourse,"

If I hadn't worked in a mental institution as a lab tech and learned the difference between a psychic and a sick psychic,

If I hadn't heard the birds' crying-song while knapping, unable to discern how I knew their cry, only to get up, open the door and see birds fluttering wildly over their lifeless friend adored,

If I hadn't heard a helicopter in Oakland fly over my house and drop something on the house at the corner that sounded like a loud *SWOOSH,* on May 13, 1985, after 2AM, on the West Coast,

If I hadn't read in the newspaper later the same morning that a helicopter dropped a bomb on the MOVE organization's home on the corner of Osage & Pine in Philadelphia, on the East Coast at 5 AM, and note a 3-hour time difference,

If I hadn't felt a patient's medication for his right eye land as if a web on my left eye, and associated molecular isomers, mirroring molecules,

If I hadn't heard an unknown Goddess whisper in my ear and shown the spelling of her name in my mind's eye,

If I hadn't found her name in the dictionary, as revealed, and learn she was the deity of love and war, my sun & rising sign,

If I hadn't seen rainbows near sun in clear skies, as if to illume answers of questioned insight,

If I hadn't been pulled outside to bow my head, point to the vastness of the night sky, and at the tip of my finger have a shooting star arrive,

If I hadn't awakened abruptly from a deep sleep to see Isis, known as Sirius, watching over me,

If I hadn't heard a voice say, "You have fidelity in the law and it will be used as your trench!"

I might not have learned that the Dogons of West Africa, once every 50 years, parade the reflection of star Amma B around A, wearing head-dresses that resemble telephone poles, because their eyes have not been corrupted,

Or that the African, Chinese, Irish, Cherokee, and Black Foot understanding of stars in me is on earth as it is in heaven,

And that the experiences, testimonies, visions, and synchronicities of blood memory I continue to speak, I may not have recognized an ancestor saying,

> *I come from Mystics*
> *who believe in hearing the inaudible,*
> *touching the intangible and*
> *seeing the invisible.*

Pamela D. Reed

Pamela D. Reed, a first-generation college graduate, is the Convenor of the Inaugural James Arthur Baldwin International Symposium. The youngest of six children, born and raised in Lake Providence, Louisiana—named "The Poorest Place in America," in 1994, by *Time* magazine—she grew up chopping cotton in the sunbaked fields of East Carroll Parish, in the Mississippi Delta. Reed went on to earn undergraduate and graduate Communications degrees from, respectively, California State University Hayward (now Cal State Eastbay) and Northeast Louisiana University (now U of Louisiana Monroe). Earning the doctorate in Temple University's storied Department of African American Studies, in 2001, under the direction of Dr. Molefi Kete Asante, was the culmination of her formal education. She has presented in myriad academic conferences around the world, from Aswan, Egypt, to Oxford, United Kingdom, to the People's Republic of China. A widely published cultural critic and public intellectual, Reed is a contributor to both the Encyclopedia of Black Studies and the Encyclopedia of African Religions. Her writings have appeared in *Diverse: Issues in Higher Education*—where she is a Guest Blogger—*The Philadelphia Inquirer, The New York Amsterdam News, The Village Voice, The Daily Voice, The Grio*, and other national publications. Reed is also an accomplished editor, having served as Guest Editor for a special issue of the *Journal of Black Studies*, "Barack Obama's Improbable Election and the Question of Race and Racism in Contemporary America" (2010). Ever multi-faceted, she also acted as script editor for the award winning, critically acclaimed film, *Motherland*. She has published numerous scholarly articles, as well as multiple book chapters, including "The Essential James Baldwin: Life & Literature, At Home & Abroad," in *Africana Paradigms, Practices & Literary Texts: Evoking Social Justice*, edited by Clenora Hudson-Weems (Kendall Hunt 2021). Presently, she is hard at work on three projects: a full-length James Baldwin manuscript, a collection of essays, and a book of personal interviews granted to her over the years by a plethora of Africana luminaries.

James Baldwin's "Everybody's Protest Novel," Distilled to its Essence:
Richard Wright and Harriet Beecher Stowe, A Marriage Made in Hell

Dread stalks our streets,

and our faces.

Many races

gather, again,

to despise and disperse

and destroy us:

nor can they any longer pretend

to be looking for a friend.

That dream was sold

when *we* were,

on the auction-block

of Manifest Destiny. (Baldwin "Song" 50; emphasis added)

A 2015 *New York Times* article asks the following question: "James Baldwin Denounced Richard Wright's 'Native Son' as a Protest Novel. Was He Right?" It features a debate between writers Ayana Mathis and Pankaj Mishra about Baldwin's seminal 1949 essay, "Everybody's Protest Novel," written at the tender age of twenty-four. Therein, Baldwin "eviscerated his mentor and benefactor Richard Wright in print... attacking *Native Son* as 'a continuation, a complement of that monstrous legend it was written to destroy,'" concludes Vanderbilt University academician and theologian Michael Eric Dyson, in his book, *What Truth Sounds Like: RFK, James Baldwin, and Our Unfinished Conversation About Race in America* (194).

Baldwin thought that their—his and Richard Wright's—"early hostile period...was ridiculously blown out of proportion." He insists that his major objection to *Native Son* was "technical," primarily the lawyer's "simpleminded" closing argument, as constructed by Wright, and delivered at the murder trial, in which he suggests that Bigger's murderous acts somehow humanized him, at long last. Mr. Baldwin reasoned that "it was simply absurd to talk about this monster created by the American public, and then expect the public to save it!" Moreover, he maintains that his harshest criticism, even for Wright's masterpiece, was actually intended for *Uncle Tom's Cabin*, suggesting a classic case of transference, of sorts, saying that when he was "dealing with Richard, [he] was in fact thinking of Harriet Beecher Stowe" and her landmark magnum opus ("James Baldwin, the Art" par. 181).

Indeed, if comments attributed to him in his 1984 *Paris Review* interview are any indication, Baldwin remained a lifelong fan of his beloved mentor, as evidenced by his high praise for Wright, and by his attempts, therein, to clarify and qualify his famously brutal critique of his literary forefather and benefactor, along with his celebrated realist tome, in "Everybody's Protest Novel," stating that he "reserve[s], in any case, the utmost respect for Richard, especially in light of his posthumous work...*Lawd Today*," which he characterized as Wright's "greatest novel," suggesting that readers "Look it up!" ("James Baldwin, the Art" par. 181).

Some might think that, since *Native Son* and *Uncle Tom's Cabin* are both works of fiction, Baldwin was making too much of Wright's Bigger Thomas and Stowe's Uncle Tom, but that simplistic perspective ignores the socializing—and propagandizing – role of art. In, arguably, one of his most important essays, "Criteria of Negro Art," W. E. B. Du Bois summed up, beautifully, the problem: since White America, almost without fail, insists on portraying Black people as beastly, unlovable, ugly caricatures in their artistic offerings, "it is the bounden duty of [B]lack America to begin this great work of the creation...preservation...and the realization of Beauty," declaring that he "shamelessly" advocates using art for the propagandistic aim of "gaining the right of [B]lack folk to love and enjoy" (101-103).

Beyond Du Bois' timeless exhortation on the power of art, Toronto Communication Studies and Creative Industries scholar, Cheryl Thompson, makes it abundantly clear why Baldwin was so affected by Wright's and Stowe's stories, and their portrayals of Black people, particularly Black men. Her essay, "The Significance of Uncle Tom in the 21st Century," concludes that "Uncle Tom will persist as long as anti-Blackness persists" (par. 22). Be that as it may, Baldwin does not believe that protest fiction is a viable remedy for America's virulent racism and, nor, White Supremacy. To the contrary, he maintains that the problem is compounded by such writings.

Sometimes called a "social novel," a "protest novel,"—as Baldwin pronounced both *Native Son* and *Uncle Tom's Cabin*—is a fictional work that dramatizes the harsh effects of at least one societal ill, in this case racism, to demonstrate how it affects the lives of its characters, who are representative of real-world people confronted with real-life situations. Although the two books were published eighty-eight years apart, Baldwin draws a direct line between them, and shines a harsh light on the traditional Christian notion of an angry God who demands absolute allegiance, lest unbelievers risk eternal damnation after death. Put another way, as Baldwin see it, one must either confess faith in Jesus, the Christ, or damn oneself to a tortuous, eternal afterlife, residing in a fiery pit called Hell.

Baldwin characterizes it as the "panic of being hurled into the flames...the terror of damnation." In other words, he implies that Harriet Beecher Stowe—and White liberal Christians, particularly those authoring protest novels—are afraid of the so-called wages of sin: dying, going to Hell, and perpetually burning in a fiery pit. Specifically, Baldwin has called this bedrock Christian doctrine a myth slash legend that amounts to a form of "theological terror" (2379). The disillusioned former child preacher further describes this phenomenon as "being caught in traffic with the devil," as was the gravely ill Florence's terrifying plight, in his semi-autobiographical 1953 novel, *Go Tell It On the Mountain*. She "remembered one phrase, which now she muttered against the knuckles that bruised her lips: 'Lord, help my unbelief'" ("Everybody's" 2377-2378).

Over three decades later, the legend of Stagger Lee[1] would serve

---

1   The legend of Stagger Lee (sometimes called Stack-a-Lee, Stagolee, or other variants) is based on the real-life story of the Black man, Lee "Stag" Shelton, by some accounts a pimp and underworld figure, who shot and killed his (also Black) acquaintance William "Billy" Lyons, who had reportedly snatched his hat off his head, in a barroom in St. Louis, Missouri. After shooting Billy, Stag is said to have matter-of-factly taken his hat back from the dying man's hand, after which, he coolly exited the night club. The

as muse, inspiring Baldwin's raw eloquence, and elegance, in his tour de force long poem, "Staggerlee Wonders," in which the iconic scribe would express similar theological sentiments about what he considers the paradoxical organizing principle of the United States of America—one nation under God—and which fuels its hegemonic ways: Manifest Destiny. This is the once long-held belief of White people that it was their heavenly charge to conquer—and save—the world, proselytizing and brutally converting the dark-skinned natives in each newly "discovered" colony around the globe (Pasha par. 7). Channeling Stagger Lee, Baldwin, evocative and in rare form, waxes poetic on the matter:

> While they are containing
>
> Russia
>
> and entering onto the quicksand of
>
> China
>
> and patronizing
>
> Africa,
>
> and calculating
>
> the Caribbean plunder, and
>
> the South China Sea booty,
>
> the niggers are aware that no one has discussed
>
> anything at all with the niggers.
>
> ....

---

sensational story inspired numerous musical renderings, beginning with its publication in 1911 and continuing with the first recording in 1923 by Fred Waring's Pennsylvanians. The who's who of Black music, including, Ma Rainey—with Louis Armstrong on cornet—James Brown, Duke Ellington, and Cab Calloway recorded the ditty. Musical legends Bob Dylan and the Grateful Dead also recorded musical accounts of the iconic folktale. The best-known, and best-selling, version was that of Lloyd Price, which topped Billboard's Top 100 in 1959 ("The Legend"; Brown).

During this long travail

our ancestors spoke to us, and we listened,

and we tried to make you hear life in our song

but now it matters not at all to me

whether you know what I am talking about—or not:

I know why we are not blinded

by your brightness, are able to see you,

who cannot see *us*. I know

why we are still here.

Godspeed.

The niggers are calculating,

from day to day, life everlasting,

and wish you well:

but decline to imitate the Son of the Morning,

and rule in Hell. ("Staggerlee" 38-48; emphasis added)

This "theological terror," Baldwin submits, is "not different from that terror that activates a lynch mob." Moreover, he suggests that a protest novel is a "report from the pit [Hell, that] reassures us of its reality and its darkness and of our own salvation...'As long as such books are being published,' an American liberal once said to me," he shares, "'everything will be all right.'" Antithetically, Baldwin argues that protest novels are "a mirror of our confusion, dishonesty, panic, trapped and immobilized in the sunlit prison of the American dream...fantasies, connecting nowhere with reality" ("Everybody's" 2379-2382).

Bottom line, in Baldwin's estimation, "*Uncle Tom's Cabin* is a very bad novel." Harriet Beecher Stowe's specific message—as is the case of the protest novel, in general—distilled to its essence, is as follows: "This is perfectly horrible! You ought to be ashamed of yourselves!" These social novels are condemned by Baldwin because they are "ostentatious" and rely heavily on "self-righteous, virtuous sentimentality," which he considers "the mark of dishonesty...always, therefore, the signal of secret and violent inhumanity, the mask of cruelty" (Baldwin "Everybody's" 2370-2371).

Baldwin refuses to even acknowledge Stowe's classic tome as a novel. Rather, he reduces *Uncle Tom's Cabin* to the rank of a long-form pamphlet, and low-rates Stowe's "powers" to the level of an "impassioned pamphleteer," in that her simplistic, sentimental message was "not intended to do anything more than prove [the obvious], that slavery was wrong; was, in fact, perfectly horrible."

In the end, though, Baldwin insists that the celebrated White liberal author never gets to the heart of the matter. That is, exactly what is it that motivates "her people"—White people—to behave in such an inhumane, savage way toward Black people? Beyond that, by his way of thinking, "the only question left to ask is why we are bound still within the same constriction. How is it that we are so loath to make a further journey than that made by Mrs. Stowe, to discover and reveal something a little closer to the truth?" ("Everybody's" 2372-2373).

Truth, however, tends to be relative; and, it is often buried beneath striations of obfuscation, which, when peeled away, like the layers of an onion, induce painful, cleansing tears. Baldwin puts it thus: "But that battered word, truth, having made its appearance here, confronts one immediately with a series of riddles and has, moreover, since so many gospels are preached, the unfortunate tendency to make one belligerent" ("Everybody's" 2373). To Baldwin, the real truth of the matter is revealed in the extensive musings of "Staggerlee."

> Then, perhaps they imagine
>
> that their crimes are not crimes?
>
> -----
>
> Perhaps. Perhaps that is why they cannot repent,
>
> why there is no possibility of repentance.
>
> Manifest Destiny is a hymn to madness,

feeding on itself, ending

(when it ends) in madness:

the action is blindness and pain,

pain bringing a torpor so deep

that every act is willed,

is desperately forced,

is willed to be a blow:

the hand becomes a fist,

the prick becomes a club,

the womb a dangerous swamp,

the hope, and fear, of love

is acid in the marrow of the bone.

No, their fire is not quenched,

nor *can* be: the oil feeding the flames

being the unadmitted terror of the wrath of God.

Yes. But let us put it in another,
less theological way:
though theology has absolutely nothing to do
with what I am trying to say.
But the moment God is mentioned
theology is summoned
to buttress or demolish belief:
an exercise which renders belief irrelevant

....

"Yeah. I would like to believe you."
But we are not talking about belief. (35-40; emphasis added)

Not only does Baldwin compare the authors of such novels to racist, hegemonic colonizers, but, more, to the pre-colonial Christian proselytizers in Africa, and, moreover, he likens the conversion of

Africans to Christianity, to enslavement. That being so, he concludes, "the aim of the protest novel becomes something very closely resembling the zeal of those alabaster missionaries to Africa to cover the nakedness of the natives, to hurry them into the pallid arms of Jesus and thence into slavery" ("Everybody's" 2382-2383). "Alabaster" and "pallid" are both used as synonyms for "White" in the preceding passage from "Everybody's Protest Novel." In "Staggerlee Wonders," Baldwin similarly refers to White people, describing them as "pink and alabaster pragmatists" (*Jimmy's Blues* 7-23). Along these same lines, Baldwin continues his scathing critique of *Uncle Tom's Cabin*:

> Thus, the African, exile, pagan, hurried off the auction block and into the fields, fell on his knees before that God in Whom he must now believe; who had made him, but not in His image. This tableau, this impossibility, is the heritage of the Negro in America: Wash me, cried the slave to his Maker, and I shall be whiter, whiter than snow! For black is the color of evil; only the robes of the saved are white. It is this cry, implacable on the air and in the skull, that he must live with. ("Everybody's" 2385-2386)

Baldwin posits that these inhumane conditions were the genesis of that "unprecedented tabernacle," the Black Church. "Subsequently, the [enslaved] was given, under the eye, and the gun, of his master, Congo Square, and the Bible" ("If Black English" par. 7). Therein, this notion of needing to be cleansed and, thus, rendered "white as snow," in order to be acceptable to the Creator—a recurrent thread throughout Baldwin's voluminous catalogue—is commonplace. For instance, "Down At the Cross," the title of his lead-off essay in the acclaimed collection, *The Fire Next Time*, takes its name from the Hoffman and Stockton hymn, of the same name. He epigraphs the lyrics of the song's first verse to open his epistle, subtitled "Letter from a Region in my Mind":

> Down at the cross where my Saviour died,
>
> Down where for cleansing from sin I cried,
>
> There to my heart was the blood applied,

Singing glory to His name!

—Hymn (qtd. in "Down At the Cross" 20-21)

The profundity of Christian mythology, and its far-reaching ramifications, is ever-present in Baldwin's compositions, which explains his decision to preface one of his signature essays with an extracted stanza of Rudyard Kipling's "The White Man's Burden," which highlights a pillar of the so-called Manifest Destiny doctrine of the West, another Baldwin focal point.

Take up the White Man's burden—

Ye dare not stoop to less—

Nor call too loud on Freedom

To cloak your weariness;

By all ye cry or whisper,

By all ye leave or do,

The silent, sullen peoples

Shall weigh your Gods and you.

(Kipling qtd. in "Down At the Cross" 18)

On this mythology, longtime CNN host Don Lemon's political treatise, *This is the Fire: What I Say to My Friends About Racism*—inspired by and modeled after *The Fire Next Time*—notes the following declaration, pulled from Baldwin's *The Devil Finds Work*: "I cannot be blamed for an ignorance which an entire republic had deliberately inculcated" (qtd. in Lemon 105).

To illustrate the danger of this country's body of myths, the Baldwinite writer invokes the memory of Breonna Taylor, the unarmed and completely innocent 26-year-old Black woman who was shot dead, in the dead of night, as she lay in bed with her fiancé Kenneth Walker, when the police stormed their Louisville, Kentucky apartment. "As the pattern evolves, the myth of good cops and bad neighborhoods sets the stage for a no-knock warrant leading to a terribly unfortunate misunderstanding for which no police officer could be held accountable" (Lemon 104-105).

What is more—in parlance reminiscent of the cynical, damning contemporary notions of "pimps in the pulpit" and "preachers who prey" (Brown; Batchelor; Marcia Dyson)—Baldwin, writing of his fragile state of mind as a teenager, in search of salvation, living in the concrete jungle called New York City, refers to the seductive nature of the "church racket"—while once again raising the specter of the "auction block," and by extension, enslavement—also in "Down at the Cross."

> I was so frightened, and at the mercy of so many conundrums, that inevitably, that summer, *someone* would have taken me over; one doesn't, in Harlem, long remain standing on any auction block. It was my good luck—perhaps—that I found myself in the church racket instead of some other, and surrendered to a spiritual seduction long before I came to any carnal knowledge. For when the pastor asked me, with that marvellous (sic) smile, "Whose little boy are you?" my heart replied at once, "Why, yours." (36-37)

At that time, Baldwin was in what he remembers as "unspeakable pain," and in search of divine intervention. He writes that "it was as though I were yelling up to Heaven and Heaven would not hear me. And if Heaven would not hear me, if love could not descend from Heaven—to wash me, to make me clean—then utter disaster was my portion" ("Down At the Cross" 38).

Richard Wright's Bigger Thomas

> Imagination
> creates the situation,
> and, then, the situation
> creates imagination.
> It may, of course,
> be the other way around:
> Columbus was discovered
> by what he found. (Baldwin "Imagination" 64)

As previously established, Baldwin does not lambast Harriet Beecher Stowe alone. At one point, he suggests, parenthetically, that we "ignore, for the moment those novels of oppression written by Negroes, which add only a raging, near-paranoiac postscript...and actually reinforce... the principles which activate the oppression they decry" ("Everybody's" 2053).

Needless to say, Baldwin does not long ignore the monstrous Bigger Thomas, produced in the mind of, at the time, America's most eminent Black "realist" writer, Richard Wright, and his magnum opus, *Native Son*, which—other than Ralph Ellison's *Invisible Man*—is arguably the best example of the use of urban realism in the African American literary tradition. Realist texts, are said to, fundamentally, strive for authenticity and brutal reality, the premise being that that there is, within every living soul, the potential for depravity, cruelty, and other extreme horrors. All that is needed to activate the monster within all of us, realism holds, is the right or, as it were, the wrong circumstances.

And Wright proceeds to craft, within the pages of *Native Son*, a string of circumstances so devastating, so terrifying for a young Black man living in a racist, unjust society, that Bigger Thomas, who originally presented as a basically good young man, albeit trapped, living in a cramped, rodent-infested Chicago tenement, with his single mother and his sister, soon morphed, into a monster who commits unspeakable acts, prompting Baldwin's fiery appraisal in "Everybody's Protest Novel." Making yet another reference to Hell in the following passage, he writes that "hatred smoulders through these pages [of *Native Son*] like sulphur fire" (2387). Bigger "dies, having come, through this violence, we are told, for the first time, to a kind of life, having for the first time redeemed his manhood" (2067-2068).

To avoid discovery, and subsequently, capture, Bigger then goes on the run, committing one senselessly violent act after another, exhibiting "a kind of nihilism that embodies existential struggle instead of mere hopelessness and meaninglessness" (Watson 298). He is ultimately jailed and tried in a court of law. According to Baldwin, it was that court scene, particularly the public defender's illogical line of defense, that drove him to so publicly critique the iconic man who generously took him under his wing when he was a young, unknown, struggling writer.

Using language that is suggestive of a metaphorical, interracial copulation, of sorts, within a "web of lust and fury," that spawns a literary offspring, Baldwin paints a vivid picture of all that he sees wrong with Wright's infamous *Native Son* protagonist.

> Bigger is Uncle Tom's descendant, flesh of his flesh, so exactly opposite a portrait that, when the books are placed together, it seems that the contemporary Negro novelist and the dead New England woman are locked together in a deadly, timeless battle…And, indeed, within this web of lust and fury, [B]lack and [W]hite can only thrust and counter-thrust, long for each other's slow, exquisite death; death by torture, acid, knives and burning; the thrust, the counter-thrust, the longing making the heavier that cloud which blinds and suffocates them both, so that they go down into the pit together. Thus has the cage betrayed us all, this moment, our life, turned to nothing through our terrible attempts to insure it. ("Everybody's" 2068-2069)

Baldwin traces the root of Bigger's problem—and by extension, Wright's—to one he identifies as, once again, theological in nature. Bottom line, for him, it all comes back to Christianity. Using imagery remarkable for a (then) twenty-four-year-old, Baldwin brings in "church-bells" to describes what can surely be termed a figurative marriage, made in Hell, between Harriet Beecher Stowe and Richard Wright, surmising that "Bigger's tragedy is… that he has accepted a theology that denies him life, that he admits the possibility of his being sub-human and feels constrained, therefore, to battle for his humanity according to those brutal criteria bequeathed him at his birth" ("Everybody's" 2069).

In the final analysis, he states what should be obvious: Black people "need not battle for [our humanity]; we need only to do what is infinitely more difficult—that is, accept it."

Here, he insists, lies the fatal flaw of protest literature: "its rejection of life, the human being, the denial of his beauty, dread, [and] power" ("Everybody's" 2069). And that, for James Baldwin—and for Du Bois, before him, in "Criteria of Negro Art"—is at the heart of the problem.

Works Cited

Baldwin, James. "Down at the Cross: Letter from a Region in My Mind." *The Fire Next Time*. Dial Press, 1963, Apple Books, books.apple.com/us/book/james-baldwin-collection-7-books-fire-next-time-giovannis/id1549605192. Accessed 17 May 2021.

---."Everybody's Protest Novel." *Partisan Review*, vol. XVI, no. 6, 1949, pp. 578-585, *James Baldwin Collection 7 Books: The Fire Next Time, Giovanni's Room, Go Tell it on the Mountain, If Beale Street Could Talk, Another Country, Notes of a Native Son, Sonny's Blues*, Apple Books. books.apple.com/us/book/james-baldwin-collection-7-books-fire-next-time-giovannis/id1549605192, pp. 2052-2069. Accessed 15 May 2021.

---. *Go Tell It on the Mountain*. Alfred A. Knopf, 1952.

---. "If Black English Isn't a Language, Then Tell Me What Is?" *New York Times*, 29 July 1979, archive.nytimes.com/www.nytimes.com/books/98/03/29/specials/baldwin-english.html?mcubz=1. Accessed 22 May 2021.

---. "Imagination." *Jimmy's Blues and Other Poems with an Introduction by Nikky Finney*. Beacon Press, 2014. Apple Books, p. 64, books.apple.com/us/book/jimmys-blues-and-other-poems/id721589877. Accessed 4 Aug 2021.

---. "James Baldwin, the Art of Fiction No. 78." Interview with Jordan Elgrably. *Paris Review*, Issue 91, Spring 1984, www.theparisreview.org/interviews/2994/the-art-of-fiction-no-78-james-baldwin. Accessed 21 May 2021.

---. *Jimmy's Blues: Selected Poems*, St. Martin's Press, 1990, pp. 7-23.

---. "Song (for Skip)." *Jimmy's Blues and Other Poems with an Introduction by Nikky Finney*. Beacon Press, 2014. Apple Books, p. 50, books.apple.com/us/book/jimmys-blues-and-other-poems/id721589877. Accessed 18 May 2020.

---. "Staggerlee Wonders." *Jimmy's Blues and Other Poems with an Introduction by Nikky Finney*. Beacon Press, 2014. Apple Books, pp. 31-54, books.apple.com/us/book/jimmys-blues-and-other-poems/id721589877. Accessed 18 May 2020.

Batchelor, Valli Boobal. *When Pastors Prey: Overcoming Clergy Sexual Abuse of Women*. World Council of Churches, 2013.

Brown, Cecil. *Stagolee Shot Billy*. Harvard University P, 2004.

Brown, H. E. *Pimps in the Pulpit*. Instep Pub, 1999.

Du Bois, W. E. Burghardt. "Criteria of Negro Art." *The Portable Harlem Renaissance Reader*, edited by and with an Introduction by David Levering Lewis, Penguin Books, 1994, pp. 100-105.

Dyson, Marcia L. "When Preachers Prey," *Essence*, May 1998, pp. 120ff. David J. Garrow. "The Man Who Was King." *New York Review of Books*, vol. 47, no. 6, p. 7, 13 Apr. 2000, pp. 40-43, "Notes," no. 19, www.davidgarrow.com/File/DJG%20 2000%20NYRBDysonMLKReview.pdf. Accessed 22 April 2021.

Dyson, Michael Eric. *What Truth Sounds Like: RFK, James Baldwin, and Our Unfinished Conversation About Race in America*. St. Martin's Press, 2018, Apple Books, books.apple.com/us/book/what-truth-sounds-like/id1303600456. . Accessed 14 May 2021.

Ellison, Ralph. *Invisible Man*. Random House, 1952.

Hoffman, Elisha Albright and John Hart Stockton. "Down at the Cross." www.hymnal. net/en/hymn/h/1066. Accessed 17 May 2021.

Kipling, Rudyard. "The White Man's Burden." *McClure's Magazine* 12 (1899), pp. 290-291.

Lemon, Don. *This is the Fire: What I Say to My Friends About Racism*. Little, Brown, and Company, 2021.

Malone, Eddie. "Long-Lost Brothers: How Nihilism Provides Bigger Thomas and Biggie Smalls With a Soul." *Journal of Black Studies*, vol. 46, no. 3, 2015, pp. 297–315., www.jstor.org/stable/24572827. Accessed 6 Aug. 2021.

Mathis, Ayana and Pankaj Mishra. "James Baldwin Denounced Richard Wright's *Native Son* as a 'Protest Novel.' Was He Right?" *New York Times*, 1 March 2015, www. nytimes.com/2015/03/01/books/review/james-baldwin-denounced-richard-wrights-native-son-as-a-protest-novel-was-he-right.html?smid=url-share. Accessed 4 May 2021.

Pasha, Kamran. "Jesus, Capitalism, and Manifest Destiny." HuffPost, 9 Dec. 2013, www. huffpost.com/entry/jesus-capitalism-and-mani_b_4406898. Accessed 27 July 2021.

Stowe, Harriet Beecher. *Uncle Tom's Cabin*. John P. Jewett and Company, 1852.

Thompson, Cheryl. "The Significance of Uncle Tom in the 21st Century." *Yes! Magazine*, 11 Feb. 2021, www.yesmagazine.org/democracy/2021/02/11/uncle-tom-racial-politics. Accessed 23 May 2021.

Wright, Richard. *Lawd Today*. Northeastern University P, 1986.

---. *Native Son*. Harper, 1940.

CLENORA HUDSON-WEEMS

Clenora Hudson-Weems, PhD—Professor, Author, Screenwriter, Producer, and conceptualizer of Africana Womanism, "an authentic, global family-centered paradigm that prioritizes race, class and gender." She is the author of four Africana Womanism books, including the Fifth Edition of the 1993 classic, *Africana Womanism: Reclaiming Ourselves* (Routledge, 2019/2020) and its sequel, *Africana Womanist Literary Theory* (Africa World Press 2004).

She is also the first to establish Emmett Till as the true catalyst of the Civil Rights Movement in her 1988 Ford doctoral dissertation, "Emmett Louis Till: The Impetus of the Modern Civil Rights Movement" (U. of Iowa), later published as *Emmett Till: The Sacrificial Lamb of the Civil Rights Movement* (1994). Her culminating fourth Till book is entitled *Emmett: Legacy, Redemption and Forgiveness* (2014).

Initiating the Nation's first graduate degrees (PhD and MA) in English with an Africana Concentration in 2000, she co-authored (with Dr. Wilfred Samuels, U. of Utah) *Toni Morrison (1990)*, the first critical study of the works of the Nobel Laureate. She is editor of *Contemporary Africana Theory, Thought and Action: A Guide to Africana Studies* (Africa World Press 2007) and *Africana Paradigms, Practices and Literary Text: Evoking Social Justice* (Kendall Hunt 2021). Two more manuscripts have been recently completed.

Chapter 1
The Need for a Definitive Africana-Melanated Womanism
Paradigm and the Question of Interconnectivity versus Intersectionality

II. Interconnectedness versus Intersectionality: Counterbalances

"The Early Image of Women's Lib was of an elitist organization made up of upper-middle class women with the concerns of that class and not paying much attention to the problems of most black women. . . . Too much emphasis is placed on gender politics." (Toni Morrison, 1971)

Toni Morrison, Nobel Laureate, in "What the Black Woman Thinks about Women's Lib," observed white women's stance, which excluded the race factor. Named and designed for them, it does virtually nothing to resolve our concerns; however, it does offer great incentives for whites and feminist theory, in that it improves their image today as a means of updating and, moreover, enhancing inclusion, indeed, a political act. Be that as it may, the question is how important is terminology, particularly relative to identity and the true level of struggle of Africana women and their families in today's conflicting society? Moreover, what is the real mission and true intent of the feminist versus the Africana womanist? Finally, does the connotation of the concept of feminism exaggerate its denotation? This could be addressed via considering the nuances of terminology. Both connotation and denotation here are one, interconnected, interwoven and interdependent upon each other for true meaning. Still, despite inconsistencies and the inapplicability of the term, Intersectionality, for Africana women, it has been widely embraced by many Black Feminists, African Feminists and even Womanists.

According to Dr. Mark Christian, an Africana scholar from Liverpool, England, in the Afterword to the 5th Edition of *Africana Womanism: Reclaiming Ourselves,* "The current academic fad phrase is intersectionality as if those of us in Africana discourse never considered the myriad of issues encountered by our communities. Race, class, gender and prioritization therein, have always been key issues for comprehending Africana Womanism." (131) He strongly proclaims and supports the long-existing presence of the prioritization of Race, Class and Gender in Africana life, prominently reflected in Africana Womanism. Indeed, its true essence dates back to the rich legacy of African antiquity wherein lies,

> ... the primacy of the centrality of family and the priority of race empowerment in the rich legacy of African womanhood and motherhood. [They descend] from a lineage of strong, proud African women activists and culture bearers, dating back to the advent of the colonization of Africa by Europe, notwithstanding African warrior queens in antiquity, [including] Queen Hatsphepsut (1505-1485 B.C.E.) of Egypt, ... Queen Nzingha (1583-1663) of West Africa [and] Queen Mother Yaa Asantewa (1840-1921) of Ghana. (Hudson-Weems, *Africana Womanist Literary Theory,* 51-52)

Grounded in this reality, Dr. Christian also upholds the insistence upon prescriptive analyses of Africana life, history and culture, and, of course, Africana Womanism remains ever resolute in recalling African traditions. To begin with, in African cosmology, the term nommo is powerful, for as literary critic, Barbara Christian, whom I debated in a 1995 television interview, contends in her book, *Black Feminist Criticism*, that "It is through nommo, the correct naming of a thing, that it comes into existence" (157-158). Feminism, which was coined by and designed specifically for white women, with Black women nowhere on its agenda, is basically inapplicable to Black women's lives. Yet some are still enameled with it, particularly with intersectionality, identifying with it and commanding acceptance of and regard for it as a fascinating methodology for defining who they are as well. Admittedly there is some improvement in the Movement, a striking contrast to what it was traditionally. Indeed, their issues and position, prevalent in this growing persona today, have shifted to a more inclusive posture. Therefore, intersectionality can only serve as a counterbalance to interconnectedness, which came first in explicating the priority of race, class and gender for Africana women; it can never be a replacement. Because of the complexity of how race, class and gender have been forced, and therefore, must be factored into the lives of Blacks in particular in contrast to that of whites, I caution that "when you buy the white terminology, you also buy its agenda" (Hudson-Weems, *Africana Womanism*, 5th Edition, 25-26). This is a truism, which speaks volumes to the importance of words and terminology and its interconnecting nature for properly addressing and explicating the whole. Hence, like interwoven fabrics of life, the Africana-Melanated family sticks together, less they risk being weakened or damaged if separated or broken apart, as in the case of separating in focusing on one aspect at a time with feminism and intersectionality.

In the Academy, intersectionality has been widely accepted by the white population. However, as it includes issues reflecting the complex reality of Africana women as well, it is beginning to galvanize more Black women, an interesting twist, as many follow them, without hesitation, perhaps a thought out dictate of modernday feminists. It must be noted, however, that these followers are not in the majority, for the true tradition of Black women has proven that Black women, in general, have never allowed upon white women to tell them what to do, which is why most Black women in Black communities do not consider themselves feminists. In fact, their course of action has served as a Blueprint for white women, who have observed Black women, out of necessity, working harmoniously with their male counterparts.

White women's inclination, then, in a somewhat similar manner, was to move "from homeplace to workplace." They also observed early on that Black women were outspoken and thus, here again, they sought to "break silence and find voice."

Morrison had summarized Black women as models back in the 80s: When you really look at the stereotypes of Black women, the worst you can say about them, that is once you disregard the vocabulary and the dirty words and deal with the substance of what is being said, it is quite complimentary ... What is being said is, that Black women are wonderful mothers and nurturers (mammies), that we are sexually at home in our bodies (oversexed), and that we are self-sufficient and tough (henpecking and overbearing). And isn't that exactly what every woman wants to be: Loving and nurturing, sexually at home in her body, competent and strong? (Morrison, *New York Times*, 1989)

Indeed, despite stereotypical descriptors/identities given to the naming and defining of Black women, they have remained the original blueprint for many. Intersectionality, a step in the right direction, expanding beyond gender issues alone, is quite appropriate in defining white women in their 3rd and even 4th Waves of Feminism today, evolving from gender-exclusivity to current inclusivity. However, it clearly offers nothing new or particularly positive for Africana women and their communities. Chapter 11 of the 5th Edition of *Africana Womanism*, entitled "Africana Womanism's Race, Class and Gender: Pre-Intersectionality," notes that

> Today, the current emphasis on the relativity of feminist activity, called "intersectionality," which was introduced by race theorist, Kimberlie Crenshaw in 1989, has enhanced the dominance of the application of the Eurocentric tool of analysis for Black life. Clearly this is not necessary, as an Afrocentric tool of analysis for Black life, particularly relative to Black women and their families, was already in place with the earlier advent of Africana Womanism. (Hudson-Weems, *Africana Womanism*, 5th Edition, 107)

Indeed, the positioning of the issues of race, class and gender in the general definition of intersectionality, as outlined in Wikipedia, suggests a conscious usage of the prioritization first established by Blacks, which strongly echoes the originality presented in Africana Womanism. Ironically, this new priority, referenced in modern feminist thought, makes it appear that the prioritization of the race factor for the family-centered Africana Womanism paradigm did not heretofore exist, thereby suggesting that this is a new phenomenon, needing only to be seriously considered.

To be sure, feminism pulls all stops in saturating the media in every area to promote its new stance, although the Africana woman had been operating from an inclusive family-centered perspective, prioritizing Race, Class and Gender for centuries.

Continuing the legacy, the 1st call for Africana Womanism in print appeared in 1989 in The Western Journal of Black Studies, later reprinted in *Africana Womanism*, 1993 and 2019:

> She realizes the critical need to prioritize the antagonist forces as racism, classism and sexism, respectively. In the final analysis, Africana Womanism is connected to the tradition of self-reliance and autonomy, working toward participation in Africana liberation. (Hudson-Weems, *Africana Womanism*, 25)

Be that as it may, however, apparently, some people need to be reminded of the fact of the new consideration of race, class and gender for the feminist, which is merely a play on that emphasis originating in the black community.

In the purest sense, intersectionality means to divide in the process of cutting between parts based upon different identities. In other words, rather than looking at Black women's concerns as a whole, it, instead, separates their issues in the process of addressing them. As it considers race, class and gender, formerly presented in the order of gender, class and race, it should retain its origin order, since, after all, that order does, in fact, reflect their true order of priorities, if, in fact, other than gender is of consideration. Another distinction is that intersectionality focuses on the overlapping nature of discrimination of different races of the same gender, specifically the female, in a format that continues to treat the components separately.

Hence, intersectionality has yet to integrate the parts, instead treating them as separate pieces or entities. Invariably referred to in earlier Africana Womanism publications as interconnection, this practice demonstrated the interweaving/blending together of the intricacies and complexities of race, class and gender as a whole. Exemplifying this is Sojourner Truth's dilemma in her 1852 oration, "And Ain't I A Woman." Before she could begin to address the absurdity of female subjugation, she as a Black woman had to first get beyond the race factor and be respected as a human being, entitled to basic human rights. It was only after her humanness, the race fact, was addressed could she move forward to address the remaining obstacles. Thus, her resounding self-actualization query, representing that interwoven nature of race, class and gender, as parts of her identity, were, in fact, parts of the whole. Although she was a Black woman, who dared to come to the all-white women's convention in Akron, Ohio to voice her opinion on matters relevant to women, she should have been welcomed as yet another woman among the community of women. However, because she was Black, she was not welcomed, as her race prohibited her from being considered a true human being. It must be here noted that her race could not be separated from her gender, and hence, unlike the white woman, she was also not considered or given the privileges of a woman, solely on the basis of race. Clearly her race and her gender were interconnected, never to be separated. This scenario reflects Linda LaRue's assessment in 1976 in her article, "The Black Movement and Women's Liberation:"

> Blacks are oppressed, and that means unreasonably burdened, unjustly, severely, rigorously, cruelly and harshly fettered by white authority. White women, on the other hand, are only suppressed, and that means checked, restrained, excluded from conscious and overt activity. And this is a difference. (218)

Indeed, this interdependence, characterizing the three key issues for Black women, makes it impossible to separate the parts of one's basic nature, activities and experiences. To be sure, the total represents the defining and joining together of the forces, an interconnected phenomenon, be it positive or negative in the end.

Consider the June 1995 Supreme Court Decision on Affirmative Action Set Asides. The ruling, affirming the unconstitutionality of racially based Set Asides for all, including Black women, has the obvious propensity for deeming Black women to be Black first rather than gender, while gender-based Set Asides for white women were ruled constitutionally solid and sound:

> When those Africana women finish fighting the Feminist battle and feminists have succeeded in realizing all their goals relative to female empowerment, the Africana woman will be left with the reality that she is both black and at the bottom.
> (Hudson-Weems, *Africana Womanist Literary Theory*, 83)

Here again, this results from the fact that the race factor will remain the ruling factor, resulting, in many instances, in her not realizing her pursuits relative to her career. In short, the fate of Black women is almost invariably determined by race first; her gender comes into consideration later, if at all. Thus, Race, Class and Gender interconnect here in the narrative of Africana people, particularly Black women, which reigns ever today.

Given the fact that the two terms, Interconnectedness and Intersectionality, have some credence, my inclination is to respect both as valid within the constructs of their distinct historical and cultural matrix and the parameters of all people and their particular experiences and persuasions. That is to say that both should remain, since both facilitate and accommodate its own audience. Neither need be eliminated in order for the other to survive, for the needs of each individual group are obviously real. Of course, both should be respected and allowed to exist freely without fear that only one can exist, for the idea of absolute applicability of a paradigm for all can only be realized if all are on equal footage, that is none is experiencing an added form or discrimination, such as racial dominance, which automatically puts the oppressed group at a disadvantage. To be sure, it is virtually impossible to address a single obstacle, when another or others have to be first corrected. At the same time, for feminism and its various collective forms, its audience can certainly appreciate its concept and terminology, with the realization that the concept, including the intersectionality signifier, should not presume to represent all women, particular Africana women. That would surely force the Africana woman to subjugate her number one obstacle, racism, while the dominant culture is allowed to continue to prioritize, though covertly so, gender as still its priority.

In the final analysis, then, let's be clear that when the Black woman succumbs to this, she will ultimately have to admit that she is still "black and on the bottom." And what an epiphany! It must be realized and accepted that Africana women should have that same right to name and define self and our movement as does the privileged other.

Indeed, Africana women should not be relegated to the level of assimilation, forced to embrace someone else's paradigm and priorities for penance—superficial acceptance and feigned political legitimacy. By now, more serious consideration for the call for the acknowledgement of the obvious pre-existence of "interconnectedness," associated with Africana Womanism for Black women, is to be respected in much the same way as one would never deemed feminism non-existent. As assessed in the new edition of the classic Africana Womanism,

> While I am not calling for a replacement of traditional, established paradigms, such as feminism, etc., for they were, indeed, created out of the needs of a particular group [white women] that had legitimate concerns or issues that needed to be addressed, I am nonetheless proposing for a broadening of the body of criticism to include yet another perspective or paradigm, which is Africana Womanism, now evolving to Africana-Melanated Womanism. (Hudson-Weems, *Africana Womanism*, 112)

To be sure, just as there is no one solution to all the problems of the universe, there is no one position for all the people of the world. We are diverse people of diverse needs, and thus, demand diversity in color, action and thought, including our philosophical and methodological preferences. According to Dr. James B. Stewart, Past President of NCBS, and Afrocentric Guadeloupe scholar, Dr. Ama Mazama, co-writers of the Foreword to *Africana Womanism*, 5th Edition, Africana Womanism is an important corrective to the continuing tendency to marginalize the experiences of Africana women and minimize their roles as active agents in the ongoing liberation struggle. Consequently, Africana Womanism is enabling Africana Studies/Africology to realize its full potential as a guiding beacon in the global battle to claim the natural rights of all people of African descent. Indeed, one commentator, general editor of Call and Response, has suggested, "Of all the theoretical models, Hudson-Weems' best describes the racially based perspective of many black women's right advocates, beginning with Maria W. Stewart and Frances W. Harper in the early nineteenth century." (p. 1379); (Stewart and Mazama, Africana Womanism, xiii)

In the final analysis, then, with reference here to the historical function of the African American Literary tradition as a corrective for historical wrongs, dating back to American slavery and the seminal role of slave narratives (like Olaudah Equiano or Gustavus Vassa, followed by

Frederick Douglass, Harriet Ann Jacobs, Harriet E. Wilson and others), Africana Womanism, too, offers opportunities for correcting continuous racist wrongs—beginning here with the mis-naming and mis-defining of Africana woman outside of her historical and current context. Indeed, Interconnectedness is more appropriate in assessing Black women's activities, although it does not rule out Intersectionality for the feminist.

As we review the powerful presence of the Africana woman, in concert with her male companion throughout history, it becomes clear that there was a real need for naming and defining Black women, justified by the very fact that such a paradigm, independently and separately designed for all women of African descent, only came about when Africana Womanism hit the scene in the mid 1980s. Although it is a global concept and still rising, it must be here noted that it is still very much needed and must be continued as our legacy for ultimate victory.

References
Anderson, Talmadge. Inside Blurb. Africana Womanism: Reclaiming Ourselves. Troy, MI: Bedford Publishers, 1993.

Aldridge, Delores P. Jacket Blurb. Africana Womanism: Reclaiming Ourselves: Troy, MI: Bedford Publishers, 1993.

Aldridge, Delores P. "Towards Integrating Africana Woman into Africana Studies" in Out of the Revolution: The Development of Africana Studies. Lanham, Boulder, New York, Oxford: Lexington Books, 2000, 191-201.

Aptheker, Bettina. "Strong Is What We Make Each Other: Unlearning Racism Within Women's Studies." Women's Studies Quarterly, 9:4 (Winter), 1981, 13-6.

Asante, Molefi Kete. Afterword in Africana Womanist Literary Theory. Trenton: Africa World Press, 2004, 137-139.

Carroll, Peter N. and David W. Nobel. The Free and the Unfree: A New History of the United States. New York: Penguin Books, 1977.

Christian, Barbara. Black Feminist Criticism: Perspectives on Black Women Writers. New York: Pergamon, 1985.

Christian, Mark. Afterword in Africana Womanism: Reclaiming Ourselves, 5th Edition. London and New York: Routledge Press, 2019.

Cowan, Connell and Melvyn Kinder. Smart Women: Foolish Choices. New York: Clarkson N. Potter, 1985.

Harris, Jr., Robert L. Book Endorsement in Africana Womanism: Reclaiming Ourselves.

Troy, MI: Bedford, 1993.

Hill, Patricia Liggins, et al,eds. Call and Response: The Riverside Anthology of the African American Literary Tradition. Boston: Houghton Mifflin, 1998.

Hudson-Weems, Clenora. "Africana Womanism: An Overview." in Out of the Revolution: The Development of Africana Studies. Lanham, Boulder, New York, Oxford: Lexington Books, 2000, 205-217.

Hudson-Weems, Clenora. "Africana Womanism: I Got Your Back, Boo," in Africana Womanism: Reclaiming Ourselves, 5th. Edition. London and New York: Routledge Press, 2019, 120.

Hudson-Weems, Clenora. Africana Womanism: Reclaiming Ourselves. Troy, MI: Bedford Publishers, 1993.

Hudson-Weems, Clenora. Africana Womanism: Reclaiming Ourselves, 5th Edition. London and New York: Routledge Press, 2019.

Hudson-Weems, Clenora. Africana Womanist Literary Theory. Trenton: Africa World Press, 2004.

Hudson-Weems, Clenora. Contemporary Africana Theory, Thought and Action: A Guide for Africana Studies. Trenton: Africa World Press, 2007.

Hudson-Weems, Clenora. "Cultural and Agenda Conflicts in Academia: Critical Issues for Africana Women's Studies" in The Western Journal of Black Studies, 13: 4, 1989, 185-189.

Hudson-Weems, Clenora. "The African American Literary Tradition" in The African American Experience: An Historiographical and Bibliographical Guide. Westport, Connecticut, London: Greenwood Press, 2001, 116-143.

Langley, April. "Lucy Terry Prince: The Cultural and Literary Legacy of Africana Womanism." The Western Journal of Black Studies, 25:3, Fall 2001, 153-162.

LaRue, Linda. "The Black Movement And Women's Liberation." Female Psychology: The Emerging Self. Sue Cox, ed. Chicago: SRA, 9176, 216-25.

Lincoln, C. Eric. Inside Blurb. Africana Womanism: Reclaiming Ourselves. Troy, MI: Bedford Publishers, 1993.

Mompati, Ruth. "Women and Life Under Apartheid" in One Is Not A Woman, One Becomes: The African Woman in a Transitional Society. Daphne Williams Ntiri, editor. Troy: MI: Bedford, 1982.

Mootry, Maria. Book Review in The Western Journal of Black Studies. Volume 18, Number 4, Winter 1994, 244-5.

Morrison, Toni. Times, 1989.

Morrison, Toni. "What the Black Woman Thinks about Women's Lib." New York Times Magazine, August 1971, 63.

Newson-Horst, Adele S. "Gloria Naylor's Mama Day: An Africana Womanist Reading" in Contemporary Africana Theory, Thought and Action: A Guide to Africana Studies. Trenton: Africa World Press, 2007, 359-372.

Ntiri, Daphne W. Introduction in Africana Womanism: Reclaiming Ourselves, 5th Edition. London and New York: Routledge Press, 1993; 2019, 1-8.

Stewart, James B. and Ama Mazama. Foreword in Africana Womanism: Reclaiming Ourselves, 5th Edition. London and New York: Routledge Press, 2019, xiii-xv.

MONA LISA SALOY

Dr. Mona Lisa Saloy is the 2021-23 Louisiana Poet Laureate. A native New Orleanian as well as a poet and folklorist, Saloy is the Conrad N. Hilton Endowed Professor of English at Dillard University in New Orleans. Dr. Saloy has documented Creole culture in sidewalk songs, jump-rope rhymes, and clap-hand games to discuss the importance of play. Her first collection of poetry, *Red Beans & Ricely Yours: Poems* (Truman State University Press) won the 2005 T. S. Eliot Prize for Poetry as well as the Pen Oakland-Josephine Miles 16th Annual National Literary Award in 2006. Her second published collection, *Second Line Home: New Orleans Poems*, was published by Truman State University Press in 2014. Saloy holds a PhD and an MFA from Louisiana State University, an MA from San Francisco State University, and a BA from the University of Washington. Her work has been published in numerous academic and literary journals, including *Africology: The Journal of Pan African Studies, Callaloo, Southern Journal of Linguistics, African American Review, Haight Ashbury Literary Journal* and most recently in the *Chicago Quarterly Review,* vol 33, Anthology of Black American Literature.

7th Ward Daily Fare: or Black Creole Talk

In the Crescent City
We live on the inside of good luck the
Right side of blessings
Past front steps and porches
We're a giving thanks & praying town
Contrary to popular opinion
There's more churches than bars!
Annually, we count the storms missing us
Laugh & Thank YOU Lord for another safe season
& in the middle of smiles
We see each other &
Wish *Y'all* well
Until we chew the fat on the gallery again
Hey, he looks like Uncle Brother . . .
Naw, he look like Jessie Hill,
Who dat?
Mr. Ooooo Poo Pah Doo his self!
Awww, they did that dude bad
Buried in old Holt Cemetery
What?
Potter's Field
No lie; that's Capoo (Black Creole for bad luck)
Oh oh gotta step
"Need to find a stump to fit & rest my rump."
Chew some pecans later
Amen!

Resurrection Sunday, Tree Top visits

Resurrection Sunday
After the Gospel Mass
At Ds House in the Neighborhood
7th Ward
No party today just cousins
Thankful for good worship
Healthy hands to bake red fish
Sweet potatoes

Tossed green salad graced with purple onions sliced peppers
Sautéed broccoli cauliflower corn sliced to tender when the
Doorbell brought a tall chocolate
Bent-over dude carrying a well-used duffle across his body along with
Water bottle sticking out
Ohhh he said he remembers me,
Not really, but Happy Easter
His greyed jeans saw better days, his head capped in a bent
Knit mostly black with red green stripes small but vivid
"D home?" Yes.
You remember me, Tree Top?
"You'se the couzin-poet
I holler "Y'all it's Tree Top!"
Tell him to come in
Tree eases into the kitchen,
Family central, slouches on a
Stool. "Sorry to come like this,
Sudden like, but Momma's gone now,
Was forced out the house &
Need to get tight for Salvation Army, who
Charge $10 a night now & no
Days work this week.
"$10 a night, that's rent!!?" D asked.
Tree *said "if he claimed crazy*
He could get free vouchers
But he ain't crazy & some things a man just can't do
His Momma didn't raise him to tell that kinda lie for $10 bucks."

Now looking into his pride of manhood,
his handsome chocolate shines though toothless.
He was one of Mush's men,
Mush, our D's father-in-law
our family crooner, jazz-base voice
"Autumn Leaves...."
His fresh greens from ground he dug
Collards to heal the earth, Creole tomatoes for flavor, *Merliton* in season
Tree Top, his Padna, caregiver for his Mom, across the street, end-
of-day sharing heavy tree removal, or barbequing on Summer days,
Gumbo on cold days, sharing a brewsky to
Jazz, Blues, Gospel, R & B every day
Occasional old-school movies in the yard.

Tree, like Mush, told me to
keep my old Toyota truck, just take care of it; danced Roots Rock with me to Marley Reggae
Made every Mush Birthday party, Crawfish boil, Sunday Suppers in the backyard:
we were together
we were safe, hugs by Mush
& his Buddies who helped change a tire, oil, or send us to the right mechanic
if they couldn't fix it.

This Resurrection Sunday, Tree Top stopped by
checked in, left with palms warmed
by buckets of food, love, & $favor
Our eyes leaked together
He would not take a ride
wanted to walk to the bus
hold our gifts in his heart
His head higher, his walk lighter,
His lips broad, he wipes leaks from smiling eyes

Years ago Before the Storm

It was hotter & more humid than now.
The ink was not dry on my *Ph D*.
My family gave me a knock-down
Dance-up back-yard party.
Cousins came from far,
Elder neighbors who loved me through the hardest days of
research and elder care of my Daddy, through the
crack epidemic that left Daddy drooling from the putrid red beans, a
layer of moldy slime swimming across the top of the big-black-iron
pot I found in the filthy mice-&-rat-infested kitchen, with only a piece
of roof dangling, roaches flying from nest to nest like birds; my family

remembered, that crack heads stole
everything not nailed down.
Didn't leave Daddy a pair of shoes. I
had to draw around his feet on cardboard for sizing; the
shoe store clerk wanted security to remove me
until I stood my ground, and left with a tan pair of huaraches and
slippers for Daddy. Doctors thought Daddy deaf and deteriorating
from dementia, but he just closed his ears and leaking eyes to the
disappointment he saw in his step kids and the transient men who
took over his home, his life with no hot-running water, a broken toilet,
the weeds growing through the bathroom floor from the dirt ground,
four feet below the claw-foot iron tub leaning through the broken floor
boards rotten from neglect.

(*Took me two years in & out of court to get rid of those niggas.*)

It was the filth and poor nutrition on top of it, that diminished this
WWII Army Sargent, Master Carpenter, into a man who babbled,
slobbered, who forgot who he knew; **my** Daddy, who used to dance
with my Mother and shuck oysters at our backyard parties growing
up. Had **no** idea what I walked into, just rolled his 300-pound body in
sheets to clean him & change bed linens until the shower was installed-
-his first shower since his Army days he sang; he was happy again,
and came back to himself fully for years, returning to stand guard on
the front porch and greet family & neighbors or what we call do(or)
popping, talk stuff about passersby. Even his doctors were shocked;
we all knew: it was **only God**, and a lot of prayers.

My new college colleagues, friends, and professors-now-friends came
and ate **Busters'** *plarines* and **Andrews'** *bananas-fo*ster *bread pudding*
with us, and danced the Second Line with us on to Duels Street and A.P.
Tureaud, laughing faces in tune to Levert's:

> *"I ain't much on Casanova.*
> *Me & Romero ain't never been friends*
> *Can't you see how much I really love ya*
> *Gonna say it you time & time again*
> *Ohhh Casanova. . . ."*

They thought my family was celebrating my degree. My cousin Larry said this backyard bash took him to our old parties, that everybody came for me, **not** for a wedding or a funeral,
"*BeBe, nobody got married and nobody died!*" he shouted.
They came for me, for watching me love Daddy back to health,
back to himself, back to our family,
and yes the Ph.D., a family first,
bringing us all together the way we were all raised,
only God we said only God.

Cicadas sang through the evening, serenading the nights until stopped only days later by Hurricane Katrina fanned across the gulf. That was our family's last time all together with long-time elders. **Mush** our Jazz crooner, the fish-net making **Leons** & great-gumbo **Cerres** no longer here. I told my family, maybe I'll write a novel about those hard days of waking up to a **Strawberry (crack-head whore)** peering over the **African beads** on my dresser, and **Daddy with no shoes**. I'll change the names to **protect the guilty**.

It was hotter & more humid years ago, the
Last time our family was all together
when nobody died &
No one was married.

"*I ain't much on Casanova. . . .* "

Elaine Brown

Elaine Brown aka Poet E Spoken is an explosive freestyle artist, History Teacher, Co-host of VENT, an online literary Empathy Circle, and My Word Open Mic. "Never afraid to normalize conversations of trauma!"

Joshua's Tree

Every since the day that you claimed
that our knuckles scraped ground
and we walked on all fours
We were still upright you see
Amendments did not change
nor legitimize legacies
So we broke bread like chains
to tell our stories
Therefore silence is forgein tongue
So all the trials triumph and tribulations
written in the blood of our ancestors
were meant to be told
It is healing for lost souls
For I myself had strayed far from this path
But voices from the past
Whispered wisdom
They said Elaine even
deep rooted systems
Of oppression have vision
They spread the Gospel of lies
In history books like religion
And although unwritten
Our voice has the power
To transform generations
When we uplift them
We must teach them that
56% of the Black race
Represented Wilmington
Under the Era Of Reconstruction
Did away with this two party system
and created Fusion
Words like diversity and inclusion

suddenly had meaning
In a port town that brought us
Over in slave ships but
We fought like hell
To control our own interests
Opened our own businesses
While White supremacists
Saw this as an act of violence
Stormed the local government
Burned Black establishments
Killed unarmed Blacke men
Women and children
And those who couldn't leave
Hid in the Black cemetery
where our ancestors dwell
And it was there
I heard the call through
The trumpet of conch shells
Grandpa Joshua, grandma Sallie
Grandma Bessie, Anne, Grandma, Juanita,
My Daddy, my brother Vernon,
Aunt Elaine, Aunt Lorretta, Uncle Sunny,
Uncle Earl, and Blest to be alive my Momma
Joan The Matriarch Yell
Tell our storiesTell our stories
Tell our stories

Akua Lezli Hope

Akua Lezli Hope is writing and dreaming from the ancestral land of the Onöndowa'ga:' also known as the Seneca, keepers of the Western Door in the southern Finger Lakes region of New York State.

IGBO LANDING

> We are incomprehensible
> to you who feel only fear
> when you hear us, spider
> silk on face, chill up back

which is a success perhaps
to have both sugar and fat
to die of excess and sloth
not like we hungry wraiths
whose forgotten flesh was sinew
whose nonexistent options were
to live death or die living
whose path was clear:
undo or be undone

Our drowned captors are silent
their injustice muzzles them

We sang the song of home going
a freedom-bound journey   as we
down drowned with determination
deliberation, avowals to never surrender
to die and return from whence we
came from where we were stolen,
to resist and not submit, calling to
our God, Chukwu, for escort, for conveyance
for admission to the next phase
existence beyond this abominable land
out of reach of horrible hands:

those who would eat our souls, bite
bit after bit, daily flay flesh
from our backs, lynch us
take our babies, steal their milk
rape our young ones, remove our tongues
and in that terrible future in which you tremble
by our whispers, lingering laments,
you would believe such theft was chosen?

and that is what frightens you
we refused to languish in longing
you hear our reverberating answers echo
through the water, slow lapping sounds
waves creeping on the land, our avowals

We consecrated our commitment
how we said no with our lives
for our lives, how we refused
that hell on land, making generations
of grist for the hideous mill of rogue
capital, the codified caprice of robbers
we brothers, sisters, daughters, sons, clear willed
strong souled, liberty-led, freedom fed
returned to mother water, singing a way
open

out of 75 only 13 were found
drowned, the rest of us lifted,
transmuted, flew

Igbo Landing is a historic site at Dunbar Creek on St. Simons Island in Glynn County, Georgia, where in 1803, 75 Igbo captives after drowning their captors and running the ship York aground, marched ashore, singing, and walked into Dunbar creek, committing mass suicide. 13 bodies were recovered the rest remain missing. In 2002 the site was declared a holy ground.

Igbo Landing II

We don't want to remember you
We peasants unendowed with vision
We mundane,   unschooled in magic
We who did not hear the trumpet
who could not hear the call of Chukwu
smell the sweet perfume of Oshun
who were too young to be initiated
or too old to lend our ears
or too tired to rise up
or too fearful to lay down our lives
who live in hope of rescue
who live in disbelief

Who live in margins and by
increments
who can live for centuries on 1/2 breath
submerged in the unbreathable
gasping, half garroted, yoked

We are the frightened and the failed
who nonetheless persist
who turned back from the
revolutionary act
from our punished
loins comes the future
from our conscript wombs
generations issue
from water to water
not dust   and with birth pains
blue wails that fill the lungs'
entry with their first breath
still knowing

we, applauded only for increase
for marrow and meat   for narrowing
contortions,   for bending
hoeing and reaping

not for inheritance
not for the welcoming of generations
still somehow loved
as flesh loves its continuance
its reflection

We don't want to remember you
stark indictment of our bleak being
Your refusal to be one with us
dark   broken   stolen
caged conscripted duped disputed
colonized cargo
fettered unfortunate losers in
history's lottery

We who write you now into being
we unwilling subjugated who
whispered you into being
who dressed the picked and disappearing bones
of your incomprehensibility into quilts of remembrance
patches of precious   precious recollection
sewn stitched summoned   annointed
despite ourselves   saved
connected into patterns of soulsong
images of your winged and watery triumph
painted with future sky, inner longings
unsuppressable, persistent   gut string
blind in our belief see now

pattern of decision tattooed on our wavering soulflesh
our lost millions   undecisioned
unmoored   untethered
living in terror
policed by Madness who still
somehow maintained memory
hid it   fed it   from armpit
to rib from mouth roof   to knee bend

o blooded land of benighted bones
our stolen teeth in mouth of its president
planted, arise in multiplicities to battle
what we don't want to remember
how unmaking is an option
how unlife is as understandable
as the struggle to be

those broken dreams became song
rice growers grew rice   iron mongers
forged   mute protections
wrought steel   spiritual blues
we told each other anyway

we told each other
while we spoke to the cotton
and the yam   and the cane whose
mills were baptized with our blood,

               our lost limbs, say   we won't remember
               we have no choice but
               to

On Design

for my nivlings

Your Harlem-born grandparents had an Isamu Noguchi
coffee table in our fifth floor walkup South Bronx apartment
where there were curtained French doors
They changed from blond wood to dark
in Queens which shocked me,
nabbing finds at flea markets and having their own
special furniture hustler in a dark store in Laurelton
— As it seemed all their dens of iniquity and rogue commerce
were dark stores made small by being crammed
with select, underpriced goods whose proprietors
like the cigar-chewing material guy on Delancey Street
had a secret knowledge of me without knowing me
i would wonder what they had said
and was jealous and possessive that these storekeeps
knew my parents well enough to presume
or that my parents allowed them
to think they knew them well enough,
to presume … i was slow
that was the hustle
i was there to play a role in
the elaborate plays they would construct
between themselves, designing
a family   a way   a life
their love

Linda D. Addison

Linda D. Addison is an award-winning author of five collections, including *How To Recognize A Demon Has Become Your Friend*, and the first African-American recipient of the HWA Bram Stoker Award®. She is a recipient of the HWA Lifetime Achievement Award, HWA Mentor of the Year and SFPA Grand Master. She has published over 370 poems, stories and articles and is a member of CITH, HWA, SFWA and SFPA. Look for her story in the *Black Panther: Tales of Wakanda* anthology (Marvel/Titan).

MetaGender Machine

Like a splinter in my mind
    driving me mad,
these thoughts, feelings
    shifting my desire,
like a fractal in my soul.

I split, revise, break into pieces,
    teleporting each hour
into another sex, amusing no one
    except myself, living outside
the boundaries, a rainbow misplaced.

What is my homeland, where can
    I live, a place of comfort, perhaps
not this planet or the next, but
    I continue to search, to
morph until I am what I am to be…

Neo-Americans

Before: we were from Senegal, Gambia,
    the Gold Coast, Biafra, Angola.
Named for the land of our ancestors,
    by the river, mountain, valley we lived near,

the work we did, the region we were
from: Kolda, Wollof, Kru, Igbo, Malembo.

Now: we are from Ohio, California,
    the East Coast, Maryland, Nevada.
Named by our parents, renamed by ourselves
    to reclaim humanity, heritage, pride,
        for the pain survived to stand tall in a
country fast to forget, slow to evolve.

The first twenty were called *Negar*. Much
    work to be done. The plan to create the ideal slave:
break them young, wipe them clean of birth culture,
    transplant inferiority, fear, helplessness.
    All slaves are African, all Africans are slaves.
Freedom was not color-blind. So they thought.

Our great-great grandparents' names forbidden in the New
    World. Slave names forced into their mouths.
Part of the plan to control, to erase our legacy. But
    humans find a way, using private names in their
    quarters to let their children know they still had
some power, some breath that could not be stolen.

We are called *African-American*, arriving at that label in steps:
    Colored => *Negro* => *Black* => *Afro-American*. Struggling
to find equality, naming ourselves: Jayla, Deion, Kimani, Elroi,
    invoking God, strength, beauty, royalty.
    All Americans are humans, all humans are equal.
Still struggling to hold these truths to be self-evident.

Now: we are Americans of African descent, conceived
    on land soaked in the blood of greed,
attacked by those still believing the original lie.
    We are born with the inherent need to be
    free, to be respected. No matter what you name us,
or what we name ourselves: We are humans—we are *Americans*.

Jewelle Gomez

Jewelle Gomez (Cape Verdean/Ioway/Wampanoag) is a writer and activist and author of the double Lambda Award-winning novel, *The Gilda Stories,* from Firebrand Books. Her adaptation of the book for the stage, *Bones & Ash: A Gilda Story,* was performed by the Urban Bush Women company in 13 U.S. cities. The script was published as a Triangle Classic by the Paperback Book Club.

She is the recipient of a literature fellowship from the National Endowment for the Arts; two California Arts Council fellowships and an Individual Artist Commission from the San Francisco Arts Commission.

Her fiction, essays, criticism and poetry have appeared in numerous periodicals. Among them: *The San Francisco Chronicle, The New York Times, The Village Voice; Ms Magazine, ESSENCE* Magazine, *The Advocate, Callaloo* and *Black Scholar.* Her work has appeared in such anthologies as *Home Girls, Reading Black Reading Feminist, Dark Matter* and the *Oxford World Treasury Of Love Stories.*

She has served on literature panels for the National Endowment for the Arts, the Illinois Arts Council and the California Arts Council.

She was on the original staffs of *Say Brother,* one of the first weekly, Black television shows in the U.S. (WGBH-TV, Boston) and *The Electric Company* (Children's Television Workshop, NYC) as well as and on the founding board of the Gay and Lesbian Alliance Against Defamation (GLAAD). She was an original member of the boards of the Astraea Foundation and the Open Meadows Foundation.

Her first novel, *The Gilda Stories,* celebrated its 20th year in print in 2011 with readings at the Museum of the African Diaspora and at the Queer Arts Festival. Her other publications include three collections of poetry: *The Lipstick Papers* (1980) and *Flamingoes And Bears* (1986), both self published and *Oral Tradition* from Firebrand Books (1995). She edited (with Eric Garber) a fantasy fiction anthology entitled *Swords Of The Rainbow* (Alyson Publications (1996) and selected the fiction for *The Best Lesbian Erotica Of 1997* (Cleis).

She is also the author a book of personal and political essays entitled *Forty-Three Septembers* (Firebrand Books 1993) and a collection of short fiction, *Don't Explain* (Firebrand Books 1997).

She has presented lectures and taught at numerous institutions of higher learning including San Francisco State University, Hunter College, Rutgers University,

New College of California, Grinnell College, San Diego City College, The Ohio State University and the University of Washington (Seattle).

Formerly the executive director of the Poetry Center and the American Poetry Archives at San Francisco State University she has also worked in philanthropy for many years. She is the former director of the Literature program at the New York State Council on the Arts and the director of Cultural Equity Grants for the San Francisco Arts Commission. She is also the former Director of Grants and Community Initiatives for Horizons Foundation as well as the former President of the San Francisco Public Library Commission. She is currently Playwright in Residence at New Conservatory Theatre Center.

Gilda Dreaming Awake

A road extends far into the future, far into the past.
One long and winding road. I move again,
this time in close circles, then twirling,
dervishing circles, green skirts
swirling, first around my ankles,
then raised above my knees
brushing your faces as I move.
On point, pivoting, burrowing
into the earth with my toe,
my body a machine for digging.
When it stops I do not;
but keep traveling, motion, traveling.
Salt over my shoulder, pale candles for our health.
I cut my hair from my head, bundle the locks
in neat packets and scatter them about the world.
I must keep dreaming to remember where they are.

My lips are parched and split. Not from
being black, being colored, being Negro
being nigger, being old or loving women.
But from the lies I've had to tell.
From the bile I've swallowed.

As I watch my body swirl in remarkable skirts
I can see rows demarcated by
the hidden locks of my hair.
There is the horizon I was too bitter to see.

In the east a sun still rises, I'm told,
And following it a sweet low moon.

Why in the dream, do I still carry a knife
for gutting? If I peer intently, I see deep
into eyes that belong to others on the road
who dream as I do: black, brown, white, old, young
short, tall, women mostly.

There are many like me. Our knives remain
sheathed. Our eyes open.
I brush fresh-cut hairs from my face
with bloody fingers. The startling red
streaks mark me and the cotton:
a ritual painting. Trails are made
deep into the rows, where others
have passed. Do I ever laugh in
the dream? Maybe at the thoughtful
baby biting her mother's breast
to prepare her for separation anxiety.

The procession of others,
The procession of myself
mirthful? Perhaps.

There's a dream I have of who I am.
In it I'm a woman with my breasts bound tight
To my body—invincible. Armored dreamer
With no obstacles in my path.
A woman with my breasts bound tight to my body,
who can breathe only with care, wasting no air,
making no easy motion.
I am not a woman ripe for splitting open
But a tightly wrapped package of
everything we need to know.

When I stop twirling, the dream may end
Or it may have a life of its own.
Black, red, purple songs that insist
upon being sung by lips, no matter how split.

The words may be as bitter as bile
or as sweet as my skin.

And through the song blood flows,
acapella, unashamed, unabridged.
We may be despairing but blood is sanguine.

When I stop moving my remarkable
green skirts and dull brown cape
nestle damply against my thighs.
I suck on the sweet bloodied tips
of my fingers for sustenance.
They are the earthy mushrooms of vision.

Our freedom always lies ahead.

Eleanor Bumpers* Reminds You: This is Not the Titanic…

"I imagine one of the reasons people cling to their hates so stubbornly is because they sense, once hate is gone, they will be forced to deal with pain."
                                                            James Baldwin

…but we are goin' down.
Y'all been drifting through history,
dancin' on the waves, clinging to a piece of
junk left over from the ship meetin' up
with—not an iceberg, but reality.

Sure is a winter night lyin' hard on you boys,
hiding your people and mine.
That cold froze your brain like
one of those science things
kept in a jar, waiting to be sliced.

There ain't no ship coming to save you
this time. No Natives gonna
teach you how to cook a turkey.
'Course there might be a group hug
at the end. But we so far from
the end we can't even see the letter
e.

Remember how you used to apologise
to your daddy for being bad? Then
he told you to go out to the alley and
bring him back a switch. That's
where we are right now.

So let go that piece of wood,
whatever it used to be
that you think is truth. Go on,
slip down in the icy water. Swim
like crazy before it freeze your butt.
If that happen they got to break your legs
to put you in a box. Come on now,
it's not going to be pretty. There's
gonna to be some crying.
And yeah, there gonna
be pain.

***

*Eleanor Bumpers, an elderly, disturbed Black woman was killed in 1984 by police with a 12 gauge shotgun when she resisted being evicted from her flat in the Bronx.

Halifu Osumare

Dance & Black Popular Culture Scholar

Halifu Osumare is Professor Emerita of African American & African Studies at University of California, Davis. She has been a dancer, choreographer, educator, cultural activist, and scholar for over forty years. She was a dancer with the New York's Rod Rodgers Dance Company in the early 1970s and the Founder of Black Choreographers Moving Toward the 21st Century, a California dance initiative, 1989-1995. She published *The Africanist Aesthetic in Global Hip-Hop: Power Moves* (2007) and *The Hiplife in Ghana: West Africanist Indigenization of*

Hip-Hop (2012) and was a 2008 Fulbright Scholar to Ghana. Her recent *Dancing in Blackness, A Memoir* won the 2019 Selma Jeanne Cohen Prize in Dance Aesthetics and a National Book Award from the Before Columbus Foundation. Dr. Osumare was awarded the 2020 Distinction in Dance for performance, scholarship, and service to the field by the Dance Studies Association. Finally, she is a Certified Dunham Instructor, and believes as her mentor Katherine Dunham did, the arts and the humanities in tandem can help evolve the human spirit.

The U.S. Has Always Been About US

Black backs bent, fingers bleeding from King Cotton
Hands stained browner from Virginia Tobacco
Body toiled, tired, and tethered to the plough
Mind smarting from the psychic pain of lashes
      but wise from the oppressed vantage place
Laying foundations for nouveau riche dreams
Building wealth for someone else's schemes
Laying groundwork for another Empire of Control
  The U.S. has always been about US

Cakewalking the sly digs
      while entertaining Massa's Guests and the World's Fantasies
Derisions of arrogant imitation, while high kicking
      and smiling all the while
The grinning Mask worn by white imitators
      not knowing the comic-tragedy
The U.S. has always been about US
The Jazz Singer wins the fame and money
      while we entertain the Massa at clubs built by Cotton
Watching from the wings
Wearing our wings of comic-tragic glory
Rolling our polyrhythmic hips, footwork faster than lightning,
      a Love Supreme moving, incomprehensible articulate phrases
America is not dancing the English Minuet on Saturday nights
The U.S. has always been about US

Racing through hundreds of years of time
The illusion of Race built on our humanity
Constructing false hopes of whiteness

>   on a fragile, crumbling hierarchy
> Blackness as hypothesis: at least you ain't a "nigger"
> Hope for the American Dream
>   as we fall into scenarios of a Nightmare constructed long ago
> Victims of a false narrative enacted over time
> Racing through 250 years on someone else's land
> Building a Race Edifice of crumbling concrete, encasing all our humanities
>   into a monument of the Exceptional Empire
> Envisioning Inalienable Rights, but blind to Human Breath
>   exhaling into the new possibility of the Collective
> Making it about not being the (Black) Other
>   While duping us into thinking we could also be the Elite
> Black Lives have always mattered
> The U.S. Has Always been About US
> And today Freedom has been expanded from 140 to 280 characters

Excerpts from
Dancing in Blackness, A Memoir (2018)

Chapter 1 - "Coming of Age in the Black Arts/Black Power Movements in the Bay Area "

(pp. 25-26)

I grew up in San Francisco, with my mother, stepfather, and three sisters, moving there from Texas in 1957 for "better opportunities for Negroes." As a child, I only infrequently went across the Bay Bridge to Oakland in the East Bay with my family to visit our cousins. But as a 19-year old, having moved away from home after graduating high school, and living in San Francisco apartments with student roommates, I began to explore Oakland and Berkeley. I took community dance classes and eventually moved to Berkeley, while carpooling with other SF State students over to the SF State University campus. Although only about twelve miles apart, Oakland is very different from San Francisco, then with a majority black population and increasingly more politically accessible to its black community. But there has always been a strong connection between both sides of the Bay.

California in general, and the Bay Area in particular, has achieved a reputation for being the bastion of American counter-culture, from politics to sexuality, and from collective social activism to the black consciousness movement. This Bay Area culture fit very well with my iconoclastic personality, and helped shape its contours. In fact, the seminal events, personalities, and social movements in the region during the late 60s was ground zero for the shift to a new cultural zeitgeist that occurred throughout the entire world, and I partook in this cultural change in my own particular way. The brewing revolutionary black cultural and political consciousness, as a part of this socio-cultural shift, would become known as Black Power and the Black Arts Movement. Cultural theorist Amy Ongiri rightfully notes that

> . . . the historical moment of both the Black Power and the Black Arts Movements was the formative movement, not only for contemporary understanding of African American identity, but also for ideas of blackness in African American cultural production, characterized by artists and intellectuals of the era as "the new thing" but naturalized into contemporary African American culture as "authentic" Blackness.[10]

Indeed, "the new thing" pervaded my undergraduate years between 1965-1968 at San Francisco State University and shaped my personal consciousness as a black female and a dancer-choreographer. San Francisco and Oakland (as well as Berkeley) had a symbiotic relationship in the development of "the new thing."

(pp. 28-29)

Meanwhile, on the heels of the Civil Rights (1964) and Voting Rights (1965) Acts, and the late 60s Black Power Movement (Stokely Carmichael had given his famous Black Power speech in October 1966 at UC Berkeley.), we forged a Bay Area version on the West Coast of the Black Arts Movement (BAM) that helped redefine, for my baby-boomer generation, who black people were becoming. In 1966 a short-lived cultural venue, the Black House, was established in San Francisco with several Bay Area playwrights and poets like Ed Bullins, Marvin X, and Jimmy Garrett. East Coast nationally recognized artists arrived to connect with the West Coast artists. Amiri Baraka (then known as

Leroi Jones), Sonia Sanchez, and saxophonist Joseph Jarman (later to become a member of the Art Ensemble of Chicago), were some of the out-of-towers who helped us think through our artistic identity. The Black House featured "revolutionary new black music" and staged plays of the new militant persuasion. Leroi Jones held community meetings to inculcate the new manifesto of the black arts movement that he and writer-theorist Larry Neal had developed on the East Coast. The basis of this manifesto, Neal said, was "radically opposed to any concept of the artist that alienates him from his community." He also proclaimed that the Black Arts movement "is the aesthetic and spiritual sister of the Black Power concept."[11]

To the end of linking the two parts of the movement, Jones also created a written "Communications Project," which was ostensibly an outline for how to implement the Black Arts Movement within the larger project of changing the consciousness in the black community, or what he called building black consciousness in general. The basic mandate of the document was to "clarify or agitate, reinterpret, or retell," the issues pertaining to the black community, including "What to do in case of riots." Jones' "Communications Project" was published in a Black Theatre issue of The Drama Review (TDR) in Summer 1968. It is a comprehensive outline of all the areas that should be addressed to get the message out to the people, including newsletters, newspapers, comic books, and posters. Politically, it clearly stated the agenda should be "anti-Vietnam, anti-genocide, and economically starting neighborhood block associations, welfare recipients organizations, and rent strikes." The cultural component is most important here, and it included reeducation about black history, philosophy, and traditions that would be inculcated through drama, poetry, mixed media, music, and dance. Therefore, dance was viewed as a legitimate medium of propaganda to help change the consciousness of the black community. Most importantly, the Black House in San Francisco is mentioned and linked to the SF State Black Student Union.[12]

Dance Becomes My Revolutionary Expression (pp. 31-32)

Dance was my tool of expression and I used my growing creative movement style to make my own individual statements about my developing black consciousness. When I first entered SF State in 1965 I joined the Negro Student Association; by the time of the infamous

1968 SF State Strike that organization had morphed into the militant Black Student Union, and we turned the campus on its head. The student protests precipitated the academic field of Ethnic Studies when SF State started the country's first Black Studies Department and eventually the School of Ethnic Studies (in which I would eventually go on to get my master's degree in the early 90s).

(p. 27)

Armed with this new revolutionary cultural curiosity, I explored my own performance approach and choreography at several venues, including the Sunday Showcases at the Black Panthers headquarters (The Oakland Learning Center) in East Oakland. The growing political militancy regarding black liberation that the Black Panther Party (BPP) represented, was not my approach, and in 1967 and 1968 I struggled with exactly how I could contribute to the movement. My answer was to take my solo choreography to the Sunday showcases and offer it as my creative furthering of the "revolution." My dance solos were welcomed at the Panther's Sunday community gatherings, and this became my personal contribution to the black power political movement and the new revolutionary consciousness at its foundation. Dance has always been central to African American culture; therefore, dance in service to social change is a valid and effective means of communicating the shifting (black) consciousness. What I performed, but they were an amalgam of what I was learning from Zak Thompson, Ed Mock, and Ruth Beckford, as well as my own developing choreographic voice from my SF State dance classes.

In late 1967, while the student demonstrations on SF State campus were heating up, right before the conservative S. I. Hayakawa was hired as President of the university, and the Black Panthers in Oakland were creating an armed resistance to police brutality, I decided to teach my own dance class as another cultural political statement. By this time, I was living in Bernal Heights above the Mission district in San Francisco, and was able to get a recreation room donated at the Good Samaritan Community Center on Potrero St. in the Mission district. It was a big hulking room with tables and arts and crafts supplies, and not really set up for dance. But it had the most important thing: a sprung hardwood floor. Long before the days of Facebook and the Internet, I created thirty hand-made flyers with crayons, and put them up in strategic spots throughout San Francisco's North Beach, the Haight-Ashbury, at the university, and in the Mission. To my amazement 35 people showed up for my dance class, which consisted of Dunham Technique from Ruth Beckford, Afro-Cuban learned from Ed Mock, and modern dance and the little jazz I had learned from Nontsizi Cayou at SF State University.

However, another component of the SF State revolutionary movement allowed me to continue to hone my abilities as a dance teacher: the "Experimental College." As an appeasement to students' growing demand for a voice in their education, particularly for non-traditional classes, the diplomatic concept of the Experimental College was created. This was an actual student-led bureaucracy and funded by the Associated Students, which accepted or reject courses taught by students teaching other students and community members using university facilities. Many SF State students exploring the hippie movement centered in the San Francisco's Haight-Ashbury district (where I lived for part of my undergraduate years), could gain experience by teaching experimental courses, from macramé weaving to astrology. These were non-credit courses, but many students got their first experience teaching through the Experimental College. The course titles reflected the times: "Witchcraft of Middle Ages Made Practical," "Alchemy for the Whole Family," "Expanding Your Consciousness with Ken Kesey's Bus Ride," "Mao Tse-Tung's Red Book Interpreted for the D Student," "Protecting Yourself During Civil Disobedience," and my course that I called "Primitive Jazz Dance."

Primitive Jazz Dance was an obviously naive appellation that alluded to my accumulated study in modern, jazz, and Afro-based dance forms available at the time.[13] In the late 60s we were not yet sophisticated about the nuances of our own colonized language, and my 1967 dance class title illuminates our own complicity in belittling African-based dance forms in those early years while, at the same time, attempting to elevate the stature of black dance. This is the insidious nature of cultural hegemony: it is imbedded in the deep structure of the language, representing the unconscious thought patterns that can often be more oppressive than overt racism. Like Foucault's search light gaze of the "panopticon," the "Master's" assessment of the "Slave" becomes internalized, remaining long after the Master has physically been extricated.[14]

(pp. 34-35)

The Bay Area, in the late 60s and early 70s became ground zero of social, political and cultural activism for the country, and what I would realize later, the world. The Black Panther Party, the Black Arts Movement, the San Francisco State Student Strike, the UC Berkeley Free Speech Movement, the Anti-Vietnam War Movement, the Free Huey and Free Angela Davis protests, and the hippie drop-out-and-tune-in counterculture all converged into a tumultuous time that shaped my consciousness and therefore the trajectory of my life. On the black cultural front an important local KQED public television series by Maya Angelou (1928-2014) emerged, Blacks Blues, Black! This was a ten part series of one-hour shows written and hosted by Maya Angelou that examined the influence of African American culture on modern American society. It included some of black dancers and theatre people, such as Danny Duncan and Blondell Breed (Mwanza Furaha) who were to become seminal in creating the local black arts scene. It also included African scholars and musicians, linking Africa and African America in poignant and entertainingly cultural ways. As Dr. Angelou was a practitioner of many of the performing arts, theater skits, children's games, singing, drumming, and dance were used to tell the story of the black American journey. This mainstream televised show was an example of the late 60s as a crucial shift in the consciousness and representation about black people in American society.

This was the socio-political context in which I developed my first sense of a black dance consciousness that has driven my career first as a dancer-choreographer (1968-1999), as a producer-cultural activist (1977-1994), and now a dance and popular culture scholar (1995-present). Little did I know in the 60s that my choice of dance (or did it choose me—it's hard to discern the difference any more) would become my platform to explore blackness in its political racial, and cultural, and postcolonial, and even spiritual dimensions. Dance was also to serve as an international language, connecting me to future students, artists, and scholars in Spain, France, Holland, Denmark, Sweden, Mexico, Ghana, Nigeria, Togo, Kenya, Malawi, Trinidad & Tobago, Jamaica, and more recently Brazil in ways that I could never have imagined. The universality of dance and music allows a bridging of cultures in dynamic people-to-people ways that connect across all kinds of borders far beyond the spoken language, physically and spiritually reaching out and connecting people. The Blacks Arts Movement-West became part of my introduction to this understanding of the power of dance and the arts.

Endnotes

[1] Arthur Jafa's theory of "flow, layering, and rupture" is cited in: Tricia Rose, *Black Noise: Rap Music and Black Culture in Contemporary America* (Middletown, CT :Wesleyan University Press, 1994), 38.

[2] Don L. Lee (Haki Madhubuti), "Gwendolyn Brooks," in *Directionscore: Selected and New Poems* (Detroit: Broadside Press, 1971), 88–90.

[3] LeRoi Jones and Larry Neal, eds., *Black Fire: an anthology of Afro-American Writing* (New York: William Morrow, 1968), 5.

[4] LeRoi Jones and Larry Neal, eds., *Black Fire: an anthology of Afro-American Writing* (New York: William Morrow, 1968), n.p

[5] Toni Cade Bambara, ed., *The Black Woman: An Anthology* (New York: Penguin, 1970), 13.

[6] W. E. B. Du Bois, *The Souls of Black Folk* (New York: Penguin, 1995), 45.

[7] Larry Neal, *Black Boogaloo: Notes on Black Liberation* (San Francisco: Journal of Black Poetry Press, 1969)

[8] LeRoi Jones and Larry Neal, eds., *Black Fire: an anthology of Afro-American Writing* (New York: William Morrow, 1968), 314.

[9] Claudia Rankine, *Citizen: An American Lyric* (Minneapolis: Graywolf Press, 2014), 135.

[10] Amy Abugo Ongiri, *Spectacular Blackness: The Cultural Politics of the Black Power Movement and the Sear for a Black Aesthetic.* Charlottesville, VA: University of Virginia Press, 2010, 89.

[11] Larry Neal, "The Black Arts Movement," *Drama Review*, Summer 1968. Reissued by National Humanities Center Resource Toolbox: The Making of African American Identity: Vol. III, 1917-1968. Accessed January 26, 2015, http://nationalhumanitiescenter.org/pds/maai3/community/text8/blackartsmovement.pdf

[12] Le Roi Jones, "Communications Project," *The Drama Review* (*TDR*), Vol. 12, no. 4, (Summer 1968), Special Black Theatre issue: 53-57.

[13] My use of the word "primitive" to describe my dance 1960s dance style did not have the academic connotation underlying Katherine Dunham's early anthropological use of the word. In 1930s anthropology, "primitive peoples" meant those without a written language or history. She therefore frequently used the term "primitive dance" in that anthropological sense, while illuminating the great sophistication of the dances within that rubric. Even after the revisionism in social sciences that challenged this ethnocentric language, she continued to use the term, representing her original anthropological connotation.

[14] See the full development of the symbolism of the panopticon in Michel Foucault, *Discipline and Punishment: The Birth of the Prism.* New York: Pantheon Books (1977).

Elijah Pringle III & Aileen Cassinetto

Elijah Pringle III is a Philadelphia poet, lyric baritone, composer, actor, and artivist. A "Best of the Net" nominee, he is the author *of At the Cornerstone, Feeding the Sparrow,* and *Second Saturday at Serenity,* and has appeared on radio, TV & stage. He has been quoted in print in *Newsweek, The New York Times, The Philadelphia Daily News,* and elsewhere. He credits his true education to five generations of teachers.

Aileen Cassinetto is the Poet Laureate of San Mateo County, California. Widely anthologized, she is the author of two poetry collections and three chapbooks. Her work has appeared or is forthcoming in the *Asahi Shimbun, The Banyan Review, Moss Trill, The Nonconformist Magazine,* the *San Francisco Chronicle,* and *Vox Populi,* among others. Curator of the reading series "POWER TO THE POETS," Aileen also organized the Peninsula Virtual Bookfest which gathered over 60 authors in a series of inspiring and vital readings and conversations in September and October 2020.

HOW TO LAUNCH AN AD CAMPAIGN USING BLACK BODIES

"Madison Avenue is afraid of the dark."
—Nat King Cole

Part 1 Cigarette
    As I look at the being of the American Negroid
    I know we can brand them and make new money.
    We can re-chain them to tobacco with cigarette.
    We've had them plant it, weed it, prone it and till it.
    Now we'll manufacture it and force them to consume.
    See psychologically smoking allows them to escape
    from their mundane being. We'll retail it "sexy cool".
    Can't get black lungs working cotton field so this
    will do. The lungs of Blacks to become cancerous.

Part 2 Malt Liquor
    Next we'll need to plaster malt liquor signs every-
    where in their barrios, especially near schools.

If they are abstemious they'll resist our efforts to
placate and pacify them with a forty-five bottle
thirty-two ounces of liquid denial will keep them
unbalanced, gifted with hangovers the next day.
Don't worry about the taste. It is the buzz the high
and as a delightful by-product we can have the
indigenous birth children of alcohol syndrome.

Part 3 Soap
We can use them to sell soap. Have their black
bodies scrub lily white to show how great it is. Or
sell Elliott's White Veneer—see how it covers
over black. Sell bleaching cream to lighten their
burden. Oh, not really but they'll buy the hoax.
Give them the lye of straightening hair. Or maybe
have them glue their minds shut with No. 33
synthetic locks. "I swing my head back and forth."
I wish we could get Willow to do our commercial

Part 4 Sweater
It all boils down to media cost. How much
will you pay to make something go away.
Like this little ~~blackface~~ balaclava sweater,
like the green hoodie with the coolest monkey,
like an ad gone awry. But you need to act
quickly. Firstly, own your bad press. Secondly,
hashtag, meme, amplify, ROI.
Lastly and most importantly, open that red sylvie.
How much will you pay in solidari-té.

Part 5 Postcards
What's better than double page spreads?
Collectible postcards! Saturate
the market with your brand. Come up
with sexy ad copy such as pregnant
black child in watermelon patch ("Oh—I is Not!...
It Must Be Sumthin' I Et!!"). Or something
more domestic, like white woman sewing
with six-cord cotton thread/black woman
laboring in cotton field. ("Wish you were here!")

Part 6 Syrup
    We all know that a ready-mix by itself
    wouldn't sell. Any foodie can add hard
    winter wheat, corn flour, phosphate compounds,
    and some salt to APF to make pancakes.
    You gotta bring in Aunt Jemima.
    Give the target audience some antebellum-
    flavored grub. For maximum reach,
    "Let ol Auntie sing in yo' kitchen."
    "I's in Town, Honey." It's all syrup or gravy!

Lakiba Pittman

Lakiba Pittman is a poet, creative artist, educator, and business consultant. She is a facilitator for Emotional Emancipation Circles sponsored by the Association of Black Psychologists and is also a trauma healing facilitator and consultant with Healing Together and Circles International. Lakiba is currently working on the 2nd edition of her self-published book *Bread Crumbs from The Soul... Finding Your Way Back Home,* which is a showcase featuring her original art, poetry and autobiographical reflections. In 2020, she opened as a feature guest poet at the Museum of the African Diaspora (MOAD) Open Mic Series in San Francisco. She has exhibited her art with The Black Woman is God art exhibits for several years in San Francisco and will be one of the featured artists at the exhibit at SomARTS in 2022. Her art has also been featured at the African American Art & Cultural Center in San Francisco. She is a Professor at Menlo College where she teaches Diversity in the Workplace, Culture in Media, and Race & Racism. She also designs and delivers specialized workshops on cultural sensitivity and competency, and on reducing bias through mindful practices. Lakiba teaches public and private classes and workshops on compassion, wellness, and self-care. She is certified by Stanford University's Center for Compassion & Altruism Research & Education (CCARE) and is a Sr. Instructor teaching Compassion Cultivation Training (CCT) workshops. She is certified as a Compassion Ambassador through the Applied Compassion Academy at Stanford University. Working with CCARE, the Compassion Institute and Compassion Corps, Lakiba develops and delivers classes, workshops, and culturally relevant compassion training throughout the Bay Area in person and on Zoom globally.

We Come to Heal the World …

I call myself Queen of the universe, of the sky
As I fly into new realities once living many years
as a caterpillar – stuck – and then I found a safe spot to transform
And within this chrysalis I began to know my true self
This metaphormosis of me becoming Queen
Re-birthing out of a cocoon of light and love
I awoke as a butterfly high in the sky
Above all seeming troubles of the day
I am alive in this new place due to miraculous callings
now crowning others to walk in ancestries
footsteps where we survive, we thrive as we vision and manifest
new ways to be soft yet powerful. With eyes lifted to imaginations
I hasten to my throne to deliver truths and wisdom and
fabrics of many colors to new soon-to-be
Queens in this now … this future day
I am because she was because you are
the one to continue this majesty.
Lift up your chin in true regality, knowing the power you sense
within is real and the time you sense is now
as you are the one to come to heal
You are the one we prayed for Oh Queen of Queens take your
Rightful place on the throne that
We might be healed by your heart, by your tone
By your art, by your music, by your rhythm, your rhyme,
Your poetry, by your touch… by your soul…
I speak to the Queens and the Queens answer
We come to heal the world…

I am the Instrument

I play within the rhythms of my own life
seeking a pathway of light and wonder
and tiny pathways and cavernous entry points.
I have no limits, no boundaries except to love fully
so, I improvise each new day and
I whisper, I sing,

I drum, I dance . . .
I am the instrument through which I play the melody of my life
I call upon the ancestors who whisper new songs
within my spirit and I don't hold back.
I give it all I've got.
I step in unencumbered, unabashedly because the world is on fire
and I am the water.
The land is dry and I am the tears
The fear is growing and I've got the love.
I am the instrument used by the holy presence
Inspired to tune you in
To resonate within your heart
To vibrate within your soul
To reverberate within your mind
Just so you can remember your purpose
I am the rock. The truth.
The light.
I am called and I answer that call
I play in beliefs
In prophecies
In stories
So that even when your ears don't hear me,
your heart does
Your soul knows
Your spirit set free
The Griot
I am Word
I am the Instrument

Antwoinette Ayers, Kathryn Bentley, Dr. Connie Frey Spurlock and Dr. Sandra E. Weissinger

Antwoinette Ayers wears several hats in the East Saint Louis greater community. She serves as the CEO of Visual Movements, which assists others in writing to visualize what their lives ultimately should be. In addition to running Visual Movements, she also serves as the Communication Director for *IAMESTL* Magazine, a magazine dedicated to shining a light on the positive people and things that make up East St. Louis. She is also a Steering Committee Member for The Winstanley Development and most recently joined SIUE Truth Racial

Healing and Transformation Campus Center. Antwoinette formerly worked as a Communications intern under the direction of Larry Perlmutter at Rise Community Development, a nonprofit housing developer, development consultant, and pre development lender in St. Louis, Missouri. She received training in the Media and Diversity Inclusion Production by Continuity StL. Certified by St. Louis Economic Development Partnership Program by Kauffman Foundation for Entrepreneurial Development.

Kathryn Bentley, M.F.A. commits herself to community-engaged arts collaborations, striving to create compassionate artistic experiences, using theater to lift social consciousness. She is an Associate Professor of Theater at Southern Illinois University Edwardsville (SIUE), the coordinator of the IMPACT Academy and the Director of the Black Studies program. She has been the Artistic Director of SIUE's Black Theatre Workshop since 2006. She has performed and directed with numerous theater companies regionally and nationally, most notably directing the groundbreaking 2019 Shakespeare in the Streets production Love at the River's Edge with Shakespeare Festival St. Louis. In 2018, she joined Bread & Roses Missouri as Artistic Director for the Workers' Theater Project and directed the company's first full length production Jailbird in 2019. In 2000, she was instrumental in developing the CHIPS In Motion program at CHIPS Health and Wellness Center in North St. Louis. This program continues to utilize performance to teach the community about pertinent health and wellness issues. Bentley is the 2020 St. Louis Visionary Awards Outstanding Working Artist.

Dr. Connie Frey Spurlock is a sociologist committed to dismantling hierarchies of oppression and building in their place flourishing relationships. She does this work by centering community-identified goals with meaningful learning experiences for area students. Frey Spurlock is founding director of the SIUE Successful Communities Collaborative, a cross-disciplinary program based on the EPIC-N model, an award-winning university-community partnership program that works to advance the needs of communities while training the next generation workforce and leadership. SSCC develops and supports partnerships between SIUE and local communities to advance resilience and sustainability. She is also a member of the SIUE TRHT Campus Center, which seeks to prepare the next generation of leaders to confront racism and dismantle the belief in a hierarchy of human value. She has been at SIUE since 2004 and is also an associate professor of sociology. Her research and teaching interests center on sustainability, research methods, and community engagement.

Dr. Sandra E. Weissinger is a sociologist committed to calling out violent systems, institutions, and behaviors. Weissinger does this work well, engaging in scholar-activism in the United States, Mexico, and Palestine. She has authored and contributed to a number of academic works. Her most recent anthologies include *Violence Against Black Bodies: An Intersectional Analysis of How Black Lives Continue to Matter* and *Law Enforcement in the Age of Black Lives Matter: Policing Black and Brown Bodies*. As part of her commitment to scholar-activism, Weissinger regularly contributes as a public lecturer, invited speaker, and community collaborator—recently obtaining funding from the National Science Foundation and Innovations in Community-Based Crime Reduction (CBCR) Program to further equity-based initiatives. Dr. Weissinger is based out of the St. Louis metro area and is an associate professor of sociology at Southern Illinois University Edwardsville (SIUE).

Beloved by Many; Abandoned by Some: The Undying and Unwavering Spirit of East St. Louis, Illinois

A Cultural Clap Back by
Sandra E. Weissinger
Kathryn Bentley
Antwoinette Ayers
Connie Frey Spurlock[1]

"Revolution is not a one time event"
Audre Lorde, Harvard University, 1982.

Being abandoned is a thief that was handed to us by those that admired us.
If the truth is told, that year in 1957—when "The Race Riot Massacre of East St. Louis"—hit our town, because a spoiled nation of greed spoke louder than building with Black folk who are rich, wealthy and creative.
We could've taken our shit back
but the laws hung us
and acquitted them from being thug members for life
while bombs dance on our streets.

We clap back.

So tread lightly...we do not stand down quietly.

---

[1] The authors acknowledge the work of SIUE TRHT Campus Center core team members— Dr. Jessica Harris, Dr. Bryan Jack, Dr. Courtney Boddie, Dr. Elizabeth McKenney, Dr. Lydia Jackson; BTW students—Rhonda Whittier, Yoseline Miranda, Tyrice Collier; SIUE Sociology students—Sean Thomas, Mario Diaz, Andrea Perez; Inaugural class of E-Storytellers— Lorenzo Savage; Dr. Eugene Redmond; Edna Patterson-Petty; Reginald Petty; Dr. Rodney Coates, Dr. Simone Williams, Darryl Cherry, Clint Collins, Dr. Wes Robinson-McNeese.

We endured the pain that left a low economic stain.
Robbed of education equity that started right here
in our promised land.
As Dr. Eugene Redmond to become Emeritus Professor of English
at SIUE.
He gave us a tiny glimpse
of pushing past the narrative of systematic educational oppression.

We clap back

We fought back.
Granddaddy worked way too hard.
Coming from the south
only to be crushed
as if his mama and daddy didn't pray for him to arrive in the place of
milk and honey flowing from the wells of economic development
and resources.

We clap back

I can't help but think: what you do see that permits you to rearrange us?
Was it your admiration of the way Katherine Dunham danced in 1942
in "Pardon My Sarong"?
No BOO! That wasn't for you.
She did that to show Black girls how not to be blue. So pardon you, I'd
hate on us too!

We clap back

Did you get upset when we were named the all American City in 1959?
It's funny how we were called "All American" and yet were treated less
than American.

We clap back

Yes, we know what you see now.
Dead lands and deserted homes
but the heart of the people here
Rich like the soil gleaning from the corn field east of the Mississippi

We keep pressing forward.
seeking the sweet bliss of opportunity.

We clap back

Left for ruins
but created music
that kept you foot-tapping through the frequency
traveled to your ear by way of Miles Davis.
He played the song "All Blues"
so that you'd feel a deep emotion from the people from his hometown.

We clap back

You thought " Left a good job for the city working for the man every
night and day" was a song lyric. Naw baby.
That was Tina Turner's life
as she witnessed father's take care business
so she can be celebrated in show business.
She rolled straight from the street of East St. Louis.

We clap back

We clap back, clap back
From the East Side to
East St. Louis
Partnering with beautiful programs such as
TRUTH, Racial Transformation Campus Center
For healing the gap
With the attempt to showcase
the glow of a broken city with beautiful people willing to unite.
We clap back
With high performances in education and intelligence
from a city with less -
suffering under the poverty line.
We clap back
We'll run circles around any opposition
We clap back
Because the football games is a family reunion

To remind us why
We are the
"THE CITY OF CHAMPIONS"
OUR BLACK IS BEAUTIFUL

Popular culture depicts East St. Louis[2] in a number of ways that reproduce stereotypes which are nasty, detrimental, and otherwise steeped in anti-Black racism. Perhaps cultural critics and those with lived experiences of navigating discrimination should not be surprised? Any time a Black space exists[3], these power plays show up in an attempt to police access and sideline artistic expression[4]. This is the legacy of colonial spaces—especially if left unchallenged by those who know that Black lives have always mattered. East Saint Louis is no exception. Despite these great odds, those who understand the costs of being silenced create and give birth to a future committed to the belief that not only is Black beautiful, it is powerful.

It is powerful.
It is resilient.
It is the voice of a people that refuse to give up their claim to humanity.

We see the humanity of residents in the ways they create space and take up space. Residents do big things in the City. They create information hubs, squaring off with those sources that refuse to show the creative energy undergirding the city's inhabitants. They become entrepreneurs, putting their crafts at the center of their activism. They protect and venerate those people who publicly challenge anti-Black stereotypes and highlight the prowess of our creative light.

---

[2] East St. Louis, or ESTL, is an Illinois city. ESTL is located just across the river from Saint Louis, Missouri. The location and name of East St. Louis is purposeful. It was created to be a city that would be used, exploited, and forgotten by the industries and workers who have, historically, walked the city streets. But just because others have abandoned a site does not mean that they have broken the spirit or backbone of the place.

[3] This use of "Black" is purposeful, as it speaks to the legacy of political empowerment shared across races to support and embolden Blackness.

[4] Consider the tragic treatment of Black cultural critics in society: Cornell West's treatment at the hands of Harvard administrators; the out casting of Steven Salita, a scholar who recognizes the connection between Blackness, colonialism, and Palestine, by the University of Illinois at Urbana-Champaign; and certainly the legacy and abandonment by Southern Illinois University in East St. Louis.

Katherine Dunham.
Miles Davis.
Jackie Joyner-Kersee.
Eugene Redmond.

They teach and lead, helping the youth to keep their faces towards the sky of possibilities.

Even with such fire, stereotypical depictions (whether purposeful or not) lay the groundwork for residents to question whether their Black is, in fact, beautiful. Scholars and news sources alike[5] document the struggle between what East St. Louisans see around them (abandonment by institutions, for example) and what they truly are—amazing and good and enough. This is the powerful, yet toxic, dynamic produced by anti-Black racism. The people who are being exploited and scapegoated are left wondering what their part is in the relationship. But as all survivors of oppression and abuse need to know, the sickness is never about them. It is always about the perpetrator. Said differently, their Blackness can never be the reason for corporate divestment and the dilapidation of building infrastructures. This is not an individual problem or cultural failure. This is a societal problem. In a place once lauded as an "All-American City," folks are navigating and grappling with and shaping what "American" is and who America is for. They do so every day and in ways that show Black Lives Matter.

An important way to make Black Lives Matter is to create spaces in which institutions commit to Black communities. In addition to human and material resources, institutions have to take responsibility for their role in furthering anti-Black racism and exploitation of Black communities. Though a relatively new endeavor, since 2019, Southern Illinois University Edwardsville has been having difficult conversations about its divestment from East St. Louis. A Truth, Racial Healing and Transformation Center was started—taking seriously the model from the Association of American Colleges and Universities (AAC&U) and designing operating papers based on a vision to "...be a model for change in the region."

---

[5] Misconstrued, Jonathan Kozal's work may lead some to this conclusion. Certainly, the news of violence (as published by the Belleville based News Democrat) can be overwhelming for those who do not have access to balanced information about community wins. Community scholars have clapped back at these unfortunate depictions of East St. Louis. For example, see the work of Lori Davis.

SIUE grapples with racism and its effects. To do so effectively, it is imperative the work is grounded in a clear understanding of our position relative to our external environment—recognizing that as a university, we do not and should not function and operate apart from the communities in which we live and work. Racism has no bounds and given its far-reaching implications, we can no longer afford to reinforce boundaries that have all too often separated campus and community; the cost is simply too high.

As a model for community-based racial healing and change, in the St. Louis-Metro East region, scholar-activists seek to dismantle the well-accepted hierarchy of human value by connecting with community agencies that are already engaged in anti-racism work, establishing new relationships between those community agencies and SIUE, and preparing college and high school students to work alongside community members as agents of social change. Those who believe that Black Lives Matter take an anti-colonial position that leverages our privilege as an economically and socially powerful institution. As equal partners with all stakeholders, we will establish authentic, trusting relationships for the upbuilding of sustainable communities where people of all backgrounds can thrive.

Scholar-activists engaged in the work of the SIUE TRHT Campus Center are committed to empowering area students with the knowledge, skills and courage to dismantle the belief in a hierarchy of human value. University students are activists at heart and, therefore, eager to develop these skills. Full of passion and ideals, they are primed to take over the world. Founded in 1999, the Black Theatre Workshop (BTW) gives space for the enormity of that fire to erupt in a theatrical environment.[6] Just as the Black Arts Movement of the 1960s was fueled by the Civil Rights Movement and the Black Power Movement, SIUE's Black Theatre Workshop has developed into a direct response to the Black Lives Matter Movement.

With the killing of Trayvon Martin in 2013, BTW's messages began to echo the universal pain and frustrations of Black youth. In honoring the notion that telling of the African-American story is incomplete without

[6] Founded by Professor Lisa Colbert, Southern Illinois University Edwardsville's Black Theatre Workshop has been a creative hub for Black students to freely express how the issues of the world impact their lives. After Colbert's transition to ancestorhood in 2002, the torch was passed to Kathryn Bentley who has been spearheading BTW as the Artistic Director since 2004.

the inclusion of voices of Latino/a, white, Asian and all ethnicities, students began to write pieces that grappled with issues of police brutality, systemic racism and racial bias in the classroom. BTW is an unapologetically Black space that is open to anyone who wants to be part of telling stories that center Blackness.

> "In recent years, the narrative in America has shifted dramatically. We have gone from the promise of hope, change, and, 'Yes We Can,' to an age more reminiscent of the Jim Crow era. A new generation of young people is witnessing, via social media and smartphones, all the hate we [7]thought had died with black and white photos in history books" Greg Fenner, 2019, Guest Director for Black Theatre Workshop.

In 2020, the BTW arts activists were challenged to deepen their artistic practice by working with Sociology senior capstone students to create the Truth, Racial Healing and Transformation E-stories—a unique collaborative project between East St. Louis and SIUE. The students jointly conducted interviews of East St. Louis residents who became the focus of the Black Theatre Workshop 2021 video production. Directed by SIUE alumnus Michael Watkins (class of 2019), this video was presented in three episodes featuring performances by BTW members.

The pieces ranged from poetry to narrative monologues that creatively brought to life the stories of these East St. Louis community heroes. One of the pieces, "A Brown Boy Born East of the River" written and performed by Tylan Mitchell, a Junior Theater and Dance major, was inspired by the interview with activist Clint Collins. Mitchell was intrigued by Mr. Collins' humility. Mitchell says, "He doesn't do what he does for recognition or praise. He's simply doing his best to pay it forward and leave behind a legacy that will make a difference in his community."

In this excerpt, Mitchell captures the dreams of a young Clint Collins as he contemplates his future:

> Generations of ancestors whose survival runs through your veins.
> Living east of the river is a Black child wondering what impact he could possibly make
> Feeling so small…

---

[7] Greg Fenner is a 2009 alumnus of SIUE's Department of Theater and Dance.

> No clue what lies ahead for his future
> Growth…
> Discovering who you are…
> Soaring above the poverty, racism, pain, hunger.
> Hungry for a future that some say you can't have.
> You are bigger than what they say you are
> The words your mother would whisper to you.
> Home is where you felt safe.
> Protected.
> Shielded.
> Loved by the people that are here to help you along your journey.
> Home is where your story begins and legacy continues. Just a brown boy born east of the river.
> Unaware of the lives you will change and light you will bring…

The group of students involved in Black Theatre Workshop 2021 is a small but passionate ensemble. Heaven Bones, Troy Caldwell-Day, Joseph King, Macnea Mackey'Harrington and Tylan Mitchell exemplify the tenacity that has been the driving force behind the 22 years of BTW. These students are clear that their role as change agents must continue even through our current pandemic:

> "I feel that SIUE's Black Theatre Workshop is contributing to the current Black Arts Movement by continuing to give the Black community a voice during this pandemic. It can feel as though you are stuck and confined to your home or school, while not knowing what to do to change the state of the world. By being in Black Theatre Workshop I feel as though our hard work and performances will reach those behind their computer screens and hopefully touch their hearts"
> Heaven Bones, BTW Student Director.

> "As a young adult, Black theater is important to me because it proves that we as Black people have many stories to tell in many different ways. It shows the power behind our words and actions and that we can't be silenced when we have something we want to share with everyone else. Black theater is a place for those who feel as though they have no other place in the world or have this creative itch that they need scratched" Joseph King, BTW Ensemble Member.

> "SIUE's Black Theatre Workshop is making massive contributions to the Black Arts Movement. This program pushes the artists involved to step out of their comfort zones and create in ways they may not be used to. They also do an excellent job of helping make Black and brown students feel welcome on this campus. BTW is the best place for Black creatives to express themselves freely in all of Edwardsville" Troy Caldwell-Day, BTW Ensemble Member.

The modern day griots of SIUE's Black Theatre Workshop are continuing a tradition passed down from their ancestors and from the leaders of East St. Louis. Through poetry, narrative monologues, song, dance and storytelling, all of the participants uphold and honor the history of the city. Additionally, they ensure future generations understand the significant intersections between Black arts and Black liberation. The collaboration between activist students and community members ensures that the legacy of the Black Arts Movement is embedded into the developing relationship between the City and SIUE. By creating artistic expression that challenges audiences to look deeply at social justice issues and acknowledge their own complicity in anti-Black racism, Black arts provide both the impetus and the method to create change agents. As stated by Audre Lorde, "[r]evolution is not a one time event." Rather, it is the clap back. The determination to be anything but a bystander.

Said differently:
"To refuse to participate in the shaping of our future is to give it up. Do not be misled into passivity either by false security (they don't mean me) or by despair (there's nothing we can do). Each of us must find our work and do it" <u>Audre Lorde</u>, Harvard University, 1984.

> We could've taken our shit back
> but the laws hung us and acquitted them
> from being a thug member for life
> while bombs dance on our streets.
>
> We clap back.

From East Side to
East St. Louis
Partnering with TRUTH, Racial Transformation and Healing
to showcase
the glow of a broken city with beautiful people.
We back with
high performances in grace, education, creativity and intelligence
from a city
suffering under the poverty line.
We clap back

Home is where your story begins and legacy continues. Just a brown boy born east of the river.

Works Cited

Farmer-Hinton, Raquel; Lewis, Joi D.; Patton, Lori D.; Rivers, Ishwanzya D. 2013. "Dear Mr. Kozol .... Four African American Women Scholars and the Re-Authoring of Savage Inequalities". *Teachers College Record*, 115: 1-38.

Kozal, Jonathan. 1991. *Savage Inequalities: Children in America's Schools*. New York: Crown Publishers.

Lorde, Audre. 1984. "Learning From the 60s." Malcolm X Weekend at Harvard University. Retrieved on February 25, 2021 from https://www.blackpast.org/african-american-history/1982-audre-lorde-learning-60s/

The Nine Network (PBS). 2003. *Made in USA: The East St. Louis Story*. Retrieved on February 25, 2021 from https://www.ninepbs.org/blogs/history/made-in-usa-the-east-st-louis-story/

Rivers, Ishwanzya D., Patton, Lori D., Farmer-Hinton, Raquel L., & Lewis, Joi D. 2021. "That Wasn't My Reality: Counter-Narratives of Educational Success as East St. Louis' Educators "Reimagine" Savage Inequalities." *Urban Education* https://doi.org/10.1177/0042085920987283

The Voice. 2015. Dear Mr. KOZOL. . . . Four African American Women scholars and THE re-authoring of Savage Inequalities. Retrieved February 26, 2021, from https://www.vialogues.com/vialogues/play/23524/

AVOTCJA

Poet/Playwright/Multi-Percussionist/Photographer/Teacher Avotcja has been published in English and Spanish in the USA, Mexico and Europe, and in more anthologies than she remembers. She is an award winning poet and multi-instrumentalist who has opened for Betty Carter in New York City, Peru's Susana Baca at San Francisco's Encuentro Popular and Cuba's Gema y Pável and played with Rahsaan Roland Kirk, Bobi & Luis Cespedes, and John Handy.

SANCTUARY

Screaming gently comes the Night
And again I face my Soul & laugh
I weave Musical webs to trap the Stars
Casting nets of Doo Wop & Cool Bop, Bomba, Jazz & Blues
A determined seeker of your mix of sweetness
An uncaged Night Bird flying freely
Ascending ... Blending ... Reveling
In the amazing acceptance of your Black bliss
Free ... like the Wind is free to catch the Moon
And I am drunk on tunes of darkness
And drunk on Songs of you

Screaming softly creeps the night
Softly ... gently ... like the cat
And I am free of daylights' terrors
Free to be me exploring a galaxy of you
Finally me ... finally free
Free of the faceless toxicity of "workaholic" horrors
God, please don't make Morning come too soon
Cause Daylight always brings down the sorrow
Of urban Sun shining on the coldness of me
Buried in the concrete
Just an artificial plastic covered world without you

And crawling loudly comes the Dawn
The Sun withers me just like a Weed

The work place lights outshine your beauty
The smell of Morning garbage kidnaps the scent of you
Once more that same old "9 to 5" horror
Tells me, "I ain't nobody!" … "I ain't no good!!!"
'Til the Sun gives up its shameless fight
And Nighttime speaks the blue-black truth
Heals me with pure undeluted power
Intoxicates me on the promise of your warm presence
Then pulls me into the darkness of your bluest Blues

I know tomorrow may outshine this evening
The Morning madness shrieks its cruel alarm
Daybreak's just a ruthless clock
An inescapable reality Bomb delivering gloom & doom
But soon … screaming gently comes the Night
Softly … screaming … comes the night
When the light of chocolate heaven again descends
And just thinking of you is enough to keep me high
Drunk on the thought of the taste of your touch
Grinning from ear to ear & living for one more dose
Of the liberating security of your rejuvenating darkness
And I'm free! … Home again
Finally really free to be me
Intoxicated on anticipation & completely drunk on Songs of you

NEVER ALONE

We have never been alone
Marcus Garvey, Arturo Schomburg, David Walker,
Ida B. Wells, Dessalines & Queen Nzinga
&
All those other incorruptible Ancestors
Who showed their contempt for slavery & servitude
By spitting in the face of evil
Jumping overboard & freeing their Souls
Proud unchained Souls
Whose restless Spirits still roam the Oceans' floor
Stamping their presence on our dreams & minds & hands
Revealing their essence in creativity all over the Globe

We were never alone
Zumbi of Palmares, Cowaya aka John Horse
Harriet Tubman & Argentina's El Negro Falucho
Our beautiful brilliant Ancestors manifest themselves
In life saving Rhythms
Rhythmic vitamins like La Bomba,
Bold rhythmic magic
Revitalizing our lives with Samba, Rumba, Landó & Yubá
They sing to us in daydreams & dance with us on stages
Their tears become our Paintings, our Books, our Poems
        &
Feed our self-esteem when life tries to get in our way
    We will never be alone
Yaa Asantewaa, Demark Vessey,
Granny Nanny, Alonso de Illescas & Gaspar Yanga…
The unstoppable freedom fighter, hero of Vera Cruz
Who reincarnated themselves in each & every one of us
    Said HELL NO!!!!!!!!
We're here; WE ARE FREE & no matter what "they" say
We're here today & we're here to stay!
We are the voice of the millions of Ancestors
Whose names we never got a chance to know
Ancestors who know
That some of us are brave enough to know their truth
To know that we were born to tell their truth
    &
Sworn to repaying their sacrifices every day with our actions
A sacred legacy written in blood forever inscribed in our Souls
An internal tattoo, an inescapable reminder
To never let us forget to remember the price they paid
For us to know that we were never alone
    that we are never alone
        and we will never, never, ever be alone

ON ROMANTICISM

I would like to fly like the Hummingbird
Floating on inspiration
&
Sing mystical songs of love

Standing still in mid air
On a cushion of metaphors
I'd love to lie back
&
Dance on the wind
Philosophizing about life
&
The joy of living
Without having to worry
about
Where the next meal is coming from
I admit it!
I would love to write pretty Poetry
About pretty flowers
&
The beauty of freedom
&
Have the time to enjoy it
but
Pretty flowers
Like freedom are pretty rare here
In my part of the City
Where even Dreams
Cost more than I can afford
&
The only flowers I get to see
Live in store windows
Or lay dead in the streets
Covered with wine & snot
&
God knows what
but
Our beautiful Children are watching
They watch
Like Urban butterflies
Hibernating in concrete cocoons
They watch & grow
&
Grow & watch
&
Never stop dreaming of becoming Poets

Amiri Baraka

Amiri Baraka, previously known as LeRoi Jones, was a writer of poetry, drama, fiction, essays and music criticism. Baraka was seen as the founder of the influential Black Arts Movement. Baraka's career spanned nearly 52 years. Baraka's plays, poetry, and essays have been described by scholars as constituting defining texts for African-American culture.

Legacy

In the south, sleeping against

the drugstore, growling under
the trucks and stoves, stumbling
through and over the cluttered eyes
of early mysterious night. Frowning
drunk waving moving a hand or lash.
Dancing kneeling reaching out, letting
a hand rest in shadows. Squatting
to drink or pee. Stretching to climb
pulling themselves onto horses near
where there was sea (the old songs
lead you to believe). Riding out
from this town, to another, where
it is also black. Down a road
where people are asleep. Towards
the moon or the shadows of houses.

Towards the songs' pretended sea.

Ka'Ba

A closed window looks down
on a dirty courtyard, and Black people
call across or scream across or walk across
defying physics in the stream of their will.

Our world is full of sound
Our world is more lovely than anyone's
tho we suffer, and kill each other
and sometimes fail to walk the air.

We are beautiful people
With African imaginations
full of masks and dances and swelling chants
with African eyes, and noses, and arms
tho we sprawl in gray chains in a place
full of winters, when what we want is sun.

Sonia Sanchez

Poet. Mother. Professor. National and International lecturer on Black Culture and Literature, Women's Liberation, Peace and Racial Justice. Sponsor of Women's International League for Peace and Freedom. Board Member of MADRE. Sonia Sanchez is the author of over 20 books including *Homecoming, We a BaddDDD People, Love Poems, I've Been a Woman, A Sound Investment and Other Stories, Homegirls and Handgrenades, Under a Soprano Sky, Wounded in the House of a Friend* (Beacon Press 1995), *Does Your House Have Lions?* (Beacon Press, 1997), *Like the Singing Coming off the Drums* (Beacon Press, 1998), *Shake Loose My Skin* (Beacon Press, 1999), *Morning Haiku* (Beacon Press, 2010), and most recently, *Collected Poems* (Beacon Press, 2021). In addition to being a contributing editor to *Black Scholar* and T*he Journal of African Studies*, she has edited an anthology, *We Be Word Sorcerers: 25 Stories by Black Americans*. *BMA: The Sonia Sanchez Literary Review* is the first African American journal that discusses the work of Sonia Sanchez and the Black Arts Movement. A recipient of a National Endowment for the Arts, the Lucretia Mott Award for 1984, the Outstanding Arts Award from the Pennsylvania Coalition of 100 Black Women, the Community Service Award from the National Black Caucus of State Legislators, she is a winner of the 1985 American Book Award for *Homegirls and Handgrenades,* the Governor's Award for Excellence in the Humanities for 1988, the Peace and Freedom Award from Women International League for Peace and Freedom (W.I.L.P.F.) for 1989, a PEW Fellowship in the Arts for 1992-1993 and the recipient of Langston Hughes Poetry Award for 1999. *Does Your House Have Lions?* was a finalist for the National Book Critics Circle Award. She is the Poetry Society of America's 2001 Robert Frost Medalist and a Ford Freedom Scholar from the Charles H. Wright Museum of African American History. Her poetry also appeared in the movie *Love Jones*. Sonia Sanchez has lectured at over 500 universities and colleges in the United States and has traveled extensively, reading her poetry in Africa, Cuba, England, the Caribbean, Australia, Europe, Nicaragua, the People's Republic of China, Norway, and Canada. She was the first Presidential Fellow at Temple University and she held the Laura Carnell Chair in English at Temple University. She is the recipient of the Harper Lee Award, 2004, Alabama Distinguished Writer, and the National Visionary Leadership Award for 2006. She is the recipient of the 2005 Leeway Foundation Transformational Award and the 2009 Robert Creeley Award. Currently, Sonia Sanchez is one of 20 African American women featured in "Freedom Sisters," an interactive exhibition created by the Cincinnati Museum Center and Smithsonian Institution traveling exhibition. In December of 2011, Philadelphia Mayor Michael Nutter selected Sonia Sanchez as Philadelphia's first Poet Laureate, calling her "the longtime conscience of the city." *BaddDDD Sonia Sanchez*, a documentary about Sanchez's life as an artist and activist by

Barbara Attie, Janet Goldwater, Sabrina Schmidt Gordon, was nominated for a 2017 Emmy®.

Additional awards include the 2016 Shelley Memorial Award of the Poetry Society of America, the Wallace Stevens Award in 2018 (presented by the Academy of American Poets), the Anisfield-Wolf Lifetime Achievement Award in 2019 and the Dorothy and Lillian Gish Prize in 2021.

A Poem for Sterling Brown

what song shall I sing you
amid epidemic prophecies
where holy men bleed like water
over the bones of black children?

how shall I call your name
sitting priest/like on mountains
raining incense
scented dancer of the sun?

where shall memory begin you
overturning cradles
rocking cemented eyes
closed flowers
opening like eastern deities under your hand?

and your words.
tall as palm/trees
black with spit
soothing the lacerated mind.

and your words.
scratching the earth
carving dialect men into pyramids
where no minstrel songs
run from their thighs.

your soul. dodging loneliness and
the festivals of Renaissance rhythms
your life
skintight with years
a world created
from love.

JUST DON'T NEVER GIVE UP ON LOVE

Feeling tired that day, I came to the park with the children. I saw her as I rounded the corner, sitting old as stale beer on the bench, ruminating on some uneventful past. And I thought, "Hell. No rap from the roots today. I need the present. On this day. This Monday. This July day buckling me under her summer wings, I need more than old words for my body to squeeze into."

I sat down at the far end of the bench, draping my legs over the edge, baring my back to time and time unwell spent. I screamed to the children to watch those curves threatening their youth as they rode their 10-speed bikes against mid-western rhythms.

I opened my book and began to write. They were coming again, those words insistent as his hands had been pounding inside me, demanding their time and place. I relaxed as my hands moved across the paper like one possessed.

I wasn't sure just what it was I heard. At first I thought it was one of the boys calling me so I kept on writing. They knew the routine by now. Emergencies demanded a presence. A facial confrontation. No long distance screams across trees and space and other children's screams. But the sound pierced the pages and I looked around, and there she was inching her bamboo-creased body toward my back, coughing a beaded sentence off her tongue.

"Guess you think I ain't never loved, huh girl? Hee. Hee. Guess that what you be thinking, huh?"

I turned. Startled by her closeness and impropriety, I stuttered, "I, I,I, Whhhaat dooooo you mean?"

"Hee. Hee. Guess you think I been old like this fo'ever, huh?" She leaned toward me. "Huh? I was so pretty that mens brought me breakfast in bed. Wouldn't let me hardly do no hard work at all."

"That's nice ma'am. I'm glad to hear that." I returned to my book. I didn't want to hear about some ancient love that she carried inside her. I had to finish a review for the journal. I was already late. I hoped she would get the hint and just sit still. I looked at her out of the corner of my eyes.

"He could barely keep hisself in changing clothes. But he was pretty. My first husband looked like the sun. I used to say his name over and over again til it hung from my ears like diamonds. Has you ever loved a pretty man, girl?"

I raised my eyes, determined to keep a distance from this woman disturbing my day.

"No ma'am. But I've seen many a pretty man. I don't like them though cuz they keep their love up high in a linen closet and I'm too short to reach it."

Her skin shook with laughter.

"Girl you gots some spunk about you after all. C'mon over here next to me. I wants to see yo' eyes up close. You looks so uneven sittin' over there."

Did she say uneven? Did this old buddah splintering death say uneven? Couldn't she see that I had one eye shorter than the other; that my breath was painted on porcelain; that one breast crocheted keloids under this white blouse?

I moved toward her though. I scooped up the years that had stripped me to the waist and moved toward her. And she called to me to come out, come out wherever you are young woman, playing hide and go seek with scarecrow men. I gathered myself up at the gateway of her confessionals.

"Do you know what it mean to love a pretty man girl?" She crooned in my ear. "You always running behind a man like that girl while he cradles his privates. Ain't no joy in a pretty yellow man, cuz he always out pleasurin' and givin' pleasure."

I nodded my head as her words sailed in my ears. Here was the pulse of a woman whose black ass shook the world once.

She continued. "A woman crying all the time is pitiful. Pitiful I says. I wuz pitiful sitting by the window every night like a cow in the fields chewin' on cud. I wanted to cry out, but not even God hisself could hear me. I tried to cry out til my mouth wuz split open at the throat. I 'spoze there is a time all womens has to visit the slaughter house. My visit lasted five years."

Touching her hands, I felt the summer splintering in prayer; touching her hands, I felt my bones migrating in red noise. I asked, "When did you see the butterflies again?"

Her eyes wandered like quicksand over my face. Then she smiled, "Girl don't you know yet that you don't never give up on love? Don't you know you has in you the pulse of winds? The noise of dragonflies?" Her eyes squinted close and she said, "One of them mornings he woke up callin' me and I wuz gone. I wuz gone running with the moon over my shoulders. I looked no which way at all. I had inside me 'nough knives and spoons to cut/scoop out the night. I wuz a tremblin' as I met the mornin'."

She stirred in her 84-year-old memory. She stirred up her body as she talked. "They's men and mens. Some good. Some bad. Some breathing death. Some breathing life. William wuz my beginnin'. I come to my second husband spittin' metal and he just pick me up and fold me inside him. I wuz christen' with his love."

She began to hum. I didn't recognize the song; it was a prayer. I leaned back and listened to her voice rustling like silk. I heard cathedrals and sonnets; I heard tents and revivals and a black woman spilling black juice among her ruins.

"We all gotta salute death one time or 'nother girl. Death be waitin' out doors trying to get inside. William died at his job. Death just turned 'round and snatched him right off the street."

Her humming became the only sound in the park. Her voice moved across the bench like a mutilated child. And I cried. For myself. For this woman talkin' about love. For all the women who have ever stretched their bodies out anticipating civilization and finding ruins.

The crashing of the bikes was anticlimactic. I jumped up, rushed toward the accident. Man. Little man. Where you bicycling to so very fast? Man. Second little man. Take it slow. It all passes so fast anyhow.

As I walked the boys and their bikes toward the bench, I smiled at this old woman waiting for our return.

"I want you to meet a great lady, boys."

"Is she a writer, too, ma?"

"No honey. She's a lady who has lived life instead of writing about it."

"After we say hello can we ride a little while longer? Please!"

"OK. But watch your manners now and your bones afterwards."

"These are my sons, Ma'am."

"How you do, sons? I'm Mrs. Rosalie Johnson. Glad to meet you." The boys shook her hand and listened for a minute to her words. Then they rode off, spinning their wheels on a city neutral with pain. As I stood watching them race the morning, Mrs. Johnson got up.

"Don't go," I cried. "You didn't finish your story."

"We'll talk by-and-by. I comes out here almost everyday. I sits here on the same bench everyday. I'll probably die sittin' here one day. As good a place as any I 'magine."

"May I hug you, ma'am? You've helped me so much today. You've given me strength to keep on looking."

"No. Don't never go looking for love girl. Just wait. It'll come. Like the rain fallin' from the heavens, it'll come. Just don't never give up on love."

We hugged, then she walked her 84-year-old walk down the street. A black woman. Echoing gold. Carrying couplets from the sky to crease the ground.

I'm Black When I'm Singing, I'm Blue When I Ain't (Excerpt from Act I)

CHARACTERS:

    REENA
    MAMA B
    TONI (Main Female Character)
    MALIKA
    DOCTOR (Male)
    ATTENDANT (Nurse) (Male or Female)

SAM (Mama B's Husband)
CATHOLIC MATRON (At Girl's Home)
BUSINESS MANAGER (For Mama B, Toni, and Reena (Male)
MARY (Toni's Mother)
JOHN (Reena's Husband)
JOSEPHINE (Reena's Mother)
CHORUS/DANCERS (3 Males)
CHORUS/DANCERS (3 Females)

Place and Time:

Act I: 1980s and 1920 in Detroit, Atlanta, and New York City (NYC)

Act II: 1940s, 1960s, and present in Baltimore, Philadelphia, and NYC

ACT I

(A room—grey and white stripes—no windows. In the center of the room is a small cot; to the left is a small desk and chair. To the right is a piano. Upstage is a child's play stove with pots and pans and a play sink. Around the room there are clothes racks; on them hang dresses, hats and other costumes for actors. A woman between 40-45 years of age is stretched out on the cot. She has on a long white hospital gown with white tights. No shoes. She wears a diamond tiara, "diamond" earrings and a diamond bracelet. She is humming a tune that seems familiar. She rises. Goes to the desk and picks up some brown paper and spreads it out on the floor, center stage. She smooths it out. Then she squats on the paper—she is humming softly and grunting.)

REENA: *(Sings)*
> The color of death is grey and white
> The color of my life is white and grey
> They are different and yet the same
> Don't ya know—I learned all this in a cabaret

(Sings)
>The color of this room is white and grey
>The color of my mind is grey and white
>They are different and yet the same
>Don't ya know—A dog licks the and it's gonna bite.

(Laughs/Grunts)

(She gets up from squatting and shakes herself. Then moves over to the play stove and gets a pot. Returning to the brown paper, she begins to spoon the imaginary feces into the pot. She continues to hum the aforementioned song. Then she takes it to the play stove and begins to cook. Removes the pot and goes to the cot and begins to eat—as she eats she glances up at the audience for the first time.) *(Extends hand)* Want some? *(Laughs)* No huh? It ain't too bad. It's solid you know. Don't look so shocked, we eats what we can when we can in this hellhole. *(Stands up)* But wait now. I haven't welcomed you properly my audience. My dear hard/playing/hard/paying audience. Here now. I'll straighten this part of my bed for you. *(Puts down pot)* There. It's smoothed out for you. Some of my space. Welcome. *(Laughs and sits down)* Such as it is. *(Extends pot again)* Are you sure you don't want any? *(Laughs a gutsy laugh. Continues to eat—concentrates on pot. Slowly looks up)* Don't look so disgusted. You there sitting in yo' middle-class conformity. You think I'm mad don't you. You should be grateful that I'm offering you this little shit. It's controlled shit. Institutionalized shit. There's so much more of it out there *(laughs)* that's running loose. And you always falling in it and always taking it too! *(She continues to eat. Looks up quickly.)* There I caught you staring again. Don't you know it's bad manners? My mother always taught me the proper things to do in North Philadelphia. "Now Reena sit up straight there girl. Remember a Black girl is bad enough, but a

hunch-backed-slouch-back-bad postured-back Black girl is the worst." My mother could always hit the nail right on the back. *(Laughs)*

I came from Philadelphia. Guess you've guessed that by now. I was a genius when I was a child. Do you hear? A mathematical and musical genius. Equations poured from my mouth and I square-rooted my rooms into the streets of Philadelphia. My hand took shape with music right before my eyes. I had a concert when I was four. I marched out on the concert stage, face greased, legs and arms greased, and played the old masters. This young 'un did in those old dudes. And when I finished, and when they had clapped for me and my mother, and we had bowed twenty-five times, we went home on the Broad street train together. And all she kept saying was, "I hope they didn't think you were too Black. I just hope they didn't care about that part of it." *(Laughs) (Stands)* But momski. I had the last laugh after all. I made everybody in here, you too my dear audience, I made everybody love Black. Didn't I my little zombies. Do you remember? When I appeared on stage in all my long and thick blackness and sang:

> "I am here Black as the nite
> I am here to bring you day
> So stretch out your hand and
> I will make Blackness the way."

(Stops and turns) Ah ha—what are you looking at huh? Ah I see you looking. Yes stretch out those eyeballs saying, wait a minute, isn't that—yes that's her. They said. I mean. I heard that ... Hee Hee Hee. You remembering me—who I am. Was. Hee, hee, hee. *(Becomes expansive)* Spirits around me. Us. Why don't you help them? They're confused by my clothes or lack of clothes. Sitting in their theater clothes. Help them. Look. They're nervous.

They're thinking she was always doing so well. Why the whole country heard her first song and knew she was heading for the top. Smiling eyes and lips announced her when she walked onto a stage. Yes. You're right. When I entered a room, music began and stopped. I walked a walk that said hunger would never populate these legs. And when the hunger came they were still eating the milk and honey of my good fortune. I ain't complaining though. But what a strange hunger those aristocrats, those well-to-do leaders of countries had. They saw me walking. Head held high. Geleed in African prints. And they convinced me that my African prints left footprints on my body. Andy they peeled me like a black banana, and I lay stripped, naked before the European Capitols of the world. A coat. A coat. All my songs for a coat! *(Laughs a wild laugh) (Moves to the cot) (Door opens. A CHORUS of three men enters. They have on white hospital gowns.)*

CHORUS: Our mothers die when they run naked on the land.
Ei—Ei—Ei.
We who are orphans must cry now to the world.
We have come to clean sin out of this place.
We have come to wash sin from the room.

CHORUS I: Singing your/people's praise is singing your/praise too.
But I have come to wash sin from your mouth.

CHORUS II: Are there no female heroes in the land? But I have
Come to beat evil from your limbs.

CHORUS III: The gates of this country are always closed to those who
Look like us.
Ay—ay—I have come to beat the evil out of your eyes.

CHORUS: Is the lady of the house at home? Has she forsaken us?

Her children? We have come to beat the evil from the room.

CHORUS I: Move evil—from the woman's body. *(Crosses self)*

CHORUS II: Move outside all ye spirits of madness. *(Sprinkles dust)*

CHORUS III: Move away O thighs carrying death. *(Pushes against the room)*

REENA: Did you mention thighs? *(Stretches back on the cot)* Did you mention the word thighs? *(Shows stockinged thighs)* Yes. These are the thighs a woman must have to be an artist. A great artist. To earn her living as an artist. And you thought it had something to do with talent or hard work. *(Laughs)* But I wouldn't lift these thighs out of bed early in the morning though. These were evening thighs, not morning thighs. These were Parisian thighs. And Caribbean thighs . . . *(Stops. A far away look covers her face.)*

CHORUS: *(Moves toward the cot)*
We have come to beat out the evil from this room.
Ay—ay—ay—Evil anywhere we find it.
Standing straight or lying down.

(Goes to her cot and surround her—crossing themselves—moving around her bed) *(She draws herself up.)*

REENA: You wouldn't know it when you saw it. Evil indeed! You three maniacs. You think it's so simple. You think my being here is simple. Your being here is simple? Do you know how old I am? I am 3,000 years old. I used to reside in the temples in Egypt and I wrote and sang the rites for funerals. What an honor it was to sing and write—what an honorable woman I was. What an honorable time that was. *(The door opens and the doctor and attendant enter.)*

DOCTOR: *(In white face)* Good morning Reena. How are you this morning? *(Stops. Changes. Moves back to couch)*

REENA: I'll be okay once you get these escapees from a Greek chorus out of here. Why do they always come to my room? I never invite them. Everyday they come and sprinkle me with goober dust then wait for some miracle to happen. I'm tired of them today. They make my head hurt sometimes.

DOCTOR: They're harmless Reena. They mean you no harm at all. They're really quite lovely—three lovely men for you.

REENA: Why do you say that? *(Somewhat agitated)* Why did you say three lovely men for me? Why do I need or want three? Why did you say that?

DOCTOR: Why do you think? Don't you remember our last conversation? Have you forgotten what happened?

REENA: *(Becomes agitated)* Get them out of here, do you hear? Three men indeed! Get them out of here.

ATTENDANT: *(Moves toward her with a straight jacket)* Shall I doctor?

REENA: *(Moves to confront the attendant)* Shall I what doctor? Don't you try to put that thing on me or I'll wrap it around your black ass.

ATTENDANT: Listen, I don't take no shit from . . .
DOCTOR: Leave her be. She's all right. Aren't you Reena? You're ready for your session, aren't you? *(Moves to desk and sits down)* *(REENA walks slowly to her cot. She's rather*

tired now and she stretches out.)

REENA: *(Begins to sing the first song we heard at the beginning of the play)*

> The color of death is grey and white
> The color of my room is white and grey . . .

DOCTOR: Who's singing today Reena?

REENA: Yours truly Doc.

DOCTOR: Who's that Reena?

REENA: Me. Reena Malone. The one and only. There ain't another like me in the world.

DOCTOR: Yes all that's true Reena. But yesterday you introduced me to your friend. What was her name? Mama B wasn't it? *(REENA turns toward the wall. She is silent.)* Wasn't that her name? Wasn't it Mama B? Are you listening to me Reena?

REENA: Yeah. I'm listening to you Doc.

DOCTOR: Mama B was her name, wasn't it?

REENA: Maybe. But it could have been Toni too.

DOCTOR: *(Leans forward—excited)* You've never mentioned another friend. *(Writes furiously)* Why didn't you tell me this before? *(Becomes agitated)* Are you serious Reena? How do I know that you're not pulling my leg? Or as you say jiving me?

REENA: *(Turns toward him)* You don't do you? That's what's so funny about all of this. You don't know for sure if I'm jiving you at all. *(Sits on edge of the cot)* Look at you. You just can't wait can you? Well you can only meet them when I want you to. *(Stands)* They can't appear unless I will it. I'm the strongest of all of them. They just some dead ladies that didn't know how to take care of themselves. I do. I know how to protect me and my interests. Dumb bitches. Dumb black bitches. Ending up playing one nighters in one-horse towns—chitterling circuit women. I'm strictly escargots my man.

DOCTOR: Snails tonite for you Reena if you introduce me to your friend again.

REENA: *(Angrily)* I said I have two of 'em. Didn't you hear me? Which one?

DOCTOR: The one you'd like for me to meet. I'm interested in the one you'd like for me to meet now. *(Softly)* Eventually I'll meet them all.

REENA: It really doesn't matter. They're about the same. Traveling around in a car in the South. Once she even had her own railroad car. Can you imagine, traveling in those days in your own railroad car. It was painted red. A sign read Same Reid presents: Mama B and her follies. You could see her coming as she toured the South. First class.

DOCTOR: What days are you talking about Reena?

REENA: *(Has retrieved her tiara, earrings and bracelet and has laid them out. While they talk she moves around the room and puts on a long fringe 20s type dress over the hospital gown. Should make her appear bigger. Wraps a fur piece round her neck. Places straightened wig on her head—bangs style—Plume type hat on her head.)* The good ol' days. Why them days where after a show you went to pigs' feet parties. You'd walk in that door in Detroit and the funk would be flying. There it all was. Liquor. Smoke. Food. Perspiration. Fine looking Browns. Funk. And you would sit down to a steaming pot off pigs' feet, collard greens, black-eyed peas and scallions. And of course some gin. C'mon y'all, I'm ready to sing. Everybody shut up. Mama B is coming out . . .

MAMA B: My name is Mama B and I'm as brassy as can be
I say my name is Mama B and I'm as loud as I can be
C'mon over here baby and take a dip in this deep, deep blue sea.
I was born in Chattanooga some twenty years ago
I say I was born in Chattanooga bout twenty years ago
I'm heading or NYC, don't like the South no mo'.
I got me a real pretty man who loves me down to me toes
Say I got me a pretty man who digs me on down to my toes
Oh how I loves that man, only the Lord hisself does know.
I say my name is Mama B and I'm a big young brassy one
Say my name is Mama B and I'm a big brassy one
If I ever leave my daddy baby, you can have this Amazon.

(During this singing the DR. and ATTENDANT leave and the lighting changes. We see REENA leaving an imaginary stage reaching for her mink and calling to her tow female singers/dancers)

MAMA B: C'mon Y'all we got a recording date, Remember? Move your yellow asses. You bitches from the North think you too cute to move. C'mon today's the day we going into the recording business. Sam. Where's Sam. Can never find that man when I need him.

BUSINESS MANAGER:
(Has white side/black side. Black side shows when speaking) I got a good deal for you Reena. You gonna record. They want you to record. Seems like Mamie done done us a favor. C'mon gal we gonna make us some money. They'll pay us $125 a side. C'mon gal. Here's a chance of a lifetime. It's a big time for us.

MAMA B: *(A nervous MAMA B, young and inexperienced, enters the studio with manager.)*

"I'm fresh from the country, yuh know I'm easy to ride
Say I'm fresh from the country, yuh know I'm easy to ride
Just climb on board me, brown skin and let me be yo only guide
I love cornbread and milk, eat it each day I can
Say I love cornbread and milk, eat it each day I can
Promise you some of the same, if you'll be my one and only man."
Hey. Stop, ya'll. I gotta spit . . . *(MAMA B spits and the music stops.)*

REENA: Did you see that? Did you see that loud mouth, uncouth fool? She stopped and spit in the middle of a record date. Did you see that white man's face congeal in disgust? He almost fainted. Lord Almighty. Of course, she didn't get the contract. How could she? She was too busy spitting. *(Laughs)*

MAMA B: *(Fighting to come out)* So what if I spit? I had to spit. I couldn't keep singing with all the spit in my mouth. But if those white companies didn't like me they eventually did sign me up anyway. I'm on stage now.

You shut the hell up. I don't share my stage with
no other blues singer when I'm on stage. That's
my audience now. So you just shut your northern
Philadelphia mouth up.

BUSINESS MANAGER:
(White side) It's a good deal Mama B. You'll get
$3,000 a year, $150.00 a piece for the next six record
dates and because we love you so much, here's a bonus
of $500.00. Yes. You and Major Records are on their
way. We'll do you up just fine Mama B. We even have
someone to print the word colored on the record.
Everybody will know who you are. . .

Afterword

Already Missing the High Priestess of "Talking Back"— A Tribute to bell hooks

There was something daring about a young black woman scholar who authored a first book on black feminism, *Ain't I A Woman: Black Women and Feminism* (1981) as an undergraduate student, reclaiming the language of Sojourner Truth titularly and conceptually. bell hooks brought the creative fire of past generations into the contemporary and so provided the example of a bold claiming of a space for Black women's ability to articulate, using the language they had and the energies that they needed to confront silencing often imposed by dominant framings of black women as angry or incoherent. Many of us remembered our own punishments for "talking back" to people who occupied places of power in our lives. That simultaneous excitement and fear at being able to voice a position that constricted all bodily systems if it remained unarticulated provided a counter rush of our own power in the process of talking back.

This is what bell hooks gave us—she used the voice she had, as Sojourner Truth did, to claim a space to speak with passion to dominant discourse. In doing so she patterned this facility for subsequent scholars, students, thinkers, community workers and activists. Black women activists and writers around the world were empowered to speak confidently of their own realities and in their own voices. She demonstrated how a "dissenting voice" of radical black feminist politics operated. Finding the courage to say what needs to be said for bell hooks was always part of a process of teaching beyond the classroom, reaching audiences beyond the academy and thereby creating generations of critical activists. To do this, she mastered literary critical analysis in studies of James Baldwin and Toni Morrison, engaged popular culture, used the essay form (and the extended monograph) and challenged regimented academic documentation patterns. She also used public conversation, video interviews and children's books to articulate multiple incisive positions.

Gloria Watkins (1952-2021), who had taken her pen name from

a grandmother who spoke incisively and from whom she also clearly acquired the permission to "talk back," impacted many with her unabashed black feminist visionary praxis, taking all of us further along the road to full self-articulation, providing the example of manifesting critical consciousness with love. "Moving away from the languages of domination" became a watchword. The presence of bell hooks and her meaning of radical praxis will endure through the numerous intellectual contributions she left us, and within the many outpourings of generations of young scholars, artists, thinkers and activists whose lives and consciousness she helped to transform. For this we honor you, dear friend and comrade!

>—Carole Boyce Davies, Professor of Africana Studies and Literatures in English at Cornell University

Text Permissions and Acknowledgments

Baldwin, James. "Amen" by James Baldwin from *Jimmy's Blues and Other Poems*. Copyright © 1983, 1985 by James Baldwin. Reprinted with permission from Beacon Press, Boston, Massachusetts.

Baldwin, James. *Blues for Mister Charlie*. Copyright (c) 1964 by James Baldwin. Copyright renewed 1992 by The James Baldwin Estate. Permission granted by The Estate of James Baldwin.

Baraka, Amina. "Hip Songs" courtesy of Amina Baraka.

Baraka, Amiri. "Legacy" and "Ka'Ba" courtesy of Amina Baraka.

Boyd, Melba Joyce. "To Darnell and Johnny." Broadside No 68, *Broadside Series*, 1973.

Brooks, Gwendolyn. "Infirm," "To the Disapora" and "The Boy Died in My Alley." Reprinted by Consent of Brooks Permissions.

Dent, Tom. *Ritual Murder* courtesy of Ben and Walter Dent. Bio with assistance from Kalamu ya Salaam.

Dumas, Henry. "Knees of a Natural Man," "Love Song" and "Son of Msippi." Used by permission of the Hentry Dumas Estate, Eugene B. Redmond, Executor.

Dungy, Camille T. "This'll hurt me more" was previously published in *LitHub*, June 2020.

Dungy, Camille T. "Metaphor of America as this Homegrown Painted Lady Chrysalis" was previously published in *American Poetry Review*, September 2020.

Dungy, Camille T. "Jamestown 2019" was previously published in *LA Review of Books*, August 2019.

Eubanks, Cole. *The Other N-Word* was published in the summer edition (2021) of *MiGoZine*.

Fitzpatrick, Liseli A. "Amazing Grace" appears in *Feminists Talk Whiteness*.

Fitzpatrick, Liseli A. "seen and heard" has been published in *Chicken Soup for the Soul* special edition *I'm Speaking Now: Black Women Share Their Truth in 101 Stories of Love, Courage and Hope*. It will appear in "A (Re)Turn to the African Girl— (Re)Defining African Girlhood Studies" Edited Collection.

Gabbin, Joanne V. Excerpt from "Introduction," Furious Flower: African American Poetry from the Black Arts Movement to the Present. Reprinted with the permission of the author. University of Virginia Press, 2004.

Jones, Quincy Scott. "knives of peace." Poet's statement: "Lines appropriated from Alain Locke, Paul Lawrence Dunbar, Amiri Baraka, Nicole Lovebreed, Claudio Segovia, Hector Orezzoli, August Wilson, Ntosake Shange, Biggie Smalls, The Rolling Stones, Jay-Z, Sonia Sanchez, Lucille Clifton, Michael S. Harper, Elizabeth Alexander, William Blake, Sterling A Brown, Langston Hughes, Nikki Giovanni, Derek Walcott, Charles Bukowski, Wallace Stevens, and The Last Poets."

Lorde, Audre. Epigraph excerpt from "The Master's Tools Will Never Dismantle the Master's House." *Sister Outsider*. Penguin Classics, 2019, p. 112.

McMillon, Kim. "Editor's Notes." Anna J. Cooper quotation from "WOMANHOOD A VITAL ELEMENT IN THE REGENERATION AND PROGRESS OF A RACE." *A Voice from the South: By a Black Woman of the South*, University of North Carolina Press, 2017, pp. 16–34.

Moore, Lenard D. "8 Haiku" has previously appeared on page 31, *African Voices: A Soulful Collection of Art And Literature*, Volume No. 13, Issue 30, Spring/Summer 2015.

Moore, Lenard D. "Haiku Sequence" has previously appeared on pages 22 and 23 in *VALLEY VOICES: A Literary Review*, Volume 15, Number 2, Fall 2015; it was reprinted on page 81 in *All The Songs We Sing: Celebrating The 25th Anniversary Of The Carolina African American Writers' Collective* (Blair, 2020).

Nicholas, Denise. *Freshwater Road*, Chapter 3, pp. 21-31 (excerpt). © 2005, 2016 by Denise Nicholas, ISBN 978-1-5728419-5-6, Bold Books, April 2016.

Randall, Dudley. "On Getting a Natural," "A Poet is Not a Jukebox" and "Booker T. and W.E.B." Reprinted by permission from the Dudley Randall Literary Estate.

Reed, Ishmael. "The Luckiest People in the World." Reprinted with Permission of the Author.

Roy, Darlene. "BAMtized," "Pen Felt Around the World" and "Black Arts Movement Warrior" have appeared in the following anthologies, journals and/or book in the same or slightly different versions: *Literati Chicago* 1988; *Drumvoices Revue* 1992, 2005, 2006, 2007, 2011, 2012; *Valley Voices* (Spring) 2018; and *Afrocenthesis: A Feast of Poetry & Folklore,* Kuumba Scribes Press, an imprint of Black River Writers, 2015.

Sanchez, Sonia. "A Poem for Sterling Brown,""Just Don't Never Give Up On Love." From *Confirmation: An Anthology of African American Women* edited by Amiri Baraka (LeRoi Jones) and Amina Baraka. New York: Morrow, 1983.

Sanchez, Sonia. *I'm Black When I'm Singing, I'm Blue When I Ain't* appears courtesy of the author.

Simanga, Michael. "A Tribute to Amiri Baraka" was originally published in the *The Black Scholar,* September 17, 2014.

Stover, Darrell. "Look Back: Amiri the Blues God Lives" and the poem "Be We We? for Amiri Baraka and Larry Neal" were originally published in *Obsidian* Vol. 14 No. 1 Spring/Summer 2013.

Walker, Margaret. "Bio." https://www.literaryladiesguide.com/classic-women-authors-poetry/11-poems-by-margaret-walker/

Walker, Margaret. "For Gwen—I969" and "For My People" from *This Is My Century: New and Collected Poems* by Margaret Walker. © 1989 by Margaret Walker Alexander. Reprinted by permission from the University of Georgia Press.

Ward, Val Gray and Francis Ward. "The Black Artist—His Role in the Struggle" appears in *Black Art Notes*. © 2020 Estate of Tom Lloyd. *Black Art Notes* was first published in 1971 by Tom Lloyd in an unknown edition.

Special citations per request of the following estates:
Lucille Clifton, "fury" from *The Book of Light*. Copyright © 1993 by Lucille Clifton. Reprinted with the permission of The Permissions Company, LLC on behalf of Copper Canyon Press, coppercanyonpress.org.
Lucille Clifton, "shapeshifter poems" from *How to Carry Water: Selected Poems*. Copyright © 1987 by Lucille Clifton. Reprinted with the permission of The Permissions Company, LLC on behalf of BOA Editions Ltd., www.boaeditions.org.
Wanda Coleman, "Emmett Till" from *Wicked Enchantment: Selected Poems*. Reprinted by permission of Black Sparrow Press. Copyright ©1990, 2020 by Wanda Coleman.

All other works in this collection are courtesy of the contributors.
Special Thanks to:
Dr. Kim McMillon for conceptualizing *Black Fire—This Time* and for her work with numerous literary estates;
Dr. Margo Natalie Crawford for the Introduction;
Ishmael Reed for the Foreword;
Carole Boyce Davies for the bell hooks Afterword;
Darrell Stover and Dr. Liseli A. Fitzpatrick for additional editorial support;
Anonymous for assistance with James Baldwin permissions;
Megha Sood for assisting with reviews;
Dr. Melba Joyce Boyd for assistance with the Dudley Randall Literary Estate;
Michael Simanga for assistance with the works of Haki Madhubuti;
Kalamu ya Salaam for assistance throughout and for Tom Dent's bio;
Sidney Clifton for her mother Lucille Clifton's work;
Dr. Liseli A. Fitzpatrick for the works of Val Gray Ward and Francis Ward;
Yoruba Richen for her mother Aishah Rahman's work;
Eugene B. Redmond for helping with the works of Henry Dumas;
Ben and Walter Dent for the work of Tom Dent;
Satoko, widow of **Mozel Zeke Nealy**, for his works;
and **Nora Brooks Blakely*** for assistance with the works of *Gwendolyn Brooks*.

*About Nora Brooks Blakely, daughter of Gwendolyn Brooks:
Nora Brooks Blakely, a former teacher in the Chicago Public Schools, founded Chocolate Chips Theatre Company (1982-2011) and was its primary playwright. Ms. Blakely is the daughter of two writers, Henry Blakely (*Windy Place*) and Gwendolyn Brooks (the first Black person to ever win the Pulitzer Prize). She founded Brooks Permissions in 2001. The company licenses and promotes her mother's work and develops programming and publications which demonstrate Gwendolyn Brooks' continuing relevance. After writing plays and musicals for decades, Nora's first children's book, *Moyenda and The Golden Heart*, an origin tale for Kwanzaa, was released in 2021. You can learn more about Ms. Blakely on her website, flyingcolorsunlimited.com.